THE WOMAN COMPOSER: CREATIVITY AND THE GENDERED POLITICS OF MUSICAL COMPOSITION

The Woman Composer: Creativity and the Gendered Politics of Musical Composition

Jill Halstead

Ashgate

Aldershot • Brookfield USA • Singapore • Sydney

Published by
Ashgate Publishing Company
Gower House
Croft Road
Aldershot, Hants
GU11 3HR
England

Ashgate Publishing Company
Old Post Road
Brookfield
Vermont 05036-9704
USA

Ashgate website:http://www.ashgate.com

Reprinted 1999

British Library Cataloguing-in-Publication Data
Halstead, Jill
The woman composer : creativity and the gendered politics of musical composition
1. Women composers – Great Britain 2. Composition (Music)
3. Sex discrimination against women — Great Britain
I. Title
780.8'2'0941

Library of Congress Cataloging-in-Publication Data
Halstead, Jill
The woman composer : creativity and the gendered politics of musical composition / Jill Halstead
Includes bibliographical references and index.
1. Women composers — Great Britain — Social conditions. 2. Women composers — Great Britain — Psychology. 3. Great Britain — Social conditions — 20th century. I Title.
ML82.H35 1977
780'.82'0941—dc21 97-2419
CIP
MN

ISBN 1 85928 183 4

Typeset in Sabon by Photoprint, Torquay, Devon and printed in Great Britain by Biddles Limited, Guildford and King's Lynn.

Contents

Preface

> The study of gender does not simply involve the study of women. Neither does it simply involve the addition of the study of women to the study of men. It involves a reconceptualization of the study of humanity so that the rectification of this particular silence (itself a consequence of a particular political agenda) results in a different understanding of the social world. To study the situation of women is, in other words, to challenge the political domination of men.*

Why are women composers still such a rarity in Britain at the end of the twentieth century? Since I myself am a female musician, the motivation to find the reason for this particular situation has been personal as well as professional. The initial stages of my research were inspired by Germaine Greer's book *The Obstacle Race* (London, 1979), which concerns female pictorial artists. This book provided an effective model for the study of women's experiences on both the personal and the professional level. Hence this book is only incidentally about the actual music that women composers have produced. Rather, it is an examination of the many factors which influence the degree to which women as a group are enabled to fulfil their musical potential. My research has been structured to address a broad range of issues, many lying outside mainstream musicology, which affect female composers' creative potential, compositional output, career and place in musical life. Ultimately, the study of women's contribution to musical composition cannot be separated from women's wider position in a society within which they lack tradition, value, authority and power. The many social changes brought about in this century seem to have done little to redress the continued gender-bias of our musical culture. (A pertinent example: the 1995 Proms season of concerts included works by only five female composers compared with some 106 male composers; it featured 50 male conductors as opposed to one female; 42 male as against 10 female solo instrumentalists.) Despite this evident bias, many people still question the need to single out women composers and musicians for special attention. It is often felt that women have more than sufficient encouragement and opportunity to become professional musicians and that therefore any 'artificial' segregation serves only to reinforce their position outside the mainstream. The belief that any music of quality will sooner or later be recognised as such, no matter who composed it, is widespread. This, coupled with the reality of a musical culture which, both traditionally and

---

* John Shepherd, *Music as Social Text* (Cambridge, 1991), 153.

currently, is male-dominated, has provided the foundation for suggestions that women in some innate way lack the ability to compose music of substance and enduring value.

My study departs from the precedent set by much of the pioneering published research about women composers, which has most often applied traditional methodology ('life and works') and anthologizing treatment to women. Although this type of research was, and is, vital to the process of reconstructing a history which actually includes women, I felt that this approach fails to pay sufficient attention to the factors lying behind the invisibility (and scarcity) of women composers as a group in the first place. My research has examined the traditions, theories (psychological and cultural) and systems (social and musical) which have led to the current situation. This approach is actually quite novel, since the study of Western 'art' music has, by and large, shown itself very resistant to the absorption of data and concepts acquired via interdisciplinary investigation. Musicologists have traditionally avoided the wider social, cultural and political issues which influence musicians and music, preferring instead to discuss music as an autonomous entity, untainted by external reality. Yet composers and their works do not operate beyond the reach of social and political influence: factors other than purely musical ones do genuinely affect the development of musicians and the production and consumption of music. Interdisciplinary study has emerged as an essential foundation on which to construct a more holistic understanding of women composers, their position and their work.

The book is divided into three parts which together broadly embrace the areas of psychology, social history and the gendered politics of music. The convergence of the many elements within these areas creates the environment in which composers (and their works) are formed. Part One of the book is an examination of the arguments against female creativity and musical ability (which are both numerous and persistent). This is a controversial area carefully avoided by many writers. However, I felt that such arguments could not be ignored, since they form the overt or tacit basis for wider discrimination against women composers. Through the study of sex differences in the realm of psychology any limits (real or imagined) to female musical creativity can be revealed. The difficulty in fully researching physical or mental sex-differentiation is that the relevant information lies scattered across many disciplines: biology, neurology, psychology, music psychology, education, social history, anthropology and doubtless others. The evidence and information uncovered through the integrated study of information from these various fields has yielded many new insights and conclusions.

Part Two of the book focuses on the social, domestic and educational dimensions which continue to affect female composers in the twentieth century. In order to gain a clearer picture of the environments in which modern women composers have developed, I elected to orient the study around the lives, education and experiences of a group of women. To do this, I assembled a study group of nine British female composers who were all born in the twentieth century: Avril Coleridge-Taylor, Grace Williams, Elizabeth Maconchy, Minna Keal, Ruth Gipps, Antionette Kirkwood, Enid Luff, Judith Bailey and Bryony Jagger. The conventional criteria for inclusion in such a group are the quantity of works written and the level of 'success' achieved. However, in a book committed to identifying factors which affect female creativity negatively, such an approach would be likely to exclude women who had suffered difficulties. Therefore the group is a highly diverse cross-section of female composers, the single connecting factor being that they have all written at least one symphonic work. This factor was a vital element in linking the study group to the extended discussion of genre which occurs in Chapter 6. I feel that the group is fairly representative, despite its small size. The lives, experiences, beliefs and musical contributions of these women have provided valuable insights and information forming the basis for wider discussions. Since published information about most of the nine chosen composers is both inadequate and limited, a large amount of original fieldwork was necessary. Only two books containing information about any of them have been published. These are *Grace Williams* by Malcolm Boyd and *The Heritage of Samuel Coleridge-Taylor* by Avril Coleridge-Taylor (the second section of this work is autobiographical). These books have been invaluable, since gathering information directly from the two composers concerned was impossible. I have also consulted many articles, published primarily in newspapers and magazines, which between them cover most of the women in the study. Unfortunately, the quality and accuracy of these publications varies immensely, so that overall they have been of limited use in compiling the biographies.* In view of the varying degrees of access to the composers and the diverse nature of the sources of information, the biographies are not equally detailed.

Part Three explores the gendered politics of musicology and the musical establishment. Musicology has often ignored women composers and thereby silenced their contribution. Many recent writings on women composers serve to illustrate the level of bias and discrimination still deeply embedded in the musical establishment. The last two chapters explore matters which are widely thought to be almost beyond political or social influence: traditions, compositional genre, musical valuation and musical perception. Yet the roles played by these elements are all affected by gender and the functional significance ascribed to this category.

Gender is an inescapable issue, however much we may wish it otherwise: it is the basic polarity upon which society is constructed and divided. Hence no woman (or man) can approach the subject of women's current social and cultural position with the perfectly dispassionate spirit of enquiry that, in theory, scientific or scholarly investigation demands. However, the subject is far too important to be avoided just because this ideal, in its pure form, cannot

* Newspaper articles which were supplied by the composers or were located in collections housed in the British Music Information Centre are often saved simply as 'cuttings'; hence page numbers (and occasionally even the name of the publication) are not always recorded. I have, wherever possible, traced such information.

be attained. Although the results of my study conform, broadly speaking, to what I would have wished to find when I began my research, I have done my best to consider all relevant evidence seriously. As this evidence is so multifarious, and because some of it is inconclusive or ambiguous in meaning, my conclusions are inevitably qualified and nuanced. Nevertheless, my main conclusion – that the low number of women composers and their comparatively low public status are due to social, cultural and historical factors rather than to biological ones – is not in doubt. This book does not propose specific remedies for the various disadvantages and injustices that it uncovers, but it does venture to suggest where action is needed.

In the course of my research I have become aware of the scepticism and criticism evoked by gender studies in music, not least from women composers themselves. Many of them feel that any special examination of their position – that is, any study which highlights problems affecting women as a group – in some way 'excuses' those who lack sufficient talent and training. Most musicians, both male and female, continue to believe that the main or indeed only factor which limits a composer is lack of talent. Women composers are desperate for their work to be judged on merit alone; they wish to be treated equally and without discrimination, whether positive or negative. However, the belief that musical quality alone will catapult women composers into the midst of the musical canon is not only somewhat optimistic but also tends in many ways to confirm that women composers of the past and present are being ignored for all the right reasons. Through my research I hope to show that the issues which surround composers and the status of their music, are connected not only with aesthetics and talent but also with history, politics, society and, above all, power.

Acknowledgements

First and foremost, I offer gratitude to the seven composers who have shared with me their lives, experiences and ideas, and who have given so generously of their time: Judith Bailey, Ruth Gipps, Enid Luff, Minna Keal, Antoinette Kirkwood, Bryony Jagger and the late Elizabeth Maconchy. I would also like to thank Mrs Marian Glyn Evans for supplying information about her sister Grace Williams.

Special thanks are due to Professor Michael Talbot at Liverpool University, who has guided and encouraged my research and has shown me much kindness.

For permission to quote extracts and to reproduce illustrations I am grateful to:

Harcourt, Brace & Company (for illustrations from *The Introduction to Psychology*)

Peter Owen Ltd, London (for quotations from *The Great Sex Divide*, by Glenn Wilson, 1989)

Yale University Press (for quotations from *The Way Men Think*, by Liam Hudson and Bernadine Jacot, 1991)

Cambridge University Press (for quotations from *Gender and the Musical Canon*, by Marcia J Citron, 1993)

The University of Wales Press (for quotations from *Grace Williams*, by Malcolm Boyd, 1980)

The University of Minnesota Press (for quotations from *Feminine Endings*, by Susan McClary, 1991)

Every effort has been made to trace all copyright holders but if any have been inadvertently overlooked, the author and publisher apologise and will be pleased to make the necessary arrangement at the earliest opportunity.

I would like to express my appreciation to the many individuals who have been of great assistance in my search for information, particularly the staff of the

Sidney Jones Library at the University of Liverpool and its Inter-Library Loans section; also Janet Snowman of the Royal Academy of Music, Kevin Porter and Mike Fuller at the Royal College of Music, Elizabeth Chambers at Trinity College of Music, the staff of the London Symphony Orchestra, the City of Birmingham Symphony Orchestra, the London Philharmonic and the BBC Philharmonic; Peter Barry Ould of Bardic Edition, Malcolm Smith at Boosey and Hawkes and Dr Malcolm Boyd.

Personal thanks are due to my family, who have helped me in innumerable ways; Clare Pugh and Lee McDonough have supplied tireless support, both practically and emotionally.

Finally, I offer my greatest thanks to my Dad and Mum, Eric and Jennifer Halstead, who have believed in me and shared my enthusiasm. Their love, support and encouragement have continued to know no bounds.

Part One: Psychology

1 Music and Aptitude

> Women, it should be remembered, only in our own era are beginning to emerge from a long period of social and economic subjection. But, it will be rightly urged, there have been great novelists and even poets during this same period [. . .] but there is no composer of even second-rate rank among women. What is the explanation? [. . .] The most frequent conjecture has been that women just don't have what it takes [. . .] it is possible to predict that there will never be a female composer of the first rank [. . .] If [. . .] she does make her appearance, she would [. . .] be a biological freak.[1]

> Virtually all of the people throughout history whose achievements are acknowledged as products of undisputed genius have one thing in common. They come from a great variety of geographical, national, social and religious backgrounds, but they are all male. Starting with names like Da Vinci, Newton, Einstein, Galton, Shakespeare, Edison, Goethe, Beethoven, Mozart, Wagner and Picasso, we might have to fill many pages before the first comparable women would appear. When we consider the claims of women for inclusion in a list of outstanding accomplishments, their contributions can be seen mostly in the fields of literature [. . .] humanitarianism [. . .] or politics [. . .], rather than science, technology, music or fine art [. . .] Few social learning theorists [. . .] would deny the preponderance of male genius, but would proffer an explanation in terms of the limited educational opportunities for women throughout history and general discouragement to achieve outside the realm of motherhood and the home. This explanation seems to be unsatisfactory on a number of counts [. . .] it would seem more fruitful to seek an explanation for the appearance of male genius in constitutional factors [. . .] intellectual, motivational [. . .] [and] temperamental.[2]

Biological differences between men and women have often been adduced to provide justification for male domination, and this has been the case in music as in many other areas. The emerging field of research which examines women's role in, and contribution to, Western 'art' music has for the most part attempted to highlight the social inequalities lying behind the observable fact that the vast majority of this musical canon has been created by men. However, there is a long tradition of arguments which state that women have not become 'great' composers (or indeed composers at all) because they are biologically or psychologically less well equipped than men to create music. These ideas have persisted throughout the twentieth century and continue to place a question mark over the extent of women's innate musical and creative abilities. Such charges must be answered, as otherwise the body of arguments which ascribe women's relative lack of contribution (or indeed, lack of distinction) in musical composition to some kind of biological or mental inferiority will surely persist, inhibiting their progress towards full integration in the musical mainstream.

The route to understanding how male and female musical aptitude may differ is complex and lies within a range of disciplines. In the course of this chapter I intend to examine sex differences in biology (genetics, hormones, brain structure, sensory perception) and psychology (brain organization, intellect, cognitive ability and types of thinking), since these areas form the basis for the various functions and abilities that we understand collectively as musical aptitude.[3]

It is an indisputable fact that men and women differ in their physiology. It is also one of the first realizations made by children in relation to themselves and those around them. The understanding of one's biological sex is fundamental to any person's identity. However, beyond the understanding of the obvious differences in internal and external sex organs, there is much confusion over how such differences may affect men and women either physically or mentally. It must be admitted that research into sex differences is a hotly contested area and is often marked by contradiction, claim and counter-claim.

A firm starting point, however, is the genetic difference. A female has two X chromosomes (XX), whereas a male has one X and one Y chromosome (XY); this constitutes the genetic sex of an individual. In the first seven weeks of development, there are no anatomical differences between a male and female foetus. The onset of the sexual changes in anatomy, and so the beginning of sex differentiation, is initiated by hormones. Contrary to popular belief, no hormone is exclusively male or female, although men carry higher concentrations of steroid hormones called androgens, particularly testosterone, whereas women carry higher concentrations of two steroids of similar structure, called respectively oestrogens and progestogens.[4] Sex hormones are very powerful chemicals, and it is only in recent years that scientists have begun to understand the effect they, and other groups of hormones, have on the human body, brain and behaviour and hence how far these hormones may dictate sex-differentiated skills, behaviour and ability.

However, before discussing this most recent instalment in the research into sex differences, I intend to confront perhaps the oldest known sex difference which has been used as the biological basis for female inferiority: that of brain size and structure. Although the basic structure of the human brain is common to both sexes, women's brains are, on average, smaller and lighter than those of men; they also vary slightly in their proportions.[5] Put simply, it was first suggested that male brains were bigger than female brains because males are more intelligent! Indeed, this was first proposed by Aristotle more than two thousand years ago.[6] From this time a clear line of neurologically-based arguments which have sought to reinforce bigoted attitudes about women can be traced. Naïve as all this may seem, the extension of this argument has provided the biological justification for the subjection and oppression of women for hundreds of years; it has underscored restrictions on female education and opportunity, by denying female capabilities across a wide range of intellectual skills.

The results of scientific data on sex differences have often been misinterpreted and used as part of the wider political opposition to women's rights. The importance assigned to the difference in brain size found between men and women emerged anew in nineteenth-century disciplines such as craniometry and phrenology, which took for granted that absolute brain size reflected intellectual capacity. For example, in 1879 Gustave Le Bon, a prominent French man of medicine, concluded:

> In the most intelligent races [. . .] there are a large number of women whose brains are closer in size to those of gorillas than to the most developed male brains [. . .] All psychologists who have studied the intelligence of women [. . .] recognize that they represent the most inferior forms of human evolution and that they are closer to children and savages than to an adult, civilised man.[7]

Such theories were said to 'prove' that women were less intelligent than men and therefore justified the legislation that denied women access to equal education (or indeed the opportunity to take control of their own lives), at a time when women were demanding equal rights across most of Europe. These supposedly 'scientific' theories had many other political applications and were used against other oppressed groups. For example, the information that European brains were larger than non-European brains was used as biological support for the continuation of slavery and colonialism. It is disturbing to witness just how unobjective scientists could be and how often they misinterpreted results to lend proof to their original theories – theories which could be loaded with prejudice.[8] The emergence and decline of the theories of inequality in mental abilities as determined by sex-linked and racial differences in brain size have always been as much social as scientific in origin. For example, only in the early 1900s, when women were proving their claim on higher education to be legitimate, achieving academic results comparable with men, was the belief in a biologically determined lack of general intelligence no longer able to be intellectually respectable.

Early in this century it was demonstrated (and widely accepted) that neither brain weight nor cerebral dimensions had any effect on intelligence. Moreover, it has been proposed that women's proportionally smaller brains only parallel their proportionally smaller bodies and that any measurements of brains should correlate brain size in relation to overall body size.[9] Yet some scientists have continued to argue that male brains are proportionally bigger than female and that the explanation for the difference in size and weight corresponds to levels of intelligence. For example, a recent piece of research suggested that even after the difference in body size was taken into account, the average male brain was still about 100 grams heavier than that of the female.[10] This led a recent review of such research to conclude:

> [. . .] many scientists deny that there is any connection at all between brain size and intelligence, although a number of recent studies have found that a weak correlation does exist [. . .] only one thing is sure. The size difference [. . .] has the same

> implications as the rest of the sex differences found in the brain: it shows that men's and women's brains are different [. . .][11]

Although it is often stressed that difference does not necessarily mean inequality, almost without exception the information is then used to support reasons for a biologically-based difference in women's social and cultural position. Scientists speak of such differences in brain size as if they were unchallengeable, but on closer inspection the methods used for assessing brain size and weight in relation to body size and weight (even at the present time) appear at best varied and at worst flawed:

> [. . .] modern students of brain size [. . .] have still not agreed on the proper measure to eliminate the powerful effect of body size. Height is partly adequate, but men and women of the same height do not share the same body build. Weight is even worse than height, because most of its variation reflects nutrition rather than intrinsic size – fat v. skinny exerts little influence upon the brain. Manouvrier took up this subject in the 1880s and argued that muscular mass and force should be used. He tried to measure this elusive property in various ways a [. . .] When he corrected for what he called 'sexual mass', women actually came out slightly ahead in brain size.[12]

Hence fact and figures which relate to sex differences in brain size should be approached with the utmost caution. Moreover, even if it is proved beyond doubt that female brains are relatively smaller and lighter, despite the difference in body size, there is still no evidence that this factor has any direct bearing on intelligence, aptitude or behaviour.[13] Indeed, to reveal the precarious nature of many of the conclusions which relate differences in intelligence to differences in brain size is not difficult:

> [. . .] the ratio of brain to body size tells us little about intelligence – if it did, we would have to expect not only dolphins, but also marmosets and even some strains of mice, to outshine us intellectually, since these species all have a more impressive brain to body-weight ratio than we have.[14]

The brain size debate is but one illustration of how science has been used to provide justification for sexual discrimination. If it can be proved that women are less capable in whatever way, it removes the onus from society to change its attitudes about women. Fighting this kind of biological determinist prejudice is a battle which has continued on many fronts throughout the twentieth century.

The greatest advances in the understanding of human intelligence have come about through the introduction of more reliable methods of testing intelligence. Indeed, intelligence tests (Intelligence Quotient or IQ tests) have become the principal basis for the measurement of mental ability across the world for some decades. These intelligence tests measure a person's ability in a number of areas: verbal reasoning, quantitative/mathematical reasoning, abstract visual reasoning[15] and short-term memory. Through the application of these tests it has been established that males and females score about the same on intelligence tests such as the Stanford-Binet and the Wechsler tests. Yet within the different test areas differences between members of the two sexes and of other subgroups (for example, those defined by race and economic class) have been found:

> Females, *on the average*, have scored higher then males on tests of verbal ability; males, *on the average*, have scored higher than females on tests of mathematical reasoning and visual-spatial skills.[16]

This was not thought to be of great importance to the overall intelligence of either sex, and most intelligence tests have been refined in order to minimize sex differences by excluding types of tests that showed a large difference between the sexes or by balancing tests that were advantageous to either sex. However, some still see a difference in the pattern of IQ test results and have used these slight differences as the basis for arguments which continue to set limits on female aptitude. One of the first extensive pieces of research into the sex-linked cognitive differences as found in IQ tests was carried out by Maccoby and Jacklin in 1975. They noted that females between one and five years of age were more proficient in linguistic skills than males of the same age.[17] The female advantage in communicative skills, fluency, comprehension, verbal reasoning and flexibility in handling verbal symbols remains throughout human development. Females are superior in reading skills. More recent research has confirmed that females are superior in verbal and visual memory.

The superior ability of males in spatial-mechanical ability has been well documented.[18] Men have a superior capacity to rotate or isolate visual images into new planes or combinations. Males have been shown to have superior mathematical ability from adolescence onwards.[19] Moreover, it seems that boys continue to improve mathematically, whereas girls seem to decline in ability from the age of 11–15. In tests of analytical ability boys of school age consistently scored better than girls, but these differences are not apparent in pre-adolescent children.[20] The slight difference in visual-spatial ability between the sexes has been put forward as a reason for men's dominance in many fields (including that of musical composition).

There is a great deal of disagreement among psychologists about the reason for the slight differences in cognitive abilities; opinions range from a biological-determinist stance to socialization theories. Traditionally, the view in the second camp was that sex differences in certain abilities were culturally imposed, being due to differences in male and female learning opportunities, and this indeed now seems to be the most obvious and likely cause of the differences. This theory is strongly supported by evidence from recent studies that although these specific differences in test results have been recognized since intelligence testing began, the differences have diminished gradually over the last 30 years.[21] It seems that both male verbal proficiency and female mathematical/spatial reasoning are improving.[22] This suggests that earlier differences in scores were due, at least in part, to differences in training and social expectation. Culturally prescribed activities encourage boys and girls to develop in different ways. A good example of this is the types of toys children are encouraged to play with. From an early age boys have access to toys which encourage objectification (trains, trucks), whereas girls receive encouragement in communication (dolls).[23] Recent research reinforces this view: at school boys are now being encouraged to take an interest in the humanities subjects and girls are encouraged to study science subjects. Whilst these different strengths in ability should be noted, it is also important to keep the differences between the sexes in perspective. The differences are only average differences and are small when compared with the variability within each group: that is, many girls will score better on visual spatial skills than many boys. This seems to be a fact conveniently ignored by those who seek confirmation of an innate mental deficiency in women.

Some researchers have tried to explain what they see as 'male' abilities, particularly spatial/mathematical reasoning, as being due to male physiology in terms of brain organization and structure, hormones and genetics. This provides a sex-differentiated biological basis for the cognitive process. At first sight, male aptitude for spatial processing may seem rather rarefied and not particularly useful in the context of a discussion of musical abilities, but, on the contrary, many have suggested that spatial processing lies at the heart of many musical faculties, especially composition.

The most recent finding to place certain limitations on the functions of the female brain in comparison with the male, particularly in terms of spatial abilities, focuses not on the debate over brain size and weight but instead on brain organization and function. Before we embark on a more detailed discussion of the research into brain sex differentiation, it seems important to state some neurological facts establishing the overwhelming similarity of human brains, regardless of sex.

The brain can be seen as divided into three sections (see Figure 1.1):

- **Central Core**
  The various structures in the central core of the brain control breathing and coordination of movement; they also act as sense receptors for vision, hearing, touch and taste.
- **Limbic System**
  The various structures in the limbic system control hormone levels and memory, but this system is primarily concerned with experiencing emotion. It is also affected by hormones.
- **Cerebral Hemispheres** (together, these are known as the cerebrum)
  The cerebrum is more developed in human beings than in any other organism. All the sensory systems project information into areas of the cortex (an outer layer of the cerebrum). This is divided in two basically symmetrical sections, described as the right and left hemispheres. Each hemisphere is divided into four lobes: the frontal, parietal, occipital and temporal. Some experts believe it is here that differences in male and female thinking are located.

Basically, it is understood that the various parts of the brain control, and specialize in, various functions and skills. The dominant left side of the cerebral cortex controls and processes language and verbal information; the minor right side controls and processes non-verbal information. The brain processes

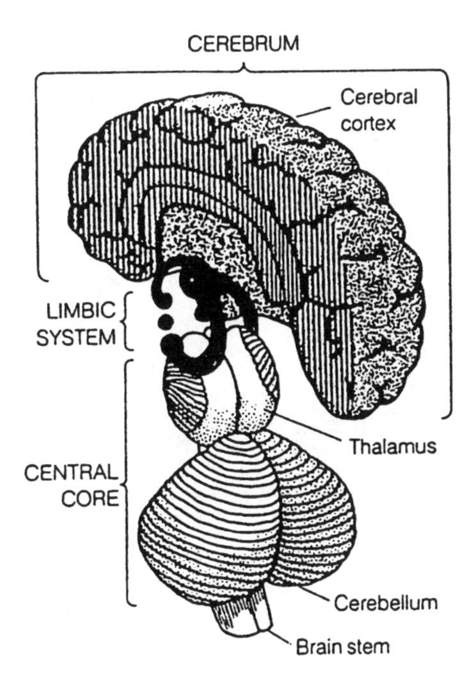

Figure 1.1 Three concentric layers of the human brain
Source: Atkinson and Atkinson, *Introduction to Psychology*

information passed from the *opposite* side of the body. For example, a visual stimulus picked up by the right eye is processed by the left side of the brain, and vice versa. This is the reason why most people are right-handed, as the left side of the brain is the dominant processor of words and verbal sounds. Only 3 per cent of people are naturally left-handed; these people have more of their language ability located in the right side of the brain.

It is important to remember that although the two hemispheres of the brain differ in their specialization, they integrate their actions at all times. Much research has been done into the localization (or lateralization) of a variety of skills and special abilities, including music, within the two hemispheres and the brain as a whole. It is generally agreed that some specialized functions occur in each hemisphere; these are listed in Table 1.1.

Variations in this arrangement are believed to result in varying levels of ability in certain functions. Significantly, aspects of brain organization known as hemispheric lateralization have been observed to function differently in men and women. Again, scientists have put forward a number of often opposed views.[24] It has been suggested that the female brain is both more *and* less lateralized than the male brain! Such extreme divergences of opinion serve only to show the difficulty of obtaining suitable objective data.

Possibly the most convincing evidence concludes that women's brains are slightly less lateralized than men's.[25] Taken very simply, this means that the

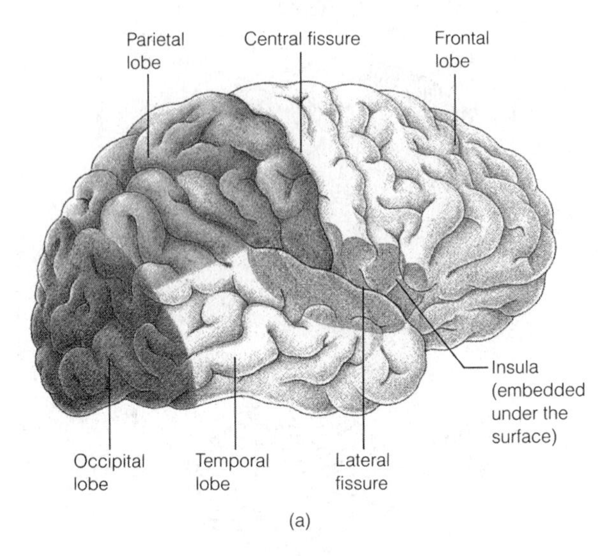

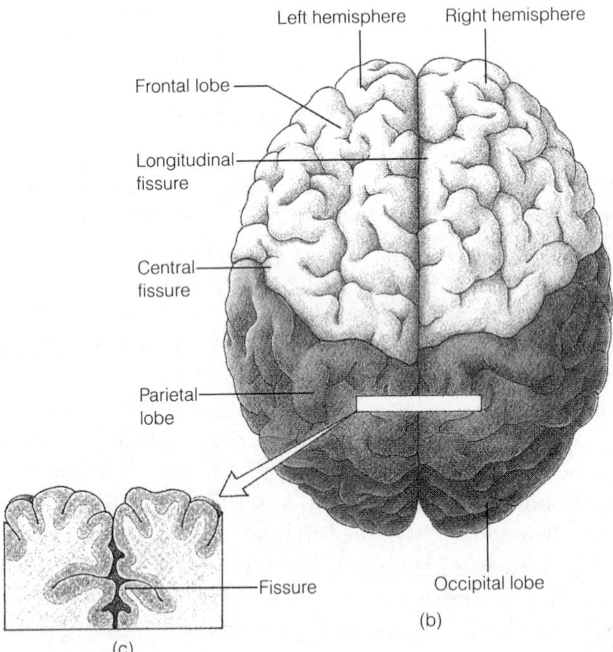

Figure 1.2 Cerebral hemispheres
(a) Lateral view. (b) Superior view. (c) Transverse section through cerebral cortex.
Source: Atkinson and Atkinson, *Introduction to Psychology*

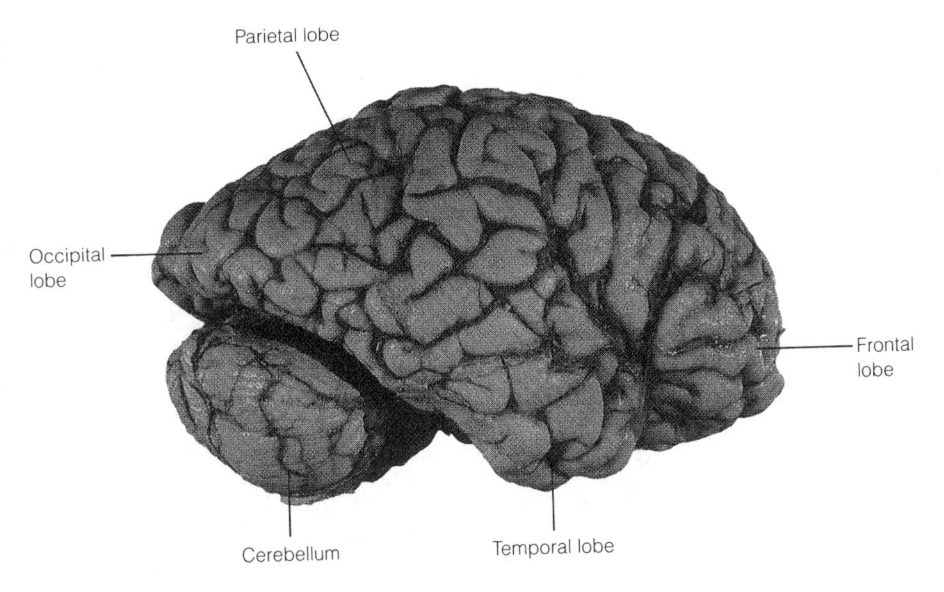

Figure 1.3 Human brain (lateral view)
Source: Atkinson and Atkinson, *Introduction to Psychology* (© Martin Rotker/Phototake, NYC)

female brain is better organized for communicating between the two hemispheres, whereas the male brain specializes its functions more strongly in each hemisphere.[26] Some investigators have noted that the anatomical construction of the female brain tends to support this theory. An observable difference in the brains of male and female foetuses is that the corpus callosum (a band of nerved fibres which connect the two hemispheres) is often larger in females. This is thought to be because the female corpus callosum has larger fibres, which makes communication between the two halves more efficient.[27] However, a number of researchers have stressed:

> It is important to emphasize that these are gender differences in the *degree* of lateralization and are small in magnitude compared to the extent of lateralization found in both men and women. The really striking finding is that the *human* brain shows hemispheric specialization.[28]

The differences in brain lateralization may indeed be slight, but they have been used to set limits on the aptitude of females rather than males. In a similar way to the conclusions drawn from the supposed differences in brain size they have been used as neurological 'proof' that social factors have little to do with the lack of female contribution in a number of areas.

The most striking example of this type of theory is the suggestion that because the female brain apparently integrates its functions to a greater degree, it is less well equipped to process spatial information (a function believed to be located mainly in the right hemisphere). In 1972 tests carried out by J. Levy confirmed that in tests of spatial ability, as found in intelligence tests, boys perform better than girls. Levy linked this information to superior right-brain

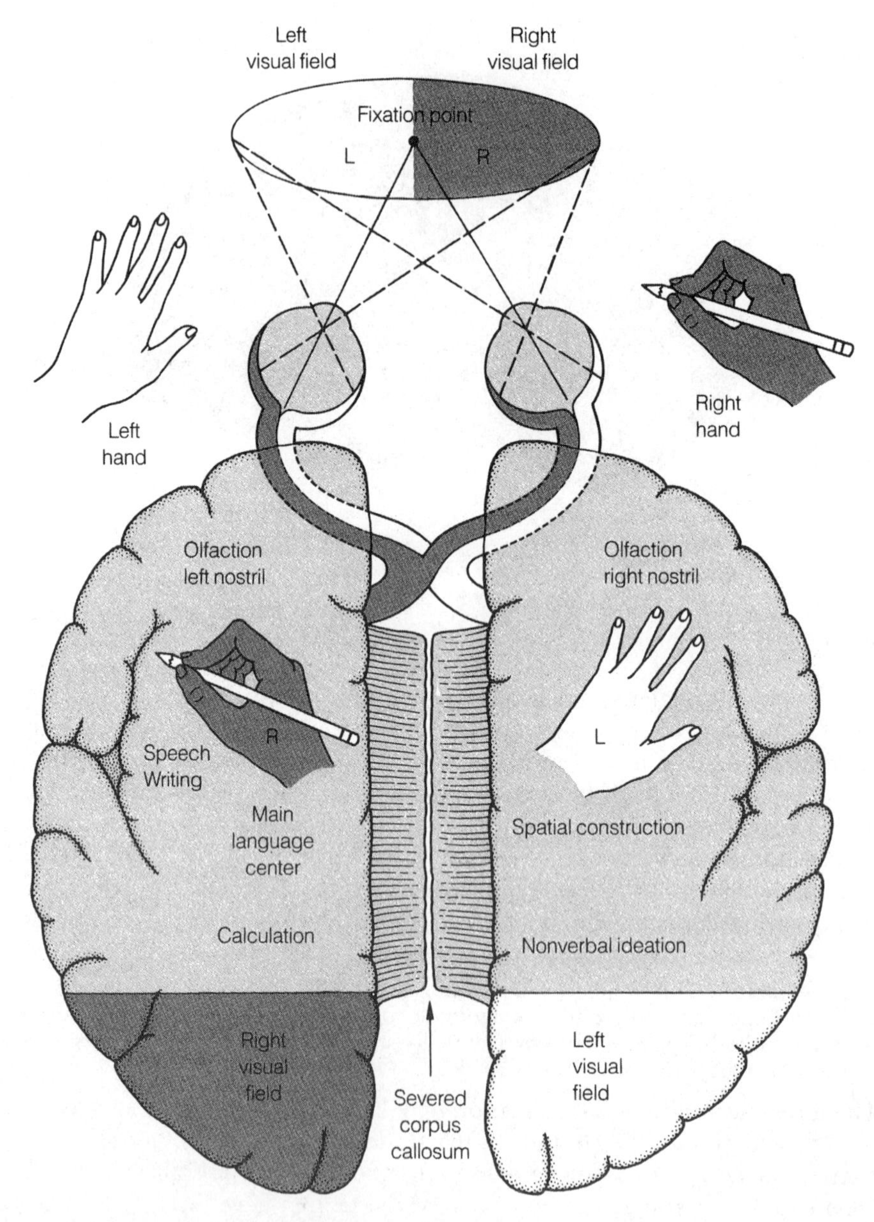

Figure 1.4 Sensory inputs into the two hemispheres
Source: Atkinson and Atkinson, *Introduction to Psychology* (Reprinted from 'Perception in the absence of neocortical commissures', in *Perceptions and its Disorders*, Res. Publ. ARNMD, Vol. 48)

functioning in males.[29] Levy proposed that females (like left-handed males) process spatial information in the part of the brain where they also process verbal information. This results in mutual interference by the two types of

Table 1.1 Specialized functions of the left and right hemispheres

Left hemisphere	Right hemisphere
Language	Comprehends simple language
Complex logical and analytical activities	Highly developed spatial and pattern sense
Mathematical computation	Can perform simple 2-digit calculations
	Responds to association of objects

Source: Atkinson and Atkinson *et al.*, *Introduction to Psychology*

information, which disrupts performance. She concluded that specialization of one hemisphere for language and the other for spatial information (which characterizes right-handed men but not women!) indicates a more perfect evolution. Women's brains suddenly became flawed through right-hemisphere deficit. This theory was given a further biological foundation when it was linked to male hormones.[30] It was proposed that larger amounts of testosterone (the predominantly male sex hormone) resulted in right-brain superiority in men. It is believed that left-handedness (resulting in a greater ability to process information in the right hemisphere) is caused by a prenatal imbalance of hormones resulting from over exposure to testosterone. Obviously, male vulnerability to excessive testosterone is greater than women's, and this seems to be validated by the greater incidence of male left-handers.[31] If it is testosterone which causes a greater distribution of processes in the right side of the brain, this could give men a natural advantage in many professions which require a great deal of right-hemisphere processing. The inference, if these theories are correct, is that it is this biologically dictated right-hemisphere superiority in men, and not social conditioning or male opposition, which accounts for a smaller accomplishment by women in professions such as music, art, architecture and engineering, all of which are thought to rely for the greater part on right-hemisphere processing.

Others have put forward the idea that sex differences in the brain are as much the effect as the cause of inequalities. Lauren Jay Harris has pointed out that girls' verbal functions mature more quickly than those of boys.[32] In turn, this leads mothers to stimulate verbal skills more in their daughters than in their sons and induces girls to rely on their dominant hemisphere to process both linguistic and spatial information.

Apart from the theories concerning the influence of hormones on differences in thinking and reasoning, some researchers have found evidence which points to the responsibility of hormonal-based sex differences for other stereotypical male behaviour:

> [testosterone] increases behavioural reactivity [. . .] It enhances persistence and attention [. . .] it makes sense that sex drive, aggression and testosterone should come together in men, along with intensity, quick reaction and visual spatial skills, in one evolutionary package.[33]

Although the effect of hormones on women has been studied to a lesser degree, some writers see oestrogen and progesterone as lying at the root of women's passivity and domestic orientation:

> Given externally, progesterone and its relatives induce calmness. And estradiol and its relatives seem to promote a sense of well-being. This may be somehow connected to the woman's essential role as mother [. . .] the evolutionary package that comes with the sex hormones [. . .] also comes perhaps with some maternal ability but more surely with a sensitivity to mood, an evenness of temperament and a general lack of volatility.[34]

However, the significance of the role played by sex hormones in terms of brain organization or behaviour is not universally accepted, and scientists often hold completely opposing views on the exact nature and purpose of hormones. It was mentioned at the start of this chapter that hormones initiate sex differentiation in the human foetus. The presence of these sex hormones, or the lack of them, plays a vital role in the masculinization or feminization of the genitalia and the onset of secondary sexual characteristics. Male sex hormones must be present at the earliest stages for a male to develop successfully; in this way, it has been suggested that in mammals, the female is the 'default' sex. Although some writers have identified the differences in sex hormones as the biological justification for sex-differentiated behaviour and social positions, other studies argue strongly against such theories:

> On available evidence the differing concentrations of androgens in males and females cannot explain human sex differences in sexual and aggressive behaviour or on psychophysical and cognitive tasks. It has been impossible to control for cultural factors. Even in animals it has frequently been possible to demonstrate that environmental factors can modify the effects of sex hormones on behaviour [. . .] Arguments using Man's evolutionary past to justify a hormonal control of human behaviour are therefore fallacious.[35]

All too often, the vital effects of learned social behaviour are not considered as part of the psychological equation. From the very first days of life a baby's sex is the fundamental factor affecting how the child is treated and expected to function. The powerful ideas imposed by social and cultural surroundings prescribe very definite roles and modes of behaviour for the two sexes. In my opinion, the passages quoted earlier that posit hormonal control of gender-stereotyped behaviour reinforce the idea that a woman is fundamentally programmed to be docile, biologically destined and psychologically content to be mother and carer. Opinions formed along these lines have lain at the foundation of a view that the limitations placed on women's cultural contribution are biologically determined and therefore inevitable. According to this view, the active, striving, dynamic, intense characteristics ascribed to the male (and here given a physiological basis in hormone levels) often lead to deviance and disaster – but are also characteristics fundamental to the intellectual motivation, drive and courage required in many creative, intellectual or physical acts.

The theory that men exhibit more extreme forms of behaviour (and intelligence) has been given an additional genetic basis, and has been linked to differences in male and female intelligence, in a number of ways. For example, when large quantities of IQ test results were analysed, it was observed that male results tend to cluster around the lower and upper ends of the scale; put more simply, men constitute both more of the most stupid and more of the most intelligent people:

> It appears that brain abnormalities, or exceptionality, are more common in men than in women. One result of this is to spread the range of IQs in men relative to women [. . .] This apparently occurs because the second X chromosome in women has an averaging effect, cancelling out extreme tendencies based on the other [. . .][36]

This has been used by some as evidence of the so-called 'hypothesis of female mediocrity' in that men seem, *more often* than women, to exhibit extreme forms of behaviour and ability; this includes those who achieve genius and greatness (in all areas), as well as those who are mentally abnormal in some way.[37] It is a fact that a higher proportion of males than females are classed as educationally subnormal. However, the two highest-ever recorded IQ scores were obtained by females.[38] So there may be slight differences in the range and variety of scores, but what conclusions should be drawn from this fact is open to debate. It is clear that whenever differences are found to exist between men and women, they will be interpreted by some as 'proof' of female deficiency or, as here, mediocrity.

It is striking that the findings of research into sex differences are used only to the disadvantage of females. A glaringly obvious example of this is the fact that female spatial 'deficiency' has been suggested as the reason for the shortage of women in certain occupational areas. Yet no one ever suggests that the male 'deficiency' in verbal, language and communication skills will disadvantage, or indeed has ever disadvantaged, male writers, politicians, poets or philosophers. If a verbal and language weakness in males can still result in a Shakespeare or a Wordsworth, it is clear that *group differences do not define the individual.* This argument proposes that 'male weaknesses' (revealed in comparison to females) erect no barriers to male aptitude – not just in average terms but also at extremely high levels of achievement. Surely the same should hold true for any 'female weaknesses'.

In the earliest scientific research the differences between male and female physiques and brains were exploited to become the obvious cornerstones of women's subjection. A century or two later, we confront the claim that it is a slight difference in innate cognitive abilities (which in fact works both ways) that accounts for women's relative lack of contribution and success in certain areas. I concur with the views expressed in Janet Sayers' ground-breaking work on the political significance of biological research. This writer suggests that the cognitive differences (based on differences in brain organization) between men and women will cease:

> [. . .] only given a situation in which women prove themselves equally competent to men in professions like engineering and architecture [and music]. In order for women to be able to do this, however, it will be necessary to struggle against the discriminatory practices that currently obstruct their entry into these professions,

> practices which are now being justified by some [. . .] in terms of sex differences in brain organisation.[39]

Differences in brain organization and cognitive abilities form part of the general argument used 'against' (in a variety of senses) women composers. In the rest of this chapter I will highlight a number of differences which are specific to musical aptitude. Obviously, the area of music psychology is vast, and I can in no way hope to give more than the briefest outline of its ideas in this and the following chapter. I intend to concentrate on those aspects of psychology and neurology which pertain to the previously discussed similarities and differences in male and female brain structure and organization.

Perhaps the greatest irony in the discussion of women and musical aptitude is the fact that in virtually all tests devised specifically to measure musical abilities (musical aptitude tests) women have been found to obtain superior results.[40] An article by G.M. Gilbert (1942) titled 'Sex differences in Musical Aptitude and Training' set out to disprove the stereotype that women had (in accordance with test results) greater innate musical abilities:

> An assumed sex difference is reflected in the social stereotype that women are 'more artistic' than men, and that the pursuit of the arts is more or less a peculiarly feminine activity. This stereotype seems to be supported by sex differences on certain tests, particularly those of musical talent.[41]

This certainly turns the whole idea of sex-related superiority on its head. However, it was concluded that:

> There is historical as well as psychometric evidence, however, that women are inferior or superior only insofar as their training is inferior or superior to that of men [. . .] their superiority in the arts has long been encouraged by superior training [. . .] Nevertheless, on the professional level we frequently find curious paradoxes where one set of stereotypes comes in conflict with another. In spite of the stereotype crediting women with superior musical talent, almost all the [professional] musicians [. . .] are male.[42]

That the arts generally are considered a 'feminine' area is not in dispute; however, the claim that women have received superior education in this area certainly is (see Chapter 4). How far musical aptitude (as measured by musical aptitude tests) is affected by musical education and training has long been debated. Many early researchers believed that musical aptitude was a totally inherited 'gift' which was unalterable by training or education. This view has often been used to combat the argument that females have been held back from achievement by lack of adequate opportunity:

> Many male geniuses have to override considerable disadvantage in their educational or social background [. . . for example] Richard Wagner had virtually no musical training but taught himself harmony by buying a book in his late teens [. . .] Social and educational advantages cannot be held accountable for the achievements of men such as [Wagner . . .] so why should disadvantage be invoked to account for the absence of female achievement?[43]

It should be noted, however, that in 1831, at the age of 18, Wagner had gained enough musical knowledge to enter Leipzig University to study music. If

Wagner had been a woman, whatever his level of genius, he would not have been allowed to enter university at that time, and so his musical development would have been impeded. The real issue is whether Wagner's genius appeared without *any* environmental encouragement or education. It must be stressed that even if this were the case, it would act as an argument against female composers only if women were proved to lack the mechanism to inherit such musical abilities.

Music history seems to provide evidence that musical aptitude of a high order is passed on through families; there have been many musical dynasties which are well documented: for example, the Bach, Couperin and Scarlatti families. Although many musicians have come from families in which musical ability was encouraged, others come from backgrounds which were unfavourable towards musical development. The conclusion reached by one investigator is:

> [. . .] we see that a home can be as musical as possible and yet no talent may appear, or it may appear in one child and not in another. It would seem then that one is or is not born with great musical capacity. Musical talent is in all probability inherited through a number of genes acting together, and without the required number of genes there can be no musical talent.[44]

Sex-linked mechanism theories of the transmission of musical aptitude would seem irrelevant when both sexes score equally well on musical aptitude tests. The evidence seems to point more to environmental factors and the development of musical behaviour as the fundamentals involved in developing musical ability:

> By saying that musical behaviour is acquired, we are not denying biological inheritance of structure. Deficient structures will obviously be limiting factors for musical as well as other kinds of behaviour.[45]

That there is a complex interplay between heredity and environment has been recorded by many researchers. A person's manifestation of musical talent can be increased by exposure to a musically stimulating environment and appropriate encouragement, this manifestation decreasing when environment and encouragement are inadequate:

> That musical talent is the result of previously acquired skills and not inherited genius should be clear by now. No great composer or performer ever achieved his goal without long hours of apprenticeship and struggle. Musical accomplishment is not the mere result of inherited inspiration but is also the product of hard work.[46]

Through extensive practice and study a person will achieve his or her full potential, but that potential is always genetically controlled. However, rates of maturation, which are heredity-controlled, can also affect musical development. Musically advanced children often have a head start which is hard to bridge for children who show musical ability later in their development. Sex differences in maturation rates are important when considering sex differences. If maturation were a relevant factor in the development of musical aptitude, females should have a distinct advantage over males, since girls mature faster than boys at every stage of development (females are more physiologically mature than males of the same chronological age until well after puberty). As physiological development is known to affect attitude and behaviour, girls possess advantages in many areas, including that of musical development. This fact has been put forward as a possible reason for some of the differences between the sexes in musical aptitude test scores which favour females.[47]

Obviously, all the evidence points to a complex interaction between inherited aptitude of many kinds, including musical aptitude, and the environment. It is the environmental factor which provides the huge sex-linked difference, for the societal environment for women is vastly different from that for men. The larger number of women entering some branches of music (singers account for a large proportion of female professional musicians) has been shown to have no genetic basis and is understood to be an entirely environmentally constructed inequality.[48] Environment greatly diminishes genetic factors, and the level of environmental effect is seen to vary according to the level of musical attainment. It seems reasonable to assume on the available evidence that there is no genetically determined difference in musical aptitude between men and women, contrary to the belief of early researchers. All this evidence points to the conclusion that natural endowment certainly plays a part in the level of the potential that a person can achieve, but this level of potential is in no way different in men as a group or women as a group.

When the area of music psychology is approached from a clinical neurological direction, it must first be acknowledged that the neurological sciences have obvious limits to how far they can understand and explain musical experiences; this is true also for other art forms, both literary and visual. Understanding the immensely complex functions of the brain and how humans create, perceive and react to art still seems to be beyond the scope of scientific understanding. However, some basic aspects of neurology and brain organization can be seen to have a direct effect on various aspects of musical aptitude.

We saw that the dimensions of the human brain often differ according to sex; this was found also to be true when studies were carried out into differences between the brains of eminent persons (including musicians) and persons of 'average' ability. The results are interesting, although inconclusive.[49] When brains are studied macroscopically, it does appear that there are some observed morphological differences in the brains of people of higher intellectual achievement as compared with those of persons of average ability. S. Auerbach, a pioneer in the study of the brains of eminent musicians, noticed certain differences in the brain structure of professional musicians in comparison with the 'average' brain:

> Auerbach concluded that in all cases so far investigated, the middle and posterior thirds of the superior temporal gyrus were strongly developed and showed great width; they were intimately connected with the equally well developed gyrus supramarginalis.[50]

I have not been able to find relevant research on the morphology of eminent women's brains, a state of affairs that could be held to imply that eminent women as group are either non-existent or, more likely, that they have not been recognized as such. If there are indeed differences in brain structure between the 'eminent' and 'average' male brain, the study of differences between 'eminent' and 'average' female brains might well reveal similar differences and quash the idea of any sex linkage. However, a morphologically well-developed brain is only one – although necessary – precondition for high intellectual achievement.

Attempts to find an anatomical localization of musical perception and expression have encountered considerable problems. Location of a specific area of the brain where musical processing occurs would perhaps go a long way to explain many elements of the psychology of music. Through continued morphological investigation, some areas of the brain have been associated with musical reception: particularly the temporal lobe and gyrus of the left hemisphere and, in association with musical expressiveness, the 'F2' region of the right hemisphere. Although it would be presumptive to conclude that this is proof of a strict anatomical localization of musical faculties, it seems likely that these abilities are controlled by varying levels of brain structure that are inborn.[51]

Much research which has suggested localization of musical abilities has been devoted to the study of cases of amusia.[52] It was found that receptive amusia corresponded with lesions of the anterior temporal areas in the dominant hemisphere (left), while lesions in parts of the minor (right) hemisphere were thought to relate to forms of expressive and vocal amusia.[53] In 1975, Scheid and Eccles concluded that structural differences in the brain indicate localization of skills within the brain:

> We suggest that the enlargement of the right planum temporal is a measurement of the musical ability built into the brain by genetic coding just as we would assume that the left planum temporal is a measure of the linguistic abilities similarly built prenatally ready for linguistic use.[54]

Special developments of the temporal lobe would be evident from birth, and therefore training would not affect this physiology, which would then indicate a totally inherited and innate musical aptitude. Much more research is needed before any of this information can be applied convincingly to any differences in abilities between the two sexes. Indeed, the most recent review of research into brain damage which affects musical performance concluded:

> [. . .] although right hemisphere damage nearly always disrupts musical functioning in musicians, left hemisphere damage often disrupts it too. It is, therefore, oversimplistic to say that music is 'in' the right hemisphere. What the complex and somewhat unsatisfactory literature on brain damage does at least show is that musical skills are just as dissociable and separately disruptable as are language skills.[55]

However, some writers have taken the lateralization of musical abilities as a right-hemisphere process as proven:

> A considerable amount of evidence suggests that in most right-handed persons the left hemisphere of the neocortex is dominant, dealing with verbal, analytic and

> executive functions, while the right hemisphere has a more visual, spatial, holistic and intuitive mode of operation. Music perception, composition and performance depends heavily on pattern-processing and so is widely held to be a right hemisphere activity.[56]

As previously noted, many scientists believe that men are somewhat better equipped to organize and process information in their right hemisphere. Does this then give men an advantage in those abilities, such as music, that appear to be located and processed in the right hemisphere? Some have been quick to cite this idea as the reason for the small number of female composers:

> There are some indications that men and women differ with respect to degree of brain asymmetry. In particular, the suggestion is that the right hemisphere of the male brain is more specialised for spatial functioning than is the right side of the female brain [. . .] If this theory is confirmed, it might help to account for the fact that, although women have written many celebrated novels over the last few centuries, they have not distinguished themselves as composers.[57]

The previously quoted opinions about sex differences in brain lateralization now become a focus for sex differences in musical processing.

It is generally agreed that human brain lateralization occurred as the result of the demands for information processing; hence the language processing area in the left hemisphere became dominant in humans. Experiments have shown that non-verbal auditory tasks are processed in the minor right hemisphere:

> This supports the indication that the central mechanisms relevant to the perception of music are located fundamentally in the minor hemisphere (the temporal lobe thereof).[58]

The evidence for right-hemisphere dominance and its corresponding left-ear superiority have come about through the introduction of dichotic listening techniques.[59] When a group of normal subjects were played a baroque melody and subsequently asked to recognize the musical passage, the subjects showed a greater level of identification if the melody was played to the left ear only, which suggests right-hemisphere superiority.[60] But despite the evidence for cerebral specialization for musical processing, its exact relation to musical aptitude remains unclear. Since music is made up of many varied components (timbre, intensity, duration and so on), when certain factors are altered – for example, if the intensity is changed – this has been seen to result in increased left-hemisphere processing and corresponding right-ear superiority.[61]

An added conceptual problem concerning music and hemispheric specialization is the correlation between the level of musical competence or experience and the pattern of cerebral organization. In tests carried out by Bever and Chiarello (1974) it was found that non-musicians got the best results when the music was played to the left ear (right hemisphere), whereas musicians got the best results when music was played to the right ear (left hemisphere). It would seem that articulate musical experience, like language, may be a process requiring the analytical abilities of the left hemisphere.[62] In addition:

> It seems that the left hemisphere advantage is not confined to musicians. People who score highly on a test of musical aptitude tend to show left hemisphere advantage,

regardless of training [. . .] as do non-musicians who consciously adopt an 'analytic' strategy in a music perception task [. . .][63]

There is a distinct connection between musical aptitude and left hemisphere advantage in musical processing. This research reinforces the opinion that most higher intellectual functions, including music, always seem to involve a greater communication between the two hemispheres of the brain and are never subject to simple hemispheric division. Music psychologist John Sloboda concluded on the information available:

There is little evidence for a single 'music centre' in the brain. Furthermore, the brain areas responsible for music seem to have a partial, but incomplete, overlap with those responsible for language [. . .] Music, if not a totally distinctive neural function, almost certainly employs a distinctive configuration of neural resources.[64]

The idea of a non-dominant music function has been advanced by Hans Borchgrevink. He concluded:

There is a close, but complex, connection between speech function and musical function. Both apparently consist of a multitude of sub-functions, many of which rely upon the same psychological mechanisms. This implies extensive possibilities of interference between the two functions, weakening the concepts of distinct and different cerebral lateralizations for speech function and musical function. Each subfunction may however be distinctively lateralized.[65]

In addition, he concluded that since rhythm and pitch/tonality are controlled by different hemispheres, virtually all kinds of musical performance require extensive inter-hemisphere processing and cooperation.

As was mentioned previously, women are believed to have less strongly lateralized brains, which are better at inter-hemisphere processing than those of males, which are more strongly lateralized. I think there is little point in implying that this may make women more able, or more perfectly evolved for higher functions, than men. The important point is that we should no longer use biologically based arguments to find the key reasons or explanations for women's lack of contribution. Psychological research yields many interesting results, especially concerning sex differences, but it should not ascribe the main reason for women's subordinate position to the nature of women themselves or to their seemingly unchangeable biology. The latter view all too conveniently removes the burden of responsibility from the patriarchal system, which seeks to control the female role and set boundaries for its operation.

However, such research has continued and must be assessed critically at every stage. Indeed, one sequel to the research which suggests right-hemisphere localization of musical abilities is the idea that musical aptitude is connected with spatial ability (believed to be localized in the right-hemisphere) and is therefore a more 'male' ability (since males achieve slightly better scores than females in this area). As mentioned previously, much research has been undertaken to explore the relationship between spatial ability and musical ability, which are seen as connected in that:

In children before and during puberty, and also in adults, high scores on tests measuring musical talent were associated with high scores on spatial tests.[66]

However, recent research suggests that this is not the case for female composers:

> Women composers tested [. . .] did not differ significantly from women non-musicians on those spatial measures that were found to be associated with musical capacities in male composers, or in male and female instrumentalists [. . .] [it was wondered whether . . .] the missing relationship between spatial ability and the ability to compose in female composers might be related to a special female style of composition.[67]

Although no such style could be identified, the wide range of tests carried out by Hassler, Nieschlag and La Motte (1990) revealed many previously unknown aspects of male and female musical processing. The tests compared male and female musicians (composers) and non-musicians in terms of musical aptitude, hormone levels, hemispheric lateralization and spatial ability and also subjected the compositions of the males and females to (blind) expert rating. The results brought out many points of interest.

First, although the relation between spatial ability and musical ability did not hold so true for female composers as for male, it was found that:

> [. . .] expert ratings for women's compositions were positively correlated with results of the Hidden Pattern Test, suggesting a relationship between the extent of creative musical ability and spatial ability.[68]

This seems to make a distinction between creative musical ability and more general aspects of musical aptitude. This aspect of spatial ability and creative musical ability would seem to hold true for female as well as male composers. It was also noted:

> In the female composers, highly significant correlations between ratings [of compositions] and the Wing [musical aptitude] tests indicate a close relationship between ability to compose and general musical intelligence; this was not found in male composers.[69]

Although this information is open to varied interpretation, it could indicate merely that women who go on to be composers have very high levels of all-round ability in music, whereas male composers do not necessarily have to display such abilities to be encouraged to pursue composition.

The tests of the hormone levels of male and female composers and non-musical groups revealed:

> [. . .] that higher evaluations of compositions were associated with lower testosterone levels [. . .] the male composer's group [. . .] had significantly lower mean testosterone levels than did male instrumentalists, and insignificantly lower mean testosterone levels than did male non-musicians. In female composers, the ratings were not related to testosterone output.[70]

This casts doubt on earlier suggestions that music was one of the abilities encouraged by 'male' hormones.

Significantly, a difference between male and female musical processing was identified:

> [. . . women composers'] pattern of functional hemispheric lateralization was a mirror image of that of male composers. For verbal processing male composers were

> the least left-lateralized of the male groups; female composers were the most left-lateralized of the female groups. For spatial processing, male composers were clearly right-lateralized; female composers [. . .] did better with their right hands/left hemisphere [. . .] In female composers, left-hemisphere functions were dominant for verbal and for spatial processing. However, a marked negative trend emerged between the expert ratings and verbal laterality indices in female composers. This outcome seems to indicate that left hemisphere superiority for verbal processing decreased with increased creative musical talent.[71]

This implies that males who possess strong creative musical ability process spatial and verbal information mainly in the right hemisphere, whereas females who possess strong creative musical ability process spatial and verbal information mainly in the left hemisphere. This difference in no way denies female creative musical ability but highlights differences in the way information is processed. Indeed, this finding has been endorsed by research carried out in 1980 into the cerebral processing of a group of professional musicians (unspecified gender). This observed that musicians vary in hemispheric domination:

> [. . .] two distinct sub-groups [. . . were found among the professional musicians tested . . .] about half of these musicians showed more right-hemisphere dominance for both dichotically presented chords and words. The other subgroup showed the opposite result. They exhibited left-hemisphere superiority for both chords and words [. . .] [it was concluded] that musicians with highly developed skills display a singular mode of thought or, alternatively, a singularly activated hemisphere.[72]

This would correspond with a situation where female composers displayed a singularly activated left hemisphere and males a singularly activated right hemisphere. Perhaps the difference might be accounted for by social influences affecting neurological development. It is clear that external stimulation helps to shape the developing brain.

It has been suggested that a relationship exists between 'anomalous dominance' and special talents (such as music). Anomalous dominance is the term used to refer to patterns of dominance (or brain organization) that differ from the standard form (that is, verbal processing and hand usage controlled by the left hemisphere, and non-verbal, spatial processing by the right hemisphere). Geschwind and Galaburda (1985) suggested that this pattern is caused by enhanced production of testosterone:

> Testosterone is assumed to retard growth within certain zones of the left hemisphere, and this is likely to result in enlargement of other cortical regions, particularly the respective contralateral area, but also the adjacent regions. The influences that favor anomalous dominance [. . .] thus may favor the growth of talents associated with superior development of certain regions, either in the right hemisphere or in unaffected parts of the left hemisphere.[73]

In the tests carried out by Hassler *et al.* it was found that male composers revealed anomalous dominance patterns for language. Also clear from the results is that female composers tended to reveal anomalous dominance for spatial processing (in that the left hemisphere dominated). However, the study did not relate this to anomalous dominance, although, clearly, spatial processing has been identified as being predominantly a right-hemisphere process.

Perhaps it is the case that in women parts of the left hemisphere are more prone to develop these special abilities, whereas in males it is the right hemisphere. This may be possible, since environmental influences are seen to affect some aspects of neurological development:

> [It has been suggested] that an enriched and stimulating environment during development can influence neocortical function, possibly providing the basis for exceptional talents.[74]

Because of differences in more general cognitive stimulation, musical stimulation may result in the development of different parts of the brain in males and females. Females are generally encouraged in verbal (left hemisphere) skills, whereas males are generally encouraged in spatial/objective skills (right hemisphere). This may have some effect on how the adult brain develops. Of course, this is mere speculation.

Perhaps the most significant result from the Hassler study was the overall finding that:

> Mean rating scores for compositions did not differ between the sexes. Most of the women's compositions, however, were rated either very good [. . .] or not so good [. . .] We suspect that the missing median level of competence in females can be attributed to the lack of encouragement of women in Western Europe to engage in the creative uses of their musical talents.[75]

The conclusion I have reached from reviewing the often contradictory information relating to the neuropsychology and psychology of music functions is that there is no firm evidence to indicate that women have a biologically-based lack of musical aptitude. The morphological study of the brain shows no difference which could account for women's lack of, or inferior, musical achievement, whether as creators (composers) or as executants (performers). There is nothing comparable with, say, their difference in physique in relation to athletic performance (although this factor has in the past been exaggerated). However, the distillation of psychological findings by the popular press and among the general public has caused many of the facts to be used to back up the age-old idea that women are incapable of producing, and often even merely of understanding, art in its many forms. For example, the simplification of the idea of specialized hemispheric skills into the commonly-held notion that the left side of the brain is the 'logical' side and the right side the 'creative' side has served to undermine women's position, since it has given rise to the tenet that men have better processing skills than women in the right side of the brain and thus are biologically destined to be the greater cultural contributors. This tenet often forms the unspoken, and sometimes doubtless unconscious, basis for arguments that explain the scarcity of women's contribution by reference to natural lack of ability.

Like general intelligence, general musical aptitude is understood to be subject first to a general factor and then to a number of specific discrete factors. A general musical aptitude is controlled by a number of separate, interacting skills; this can be observed particularly when musicians working in separate branches of music show differential aptitudes for different skills (for example, playing a prepared piece, sight-reading or transcribing music by ear). Obviously, creative skills are vitally important for the translation of 'raw' musical aptitude into musical composition. Musical composition constitutes just one area of the general function of creativity. Tests have been constructed to measure a person's creative potential, and the results of such tests would seem highly relevant to the current discussion of possible biological justifications for the lack of female composers.

There appear to be three main methods by which psychologists examine creativity. The first is to analyse the creative product: a scientific invention or a work of art; the second is to examine the creative person and attempt to identify any personality traits or behaviour that might underlie creativity (this will be discussed in Chapter 2). The third is to examine 'creative thinking', a property that can be measured by creativity tests. Generally, two types of thinking can be distinguished.

- **Convergent thinking:** this is the process of finding one correct solution to a given problem: a process of narrowing down.
- **Divergent or lateral thinking:** this type of thinking generates a number of different possible solutions to an open-ended question.

Obviously, divergent thinking is a fundamental indicator of the potential for creativity. Creative thinking is measured by two methods: i) finding as many feasible uses for a given object as possible; ii) creating a story or picture for a given title or image. In contrast to standard intelligence tests, where only one correct answer is acceptable, creativity tests allow any fresh response. Yet it is precisely here that the difficulty in testing creativity arises. Anyone – male, female, young or old – has the potential to be creative; even a small child can create a unique picture. But this picture will not be considered as impressive as a masterpiece by Rubens. So originality is not the only criterion appropriate for measuring creativity: the really important factor is not the quantity of ideas produced by a person, but whether that person can select and develop the good ideas among them.

Research has found no significant differences between the sexes on measures of fluency (number of responses) and originality (unusualness of response).[76] Other research has noted a verbal superiority of girls in divergent tests, a situation that reflects the general superiority of female verbal fluency.[77] Some tests have shown that boys evidence greater originality, but other tests have failed to reach the same conclusions. In some recent research into sex-differences in divergent thinking it was found that straightforward tests of ability might not present a full picture of sex differences; instead, styles and levels of ability were tested in the hope of obtaining a more accurate picture.[78] The conclusions of this work are both interesting and surprising:

> It seems reasonable to conclude that there exist characteristic sex-typed divergent response styles, [. . .] and that these styles are more clear-cut than are sex differences in divergent thinking 'ability' [. . .] The results appear to reflect the developing interests of boys and girls along culturally prescribed lines.[79]

For example, boys performed better in producing mechanical-scientific, sport-games responses but produced fewer domestic responses. In contrast, girls produced more domestic and life responses, thus reinforcing the traditional stereotypes of male and female areas of interest. The finding that children respond creatively along the lines of thought imposed by society was tested also by asking the children to complete the creativity test as if they belonged to the opposite sex. The results show that sexually stereotyped responses are not concrete, since males and females are perfectly able to act out opposite-sex response styles:

> [. . .] it seems clear that these styles are not fixed, unmodifiable features of psychological functioning. Children [. . .] cannot only perceive their essential characteristics, but are evidently capable of enacting them with considerable accuracy. We need to maintain a clear distinction between the overt, behaviourial manifestations of sex-typing and their covert, cognitive determinants.[80]

This report seems to reveal that women have the potential to be as creative as men and even to produce the same sex-typed responses. The general tenor of reports into creativity shows many personality and environmental traits to be of fundamental significance to the success of any potentially creative person. Liam Hudson reported that the most important factors behind creativity are not intellectual but personal.[81] Even when one takes into account different styles of response, females score as well as, and often better than, males. Yet the distribution of men and women in creative jobs does not mirror this finding. This is thought by Hudson to be because conventional creativity tests measure only the abstract nature of creativity; as in many other areas, a creative person needs more than abstract ability to succeed. In any consideration of the position of women as creative artists the whole picture has to be surveyed, since the many other interacting areas of personality, which include social conditioning, self-esteem and one's sense of identity, all play vital roles in shaping the creative person. These areas will be covered in more detail in Chapter 2.

In music psychology little has been written specifically about sex differences in musical aptitude. Jacob Kwalwasser mentioned the subject in his book *Exploring the Musical Mind*, as did Rosamund Shuter in *The Psychology of Musical Ability*. Kwalwasser and Shuter disagree about the overall results of musical aptitude tests in relation to sex. Shuter found that:

> [. . .] on the whole, male subjects tend to make about the same scores as females on musical ability tests.[82]

Whereas Kwalwasser notes:

> It is an interesting fact [. . .] that when American boys and girls are compared the superiority of the girls is firmly established.[83]

So once again psychologists interpret similar test results differently, posing many more questions than they answer. Moreover, the results of the musical aptitude tests show a parallel with IQ test results. Although the overall scores are equal, there do nevertheless seem to be sex-linked differences of ability uncovered in subtests.[84]

Investigations involving American children seem to show a clear female advantage on most of the Kwalwasser-Dykema Music tests. Tests carried out in Europe appear to confirm these results; England showed the greatest difference favouring girls anywhere in Europe.[85] In all these tests males consistently achieve higher scores relating to time, intensity and quality of discrimination. On the other hand, women tend to achieve higher scores in tests measuring sensitivity to melody, harmony, pitch and consonance, and in tests of memory.

Shuter's review of test results for musical aptitude and appreciation seems to be the most comprehensive and reliable. She concluded that men are on the whole more sensitive to phrasing and rhythm, while they seem less perceptive of changes in intensity; conversely, women have a strong perception of intensity and are less perceptive of rhythm:

> The greater appreciation of phrasing found among the male group agrees well with the view that boys are usually more interested than girls in how musical compositions are constructed, since it is through phrasing that the construction of a movement is made clear [. . .] There may indeed be some qualitative differences underlying the differences in scores between the sexes which are quantitatively quite small.[86]

This corresponds to the stereotype that boys are more interested in how things work (implying a greater interest in objects, science, engineering and so on). If boys are indeed more interested in how musical compositions are structured, this implies in itself that they will be more inclined towards composition.

Male and female differences in sensitivity to rhythm have been related to stereotypical male and female characteristics, males being extroverts and females introverts. Jung put forward this view of male and female character, which was taken over by the music psychologist H. Wing for his explanation of the sex differences found in his musical aptitude and achievement tests. Wing noted that after the age of 14, girls excelled at tests of musical appreciation and also that women make up the majority of listeners and concert goers. The Jungian idea of women as naturally introverted and men as naturally extroverted might explain why women constitute the majority of listeners.[87] Introverts, according to Wing after Jung, are more inclined to gain pleasure through the listening experience or the composing experience if the persons in question have any creative drive.[88] Extroverts will be attracted to the rhythmic drive of music and are more likely to become performers and conductors. Introverts will be interested in using music as a vehicle for the expression of emotion and will be therefore more interested in, and perceptive of, changes in dynamic, these being music's most accessible means of expression. Applying such broad stereotypes to all males or all females is highly controversial. Firm evidence must first be provided that such sweeping generalizations have some kind of basis in reality before such theories can be accepted (see Chapter 2).

The results gained from the Kwalwasser-Ruch Musical Accomplishment tests were reviewed for sex differences. It was noted:

> Starting with a small advantage, the girls increase their lead steadily [. . .] It is clear that talent differences based on sex are relatively small, yet accomplishment score differences are considerable and sex-linked.[89]

Kwalwasser also puts forward the idea that society plays a significant role in discouraging boys from the serious study of music when they are young. Music, like other artistic professions, is commonly viewed as unreliable financially and sometimes as frivolous and improper. To the middle class, professions such as medicine or law are held in much higher esteem, and boys are encouraged to pursue such high-status careers for both social and financial reasons. It is much more important for a young male to aspire towards this type of career than it is for a female, since the male is viewed as the 'provider'. Young females are on the whole thought not to require high-status, high-salary careers, since they will bear children and need to be provided for by a male partner. This leaves girls free to concentrate on things often viewed as trivial and frivolous (such as fashion and beauty), and this freedom may extend to a limited study of, and participation in, music.

Kwalwasser also addresses the reality that at school (and amateur) level many more girls than boys are interested or active in music. Despite this, the vast majority of creative and professional performing musicians are, and always have been, men. Discussing a number of possible reasons for this apparent contradiction, Kwalwasser reviews research into aesthetic responses and argues:

> [. . .] the appreciation of art is to a large extent sublimated desire, which is in line with the modern hypothesis which attributes art activity and response to escapism.[90]

Taken at face value, this statement would actually make women eminently suited to composition and artistic expression of all kinds. As females are more circumscribed in their play and engage in a smaller range of activities than boys, they tend to be more supervised and protected as children (and as adults). Obviously, their geographical restriction and lack of freedom could very well lead to a strong need for sublimation of emotion and unfulfilled desires through music and the other arts.

This hypothesis seems very attractive. Yet only one paragraph later, Kwalwasser is repeating the Victorian misconception of woman being much more suited to monotonous work, less susceptible to boredom and having a greater tolerance of being 'thwarted'.

> When the circumstances are favorable, genuine artistic creation may favor the male merely because he is more restless when thwarted.[91]

Having seen the possible effect of the massive restrictions and pressures placed on women by the concept of femininity, Kwalwasser suddenly uses the misconceived idea of women's placidity as the instrument of their downfall when it comes to '*genuine* artistic creation' (my emphasis). His unspoken assumption seems to be that, when young, females are very aware of their oppression and have a need for other outlets of desire. As adults, however, females lose this sense and become resigned to their fate and tolerant of their status. Others may well reflect that this loss of spirit is perhaps the inevitable result of the female being consumed by patriarchal culture and learning over time that it is easier to be carried along than to fight the overwhelmingly inevitable.[92]

Kwalwasser subsequently suggests reasons for the male lack of interest in music when young, turning the whole idea of female sex-discrimination and disadvantage in music on its head:

> Trailing the girls during the formative period, the boys quite naturally lose their confidence and interest in art activities. Sensing inferiority and failing to realize that the time differential will ultimately equalize the sexes, boys are more likely to withdraw from participation in the arts, in a state of mind bordering on defeat. This sense of inferiority inevitably takes its toll [. . .][93]

Patriarchy is so totally saturated with the doctrine of the male being first that even the slight advantage shown by school-aged girls over boys has to be confronted, since it has unacceptable consequences. The male student must be given special provision to guard against the disadvantage of seeing himself as inferior to the female, since this is so highly destructive of the young ego. For males who feel this kind of defeat and inequality, it is necessary only to look around them at the wider society and culture to feel their ultimate power. Most of the teachers (except in a boy's earliest years), scientists, inventors and composers they have learned about (and from) are men; in no way could their momentary sense of inferiority become permanent, since men are so powerful in our culture. But what of the female students? How huge and insurmountable is their sense of defeat and inferiority when they look around them at women's position in society? If it is generally agreed that a sense of inferiority and the hopelessness of being perceived as being second-best tends to dampen creativity, why has nobody applied this idea to women?[94] I submit that it is via this route, above all others, that women as creative artists are destroyed, defeated and derailed, acquiring a life-long lack of confidence. Sense of identity, state of mind, and social expectation are rarely examined in the debate about the female composer. Yet it is in these areas that some of the answers needed to explain the inequalities are to be found.

If, as many have suggested, females get such strong encouragement at an early age, while males are actively discouraged, what happens to tip the balance so completely in the direction of male domination? Psychologists appear to agree that school-age girls achieve better scores on musical tests than boys. So what goes wrong? At what point do women forego their advantage and accept their destiny of becoming invisible or, at best, minority figures in music, specifically musical composition? Shuter concludes:

> [. . .] if a woman of talent encounters prejudice when she seeks employment in an orchestra, there would seem to be no such barriers to prevent her composing [. . .] It seems unlikely that women students whose compositions showed real merit would be refused tuition and encouragement. Yet [. . .] a concert of works entirely by women composers is still a novelty [. . .] there may be some genuine sex difference here. Perhaps the highest level of musical genius occurs much more rarely among women [. . .][95]

This statement raises a number of issues. Shuter concedes that discrimination against women may restrict talented females. However, she sees this as applicable to performers, not composers. If it is recognized that such sexual discrimination exists in the musical world, why should it be that female composers are exempted from its effects? That a woman of real talent would be denied performance opportunities but never composition opportunities would seem ridiculous. Herein, perhaps, lies the real essence of the argument against women composers. Psychologically speaking, there seems to be no barrier, no lack of grey matter, no proven lack of intellect or of musical aptitude. Yet we still have so few female composers, and of these, none is perceived to be in the first rank. Frustratingly, there seem to be no factual, objective answers in terms of woman's biological destiny. When people cannot see a physical obstacle, they presume that no obstacle is present, placing the responsibility for lack of success ultimately on women's innate lack of aptitude. Sadly, this leaves many to reach conclusions similar to those of Shuter's: basically, women cannot and do not compose at the highest levels of the profession because – only men do! Many find it inappropriate to suggest social and educational disadvantages as the root of the difficulties faced by female composers, since music is often perceived as an area of 'feminine' interest. As a hobby or amateur interest, music has been allowed to women. But this should not be confused with the professional world of music, which has always been viewed as 'masculine'. In particular, the cultural authority with which 'great' composers (conductors and instrumentalists) are invested has rarely allowed space for a female equivalent. This view is entrenched firmly in the conscious and unconscious mind of the musical establishment, and of the population generally. Its effects can be devastating, for it places a woman attempting a career as a composer in a severely disadvantaged position. Socially constructed barriers which face female composers come in many different forms. Some have political (legislative) and social manifestations, while others, like the ones encountered throughout this chapter (often interpreted as 'natural difference'), operate on a much more personal level. The next stage in exploding the myths of biological difference as the root of disparities in male and female musical achievement is the study of personality and temperament. This is the other area of psychological difference which, it has been suggested, disadvantages female composers.

Notes

1 Ashley Montagu, 'Why Wagner Was No Lady', *High Fidelity Magazine*, March (1958), 34 and 137.
2 Glenn Wilson, *The Great Sex Divide* (London, 1989), 97–99.
3 Music psychologists have often had great difficulty in answering the question 'What is musical aptitude?' Even the terms 'musical ability', 'musical aptitude' and 'musical talent' seem to denote, for different psychologists, quite different levels of innate and learned aspects of music. For present purposes I use the term 'musical

aptitude' to describe the native latent ability, the *potential* musical facility of an individual before any aspect of musical ability has been acquired via training.

4 Peter R. Messent, 'Female Hormones and Behaviour', in John Archer and Barbara Lloyd (eds), *Exploring Sex Differences* (London, 1976), 185.
5 John Nicholson, *Men and Women: How Different Are They?* (Oxford, 1993), 87.
6 Aristotle, *Physiognomonica*, in W.D. Ross (ed.), *The Works of Aristotle*, 6 (Oxford, 1913), 809.
7 Quoted in Stephen Jay Gould, 'Women's Brains', *New Scientist*, 80 (1978), 365.
8 *Ibid.*, 364–366.
9 Robert Pool, *The New Sexual Revolution* (London and Sydney, 1994), 131–132.
10 *Ibid.*, 132.
11 *Ibid.*, 135.
12 Gould, 'Women's Brains', 365.
13 Pool, *The New Sexual Revolution*, 128.
14 John Nicholson, *Men and Women: How Different Are They?* (Oxford, 1993), 87.
15 Abstract visual reasoning involves the ability to isolate visual images into new planes or combinations, reading maps and blueprints. It is also called Visual Spatial Ability.
16 Atkinson and Atkinson *et al.*, *Introduction to Psychology*, Tenth Edition (San Diego, 1990), 455.
17 E.E. Maccoby and C.N. Jacklin, *The Psychology of Sex Differences* (London, 1975), 63–133.
18 For example, J. Levy and M. Reid, 'Variations in Cerebral Organization as a Function of Handedness, Hand Posture in Writing, and Sex', *Journal of Experimental Psychology*, 107/2 (1978), 119–144. C. Hutt, *Males and Females* (Harmondsworth, 1972). Maccoby and Jacklin, *The Psychology of Sex Differences*, 351.
19 Maccoby and Jacklin, *The Psychology of Sex Differences*, 352.
20 The term 'analytical ability' can have several meanings. It is used here to describe the ability to respond to one aspect of a stimulus situation without being influenced by the background or 'field'.
21 A. Feingold, 'Cognitive Gender Differences are Disappearing', *American Psychologist*, 43 (1988), 95–103.
22 J.S. Hyde and M.C. Linn, 'Gender Differences in Verbal Ability: A Meta-Analysis', *Psychological Bulletin*, 104 (1988), 53–69.
23 J.S. Eccles and J.E. Jacobs, 'Social Forces Shape Math Attitudes and Performance', *Signs*, 11 (1986), 367–389.
24 Most of the relevant studies on this topic were reviewed in J. McGlone, 'Sex Differences in Human Brain Asymmetry: A Critical Survey', *Behavioural and Brain Sciences*, 3 (1980), 215–227).
25 Richard Epro, 'Skills and Aptitudes', in Anne Campbell (ed.), *The Opposite Sex* (London, 1989), 90.
26 J. Archer and B. Lloyd, *Sex and Gender* (Cambridge, 1985), 234.
27 Campbell (ed.), *The Opposite Sex*, 90.
28 Archer and Lloyd, *Sex and Gender*, 234.
29 Jerre Levy, 'Lateral Specialization of the Human Brain: Behavioral Manifestations and Possible Evolutionary Basis', in J.A. Kiger (ed.), *The Biology of Behavior* (Oregon, 1972).
30 A. Buffery and J. Gray, 'Sex Differences in the Development of Spatial and Linguistic Skills', in *Gender Differences: Their Ontogeny and Significance*, C. Ounsted and D. Taylor (eds) London: Churchill Livingstone, 1972, 123–157.
31 Nicholson, *Men and Women: How Different Are They?*, 103–104.

32 L.J. Harris, 'Sex Difference in the Growth and Use of Language', in E. Donelson and J Gullahorn (eds), *Women: A Psychological Perspective* (New York, 1977).
33 J. Durden-Smith and D. DeSimone, *Sex and the Brain* (New York, 1983), 96.
34 *Ibid.*, 97.
35 Lesley Rogers, 'Male Hormones and Behaviour', in J. Archer and B. Lloyd (eds), *Exploring Sex Differences*, 177–178.
36 Wilson, *The Great Sex Divide*, 107–108.
37 Nicholson, *Men and Women: How Different Are They?*, 91.
38 Nicholson, *loc. cit.*
39 Janet Sayers, *Biological Politics: Feminist and Anti-Feminist Perspectives* (London, 1982), 103.
40 Musical aptitude tests usually require the subject to listen and make judgements about short extracts of music. No tests rely on acquired musical skills or knowledge.
41 G.M. Gilbert, 'Sex Differences in Musical Aptitude and Training', *The Journal of General Psychology*, 26 (1942), 19.
42 *Ibid.*, 29.
43 Wilson, *The Great Sex Divide*, 98–99.
44 Jacob Kwalwasser, *Exploring the Musical Mind* (New York, 1955), 7.
45 R.W. Lundin, *An Objective Psychology of Music* (New York, 1967), 221–222.
46 *Ibid.*, 222.
47 In the study group of nine British woman composers all but one showed musical aptitude before the age of five, a phenomenon shown to be common among the vast majority of professional musicians.
48 R.T.C. Pratt, 'The Inheritance of Musicality', in M. Critchley and Henson (eds), *Music and the Brain. Studies in the Neurology of Music* (London, 1977), 29.
49 Alfred Meyer, 'The Search for a Morphological Substrate in the Brains of Eminent Persons including Musicians: A Historical Review', in M. Critchley and R.A. Henson (eds), *Music and the Brain: Studies in the Neurology of Music*, 255–281. Although the study was entitled 'eminent persons' and not 'eminent men', it should be noted that there were no women included in this study or in the extensive reviews of previous research.
50 *Ibid.*, 264.
51 N. Wertheim, 'Is there an Anatomical Localisation of Musical Faculties?', in Critchley and Henson, *Music and the Brain*, 291.
52 'Amusia is a collective term denoting the loss or impairment of musical capacity as a consequence of brain disease.' R.L. Benton, 'The Amusias', in Critchley and Henson, *Music and the Brain*, 378.
53 Wertheim, 'Is there an Anatomical Localisation for Musical Faculties?', in Critchley and Henson, *Music and the Brain*, 291.
54 P. Scheid and J.C. Eccles, 'Music and Speech: Artistic Functions of the Human Brain', *Psychology of Music*, 3–1 (1975), 21.
55 John A. Sloboda, *The Musical Mind: The Cognitive Psychology of Music* (Oxford, 1985), 263–264.
56 Glenn Wilson, *The Psychology of the Performing Arts* (London, 1985), 143.
57 *Ibid.*, 144.
58 Juan G. Roederer, 'Physical and Neuropsychological Foundations of Music: The Basic Questions', in Manfred Clynes (ed.), *Music, Mind and Brain* (New York and London, 1982), 44.
59 Dichotic listening techniques involve playing music so it can only be perceived by the left or right ear at any one time.
60 D. Kimura, 'Left-Right Differences in the Perception of Melodies', *Quarterly Journal of Experimental Psychology*, 16 (1964), 355–358, cited in Maria Wyke,

'Musical Ability: a Neuropsychological Interpretation', *Music and the Brain*, 160.

61 Maria Wyke, 'Music Ability: A Neuropsychological Interpretation', 165.
62 T.G. Bever and R.J. Chiarello, 'Cerebral Dominance in Musicians and Non-Musicians', *Science*, 185 (1974), 537–539.
63 Sloboda, *The Musical Mind*, 264.
64 *Ibid.*, 265.
65 Hans Borchgrevink, 'Cerebral Lateralization of Speech and Singing after Intra-carotid Amytal Injection', in M. Taylor Sarno and O. Hook (eds), *Aphasia: An Assessment and Treatment*, cited in Hans Borchgrevink , 'Prosody and Music Rhythm are Controlled by the Speech Hemisphere', *Music, Mind and Brain*, 151.
66 Marianne Hassler, Eberhard Nieschlag and Diether De La Motte, 'Creative Musical Talent, Cognitive Functioning, and Gender: Psychobiological Aspects', *Musical Perception*, 8 (1990), 36.
67 *Ibid.*, 36.
68 *Ibid.*, 46.
69 *Ibid.*, 43.
70 *Ibid.*, 42–43.
71 *Ibid.*, 45–46.
72 H.W. Gordon, 'Degree of Ear Asymmetries for Perception of Dichotic Chords and for Illusory Chord Localization in Musicians of Different Levels of Competence', *Journal of Experimental Psychology: Human Perception and Performance*, 6 (1980), 516–527, cited in Hassler, Nieschlag and La Motte, 'Creative Musical Talent', 45.
73 Hassler, Nieschlag and La Motte, 'Creative Musical Talent', 35–36.
74 M.C. Diamond *et al.*, 'Plasticity in the 904 day old Male Rat Cerebral Cortex', *Experimental Neurology*, 87 (1985), 309–317, cited in Hassler, Nieschlag and La Motte, 'Creative Musical Talent', 44.
75 Hassler, Nieschlag and La Motte, 'Creative Musical Talent', 46.
76 M.A. Wallach and N. Kogan, *Modes of Thinking in Young Children* (New York, 1965). H.J. Klausmeier and W. Wiersma, 'The Effects of IQ Level and Sex on divergent Thinking of Seventh Grade Pupils of Low, Average and High IQ', *Journal of Educational Research*, 58 (1965), 300–302.
77 Campbell, *The Opposite Sex*, 214.
78 David J. Hargreaves, 'Sex Roles in Divergent Thinking', *British Journal of Educational Psychology*, 47 (1977), 25–32.
79 *Ibid.*, 31.
80 Hargreaves, *loc. cit.*
81 Liam Hudson, *Frames of Mind: Ability, Perception and Self-perception in the Arts and Sciences* (London, 1968). Hudson's tests were carried out on an unrepresentative sample of 14–18 year old grammar and public school boys. However, his findings are interesting in that they echo the results of other research. When the boys were asked to respond to the use of objects tests as if they were someone else (stereotyped as either highly artistic or scientific) they could adjust their thinking accordingly to be divergent or convergent.
82 Rosamund Shuter, *The Psychology of Musical Ability* (London, 1968), 88.
83 Kwalwasser, *Exploring the Musical Mind* (New York, 1955), 79.
84 It must be noted that results often give conflicting evidence perhaps suggesting the difficulty in obtaining information accurately.
85 Kwalwasser, *Exploring the Musical Mind*, 81.
86 Shuter, *The Psychology of Musical Ability*, 91.
87 However, according to recent research this depends very much on the style of the music.

88 Herbert D. Wing, *Musical Ability and Appreciation* (PhD thesis, London University, 1941), cited in Shuter, *The Psychology of Musical Ability*, 88–90.
89 Kwalwasser, *Exploring the Musical Mind*, 83.
90 *Ibid.*, 75.
91 *Ibid.*, 76–77.
92 I use the terms 'patriarchy' and 'patriarchal' in the technical sense (of institutionalized male dominance) in which they are employed by feminists.
93 *Ibid.*, 77–78.
94 The often overlooked factor of morale as it affects achievement is relevant to many other disadvantaged social groups: occupational, national, racial and so on.
95 Shuter, *The Psychology of Musical Ability*, 93.

2 Music and Personality

> Another possible source of the preponderance of male achievement in the world is constitutional personality and motivation. Men tend to be more assertive, ambitious and grandiose in their schemes than women, and more single-minded in seeking recognition and greatness. Aggressiveness and dominance are characteristics of males in all human societies [. . .] women who do compete with men in traditionally male occupations [. . .] show signs of having been exposed to more male hormones than women in more typically feminine roles [. . .][1]

In this chapter I intend to focus on how sex differentiation of temperament and personality may affect the fulfilment of musical potential in females. As the above quotation demonstrates, there is an opinion that women as a group 'naturally' lack the necessary motivation to contribute and achieve in a wide range of areas. Conveniently, this provides yet another seemingly impossible obstacle to female equality, and is therefore an issue which must be examined in the search for factors which affect the potential of musically creative women.

Many people believe that men and women differ fundamentally in their basic personalities and that these differences then form the basis of further sex differences in interest, attitude and occupations. Viewed thus, having the innate musical potential to become a composer forms only one component in the set of psychological 'abilities' required for success. Music psychologists agree that dimensions outside aptitude and cognition are vital contributory factors in the development and realization of musical potential:

> [. . .] even when a comprehensive description of musical abilities has been well-defined, it is important to consider that this would still represent a restricted view of the whole musician: aspects of temperament and motivation combine with abilities and integrate to produce an overall picture.[2]

Indeed, in the wider sense, an individual's personality and temperament have been proved to be enormously influential with regard to the type of occupation to which he or she will be drawn. Some writers have suggested that occupational personality profiles directly reflect the task description, and so choice of occupation can be seen as the very expression of personality.[3] This perspective has been adopted by those who seek to explain sex differentiation of occupations and labour as a 'natural' expression of the different characteristics between the two sexes. Some researchers continue to believe that certain stereotypes are universal, there always being:

> [. . .] a basic divergence between the sexes: male tilting toward achievement in work, sports, technology, and public life; females, toward affiliation, often expressed in the private domain through service, caring, teaching and art.[4]

> A major reason why men and women gravitate towards different occupations seems to be that of interest. Men seem naturally more intrigued by abstract ideas, mechanics and science, as well as personal success and power, and women appear to be more interested in art, religion, child development and interpersonal relationships.[5]

These ideas reinforce the common belief that men are 'by nature' logical, profound, technical and ambitious, whereas women are 'by nature' intuitive, refined and caring. Throughout the course of this chapter the biological basis on which such statements are founded will be examined and questioned. Yet, even if such ideas proved to be true (and based on unchangeable sex differences), a glaring contradiction in the biological determinist theory is revealed. Despite the fact that the arts and music are depicted as areas of 'natural feminine' interest, they have been (and still are) staunchly male-dominated. By this reasoning, 'natural interest' on the part of women would seem to have no basis in 'natural' ability, unless it is directly related to their reproductive role! How is the contradiction of music's perceived 'femininity', yet its domination by men, to be explained? Before this controversy can be discussed, it is vital to establish a number of points. First: which traits define masculine and feminine personalities? Second: how far do masculine and feminine traits characterize musicians and composers? Third: are masculinity and femininity the 'natural' personality profiles of males and females?

Traditionally, the healthy or 'ideal' personality has been regarded as one which conforms to the appropriate sex-role identity: that is, masculine male, feminine female.[6] The exhibition of inappropriate characteristics for either sex has been perceived generally as a sign of maladjustment and even mental instability; this situation is reflected in the trait types for masculine and feminine being oppositional and exclusive. Table 2.1 catalogues some of the most commonly perceived sex-differentiated personality characteristics in Western Culture.

The search for how far such categories apply in reality has been the subject of much research. One of the earliest studies of the question was carried out in 1936 by Lewis Terman and Catherine Miles. They devised a masculinity-femininity test (M-F test) in an attempt to establish how far a person conforms to, or contradicts, sex-stereotyped personality traits and, in turn, which factors influence the degree of conformity to such stereotypes.[7] The main purpose of the test was to define more objectively those aspects of personality in which the two sexes differ. The general comparison of male and female M-F scores revealed some interesting results, as did the comparison of selected groups of the population. When the M-F scores were examined in terms of age groupings, male and female scores showed a general parallel movement, although they were far from close in any period. Up to the age of about 20 years, there seems to be a strong tendency for masculinization of both sexes. After this time

Table 2.1 Commonly perceived male/female personality characteristics

Masculine	Feminine
Aggressive	Passive
Unemotional	Sympathetic
Brave	Nurturant
Decisive	Friendly
Independent	Yielding
Assertive	Shy
Strong	Childlike
Analytical	Intuitive
Dominant	Submissive
Initiative	Sensitive

Source: I.K. Broverman, S.R. Vogel *et al.*, 'Sex Role Stereotypes: A Current Appraisal', *Journal of Social Issues*, 28 (1972), 59–79

the tendency is for increased feminization in both sexes until death. It should be noted that male M-F scores show a greater fluctuation throughout life than female M-F scores.[8] The test confirms that sex-differentiated personalities do indeed exist, but are by no means stable (see Figure 2.1).

Moreover, education was found to influence the M-F scores, in that males exhibit their most masculine behaviour when they pursue their education beyond secondary school level. For females, higher education has a much greater masculinizing affect than for males. This seems to indicate that education encourages individuals to be more assertive, confident and independent (all of which are classed by the investigators as masculine traits). A small positive correlation was found between intelligence and masculinity, although this association was contradicted when males in higher education who gained 'high-scholarships' tested as more feminine than those males who gained 'low-scholarships', in the sense that a difference in areas of interest was observed. High-scholarship males were more inclined towards cultural interests (feminine), whereas other males were inclined towards mechanical and athletic interests (masculine).[9] Further confirmation of this link occurred when male and female athletes were tested: their scores were the most strongly masculine, this being more marked for females than males. Females drawn towards this 'masculine' area of interest accordingly exhibited the most masculine behaviour.

When men and women of corresponding age yet differing intellects were tested on the M-F scale, they yielded the following results. Three groups of males (teenagers, college students in their twenties and men in their middle years) exhibiting superior intellectual ability were compared with three groups of average ability. The more gifted intellectual boys and middle-aged men exhibited more feminine scores than did those of average intelligence, yet the college students in their twenties tested as more masculine. When the same three age groups of superior intellectual women were tested against women of

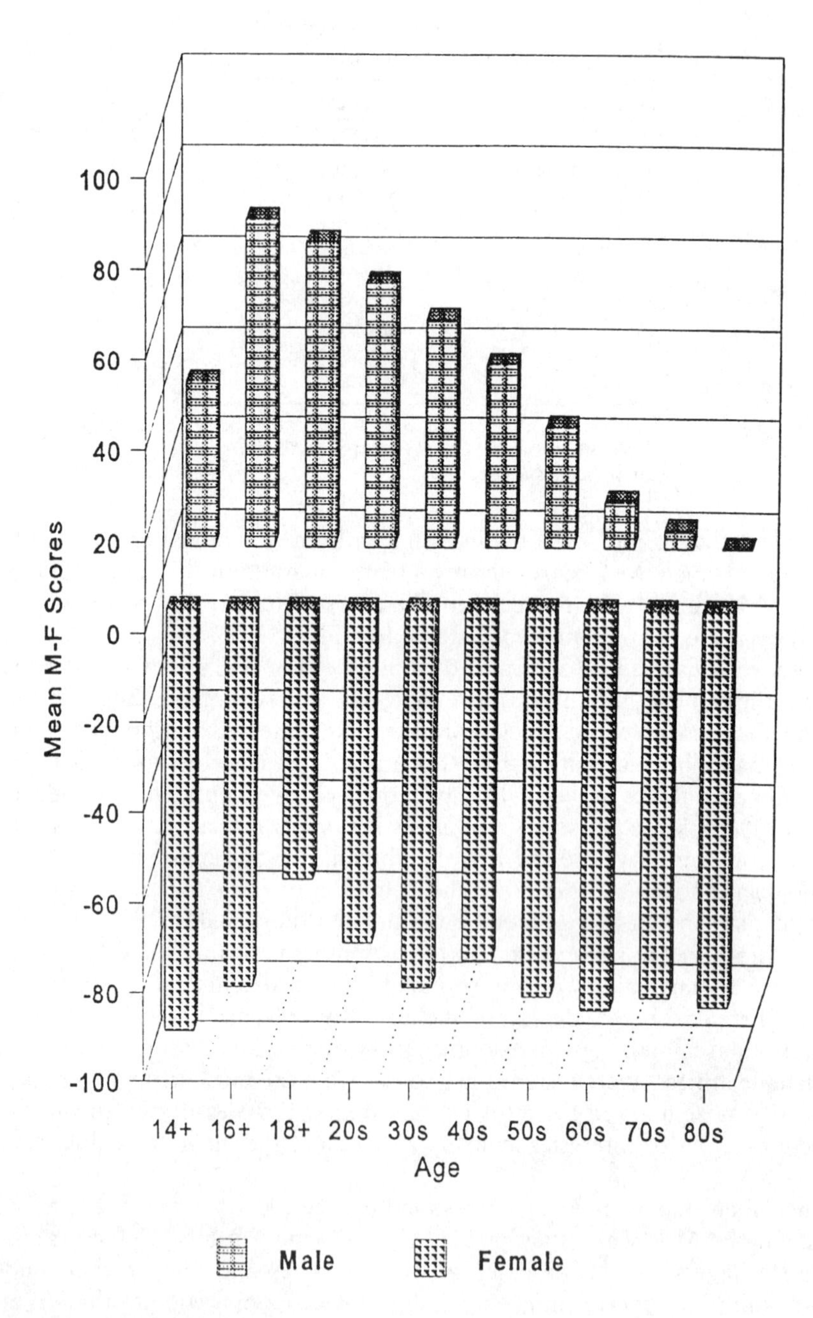

Figure 2.1 Age trends of mean M–F score
Source: Terman and Miles, *Sex and Personality*, 123

average intelligence these also diverged from the general population norms of corresponding age. All three female groups of superior intellect tested as more masculine than the three of average intellect, the middle-aged women emerging as the most masculine.[10]

These results suggest that high intellectual ability, or some factor connected with it, inclines women to be more masculine and men to be more feminine. This evidence has been reinforced in more recent studies:

> [. . .] greater intellectual development has been correlated quite consistently with cross sex typing, that is, with masculinity in girls and with femininity in boys. Boys and girls who are more sex typed have been found to have lower overall intelligence, lower spatial ability, and lower creativity.[11]

Indeed, strong sex typing, according to these results, would appear to be positively detrimental to musical composition, since spatial and creative abilities have proved to be significant for the development of creative musical ability. Clearly, how far an individual is 'masculine' or 'feminine' can depend on a number of external factors (such as education) and would appear not to be unchangeable throughout an individual's lifetime.

Occupation and interests have also been shown to exert a strong influence on the M-F scores of both sexes:

> Age, education and intelligence explain only the differences between the large general-population groups. Special groups selected with respect to occupation or other characteristics do not always conform to the expectations based on the findings for the general populations.[12]

The extent to which men and women tested as masculine and feminine was found to be influenced by the nature of the occupations with which they were involved. Men in occupations which exhibited the most masculine characteristics are listed below in an order proceeding from the most to the least masculine:

1. Professional engineers and architects
2. Professional businessmen: lawyers, salesmen, bankers, executives
3. Professional physical-social welfare group: teachers, physicians, surgeons, dentists
4. Mechanical occupations
5. Clerical and mercantile occupations
6. Building occupations
7. Farming occupations
8. Policemen and firemen
9. Vocational groups: journalists, clergymen, artists

Among the nine occupational groups, the last, described as the vocational group and including artists, proved to be the most feminine of all those considered. Although male musicians were not tested as a specific group, all the evidence from other contexts justifies their inclusion in this category. Compared with other groups of similar intelligence, class 9 is significantly more feminine:

> All these comparisons indicate the unique position of the vocations on the M-F scale. Whether by reason of nature or nurture or by influence of both, the members of class 9 have formed mental habits that register on the M-F test in responses widely divergent from those of the common run of males.[13]

Male artists seem to defy the conventional patterns of sex-differentiated personality. This conforms to the notion that artistic ability is a 'feminine' area, in that it attracts those with personality profiles which display high levels of femininity. Terman and Miles suggested that this may be because 'culture'[14] has had a feminizing effect on men:

> The vocational group rates at a point near the average score for the total [male] population in their sixties. Culture has therefore had for this group an effect similar to that of advanced age.[15]

Since much of Western culture has been traditionally dominated by men, one is led to ask, 'Why should culture make men more feminine?' – a point which will be discussed later in the chapter.

That 'femininity' is important to artistic occupations was confirmed by the female occupation group test results. Female occupations are listed below in order of those tested as the most to the least feminine.[16]

1 Gainful domestic employment
2 Vocational – artists, musicians
3 Housewives
4 Business
5 Professional

Female musicians rate as one of the most feminine groups, yet they are still assumed to be above the average for intelligence and training (intelligence supposedly producing increased masculine scores in women):

> Their position below the average on the M-F scale may be attributed in part to less than average ability in those traits which exhibit themselves in dominating and directing other people.[17]

The female musician, like women in other fields, would seem to be hampered by a lack of independence, assertiveness, leadership qualities and other masculine traits which would assist her to fulfil her potential at the highest levels of achievement. The comparison of male and female musicians indicates that many male musicians exhibit more feminine behaviour, which contradicts stereotypical ideas of masculinity, yet female musicians do not contradict the feminine personality. This observation, borne out by the Terman and Miles tests, suggests that individuals who exhibit feminine personality traits are actually better suited to artistic behaviour, leaving women, whether by nature or nurture, well placed to excel in music. In reality, however, the feminine aspects of male creative artists are only feminine when compared with a masculine personality. Figure 2.2 reveals the actual difference in the M-F scores: even the most feminine male artists are still some 90 points more masculine than female musicians!

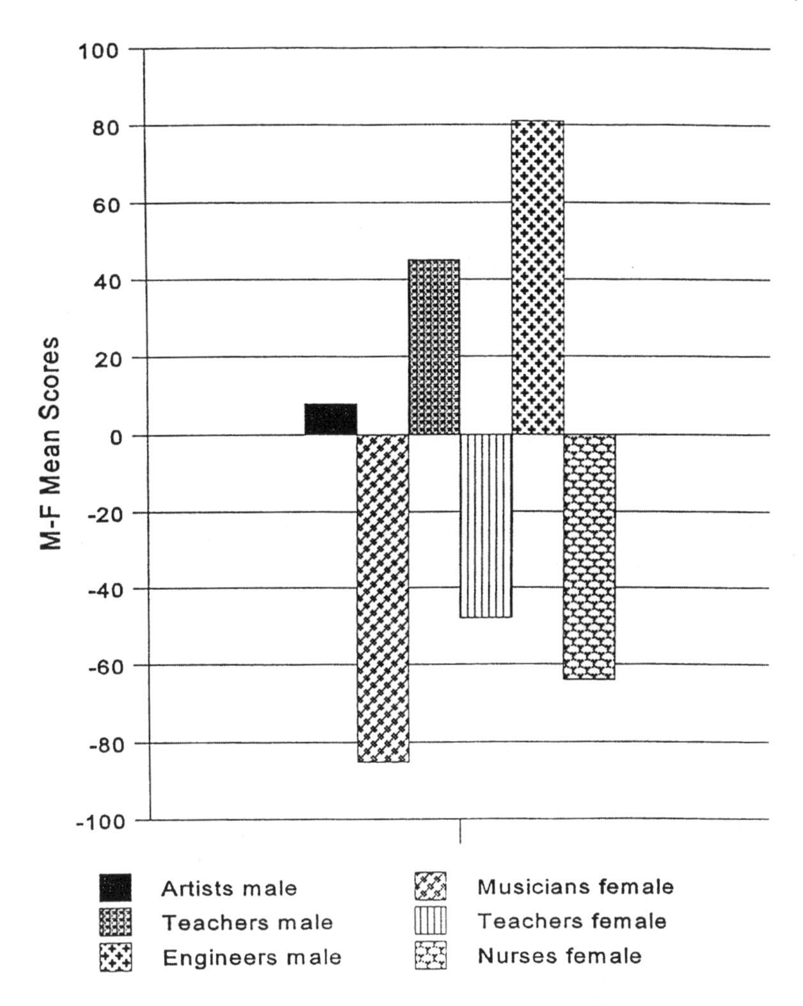

Figure 2.2 Mean M-F scores of selected occupational groups
Source: Terman and Miles, *Sex and Personality*, 159, 179

The Terman and Miles study, though important, was compiled some 60 years ago, and more recent research has reached somewhat different conclusions. Anthony Kemp's work on the personality profiles of musicians, completed in the late 1970s and early 1980s, suggests that musicians can be distinguished from non-musicians by certain aspects of their personality, and that personality structure determines which branch of the profession an individual is likely to enter. Kemp found that the personality profiles of musicians could be divided into four distinct subgroups: performers, teachers, composers and conductors:

> [. . .] each requires different forms of talent and [. . .] this results in different personality patterns.[18]

In this way musicianship is only a base from which musical talent is then variously channelled. Such channelling seems to be strongly influenced by personality. For example, a conductor needs a high degree of command and strength of character to be successful, as the job entails leading a group of individuals towards a common goal. An individual who has a high level of musical talent may be discouraged or, indeed, found inadequate as a conductor because of a lack of authority and leadership qualities.

In an article published in 1982 Kemp explored the significance of sex differences in the personality structure of musicians.[19] When personality tests were carried out on undergraduate students, sex differences were found, in that:

> [. . .] men [. . . scored] significantly higher on emotional stability, dominance, adventurousness, suspiciousness, radicalism, self-sufficiency and self-sentiment: women, on the other hand, emerged as more outgoing, sensitive, astute, guilt-prone and tense.[20]

Similar tests were then applied to three groups of musicians (secondary school level, college level and professional) and corresponding groups of non-musicians. It was observed that musicians tend to reveal a sex-identity ambivalence, in that female musicians often exhibited masculine traits and vice versa. This suggests that for musicians:

> [. . .] temperamental requirements cut across the accepted sex-identity stereotypes, and it may be incidental that these tend to be sex-biased. However, the fact that aloofness and self-sufficiency appear to be male traits might account for the male domination of many aspects of professional music for so many years in times when sex stereotyping was perhaps more rigidly imposed by society than at present. On the other hand, the other musicianship-linked trait of sensitivity, being female-biased, would account for the common attitude towards music and musicians as being somewhat effeminate.[21]

Kemp concluded that:

> Psychological androgynous persons appear to be best endowed with the wider range of temperaments necessary for success in music. Those with more highly stereotyped and rigid self-concepts in connection with sex-identity would seem misfitted in the music profession [. . .][22]

This conforms well to the traditional view that male artists are 'feminine', but not particularly well with the idea that female musicians are also more 'feminine'. It was noted that:

> [. . .] female musicians frequently displayed greater divergence than the male musicians from their respective groups of non-musicians [. . .] Factors A [outgoingness] and Q2 [self-sufficiency] were shown [. . .] to be sex-linked [. . .] and thus there interaction can be interpreted in terms of the female musicians assuming levels of introversion which appear more appropriate for males in the general population.[23]

It is implied that female musicians have to exhibit behaviour which is further from the 'gender norm' than males. This would seem a vital point as it suggests that women must diverge from their peer groups to a far greater extent if they are to fulfil their potential in music. This contradicts the Terman and Miles tests which found female musicians to be feminine and therefore conforming to their sex type.

In 1982 Kemp concluded a study which attempted to identify specifically the profile of personality characteristics for composers (male and female). It was found that:

> The comparison between the composers and non-composers suggested that creativity in music was linked to [. . .] factors of introversion, subjectivity and lower moral upbringing [. . .] Other more contentious results [. . .] showed significant levels of aloofness, desurgency, and lower self-sentiment.[24]

Kemp believed that the lower 'moral upbringing' identified in composer profiles should be more accurately interpreted as a refusal to be bound by rules and external pressures. The trait of introversion was defined as a vital characteristic of all musicians, but particularly of composers. The term 'introversion' is often understood to imply shyness and a certain lack of confidence, believed to be a feminine trait. However:

> The broad concept of introversion [. . .] especially when it is linked with pathemia and subjectivity, must not be viewed as a timid withdrawal from social involvement. It is highly indicative of strength of the inner person and his colourful, imaginative and symbolic thought processes [. . .] Viewed in this way, the extreme introversion of the composer is easily reconcilable with the clear manifestation of independence [. . .][25]

It was also reported that composers who possessed a 'degree of originality' were:

> [. . .] identifiable by levels of introversion and subjectivity over and above those of musicians generally [. . .] composers displayed levels of expediency, which were clearly unacceptable in the more persistent performers, as well as radicalism, imagination and self-sufficiency.[26]

When compared with other groups of creative people such as scientists and architects, similarities were found:

> [. . . they] also exhibited the same characteristic profile of dominance, self-confidence, spontaneity, freedom from conventional restraint and inhibition, independence and autonomy [. . .] they also showed that the more creative were not especially sociable, or of a participative temperament, but somewhat self-centred.[27]

Other research has linked artistic creativity with higher levels of ergic tension (driven, over-wrought, frustrated).[28] The personality profile of the composer which emerges from this research can be summarised (Table 2.2).

The conclusion seems to be that the musician's reputation for 'femininity' is only partially justified; indeed, there are many personality factors vital to composers which our society would class as 'masculine' traits. The popular belief that musicians are 'feminine' may apply to males to a certain degree, but the finding that female musicians require greater cross sex-typing suggests that the development of the personality characteristics necessary to realize female potential may be more problematic.

Studies which focus specifically on female composers are rare – a fact which has made any wide comparison of results difficult. However, a study carried

Table 2.2 Personality profile of a composer

Composer	Masculine	Feminine
Introverted	Independent	Introverted
Subjective	Non-conformist	Subjective
Radical	Self-centered	Emotional
Independent	Radical	
Imaginative	Imaginative	
Non-conformist		
Self-centered		
Emotional		

Source: J. Freeman, H.J. Butcher and T. Christie, *Creativity: A Selective Review of Research*, Second Edition (London, 1971), cited in Kemp, 'The Personality Structure of Composers and Performing Musicians', 74

out by Laree McNeal Trollinger (1979) has proved a vital source of information.[29] Trollinger identified personality as an important factor in the cultivation of female musical potential:

> Contemporary women have achieved social, vocational, and educational privileges unknown in the past. In spite of this, because society sanctions many behaviours which promote creativity as being 'unfeminine', women will likely continue to create less in quality and quantity than men [. . .] music educators need to know biographical and personality factors which encourage or inhibit creative behaviour in the female musician.[30]

This corresponds with the finding that many personality characteristics in composers are 'masculine' rather than 'feminine'. Trollinger's study attempted to indicate the biographical and personality factors which emerged from a group of women who were described as highly creative. In this way, Trollinger located the personality characteristics which were evident in women who had successfully fulfilled their creative potential. A group of highly creative women (HIC) were compared with similar women who were much less creative (LOC) and a group reflecting the 'norm' of female Standford University students. Certain factors emerged in the personalities of HIC women which Trollinger felt must be of significance to musically creative women.

In terms of personality structure the HIC women were found to have androgynous personalities, confirming the findings of the Kemp research. Both the LOC and HIC women showed higher levels of masculine identity than other Standford students; the HIC women also had a strongly developed feminine identity, in that they displayed, in addition to a range of masculine characteristics, a full range of feminine characteristics and appeared more feminine that other college females. It was found that HIC women could identify freely with both males and females, whereas LOC women identified predominantly with women. In this way HIC women used both male and female figures as sources of inspiration.[31] This flexibility in identification allowed the HIC to perceive a wide range of behaviour and roles as appropriate for them.

In addition, Trollinger identified certain distinctive traits in the personalities of HIC women, qualities that may have some bearing on the fulfilment of creativity:

> The trait most differentiating HIC from LOC creative women musicians was the willingness of the former group to take a risk [. . .] the finding of this trait in HIC women is indeed distinctive in our society. For reasons of species survival, the protection and security of females has received primary emphasis in most cultures. Most women are taught to seek security in marriage and career; however parents and teachers of HIC women did not put security foremost during the formative years of these women. As a result HIC women emerged [. . .] freed to experiment, explore and discover.[32]

The idea that HIC women were less constrained because of their sense of independence, which in turn allowed exploration and experimentation without fear, corresponds to the general profile for composers identified by Kemp. Trollinger identifies the overall reluctance on the part of females to take risks in terms of evolutionary theory. If this basis for female personality traits proved to be correct, it would form a 'natural' barrier to musical creativity in females.

Other traits which distinguished the HIC women were a willingness to defend their beliefs, a trait which can prove decisive in the formulation and achievement of goals:

> Without philosophical foundations creative persons will lack direction for their creativity. In music itself these beliefs will be manifested in aesthetic choices, musical qualities that are emphasized, and attention to details of the craft. Through the act of sharing musical products, beliefs concerning the functions of music for humanity will be declared.[33]

A composer shares his or her aesthetic convictions and understandings through the musical composition. For an individual to present his or her ideas, emotions and beliefs to the world in the form of an artistic product requires self-belief, confidence and conviction. Other related factors which distinguished HIC women were identified as forcefulness:

> A forceful personality has the power to compel listeners, to influence affective responses, to manipulate overt behaviors, and to cause changes.[34]

And ambition:

> The source of HIC subjects' ambition may be found in their childhoods when parental and teacher expectancies focused their goals on high, atypical achievements.[35]

Traits of self-awareness also proved important to the fulfilling of potential in HIC women, as did self-reliance and conceit:

> [. . . It is believed] that lack of self-esteem plus environmental pressure inhibit the desire to be creative. This may be true, for the musician who lacks self-esteem will seldom attempt to go beyond the status quo in creative production, performance, administration, or teaching.[36]

Traits of ingenuousness – childlike behaviour, theatricality and less conventional behaviour – were also found to distinguish very creative women:

> HIC women musicians had strong tendencies to resist conforming to societal restraints, especially manifested in their preference for unconventional female careers.[37]

All the traits which identified the highly creative women are to be found in the composer profile compiled by Kemp. The most striking finding of the Trollinger research is that nearly all of the traits which were found to be distinct in creative women were masculine: for example, self-reliance, forcefulness, ambition, rebelliousness, self-centredness. These traits were exhibited in addition to a range of feminine traits, although these were not seen as distinctive in the HIC women. Clearly, HIC women are those who, in addition to possessing high levels of musical ability, have been able to develop a range of traits and characteristics which allow sensitivity and emotion (feminine), alongside independence and non-conformity (masculine). If such 'masculine' traits occur 'naturally' in the male, the chances of women composers developing such abilities to service their innate musical ability would be severely limited. However, even if this theory proved to be correct, it would create another contradiction. If women and men are 'naturally' sex-typed to exhibit appropriate characteristics, why is it that the male musician alone has been able successfully to cross sex-type and exhibit so many feminine characteristics necessary for musical creativity?

Now that we have established which personality traits (feminine or masculine) are of significance to a composer, it is possible to begin to tackle the real issue. Of fundamental concern is how males and females develop sex-differentiated personalities in the first place. Why should certain personality traits be presumed to be 'masculine' or 'feminine' and therefore more 'naturally' inherent in the male or female personality? The traditional explanation is that such differences are the very expression of physical and psychological sex differentiation. Yet to accept such a theory is to accept male domination as natural, since many masculine characteristics are linked to achievement and 'greatness'. However, if masculine and feminine categories are wholly or largely imposed by society, women may once again be at a disadvantage because of the imposition of artificial constraints on their abilities. A refutation of the arguments which state that sex determines personality requires an excursion into fields far removed from traditional musicology.

The formation of personality in humans is a complex process, but it can basically be understood as arising from the combination of temperament and character.

An individual's uniqueness is derived from the inbuilt or genetically dictated constellation of traits that constitute temperament. Temperament is then moulded and influenced by the group of traits emphasized and encouraged by society and culture; the result can be defined as a person's character.[38] There is a long history of arguments and theories which posit that female inferiority and male superiority stem from the inheritance of a basic temperament linked to sex. This supplies a biologically dictated foundation for inequality in achievement between the sexes. Such arguments, like those in the previous chapter, seek to 'explain' women's lack of cultural contribution as part of their biological/psychological inheritance, conveniently removing the burden of responsibility from a society in which women are in reality discriminated against.

One of the first large-scale investigations into the links between sex and personality was the study carried out by Terman and Miles in 1936. Their findings proved inconclusive:

> Masculinity and femininity are important aspects of human personality [. . .] they are one of a small number of cores around which the structure of personality gradually takes shape. The masculine-feminine contrast is probably as deeply grounded, whether by nature or nurture, as any other human temperament presents.[39]

Masculinity and femininity are important areas of human personality, yet how far this behaviour is imposed or inherited remains unresolved. Correspondingly, the nature verses nurture personality debate has continued in various forms for many decades and remains very current.

Since reproduction via sexual intercourse is the whole purpose for the existence of two sexes rather than just one, it is perhaps the most appropriate starting point for an investigation into the origins of sex-differentiated temperament and the development of gender-stereotyped character traits:

> The question may be raised as to whether the primary biological sex differences associated with reproductive functions predispose the individual toward psychological differences that bear on the respective roles they are expected to play in society.[40]

Indeed, many types of human temperament and behaviour are assumed to be rooted in reproductive physiology. The fact that women are physically less strong and bear children seems to be the foundation of this reproductive basis of the feminine temperament (defined as dependent, passive and sympathetic). Motherhood, or just the potential to bear children, has been assumed to impose upon women certain instincts: gentleness, nurturance, self-sacrifice, vulnerability and dependence on others. In evolutionary terms, female dependence has been viewed as an extension of the imperative that a female should find a reliable long-term mate to protect and provide for her and her children (a factor highlighted by Trollinger); this situation, coupled with less physical strength than the male, has reinforced the idea of the female as vulnerable and in need of male protection. On the other hand, the reproductive role of men has always been presumed to be quite different and much less involved with rearing children. The male role has been viewed as that of provider and protector, the male's greater physical strength predisposing him towards greater adventurousness and independence. Researchers who have tried to identify the natural origins of sex differences have based their theories mainly on human evolution to explain behaviour:

> It is widely accepted that physical gender differences have developed as a result of specialization of function and reproductive competition, and there is every reason to suppose that mental and emotional differences have evolved in parallel [. . .] If it is

> advantageous to females to nurse offspring [. . .] [and] prepare them for adult life [. . .] then they will tend to have a greater capacity for physical endurance, nurturance and attachment, a preference for security, and social and communicative skills.[41]

The idea that the sexes differ in reproductive motivations forms another foundation for a theory of personality based on reproductive physiology. For example, the male has vast quantities of gene-carrying sperm which allow him to couple with a number of females, producing many different offspring. The continuation of the male genetic line is rendered less certain when he pairs with only one female, whereas a female's potential for producing large quantities of her own genetic line is limited either way. The universal enforcement of monogamy on females has been seen as a means whereby the male can be sure of the continuation of his own genetic line. This evolutionary biological 'argument' is a good example of how a supposedly biologically defined temperament (male promiscuity and female restraint) then becomes the basis for a certain type of behaviour (male control of female fertility). Many other types of sex-differentiated behaviour are believed to have evolved in this way. A pertinent example is the way this kind of argument has even been used to 'explain' male achievement and female non-achievement in music:

> [. . .] male creativity and productivity [may be motivated . . .] to gain access to females. The males of the species have to provide some kind of performance or display [. . .] Building the Taj Mahal [. . .] painting pictures, composing symphonies and operas, and making Nobel-prize winning contributions to science – all, ultimately, may be motivated by a need to impress women.[42]

The basic reproductive behaviour of the sexes is used as the foundation for male achievement, differences in male and female interests (which then translate into employment patterns and labour allocation) and ultimately women's under-representation in a whole range of areas.

If this biological basis for temperament and behaviour were correct, it would be reasonable to assume that it would be common to all societies and cultures across the world, and would remain relatively stable over time. Much research points to the fact that gender differences in personality do exist in all societies:

> The cross-cultural literature does make it clear that sex differences are generally important from a social and behavioural standpoint. Gender seems to be a basic distinction of social organisation in all societies.[43]

However, much other research has suggested that while sex-role differentiation is always found, the concept of what constitutes a male or female personality can take a rich diversity of forms.

The eminent anthropologist Margaret Mead examined a number of different 'primitive' societies in New Guinea to ascertain whether they differentiated sex in the same way as Western industrialized societies.[44] She found that different tribes perceived masculine and feminine characteristics differently. In the Mundugumor tribe, both sexes exhibited the temperament and personalities we would describe as masculine. The women and men alike were athletic and assertive, detesting childbearing and -rearing. The children were taught to be independent and hostile from an early age, which left males and females with very similar personalities.[45] In another tribe, the Tchambuli, the masculine and feminine differentiation of personality was completely reversed. The women were independent, unadorned and assertive while the males were skittish, highly interested in personal adornment, art and trivial gossip. Mead's observations of this tribe point to the fact that imposed sex-differentiated characteristics have a profound effect on the development and potential of either sex. She states:

> [. . .] this is the only society in which I have worked where little girls [. . .] are more alertly intelligent and more enterprising than boys [. . .] the minds of small males, teased, pampered, neglected and isolated [. . .][46]

In other words, when a group of people are expected to behaviour in a certain way, society moulds their behaviour accordingly. Other researchers have found examples of differences in temperament within the context of cultural patterns more similar to our own. For example, in Iran, a strongly patriarchal society, women are considered unemotional and calculating, whereas men are seen as emotional and sensitive.[47] This and other cross-cultural research seems to show that Western ideas of masculine and feminine temperament are neither inevitable and 'natural' nor rooted in the reproductive role.

Despite the variety of personality traits which were found in men and women from different cultures, two traits are predominantly associated respectively with each sex: passivity with females and aggression with males. These traits have been put forward as the basis for a host of related traits which work to fulfil or inhibit creative and intellectual potential. Since aggression and passivity are fundamental to Western sex-differentiated personality, they require greater scrutiny.

Passivity is a broad concept covering many aspects of human behaviour, from the amount of mental competitiveness to actions (or the lack of them) during sexual intercourse. However, the main behavioural manifestations of passivity are: lack of physical movement, submissiveness, lack of aggression, dependency and a greater need for security and social approval – all traits which are thought to lie at the core of the feminine personality.[48] The stereotypes of the 'feminine passive' and 'masculine active' personalities are ones which assert themselves in many races and cultures and translate into many areas of life: men work outside the home, women within; men provide, women tend, and so on. There is much evidence to show that males are more *physically* aggressive than females. Indeed, most of the overt undesirable aggressive behaviour such as violent crime is caused by male aggression.[49] However, the term 'aggression' is used widely to describe a whole range of behaviour from the undesirable, violent, criminal and antisocial to the desirable, assertive, independent, outgoing, ambitious and competitive. Across all cultures, males have been found to show more physical and verbal aggression than females as early as social interaction begins.[50] However, this does not necessarily imply that females are more submissive, for, although less frequently than males, females also show aggression.

The most extensive research which has attempted to identify just how far such sex-stereotyping occurs in reality was carried out by Maccoby and Jacklin in 1972.[51] They reviewed more than two thousand books and articles on the subject of the psychology of sex differences with the intention of providing a broad overview of the findings of research into sex differentiation. They concluded that there was a tendency for boys to be slightly more physically active than girls, but that this trait was not consistent for all ages and conditions.[52] In dealing with frustration young boys demonstrated a greater tendency to show negative emotion after the age of eighteen months. Boys attacked barriers placed between them and their mothers more energetically than girls. It was shown that young girls also exhibited this sort of response to frustration, but that they decreased the amount of emotional volatility and intensity as they reached puberty, whereas boys did not. Importantly, it was found that in both sexes the passive-dependent personality was usually connected with poor performance on a variety of intellectual tasks, whereas the independent personality tended to excel.[53] However, on some tests the correlation between personality and performance was stronger for boys than for girls. This broadly confirms the findings of the Terman and Miles study, where a link was found between intelligence and 'masculine' characteristics. There is evidence that dependency in young children exhibits no sex differences and that seeking comfort through close proximity to a familiar adult is a universal behaviour in human children and not one found predominantly in females. However, other studies show that male babies of about three months are treated differently, receiving fewer touches, cuddles and visual or verbal attention; this would appear to prepare and encourage them to be more independent and perhaps more aggressive.[54]

The idea that women are more timid and fearful (traits linked to passivity) is not upheld by observational studies, which have shown no difference in timidity between the sexes.[55] However, self-reports and ratings of children by teachers show females in general to be more timid. Males appear much less willing to admit fear or anxiety, even if they experience it. Maccoby and Jacklin concluded that the passivity was not the fundamental identity of women.[56] However:

> It is possible that girls' self-attribution of fearfulness does impose restrictions on their adventurousness in exploring new situations. But it is equally possible that a boy's tendency to lose his temper interferes with constructive, active coping behaviour [. . .] that is just as severe an impediment to ongoing activity as timidity would be.[57]

The restrictive influence of a society which expects females to behave in this way illuminates the socially constructed obstacles and restrictions of behaviour imposed on the female, and male, personality. Fear and timidity are not limited to contexts of physical confidence; their effect can spread to many areas of behaviour. A woman is much less likely to undertake an occupation or activity which to her seems adventurous or risky if she perceives herself to be timid; this applies in the intellectual and physical sense. Obviously, the higher degrees of achievement, academical or professional, will be hindered fatally by timidity. This is pre-eminently true of music. To present a composition to be played in public and to lay oneself open to possible criticism requires personal courage and confidence. To undertake willingly a publicly visible act, musical or otherwise, requires an independent spirit and a degree of self-confidence encouraged less often in women than in men. This is a fact confirmed by the distinctness of the highly creative group of women examined in the Trollinger study. The trait which most distinguished them from the other groups was their freedom to explore and take risks. On the whole, women will be able to develop in this way only if they do not perceive themselves to be timid or constantly in need of support and protection.

Biologically-based explanations of male aggression have focused on sex differences in physical size and strength, both of which facilitate and encourage male aggression. Rosenblatt and Cunningham state:

> [. . .] it seems that males are better equipped physically and temperamentally than females for physical aggression.[58]

Some results indicate that testosterone is present in higher levels in more aggressive individuals (both male and female), but it is not clear whether this is the cause or the consequence of aggressive actions:

> [. . .] in mammals (including humans) of both sexes, androgen levels are increased as a result of positive, exhilarating experiences and successful achievement of sexual, aggressive, and status-related goals. Decreased androgen levels result from frustrating experiences, such as social isolation, defeat, denial of access to sexual outlets, and loss of status.[59]

If environment and experience influence hormone levels then the more stimulating the environment and opportunity, the greater would be the potential for aggressive and assertive behaviour. For women the access to such opportunities is limited in comparison with men. Clearly there is strong evidence to suggest that hormones alone are not responsible for behaviour but rather they interact with external forces, a point established in the previous chapter:

> [. . .] support for a general theory stating that male sex hormones promote aggressive and sexual behaviour must be immediately qualified by exceptions where androgens play a minimal role compared to past experience [. . .][60]

Indeed, aggressive male behaviour is observed from about three years onwards, long before the rise in the level of testosterone at puberty.[61] The fact that aggression is less restricted in men and is encouraged by adult reinforcement during childhood points to:

> [. . . the] possibility that the two genders have the same degree of motivation to be aggressive but that men are more likely to act out such violent impulses than women.[62]

Society expects, and therefore encourages, men to react in aggressive and dominant ways. The more desirable manifestations of aggressive behaviours are vital for the realization of full intellectual and creative potential. Women are clearly disadvantaged if society sanctions these types of behaviour only in men.

The evidence that society plays a decisive role in shaping gender identity is overwhelming. It seems very likely that the two sexes do not inherit a sex-associated blueprint of temperament related to reproduction or any other simple factor. A more likely thesis is that we inherit temperament individually. This *genotype* forms the blueprint upon which a complex set of environmental interactions then work:

> In shaping the personality, genetic and environmental influences do not act independently of one another but are intertwined from the moment of birth.[63]

Our society places much functional significance on the sex differeniation of reproductive behaviour. This in turn forms the basis for behaviour which seems quite removed from the original source, for example, male protect and lead (men become politicians) and female care for children (women become nurses). As individual temperament appears to be flexible in both sexes, how and why do the social and cultural concepts of gender-appropriate character develop? It is apparent that gender stereotypes of character exist to enable society to function successfully by assigning roles within the community. But this does not mean that the stereotyped characters are extensions of natural temperament or that they are fair, or of benefit, to the individual. It seems that personality stereotypes become established in many cultures primarily as 'practical' solutions to problems of labour allocation. In the reality of a patriarchal society the solutions to many of these problems is to tie females to domestic and child-rearing responsibilities, a role generally accompanied by low status and financial dependence. This prescribed female role then gives men the freedom to work outside the home, facilitating their high status, financial power and independence.

In any society the ruling classes appropriate and delegate status and power by a number of means, including labour allocation. When a range of cultures and societies are considered, a universal tendency to divide labour according to sex is found, with men taking the positions of power and work carrying high social status. Yet what labour is deemed appropriately masculine and feminine in one culture may be quite different in another. The variation in cultural definitions of character is clearly associated with the work thought appropriate for each sex to carry out.

Contrary to what is often believed, the male advantage of strength alone does not suffice to define sex-appropriate labour. In most societies around the world women collect 30–40 per cent of the food, and this responsibility includes many physically demanding tasks such as collecting water and firewood. Interestingly, much male work is more likely to require a far higher level of mobility and cannot be carried out with interruptions from children.[64]

The nursing of children and the distraction from work by the same children are two important factors associated with the development of female labour allocation and participation in many societies.[65] Because of the small number of young produced and the restrictions placed on females on account of the prolonged period of rearing, it is assumed that human survival depends on long-term pair bonding and cooperation between male and female. However, a healthy pregnancy does not place restrictions on most types of work, and recovery from a normal delivery is swift. Rather, the greatest imposition on female behaviour comes from nursing, feeding and long-term child-rearing.

Labour and role allocation form the basis upon which sex-differentiated personality is imposed. It appears that once a role has been established, the sex assigned to it is socially and physically conditioned to fulfil it successfully:

> The requirements of work seem to underlie how people are brought up, what their sources of power and status are, what their skills and interests are, and even the extent of such sexual dimorphism as muscle size.[66]

This points to the difficulties involved in changing established patterns of behaviour. As the majority of anthropological data reveals, there are some aspects of sex-role differentiation which are observed in most cultures: however, many others are not. This seems to show that most temperamental and behaviour differences which are perceived between the sexes are not biological – genetic, sexual, reproductive, size- and strength-related in origin.

Much of the information discussed above is drawn from the observation of 'primitive' societies and their division of labour. Clearly, Western societies have evolved from similar patterns. However, we have now become an advanced technological society, so why are men and women still perceived to be such different creatures? The fact seems to be that over a very long period of time, starting with the primitive divisions of labour, the sexes have developed two separate historical traditions in terms of gendered personality, work and culture:

> Women and men really live in two different worlds, with two interlocking sets of values [. . .] These semi-articulated beliefs (seen not as 'beliefs' but as 'how things are') have been built into theories of behaviour, psychology, 'human nature', religion, etc., over several thousand years.[67]

Changing the basis and orientation of these 'worlds' so as to make male and female experience and attitudes more similar and less restrictive requires much social and cultural change.

Psychologists have developed a number of theories for how society exerts pressure on individuals to conform to gender-stereotypes.[68] The socialization theory of human personality sanctions environmental explanations of aggression, nurturance and other temperamental and behavioural gender differences. These social learning theories work on the basic premise that humans (and, indeed, all animals capable of learning) learn a certain behaviour when that behaviour is reinforced by reward. In addition, humans are capable of imitative learning, whereby they will imitate or avoid certain types of behaviour after observing the consequences when others take such action. The most important components of social learning theory are passed on through imitation, observation and reinforcement.[69] In this way gender roles and appropriate behaviour are learnt very early in a child's development from a number of sources such as parents, peers and society at large (in technological societies: books, media images and television).

Correspondingly, there are usually very strong links between the techniques used to care for and control children and the individual adult personality.[70] For example, if the gender-stereotype requires males to be unemotional, the male child will be punished or ridiculed for showing emotion and will, conversely, be rewarded for being tough and unemotional: therefore he will be much more likely to adopt the latter behaviour despite his natural inclinations of temperament. As males are encouraged in displays of aggression, independence and physicality, so females are restrained from such behaviour. Evidence supporting the idea that males are more aggressive because aggressive behaviour is more accepted, and in some forms rewarded, in males is a good example. As children develop, they become directed increasingly by peer pressure to conform to gender-stereotypes; in addition, as children experience more social interactions they become inclined to imitate those most similar to themselves.

It has also been observed that role-modelling – that is the imitation of behaviour of a person perceived to be similar – may have a connection with appropriate gender-typed behaviour. Parents play a major role in sex-typing the behaviour of their children:

> Their attitudes towards their own gender roles and the way they interact with each other will influence the child's view. In addition, parents shape sex-typed behaviour in numerous ways: by the toys they provide, the activities they encourage, and their responses to behaviours considered appropriate and inappropriate for the child's sex.[71]

In a study carried out in 1980 it was found that pre-school female children who chose to play with stereotypical masculine toys (toy soldiers and trucks) were punished by lack of attention by their parents and were ridiculed by other children for such behaviour. Male children of the same age, on the other hand, were rewarded and encouraged for playing with such toys.[72]

However, it has been observed that even in families where parents consciously try not to sex-type their children, the children nevertheless demonstrate stereotyped gender behaviour.[73] This provides strong evidence that children never learn their roles simply from one person or one model. Gender concepts would appear to be learned in relation to society at large rather than just within the family context. For example, if a woman had a job that society classed as 'masculine', for example as a bricklayer, her daughter would probably still feel that this was an exceptional career for a woman. Most of the signals about appropriate work for women do not come from the family but via the information received from peers, books, television and general observation.[74]

Social learning theory seems to hold many of the answers to how children become gender-typed, but there are some general reservations about the extent to which it can explain gender differences:

> [. . .] doubts have been raised as to whether the different learning conditions acting on boys and girls are sufficient to explain all the observed gender differences. Such doubts have led some psychologists to suggest either a major or minor role for biological maturation [. . .] it is felt that the part played by the child is underestimated [. . .][75]

Cognitive development theory provides a more integrated approach to how people learn their gender-appropriate behaviour. Basically, this approach suggests that children build masculine or feminine personalities on an innate sense of gender identity. A child is understood to have a sense of gender identity – I am a girl or I am a boy – by the age of three.[76] As a child develops, its way of thinking about gender changes, passing through a series of stages until adulthood:

> Girls want to do stereotypically feminine activities because these activities are consistent with their female gender identity, and not – as social-learning theory would suggest – in order to win rewards.[77]

This suggests that in a society where all manner of occupations, personality traits and attitudes are defined as 'feminine' or 'masculine', children will adopt the ones deemed appropriate for their gender identity. But again, this theory does explain fully how gender-specific behaviour is developed. A girl must first understand she is a girl before giving preference to feminine activities, yet, children who do not understand their gender identity still exhibit gender-appropriate behaviour.[78] For example, from the age of two boys are more likely to show the gender-appropriate physical aggression and 'rough and tumble' play.[79] Some have implied that this sort of behaviour must be biologically determined since it cannot be attributed to social influence or shaping.[80] However, this is probably not the case:

> There is now abundant evidence that such 'shaping' occurs from the earliest infancy onwards. As Maccoby and Jacklin acknowledge, boy babies are stimulated more than girls babies to 'gross motor behaviour', girls being treated as though 'they were more fragile than boys'.[81]

This kind of stimulation will encourage males to be more physically vigorous than females, facilitating the more extroverted mental attitude expected of males.

From the evidence it is clear that to be successful in many situations, from higher intellectual functioning to professional success, women and men are required to override the stereotypical concepts of masculine and feminine behaviour. It is clear that to fulfil their potential people are better placed if they are less strongly stereotyped. This sharply contradicts the long-held belief that the most psychologically healthy individuals exhibit the most strongly sex-typed behaviour (that is, masculine males and feminine females). Eminent psychologist Sandra Bem concluded:

> This sex-role dichotomy has served to obscure two very plausible hypotheses: first, that many individuals might be 'androgynous' [. . .] and conversely that strongly sex-typed individuals may be seriously limited in the range of behaviours available to them as they move from situation to situation.[82]

Bem's research has confirmed that individuals who manage to exhibit the appropriate behaviour, regardless of their sex type, are much better able to cope:

> [. . .] the highly sex typed person becomes motivated – during the course of sex role socialisation – to keep his or her behaviour consistent with an internalized sex role standard; that is, he becomes motivated to maintain a self-image as masculine or feminine, a goal which he presumably accomplishes by suppressing any behaviour that might be considered undesirable or inappropriate for his sex.[83]

The results are consistent with the idea that androgynous individuals behave in a great variety of ways depending on the situation; for example, they exhibit independence when under pressure to conform or demonstrate playfulness in other interactions. However,

> In contrast, all of the nonandrogynous subjects were found to display behavioural deficits of one sort or another, with the feminine females showing perhaps the greatest deficit of all.[84]

In a society which demands strong sex-differentiation in personality it is clear that individuals of *both* sexes will suffer from having to act out restricted roles. However, the imposition of the feminine personality model leaves many women:

> [at a] disadvantage in many areas of life. [. . .] high feminity in females has consistently been correlated with high anxiety, low self-esteem, and low social acceptance.[85]

Despite consistent evidence to the contrary, the repercussions of adopting appropriate gender characteristics continue to be cited:

> In his popular advice manual, *Pregnancy*, Gordon Bourne even goes as far as to suggest that such deviance [masculine females, feminine males] can lead to infertility! He writes: 'From a purely biological aspect the masculine type of female and the effeminate type of male are not good vehicles for reproduction and the procreation of the human race'.[86]

This highlights the potency of gender stereotypes of personality and the consequences of deviation from them. Socially defined behaviour, when exerted over a long period of time, becomes able to exert strong psychological pressures on the behaviour of individuals.

This socialization of human behaviour offers many points for deliberation when one considers the position of women composers and musicians. It has been stressed many times in this and the previous chapter that music, the arts and even culture itself, are perceived as 'feminine' areas of interest and activity. This had led many to believe that there are no socially created obstacles to stop women becoming musicians – in the way that such obstacles confront women who wish to become scientists, for example. This argument obscures the reality of the situation, where the musical profession and the traditional Western music canon are male dominated. In terms of the socialization theories discussed earlier, women may be encouraged to study music as an accomplishment in childhood and adolescence, since this conforms to the gender-appropriate behaviour for their sex and is therefore commendable. Yet after this point the musical stereotype suddenly emerges as 'unfeminine'. As soon as the position of those who practise music becomes socially and culturally significant ('professional'), their occupations become widely regarded as 'masculine' and more suitable for males. This can be linked both to the physical reality that members of this group are primarily male and to the fact that the behaviour which accompanies such occupations is deemed 'masculine' (competitiveness, creativity, leadership). In addition, musicians at the highest levels of achievement are considered to exhibit 'genius' and are held in the highest possible cultural esteem. This position of great power and supreme cultural or artistic authority has traditionally been reserved for men. If a female seeks confirmation of her gender identity from the gender-appropriateness of her occupation, the male domination of the musical profession (specifically, the roles of composer, conductor and musicologist) makes such confirmation unlikely, tending to deflect her from commitment and interest in those areas. Other areas of music can provide a more positive gender-role identification – for example, performance (especially vocal) and music-teaching – since more females already participate in such occupations. For more women to be encouraged to be composers and conductors, however, the dominant stereotypes must be deconstructed.

From the evidence I have considered it is clear that although music may in some ways be considered a 'feminine' area of interest, many of the personality traits which are especially important to composers, and, indeed, to other musicians, are perceived as 'masculine'. This is not to underestimate the great importance of 'femininity', especially to male musicians who need to develop this side of their personalities within a culture which all too often discourages such behaviour. If, as some of the research suggests, the stereotype of the artistic 'feminine' male is correct, there are those who may voice the idea that restrictive gender stereotyping acts to constrain male as well as female composers.

The main reason why music has so frequently been characterized as feminine is because of its 'emotional' and 'expressive' dimensions. This stems from the age-old belief that women are the embodiment of unfettered emotion without reason. Moreover, the idea that women are unable to control their emotions has traditionally been an argument used against female intellect; this has been evident in discussions which give reasons for the lack of women in music:

> Conceding that music is the highest expression of the emotions, and that woman is emotional by nature, is it not one solution of the problem [lack of women composers] that woman does not reproduce them because she herself is emotional by temperament and nature [. . . whereas man] sees them [emotions] in their full play, and can reproduce them in musical notation [. . .] to treat emotions as if they were mathematics, to bind and measure and limit them within the rigid laws of harmony and counterpoint [. . .] is a cold-blooded operation possible only to the sterner and more obdurate nature of man.[87]

Here, musical creativity is put forward as being possible only in men, who are by nature 'masculine'. It seems that males can exhibit irrational female traits but they can balance this with their logical, intellectual nature – a side which women clearly lack. The debates which have surrounded the 'nature' or 'temperament' of women have frequently been forums for the belief that women just cannot think like men and are therefore less intellectual and, by extension, inferior.

Concepts which link music and femininity are much better understood when they are viewed as part of a much wider stereotype of male genius. Christine Battersby's research into gender and genius catalogues the history of 'male genius', which is littered with references to the paradoxical femininity of the great male mind, a notion which has been around for some two thousand years:

> Woman's inferiority had been rationalised by the writers of the Aristotelian tradition as a deficiency of judgement, wit, reason, skill, talent and psychic (and bodily) heat. Women had been blamed for an excess of passion, imagination, sexual needs and for vapour-inspired delusion and irrationality. But if we look at the aesthetic literature of the late eighteenth century, we will see that the greatest *males* (the natural 'geniuses') were being praised for qualities of mind that seem *prima facie* identical with Aristotelian femininity [. . .] A man of genius was *like a woman* [. . .] but was *not a woman*.[88]

In similar vein, at the turn of the century, Otto Weininger wrote an influential study entitled *Sex and Character*, which identified the supposed impossibility of female artistic genius:

> Whilst there are people who are anatomically men and psychically women, there is no such thing as person who is physically female and psychically male [. . .] A female genius is a contradiction in terms, for genius is simply intensified, perfectly developed, universally conscious maleness.[89]

Clearly the concept of femininity in 'men of genius' in no way allowed for a female equivalent. The male mind could benefit from the feminine, whereas the female mind could not reap the same rewards from the masculine. One might have thought that the recognition of 'femininity' in the male musician would bestow an advantage on female musicians because of their 'natural' endowment of femininity. Yet this does not happen:

> It is hard to think through the implications of the fact that 'feminine' – generally used as a sneer-word in reference to art works by *women* – takes on much more positive connotations when applied to *males*.[90]

This leaves the female artist and her creation in a severely disadvantaged position. Earlier, I suggested that if male composers need to be cross sex-typed feminine, they may suffer a problem similar to that of female composers, who have cross sex-typed to be more masculine. However, when the historical context of the 'feminine' male mind is considered, an established model is uncovered, whereby 'feminine males' are regarded as far from inadequate or maladjusted males, but rather, in many cases, as 'supermales'. This was confirmed by the Terman and Miles finding that the males who were academically the most successful ('high-scholarship') were more interested in culture (ideas, knowledge, refinement, the arts) and tested as more feminine. When a male aspires to an artistic profession, he is required to break the general mould of masculinity, but the benefits of potential adulation and greatness far outweigh any drawbacks. In addition, history provides a wealth of male role models of this kind by which other males can be reassured and inspired. Femininity in this sense has nothing to do with females: those who suggest that it has, misunderstand the respective position of the sexes in relation to personality characteristics.

Clearly, aspiring female composers need to be encouraged to develop a range of characteristics enabling them to fulfil their creative potential beyond the level of mere accomplishment. But so long as high levels of achievement and success continue to be associated mainly with males, women suffer disadvantage. A parallel psychological argument against female achievement (in all areas) is the one which claims that women view success as 'unfeminine' and so avoid it. Tests carried out by Matina Horner have revealed, even in the last decade, that men and women still perceive competitiveness, intellectual achievement, competence and leadership with positive mental health and masculinity, whereas all these traits were considered in conflict, or inconsistent with, femininity.[91]

> Among women, the anticipation of success especially against a male competitor poses a threat to the sense of femininity and self-esteem and serves as potential basis for becoming socially reflected – in other words, the anticipation of success is anxiety-provoking and as such inhibits otherwise positive achievement-directed motivation and behaviour.[92]

This situation highlights the many obstacles which face females who wish to succeed in music, as in many other areas. When a woman's work in music, as composer of performer, becomes professional and visibly public in nature, it is no longer a simple accomplishment but a highly complex development of talent and ability. Hence the gender-appropriateness of music as a skill abruptly changes when it becomes more high level, public and competitive; this is doubtless true also of many other 'feminine areas' – for example, caring (medicine), cookery or teaching. For women who enter music, the path to the low levels of achievement may indeed be encouraged, so that their concept of femininity in this area is never challenged. However, by the time a woman reaches the stage of becoming professional, there is an increased need to exert more masculine behaviour in order to succeed; at this same stage females are also limited in their choice of female role models capable of reinforcing the gender-appropriateness of professional musicianship. Strongly sex-typed behaviour of any sort is difficult to reverse in adult life, since to a great extent the sex-differentiated core of personality has already been established and would require individuals to rethink the whole concept of personal identity, were they to change.

Gender-defined behaviour is very restrictive for women in our society. Having the basic potential – aptitude – is not enough: natural ability needs to be coupled with social skills to realize this potential in a male-dominated system. Obviously, individuals may have inclinations of personality which are inherited, yet I think that the evidence shows that much larger forces are at work; these forces often divide and define in terms of sex. Although these factors can have a restrictive effect on certain sections of the male population as well, the restrictions are imposed mainly on females. The 'feminine' male in part contradicts the convention, but he has proved a successful vehicle for originality and cultural contribution: he may indeed be considered feminine, but this will always be safely confined within the boundaries of the physical male, resisting any female equivalent. Hence it appears far easier for men to develop such cross sex-typed behaviour, whereas for women there are few role models and little chance of achieving iconic status and authority. For women, the path to success through the development of masculine traits is altogether more difficult. Masculine traits in women are often portrayed as unnatural and un-nurturant – values which lie at the core of the socially imposed feminine personality.

I feel that male and female creative talent, though stemming from the same human aptitude, is moulded in very different ways by Society's treatment of the individual as classified by sex. In this and the previous chapter it has become clear that there is no proven biological predisposition for either sex to be more successful than the other in music. However, Society exerts such a pervasive influence over the two sexes in terms of behaviour, personality and spheres of interest that men and women effectively become two differently programmed sections of the human race. In recent times the understanding of the restrictions imposed on women by socially constructed femininity has resulted in a gradual erosion of rigid sex-type socialization. To alter the situation further and make the achievement of potential and the gaining of success in the public arena an equally obtainable goal for women, we must surely look to Society and in particular to the structures of the family, the education system and the professional world. The disadvantages of a system which imposes a limited range of characteristics on creative women must be identified, challenged and deconstructed if there is to be any hope of eventually removing the obstacles and discrimination imposed by the current sex-differentiated poles of personality.

Notes

1 Wilson, *The Great Sex Divide*, 108–109.
2 A.E. Kemp, 'The Personality Structure of Composers and Performing Musicians', (D.Phil. thesis, University of Sussex, 1979), 1.
3 *Ibid.*, 2.
4 John P. Seward and Georgene H. Seward, *Sex Differences: Mental and Temperamental* (Toronto, 1980), 25.
5 Wilson, *The Great Sex Divide*, 140–141.
6 Sandra L. Bem, 'Probing the Promise of Androgyny', in Mary Roth Walsh (ed.), *The Psychology of Women: Ongoing Debates* (New Haven and London, 1987), 206.

7 Results were calculated on a scale where 100 was the most masculine score and − 100 was the most feminine score possible.
8 Lewis M. Terman and Catherine Cox Miles, *Sex and Personality* (New York and London, 1936), 122–124.
9 *Ibid.*, 121.
10 *Ibid.*, 148–154.
11 Sandra L. Bem, 'Sex Role Adaptability: One Consequence of Psychological Androgyny', *Journal of Personality and Social Psychology*, 31 (1975), 635.
12 Terman and Miles, *Sex and Personality*, 156.
13 *Ibid.*, 177.
14 Cultural interests are defined as greater interest and exposure to religion and the arts, concepts of social welfare and the degree of social interaction with others.
15 Terman and Miles, *Sex and Personality*, 176.
16 Terman and Miles, *Sex and Personality*, 179. It may be observed that the female list of occupations is extremely limited compared to the male list. This accurately reflects the restricted opportunities for females at the time it was complied.
17 *Ibid.*, 193.
18 *Ibid.*, 3.
19 A.E. Kemp, 'The Personality Structure of the Musician: III. The Significance of Sex Differences', *Psychology of Music*, 10 (1982), 48.
20 *Ibid*, 48.
21 *Ibid.*, 53.
22 *Ibid.*, 54.
23 *Ibid.*, 53.
24 A.E. Kemp, 'The Personality Structure of the Musician. II. Identifying a Profile of Traits for the Composer', *Psychology of Music*, 9 (1981), 69.
25 *Ibid.*, 72.
26 Kemp, 'The Personality Structure of Composers and Performing Musicians', 73.
27 *Ibid.*, 50.
28 J. Freeman, H.J. Butcher and T. Christie, *Creativity: A Selective Review of Research*, Second Edition (London, 1971), cited in Kemp, 'The Personality Structure of Composers and Performing Musicians', 74.
29 Laree McNeal Trollinger, 'A Study of Biographical and Personality Factors of Creative Women in Music' (D.M.A. thesis, Temple University, 1979).
30 *Ibid.*, 1.
31 *Ibid.*, 244.
32 *Ibid.*, 262.
33 *Ibid.*, 263.
34 *Ibid.*, 264.
35 *Loc. cit.*
36 *Ibid.*, 266.
37 *Ibid.*, 267.
38 Rhoda Metraux (ed.), *Margaret Mead: Some Personal Views* (London, 1979), 240.
39 Terman and Miles, *Sex and Personality*, 451.
40 Seward and Seward, *Sex Differences: Mental and Temperamental*, 5.
41 Wilson, *The Great Sex Divide*, 112.
42 *Ibid.*, 111–112.
43 P.C. Rosenblatt and M.R. Cunningham, 'Sex Differences in Cross-Cultural Perspective', in Archer and Lloyd, *Exploring Sex Differences*, 72.
44 Margaret Mead, *Sex and Temperament in Three Primitive Societies* (New York, 1950). Originally published in 1935.
45 Margaret Mead, *Sex and Temperament in Three Primitive Societies*, cited in Ann Oakley, *Sex, Gender and Society* (London, 1985), 54.

46 Margaret Mead, *Male and Female*, (Harmondsworth, 1950), cited in Ann Oakley, *Sex, Gender and Society*, 55.
47 Oakley, *Sex, Gender and Society*, 57.
48 I use the term feminine to describe all behaviours and characteristics believed to be *more common* among females. However, these types of behaviour are not exclusive to females and can be exhibited also by males.
49 Rosenblatt and Cunningham, 'Sex Differences in Cross Cultural Perspective', 77. Also see Ann Oakley, *Sex, Gender and Society*, 66–67. These statistics show that men have a much higher tendency to crime and deviance; even when women commit crime, it conforms to a sex-differentiated pattern, males committing more violent and sex-related crime.
50 Maccoby and Jacklin, *The Psychology of Sex Differences*, 352.
51 Maccoby and Jacklin, *loc. cit.* This piece of research has become a classic reference text, aiding psychologists to sort through the often diverse and contradictory evidence on the nature of sex differentiation of temperament and personality.
52 Maccoby and Jacklin, *The Psychology of Sex Differences*, 177.
53 Eleanor E. Maccoby, 'Sex Differences in Intellectual Functioning', in Eleanor Maccoby (ed.), *The Development of Sex Differences* (London, 1967), 35.
54 S. Goldberg and M. Lewis, 'Play Behaviour in the Year-Old Infant: Early Sex Differences', *Child Development*, 40 (1969), 21–31, cited in Carol Travis and Carole Offir (eds), *The Longest War*, (New York, 1977), 50–51.
55 Maccoby and Jacklin, *The Psychology of Sex Differences*, 189.
56 *Ibid.*, 190.
57 Maccoby and Jacklin, *loc. cit.*
58 Rosenblatt and Cunningham, 'Sex Differences in Cross-Cultural Perspective', 79.
59 L. Ellis, 'Developmental Androgen Fluctuations and the Dimensions of Mammalian Sex', *Ethology and Sociobiology*, 3 (1982), 171–179, cited in Archer and Lloyd, *Sex and Gender*, 143.
60 Lesley Rogers, 'Male Hormones and Behaviour', in Archer and Lloyd (eds), *Exploring Sex Differences*, 161.
61 It should be noted that males are exposed to more testosterone prenatally, so that some researchers believe that this exposure affects behaviour and development throughout life.
62 Archer and Lloyd, *Sex and Gender*, 125.
63 Atkinson and Atkinson *et al.*, *Introduction to Psychology*, 499.
64 *Ibid.*, 77.
65 *Ibid.*, 74. Five separate pieces of research were used to validate this finding.
66 Rosenblatt and Cunningham, 'Sex Differences in Cross-Cultural Perspective', 73.
67 Shere Hite, *Women as Revolutionary Agents of Change: The Hite Reports 1972–1993* (London, 1993), 303.
68 These theories are generally categorized as social learning theory and cognitive-development theory. Also relevant is psychoanalytical theory on the Freudian model, which links genital differences, the subconscious mind and the behaviour and psychology of men and women. A fuller discussion of this field and its relation to music is deferred to Chapter 7.
69 Campbell, *The Opposite Sex*, 32–33.
70 Oakley, *Sex, Gender and Society*, 59.
71 Atkinson and Atkinson *et al.*, *Introduction to Psychology*, 96.
72 J.H. Langlois and A.D. Downs, 'Mothers, Fathers, and Peers as Socialization Agents of Sex-Typed Play Behaviours in Young Children', *Child Development*, 51 (1980), 1237–1247.
73 Campbell, *The Opposite Sex*, 35.
74 Loc. cit.
75 Archer and Lloyd, *Sex and Gender*, 264.

76 Margaret W. Matlin, *The Psychology of Women* (New York, 1987), 51.
77 *Ibid.*, 51–52.
78 *Ibid.*, 52–53.
79 Janet Sayers, *Sexual Contradictions: Psychology, Psychoanalysis and Feminism* (London, 1986), 6.
80 Maccoby and Jacklin, *Psychology of Sex Differences*, 242.
81 Sayers, *Sexual Contradictions*, 7.
82 Sandra L. Bem, 'The Measurement of Psychological Androgyny', *The Journal of Consulting and Clinical Psychology*, 42 (1974), 155.
83 Bem, 'Sex Role Adaptability: One Consequence of Psychological Androgyny', 634.
84 Bem, *loc. cit.*
85 *Ibid.*, 635.
86 Sayers, *Sexual Contradictions*, 28. Sayers is quoting Gordon Bourne, *Pregnancy* (London, 1972), 27.
87 George Upton, *Woman in Music* (Boston, 1880), in Carol Neuls-Bates (ed.), *Women in Music: An Anthology of Source Readings from the Middle Ages to the Present* (New York and Cambridge, 1982), 206–207.
88 Christine Battersby, *Gender and Genius* (London, 1989), 8.
89 Otto Weininger, *Sex and Character* (London, 1906, translation of 1903 German edition) 188–189, cited in Battersby, *Gender and Genius*, 115.
90 Battersby, *Gender and Genius*, 7.
91 Matina S. Horner, 'Toward an Understanding of Achievement-Related Conflicts in Women', in Mary Roth Walsh (ed.), *The Psychology of Woman: Ongoing Debates*, 169–170.
92 *Ibid.*, 183.

Part Two:
Education and Social History

3 Parents, Marriage and Motherhood

> Men compose symphonies, women compose babies.
>
> *Time Magazine*, 10 January 1975

> Like many talented women Elisabeth Lutyens [1906–1983] tried, unsuccessfully, to juggle the demands of a career, husband, and four children, sliding deeper and deeper into despair. She wrote to her mother: 'I have had NO encouragement in anything I have undertaken [. . .] For years you've all given me the pit and the pendulum, your children or your music [. . .] One day – I'll show you all.'[1]

The social status and domestic role of women as a group, compared with men as a group, raises many issues which cannot be ignored when examining the cause of inequalities between male and female musical creation and contribution. In terms of the division of labour and social status, females and males are still very differently placed in twentieth-century Britain, and the effect of this reality must be ascertained carefully because of its possible prejudicial effect on the work of female composers. The introduction of social and domestic issues into musicology is not achieved without difficulty, since traditional research has most often omitted social commentary as being irrelevant to musical (and even biographical) matters. This omission renders invisible the important and influential social and domestic experiences of women composers and the consequences for their work. However, many of the problems directly affecting women's participation in musical creativity are revealed only when common aspects of the female experience are exposed:

> Social history [. . .] starts from experiences of a particular group [. . .] and [it] heeds the experiences of daily life, not only momentous events. Historical women in music could benefit from this approach. It begins with women's actual experience in music rather than some set of preconceived categories that reflect male experience.[2]

To achieve a more detailed understanding of women composers' situation in Britain, I have chosen to devote this chapter to the experiences of a group of nine British female composers, the prime focus being the influence of their family and domestic concerns on their respective creative development and output.[3] Obviously, the domestic circumstances of an individual change over time from the initial biological family unit to a marital or independent unit. Through an examination of the composers' own statements and recollections, a clear picture of the shared experiences and common obstacles facing women composers will emerge.

It must be acknowledged that generalizing about the experience of women as a group holds great difficulties, since women from different backgrounds and social classes are often treated differently by society. The social class of any individual is still highly influential in relation to the kind of aspirations he or she holds and the interests and opportunities which are afforded to him or her. The nine women composers in my study group come from a variety of backgrounds, but they can all be defined as middle-class. To define families as middle-class is really to point to their common attitudes, principles and occupations. All the biological families under consideration had to work for a living, but their work was always non-manual. The financial status of a middle-class family can vary from just adequate to affluent, and this is borne out by the study group.

Before I discuss the personal experiences of the study group, it is important to highlight the political events which have fashioned women's status in Britain, and have brought about many changes in their social role and status in the course of the twentieth century. The campaign for increased rights for British women had emerged as a significant force only in the latter part of the previous century. Up to that time, British women had been without basic civil rights in the modern sense and therefore had little power or control over their own lives. Only in the late nineteenth century was significant legislation passed which gave women as a group elementary personal rights. For example, married women gained the right to control their own earnings in 1878 and the right to own their own property in 1882. Women over 30 were granted the right to vote in 1918 (women became able to vote at the same age as men – 21 – only in 1928). In 1878 the University of London became the first university in England to award degrees to women; subsequently, in 1919, women were allowed to become lawyers, jurors, judges and members of Parliament. In 1925 women gained equal rights over child custody.[4] These and other reforms empowered women as never before, but they by no means allowed women status and rights equal to those of men, and many inequalities remained.

For much of the century, issues related to marriage and fertility have proved central to how far any woman could fulfil her potential. Throughout the twentieth century marriage has remained a common experience for women of all social classes. Women's status within marriage has often reflected their lack of basic rights. For example, women obtained the right to gain a divorce only in 1923 – but it must be remembered that divorces were very difficult to obtain right up to the late 1960s.[5] Once divorce became easier, one of the primary reasons for the substantial increase in the divorce rate was women's dissatisfaction with the inequalities so often entailed by marriage.[6] Marriage, for women, has traditionally held many restrictions and responsibilities; the traditional role of wife and mother was, for middle-class women, their sole priority. In general, the 'middle-class lady's' world throughout the period 1900–1950 was still predominantly home-centred, and there was a very clear separation between the role of the husband as provider and head of the family and that of the wife as 'homemaker' and mother. Yet this distinction was by no means the same for the working-class woman. Her role was less rigidly defined, since financial demands made it imperative for her to take some form of paid employment. However:

> By World War II both the prescribed roles and the reality of married middle class women's experience had changed and the changes within marriage were more dramatic than for working class women. Middle class married women were no longer assumed to be passive, weak and 'naturally' inferior, although men remained very much the dominant partners.[7]

Progress made in terms of women's health and reforms to the property and marriage laws benefited, on the whole, only middle-class women.[8]

Without doubt, the gradual introduction of family planning throughout this century has given women their greatest enabling force for equality. The size of the average family had been decreasing since the mid-nineteenth century from an average of six to two children per marriage.[9] Having a child could be a physically dangerous event for women up until the mid-1930s. Throughout the Victorian and Edwardian eras maternal mortality rates were about five deaths per thousand live births.[10] The real figure for maternal deaths when miscarriage and still births are included would be much higher.[11]

The gradual introduction of contraception to married women in the 1920s made a huge difference to the health and quality of life for many women. Marie Stopes opened the first private birth control clinic in London in 1921. However, access to birth control via government-run clinics became available only in 1930, and then only to married women who would be in serious physical danger if they became pregnant. Access to birth control as a right bound up with individual freedom was not acknowledged by the British Parliament until 1967.[12] Contraception meant the ability to control the number and frequency of pregnancies which has resulted in smaller families and less of the female life cycle spent bearing children. However, this did little to change women's position of responsibility in terms of their domestic situation when they had children.

The main area of female existence which had not been subjected to effective reform was, and is, women's socially prescribed domestic role. Women provide the mainstay of domestic and child-care work and continue to take the main responsibility for the emotional welfare of their families. Although social reforms opened up new areas of life in the early part of our century, basic attitudes towards women as wives or mothers remained largely unchanged. There was, and still is, substantial pressure on women to raise children and take full responsibility for domestic matters. This pressure has manifested itself in a number of ways. For example, between the First and Second World Wars, at a time when many middle-class women were beginning to work outside the home, legislation known as the 'marriage bar' was introduced. This literally barred married women from paid employment:

> During the early twentieth century and increasingly during the inter-war years the ideology of motherhood was reinforced legislatively by the marriage bar, which was applied chiefly to professional women and which served firmly to delineate the

> world of married women from that of men at a time when it was becoming widely acceptable for single middle class girls and women to go out to work.[13]

Child-rearing and domestic work, even in the 1990s, is considered by many as the 'natural' priority of the female, as opposed to the male. The fact that women physically give birth to children is seen by many as justification for the assumption by the mother of full responsibility for the care of that child into adulthood:

> The new mother [. . .] flooded with sex-specific hormones, bonds with her baby. Wanting, more than her mate, to be with and cosset her baby she stays with it [. . .] tolerance for repetition further incline her to assume these tasks. Meanwhile her mate, preferring status and control of the physical environment, is out hunting mastodons or closing a deal. Resources are used more efficiently if the mother also assumes care of whatever counts as home.[14]

This statement made in 1992 by Professor Michael Levin illustrates the prevailing social attitude of a biological basis for women's domestic responsibilities, which consequently leaves little room for negotiation of roles within families and ensures that most women continue to take full responsibility for the home and family, leaving men free to concentrate on their careers and personal development. Women who wish to have a family life and fulfil their potential usually find themselves in a position of having to combine the roles of wife, mother and worker. Coping with domestic responsibilities makes competing for career opportunities, gaining experience and developing at the same rate as a male very difficult. This applies to female musicians and composers as it does to every other occupation. It is perhaps above all this kind of imbalance which can still handicap a woman who wants to make a professional career in which she competes directly with men.

There is clear evidence that many women still suffer from the same social inequalities as were experienced by women of previous generations. The family built around marriage and children seems to be the cornerstone of human society, yet built into this structure are many of the inequalities which have not been removed or even considered by the legal reforms. Many see the fact that women have gained increased social rights and have established themselves as members of the workforce as proof of the end of sex discrimination. However:

> [. . .] others suggest that women have simply added paid employment on to the burden of housework, so that while the form of inequality has changed, the degree has not.[15]

The idea that men and women now have truly equal opportunity is not supported by the evidence of the domestic and emotional demands faced by the majority of women. While there remains such disparity between the social roles and domestic experiences of men and women, the inequalities will continue unchecked.

It has often been conceded, surely correctly, that female composers in previous centuries were severely hampered by lack of encouragement and opportunities from their biological families and then also restricted and burdened by their domestic responsibilities. Equally, it is often assumed that today this is no longer the case: in the twentieth century any woman who has sufficient talent and ambition can, allegedly, become a composer on an equal footing with her male contemporaries. However, while women's status and opportunities have certainly improved, numerous inequalities remain undiminished, as the lives of the study group of composers now testify.

Avril Coleridge-Taylor (b. 1903)

Avril Coleridge-Taylor, born Gwendolen Coleridge-Taylor, in South London in 1903, is the oldest of the composers in this study.[16] She is the only woman in the group to have an immediate relative who was also a composer, her father being Samuel Coleridge-Taylor. Samuel Coleridge-Taylor was partly of West African descent and was often subjected to terrible racial discrimination and abuse; indeed, his own father had left England because of the intolerable prejudices he suffered as a practising doctor. After living with his mother in some poverty, Samuel was 'discovered' by a well-to-do patron and entered the Royal College of Music at the age of 15. Coleridge-Taylor married a fellow student from the Royal College of Music from a prosperous middle-class background. Jessie Fleetwood Walmisley had come from a musical family, being the niece of Thomas Attwood Walmisley, a Victorian composer. After their marriage, Jessie Coleridge-Taylor confined her musical participation to assisting the advancement of her husband's career as a composer. This was the usual function for a married woman at this time, as the similar case of Alice Elgar illustrates. So Avril Coleridge-Taylor was born into a family of musicians who, although middle-class in status, were often not fully accepted by their contemporaries.

Family life was for Avril a very mixed experience, ranging from the complete joy and adulation with which she remembered her father and the unhappiness and anger which accompanied any experience brought about by her mother. The early influence of a much-idolized father who was a composer is without doubt the most prominent aspect of Avril's early musical development. Consequently, expression through musical composition was a natural process from her earliest childhood:

> Quite early in life I began to feel a sense of music within me that was anxious to make its way out. Not only did I want to write music – as I had seen my father do – but to express myself through beautiful sound. So, before I was twelve, when most other children amused themselves by playing games, I was concentrating on composition.[17]

She resolved early in life to follow in her father's footsteps. From his example she was able to decide immediately that she wanted to be a composer. She identified with him completely and even modelled herself on his personality.[18] Samuel Coleridge-Taylor encouraged his daughter's musical talents, and his influence on her was enormous:

> Nearly every night I had fallen asleep to the strains of his music. He allowed me to remain in the room with him during the day while he composed. Often he would give me a sheet of manuscript paper and a pencil so that I could 'write music' too![19]

Yet after her father's sudden death in 1912, when Avril was only nine years old, she received very little formal tuition in music, harmony or even piano-playing. Avril claims that she taught herself to play the piano sufficiently well to tackle difficult pieces by Beethoven, Schumann and, of course, her father.[20] It appears that her mother completely ignored Avril's musical potential and that it was only on the insistence of an associate of her late husband that any further musical training was arranged:

> I never quite understood whether my mother chose deliberately to ignore my musical gift, but whatever her motive the fact remained that she did little to encourage it, but everything to hinder it.[21]

It is difficult to understand her mother's motivation for such behaviour. Since she was a trained musician herself, one would perhaps have expected a wealth of encouragement towards her talented daughter – but perhaps she felt jealous that Avril would one day be in a much better position to concentrate on a career in music and thus fulfil some ambitions that she herself had been unable to fulfil. Avril maintained this was the case: 'People said Mother was jealous.'[22] All the evidence indicates that even though Avril came from a musical family, her development as a musician was by no means without obstacles or discouragement.

Family life, and particularly Mrs Coleridge-Taylor, perpetually exerted pressure on Avril, forcing her to take time off from her studies:

> My mother was almost totally uninterested in what I did, insisting, however late I arrived home, that I washed dishes or otherwise made myself useful. In the end the doctor diagnosed heart strain and I had to have complete rest for several months.[23]

When World War One broke out, Avril's brother, Hiawatha, joined the French Red Cross, so her studies were again disrupted, since she had to spend more time at home to give 'companionship' to her mother. At this time Avril managed to secure engagements, fulfilling a variety of roles as a singer, actor and reciter. Because of her age and sex, she was chaperoned to such events by her mother, who continued to be obstructive.[24]

As Avril grew into adulthood, the relationship with her mother deteriorated further. Mrs Coleridge-Taylor actively sabotaged any budding relationships upon which Avril embarked:

> Her jealousy on account of my youth was obvious, so she tried to prevent any form of happiness that precluded her.[25]

Avril's bitterness is clear – but at this time it was normal for many young women to have little say in the choice of associates. The practice of 'arranged' relationships and marriages was very much an upper-class preoccupation. For this social group, money, power and status could be lost or gained on account of a marriage, so any potential match was closely vetted. Avril seems to have been subjected to this kind of scrutiny in her personal relationships, her mother always rejecting any man Avril became involved with through her own choice. Avril even recalls how her mother:

> [. . .] pushed her into the company of an elderly rake – a real 'man about town' – whose behaviour I found most objectionable, but Mother looked on him with approval. He was very wealthy, and he was married.[26]

This man wanted Avril to become his mistress in exchange for a luxurious lifestyle, an offer she rejected. Avril quite obviously felt that this situation had been 'set up' by her mother for the financial gain of the family.

Partners can be most influential in the life of a composer, and this is true for male composers. However, for women a close relationship or marriage can often restrict their work even to the extent that compositional activities are silenced. This was true of Averil Coleridge-Taylor. In her autobiography a great amount of detail is given about her romance with a flautist named Joseph Slater. This relationship seems to have been an inspiration, encouraging her to compose a number of pieces for flute and piano which they performed together. They became engaged in 1920. The power of Mrs Coleridge-Taylor over her daughter continued, and she soon put a stop to this relationship by refusing to allow the couple to meet. Of her first marriage Avril simply states:

> In due course I married Harold Dashwood [. . .][27]

She makes no mention of how they met or the circumstances of their engagement. Perhaps Avril's silence on the matter suggests that it was initiated and arranged by her mother. It is clear that her life was still closely restricted.[28] Immediately after her marriage Avril became pregnant; there seems to have been little choice in this matter on account of her ignorance of sexual matters:

> Our honeymoon over we returned to London [. . .] where we prepared for what we coyly used to term a 'happy event'. I hardly knew whether to be pleased or not. All my life I had been kept in complete ignorance about matters related to sex.[29]

The birth of her first child had an adverse effect on her musical development, making her unable to work for some time.[30] As a wife and mother, Avril took care of all the financial, domestic and child-care arrangements. Her husband proved unable to contribute to the family income, which aggravated their difficulties. Dashwood worked in the motor trade, and it seems clear that Avril really needed the stimulation and understanding only to be found in a partner who was also musical or artistic. Eventually, the family were forced to sell their house and move into a rented unfurnished room. Following a long illness, Avril separated from her husband. During the seven years of her marriage she had composed nothing. However, after the separation from her husband her new-found freedom allowed her once again to compose:

> During the trial separation, which was what the doctor recommended, I found the inspiration to compose again.[31]

The doctor also recommended that she change her name in order to help her forget the misery of her life up to that point. This somewhat unorthodox 'treatment' seems to reflect the severity of the problems created by her domestic situation. She changed her given name from Gwendolen to Avril. This new start was marked by the completion of an orchestral piece, *To April*:

> It was not meant to represent or be an impression of the month, but an expression of the kind of new life I wished to lead.[32]

She remarried about seventeen years later, in 1945. Her new husband was Bruce Solmes Coates. He was musical, and together they founded the Coleridge-Taylor Musical Society and the Coleridge-Taylor Symphony Orchestra, of which he was the manager and secretary. This marriage seems to have been less restrictive. With no children to look after, Avril continued to conduct and compose. After their divorce in 1952 Avril travelled alone to South Africa, where she worked for a time. She was eventually forced to come back to England because of the racial policies of the South African government. Avril has continued to compose and work well into her old age.

Grace Williams (1906–76)

Grace Williams came from a quite different social background from that of Avril Coleridge-Taylor. She was born in 1906 in Barry, South Wales. Both her parents were school teachers. Accordingly, the Williams family had an obvious knowledge of and interest in education, which ensured that Grace was able to give full attention to her school work. Grace seems to have been most influenced by her father in terms of her musical development. He conducted the Romilly Boys Choir. Grace accompanied his choir rehearsals and benefited from his extensive collection of gramophone records. He taught Grace to play the piano, although she was never entered for any formal music examinations.[33] Practical music-making with her father and brother was a central part of family life.[34] These close family relationships seem to have been the most important ones of Grace's life. Indeed, she moved back to live with her parents when she was in her early forties and remained in the family home until her own death in 1976.

Grace had various romances in her student days, but there was only one serious relationship, which occurred when she was in her late thirties. Grace never married, but in this brief relationship she was subject to some of the emotional pressures which can be imposed by a partner. Grace met, and became close to, a Polish immigrant named Zen Sliwinski, when she volunteered to teach English to immigrant factory workers during the Second World War. Sliwinski was not a musician and was apparently jealous of the energies and attention composition demanded from Grace. Many feel that it was his disapproval which caused the temporary cessation and subsequent lower output of compositions in the decade following the Second World War.

When Sliwinski suddenly left for South Africa in 1949, Grace was devastated by his departure. She seems to blame Sliwinski completely for her both stopping and restarting composition:

> If *he* hadn't taken himself off to S. Africa I shd. never have had the misfortune to return to composing. I shd. have had more respect for myself if I'd died of a broken heart but alas, a few days after he'd gone I began to feel free again.[35]

In his biography of Grace Williams, Malcolm Boyd seems convinced that the main reason for Grace remaining single was her desire to concentrate on her composition:

> Her decision to forego the joys and satisfactions of marriage and motherhood and to look for fulfilment as a composer must [. . .] have cost a great deal to someone whose personal relationships were so warm and whose love of children was spontaneous and genuine.[36]

This may indeed be true. Perhaps Grace was torn between her need to focus on her composition and her need for close personal relationships, knowing that one can so often be a distraction from the other. It seems possible that she felt that her need to compose was also the source of her sometimes isolated and lonely existence; this dilemma could in some way explain her recurrently hostile and disapproving attitude to her own work:

> I have now succeeded in putting composing out of my mind for good [. . .] It's a grand feeling to be free of it, and not having it tugging at my conscience any more [. . .] The difference in me since I stopped composing is amazing.[37]

However, following a brief reunion with Sliwinski in 1970, Grace stated:

> All my (non-composer) friends think it was a lovely thing to happen to me after all these years of being shut up alone with my composing – but I have no regrets.[38]

The decision to remain single carried a certain amount of disapproval from society at large at this time. Marriage was seen not just as an option for women but the *only* option, whether a woman wanted to work or not:

> For all women marriage conferred a higher status than spinsterhood, which connoted a failure [. . .] marriage remained the normative expectation of women of all classes to the end of the period [1950 . . .] a majority of spinsters faced an often lonely and marginal life in their parents' home or in the households of a male relative.[39]

It is clear that women from many occupations have had to (and still do) balance their careers and family life. The difficulty of choosing between having a family and concentrating on composition is a dilemma from which male composers are spared.

Elizabeth Maconchy (b. 1907)

Elizabeth Maconchy was born in 1907 in Hertfordshire to Irish parents. Maconchy's first twelve years were spent in England. Between 1919 and 1923 the family relocated to Dublin, where Mr Maconchy found employment. When he died suddenly in 1922, his wife took the courageous decision to move back to London, primarily so that Elizabeth could attend the Royal College of Music. The move back to England was accompanied by a drop in the family's standard of living. Uprooting an entire family and enduring a decline in living standards simply so that a daughter could obtain a good music education was, to say the least, an exceptionally uncommon step to take in the 1920s.

Elizabeth Maconchy is the only composer in the present study who came from a family which contained no active musical role model. However, like many middle-class families at this time, they did own a piano and, as Maconchy admits:

> My father had a natural feeling for music and played the piano in an amateurish way.[40]

The key point is that music, although not practised in any regular way, was valued. Maconchy's talent was both recognized and encouraged at an early age, and was allowed to develop through adequate tuition.

Maconchy married shortly after leaving the Royal College, aged 23. Her husband, William LeFanu, was not a musician but had a good musical education and a keen interest in music. Throughout their 54 years of marriage his emotional and financial support has without doubt freed Maconchy, allowing her to concentrate to a great extent on her composition. LeFanu states:

> I have done what I can to encourage Elizabeth and in a way we have led separate lives. I was working in London all day so we only came together in the evening [. . .] I have always kept in touch with her music [. . .] we attend concerts together [. . .][41]

Maconchy primarily took responsibly for child care, although this did not have an overtly adverse effect on the smooth continuation of her career. It has been suggested that:

> She was mainly occupied during the war years in bringing up her family [. . .][42]

But this seems not to be the case, for between 1939 and 1948 her output included String Quartets Nos 4 and 5 (1943, 1948), a Sonata for Violin and Piano (1944), a Concertino (1945) and a Symphony (1948). Without denying the fact that Maconchy has considerable creative drive, it is pertinent to consider some other influential determinants.

Maconchy was much older than the average mother when she had her two children (she was 32 and 41 years respectively). In 1930 an average woman would have been 30 years old when she gave birth to her *last* child.[43] Being an older mother, Maconchy had, partially at least, already established herself as a composer. The extended interval of nine years between the birth of her daughters also points to her being less stretched domestically – that is, by having only one small child to look after at any time. Maconchy assumed the traditional role within marriage of being supported financially by her husband. Often, this is seen (with justification) as a restrictive factor in terms of female autonomy and independence, yet Maconchy's marriage has, in many ways, been a great source of support to her work. For example, she has never been compelled to seek paid employment outside composition to contribute to the income of the household:

> I have mainly been supported by my husband. I do now contribute to the family income, but when I was younger it was negligible.[44]

Over the years Maconchy has produced many works (more than 100 in total), a fact which seems to contradict the theory that a woman's domestic situation can affect her work profoundly. Yet when her personal life is examined, it is obviously a 'benign' adaptation of the traditional dependent role of a wife – one predicated on the husband's uncommonly supportive attitude to his wife's work. Sadly, in this and subsequent generations such understanding and support (which are extrinsic to the essential, traditional structures of middle-class married life) are rare. Maconchy herself summarizes:

> Combining the two [composition and family life] proved nearly impossible but I always made sure there was someone to push the children in the pram for an hour or two. The rest of my writing I did when they were asleep. Things would have been much harder if I hadn't married a man sympathetic to my work.[45]

Minna Keal (b. 1909)

Minna Keal (née Nerenstein), born in the East End of London in 1909, was the daughter of Jewish Russian immigrants. Her family were not musical but they loved to sing; vocal music played a large part in their Jewish Orthodox religion. Mr Nerenstein ran a Hebrew publishing business, assisted by his wife. Keal's childhood was unusual in that her parents had high expectations for her in terms of education and encouraged her development:

> My mother was always supportive. If I'd decided to be a baker [. . .] or a dressmaker she would have supported me. She always felt that whatever I wanted to do was important [. . .] We were brought up in an atmosphere where it was taken for granted that you did whatever you were capable of doing and there wasn't anything special about that.[46]

She was an extremely bright student and was preparing to study modern languages at university when her father died suddenly in 1926. This forced a total change in her life. It was decided that she should not go to university since this meant leaving her mother alone to run the publishing business. Keen to continue her education, Keal opted instead to pursue her talent for music at the nearby Royal Academy of Music. In her first year she excelled and was offered a bursary for her second year of study. However, family pressure caused her to give up:

> They said, 'How can you be studying when your mother is struggling in the business?' I felt awful. I felt guilty [. . .][47] [. . .] I was getting more and more demands on me to look after the business, and I was spending more and more time on my composition and it was quite incompatible, so I decided I would have to give it up.[48]

Keal needed confirmation that her ability as a composer was worth pursuing further. Sadly, no such support was offered:

> If people had come and said: 'You can't give it up: you are so good', perhaps I would not have given it up, but nobody did [. . .] So I decided that if I was really good they would have been begging me to stay, and as no-one did I obviously couldn't be much good.[49]

Keal's early works were of a very high standard. Indeed, one of her student pieces was published in 1989. Ironically, this is the only work she has ever had published. The lack of support from the Royal Academy for Keal to continue her studies is indicative of the general attitude towards women's education and prospects at the time. Yet Keal feels that the pressure brought to bear on her by her family to leave her studies was not connected with her gender:

> I don't think I had to give up music because I was a girl, I think if I had been a boy I would still have had the same conflict of interest [. . .] The only difference is that maybe people wouldn't have expected me to give it up. It isn't how you feel yourself: it is expectations.[50]

In the early decades of this century women were still expected, in the popular imagination, to be dutiful wives and daughters who would sacrifice whatever was necessary for the sake of their families. Admittedly, Keal often states that if she had attended university to study languages, as planned before her father's death, she would have kept music only as a hobby. This attitude was probably promoted by her upbringing, since she came from a family where the notion of being a professional composer was unheard of:

> I composed a little tune, and in those days people were not encouraged to; you were only a composer if you were a genius – ordinary people never tried to compose.[51]

The idea that one had to be an artistic genius to become a composer may have discouraged her from thinking she could make a success of such a rarefied career, leaving her instead to aspire to a rather more 'accessible' career in languages.

Keal met her first husband, Barnet Samuel, when she was 16 years old. They eventually married in 1931. She openly acknowledges the pressures on young people to marry:

> I fell in love with him [Samuel] [. . .] so immediately the families got together and you had to settle down [. . .] I was never proposed to: I was more or less told that I was engaged and would be getting married.[52]

Although she did not plan to have any children, her son was born in 1934. Keal acknowledges the responsibilities faced by women composers with families:

> [. . .] a woman composer is quite different from a man composer. Whereas a man might share in the children, he feels biologically independent.[53]

Before she separated from her first husband, Keal became politically active in the Communist Party. This provided the impetus for her to reject her Jewish upbringing and break off the ties to the family business. During the Second World War she moved to Slough, taking a succession of jobs to support herself and her son. She met her second husband, Bill Keal, whilst working as an aircraft progress chaser. They married in 1959.

When Keal retired, she returned to composition after a break of 46 years. She acknowledges the support given by her husband, although in recent years, after his health began to fail, problems have arisen:

> For years Bill took all the chores from me. It was really thoughtless of me, and I should have insisted on doing something – but I didn't, because I was so anxious to get on with my music [. . .] Later he used to say to me: you have an obsession [. . .] I would have been the same in his position. I do not blame him at all, but it was extremely difficult for me. I went through hell for a couple of years. But I still went on composing: I would not give it up.[54]

Even though her composing years have been free from child-care demands, Keal still has many domestic and emotional responsibilities, not least the care of her husband since his ill health:

> People don't always realise that I am a composer, but being a wife is just as important to me as being a composer [. . .] you have a maternal instinct and that maternal instinct goes into your marriage [. . .] it is a different relationship, but it has an element of mothering and of caring [. . .][55]

A family's emotional welfare is often seen as a female responsibility, whereas the financial welfare of the family is traditionally the male preserve. Women are socialized to bear the brunt of the emotional pressures of family life. Often, this is achieved through sacrificing their own needs to those of their family. This kind of demand on women composers can often prevail over their aspirations to compose. Minna Keal's reasons for not continuing her career in music are varied but stem mainly from family pressure and her own lack of confidence that she could actually fulfil her musical ambitions. The success she has had since restarting composition has given her the momentum she needed to keep composing, no matter what the difficulties may be.

Ruth Gipps (b. 1921)

For Ruth Gipps, born in East Sussex in 1921, her formative musical education seems to have instilled her with quite different priorities from those of Minna Keal. Gipps' parents were both trained at the Frankfurt Conservatoire, although her father never made a career as a practising musician. Mrs Gipps developed a career as a music teacher, and their family home 'doubled' as her music school. Accordingly she oversaw all aspects of her three children's musical development and education. The Gipps children were surrounded by music; indeed, music education was a top priority from the start of their lives. Unsurprisingly, they all chose careers in music.

Ruth Gipps is the only composer in the present group who was introduced to public performance as a small child. She made her piano-playing debut in

1925, aged 4. This is some measure of her mother's ambitions for her young daughter. Mrs Gipps was both well-educated in music and knowledgeable about professional life. This, coupled with Ruth's natural talent, made for the best possible start for a budding musician. Mrs Gipps recognized the potential of her daughter and provided her with all the facilities to develop her talent: these included not only piano lessons but also lessons in harmony and music history. Although Ruth describes her childhood as a very happy time, it was sometimes viewed by others differently:

> Mrs Gipps was often criticised for pushing her child too hard and was even accused of having composed some of Ruth's earliest compositions.[56]

Mrs Gipps may have forced Ruth's musical development, but she seems only to have been reacting to the degree of ability her daughter clearly possessed. There is no doubt that this excellent musical environment helped Ruth to develop her full potential as a child and gave her an advantage over many other students when she entered the Royal Academy of Music at the age of fifteen.

Gipps married Robert Baker in 1942, at the age of 21. Baker has been a professional clarinettist throughout his working life, and the couple have always seen themselves as colleagues. Gipps' very definite views on marriage obviously influenced their domestic arrangements:

> Marriage could not in any way alter my attitude to my work; life without work would not be life [. . .]
>
> We both defined our positions clearly as soon as we got engaged; mine worded, 'I will not darn your socks, but I will earn my living.'[57]

Gipps was brought up to be highly independent and this, coupled with a naturally forceful personality, meant that she felt no dilemma about whether her work would affect her role as wife and mother. The birth of Gipps' son in 1947 did not restrict her performing or composition work. At this time, when a pregnancy became visible a woman was expected to retire from public view, but Gipps defied convention.[58] Not only did she continue with her concert engagements but she also obtained a D.Mus. at Durham University. Following the birth of the child, a nursemaid was employed (she looked after him in return for piano lessons). This arrangement freed Gipps from many domestic pressures and was fundamental to her being able to continue her composition.

> My son need never feel that I gave up anything for him; we started on equal terms. Never shall I be able to say, 'After all I've done for you'.[59]

Antoinette Kirkwood (b. 1930)

Ruth Gipps' attitude to, and practical arrangements for, domestic responsibilities could not offer greater contrast to those of Antoinette Kirkwood, who was born seven years after Gipps, in 1930. Kirkwood came from a family with a strong army tradition; her father was a major who had served in India. Kirkwood's mother was a semi-professional *Lieder* singer who had wanted to study music in Leipzig but had been forced to follow her father to India. Music was a part of everyday life for Kirkwood, an environment created by her mother:

> I remember at a very early age finding the notes at the bottom of the piano for the accompaniment to Borodin's song 'Dissonance', which my mother used to sing; this was the favourite of all my mother's songs and a very important musical experience for me.[60]

Her parents did not believe in examinations; this meant that, like her mother before her, Antoinette did all her studying privately and obtained no formal musical qualifications.

Until her marriage to writer Richard Phibbs, when she was 31, Kirkwood had produced at least one work each year. However, after her marriage in 1961 she produced no new works for almost 20 years. Married life obviously had a dramatic effect on her creative work. Within the first four years of marriage Kirkwood had three children:

> I knew that when I had children it would mean a very big change for me [. . .] I think it inevitably changes you and causes you to develop differently as a result.[61]

Kirkwood's main musical experience for some time after her children were born was their education:

> [. . .] my husband had decided that he wanted them to have a musical education. He said, 'My children are not going to get a classical education so I want you to see to it that they have a musical education [. . .]'[62]

The cessation of her composing work was due entirely to her domestic responsibilities, which included extended periods of caring for her husband and mother, who both became terminally ill.

Enid Luff (b. 1935)

Enid Luff (née Roberts) was born in 1935 and was the eldest of five children. Her father was a Presbyterian minister, and her mother was a teacher. Neither of her parents had had any sort of music education, but her father in particular was very musical. They made sure that all their children were given a good education which included music:

> It was in the family programme [. . .] children's opinion was not asked in those days; music was just one of those things that was part of life.[63]

Her father also published poetry and read widely on philosophy and theology. However, Luff did not benefit from this intellectual opportunity, and their relationship illustrates some of the attitudes of the time:

> [. . .] a father had a relationship to a daughter which was always a relationship with someone who was going to grow up to be a wife [. . .] there was no other view around at the time [. . .][64]

Enid Luff's early years were difficult. Her father served as an army chaplain during the Second World War, and his absence resulted in great stress for the family, both emotionally and financially. These early experiences left her '[. . .] mixed up, difficult and very nervous'.[65]

Like many children from large families, Luff was responsible for looking after the younger children, which often left little time for herself. All her piano practice had to be planned in such a way as not to disturb the other children:

> For composing I had to save up my pocket money and go to buy a little manuscript book, and go and hide in the corner and do it in my head: which means I developed very good mental hearing [. . .][66]

The strongest mark on her musical and creative development was made by her mother's attitude towards her daughter's talents. Mrs Roberts was a very intelligent woman who had graduated from university; until her marriage she had been an intellectually active person:

> But once she got married she ditched all that and devoted herself to be a minister's wife and a good mother. It is a terrible waste. When I think over her life, I think she was damaged by it [. . .] Because she had repressed all this in herself, it was very painful to see it in her children, and she could not tolerate it. Subconsciously, she would repress what I was doing [. . .] In the end I repressed it in myself – it is self-defence: a person can't cope with that sort of conflict.[67]

Through this repression Luff became very secretive about the first small pieces she composed. She was an extremely creative child who would dance around to the music she heard internally, so the repression of this creative spontaneity was difficult to endure. In addition, the school she attended pushed her to concentrate on languages, not music; in 1953 she went to Newnham College, Cambridge, to read for a degree in Modern Languages.

In 1956, on leaving Cambridge, Enid married Alan Luff who, like her father, was a church minister. They have had four children:

> It has been a very happy marriage [. . .] I loved having the babies, but all through it I was wanting to do the music [. . .][68]

It was not until Luff was in her thirties that she felt she could once again heed her inner calling to create:

> It came home to me suddenly I had to do this [compose] [. . .] it was really quite a crisis, because I knew I would have thrown my life away if I had not done it. So I did, at great personal cost to everybody.[69]

Luff began a degree in music at the University College of North Wales at Bangor, aged 36 and with the responsibility for three young children. She became pregnant with her fourth whilst studying. This was far from an ideal atmosphere in which to return to music study, yet despite the difficulties she was successful and went on to gain an M.Mus. degree. Her husband's financial support has released her from some burdens, and this has been particularly useful since all the children left home:

> [. . .] I don't have to earn my own living; on the other hand, in the same context there was a lot of responsibility at home [. . .] Bringing up the children was not

> simple [. . .] I have to run the house and live alongside my husband; he accepts that I have a profession and a life to live.[70]

The stresses of caring for a family and trying to concentrate on composition and the associated pressures of promoting works highlight the conflict many women face when they want to continue to compose and have a family:

> It is murder – the conflict is there all the time, and it was quite genuine when the children were small, because they are very demanding. You are not your own person: you are competing with a vulnerable and helpless person, and it is very difficult because the conflict transfers inside you [. . .] You need to write, but you have these babies and one is going to damage the other [. . .][71]

Clearly, the greatest difficulty faced by many female artists is how to balance family and professional life.

Judith Bailey (b. 1941)

Judith Bailey was born in Cornwall in 1941. Neither of her parents was a professional musician, but both could play, and had a keen interest in, music. Judith was encouraged to play the piano and clarinet and went on to study at the Royal College of Music:

> I had this impulsive dream as a child that it would be very nice to be a composer and conductor. Nothing could have been more impractical [. . .] When I was about four, I would get a knitting needle and stand up and beat time to the radio, and people used to say, 'Ladies don't conduct', and I thought I don't really suppose they do [. . .] but it was just something that interested me very much.[72]

Bailey was an only child and had strong support from her parents. Her father in particular gave practical assistance by helping her to practise and explaining aspects of music theory. Playing duets with her father was a regular event. Like Minna Keal, Judith Bailey's father died when she was in her second year at the Royal College of Music. In contrast, Bailey was encouraged to continue her work:

> I went back to my mother and said 'Will I have to give up my studies and come home and help you?' She said: 'No, of course not'. She was wonderful and unselfish; both my parents were, and also absolutely intent that I should be independent.[73]

This seems to underline yet again the emotional strain relationships of all kinds can be for women. Women continue as the mainstay of the support and care of children and the aged. Like Grace Williams, the other unmarried composer in the study, Bailey took on the responsibility for looking after her mother in her later years.[74] Bailey obviously felt a strong motivation to be independent and make her own way in life – an attitude which has stood her in good stead for a career in music and in some way shaped her attitude to marriage and children.

In and around her family Bailey was exposed to many unmarried role models, and her parents never put any pressure on her to get married:

> They were not the sort of parents who said: ' We do think you ought to get married and have a family' [. . .] I had two great aunts who were not married; they ran a

> school [. . .] We had all kinds of bachelor people in the family, and it was looked on that some people were happier not being wed, so I think it was a conscious decision [. . .][75]

Bailey feels her career has benefited from her not having children in that it has not made demands on her time:

> If a man is writing music, it is usually his wife who does all the other things in the house [. . .] I love home-making, which is a very female thing, but not to the extent that I want to sink my life into catering for a man and children [. . .] I would rather remain single and do my own thing.[76]

It is not just the practical, domestic responsibilities but also the emotional support which so often is at the heart of family life, and is usually provided by the female, that can drain and distract from creativity. The two composers in the study who remained single were born 35 years apart, yet the feelings they had towards family life are very similar. The predicament of choosing between personal relationships and composition is highly unsatisfactory: whichever option is rejected is bound to be at some personal cost.

Bryony Jagger (b. 1948)

The youngest composer in the study, Bryony Jagger, was born in 1948. Her father was a schoolteacher and her mother was a housewife. Neither parent was particularly interested in music, so music was not a very important aspect of family life. Consequently, Bryony's earliest vehicle for self-expression was writing. She wrote a 50-page novella when she was only ten. Her parents always encouraged her writing talents possibly because as a child Jagger always showed many more verbal than musical skills. Of music Jagger states:

> I didn't show any musical ability as a child [. . .] I had music lessons because it was the done thing, not because I showed talent. I didn't know why people played or listened to music and I wasn't interested in it.[77]

Her eventual initiation into music was a quite dramatic experience:

> [. . .] the most momentous event in my life for its effect on the rest of my life was listening to Osian Ellis singing Welsh folk-songs and suddenly understanding what music was about and that I had to write it. You don't have mystical experiences everyday [. . .] It did turn me from an unmusical child into a budding composer.[78]

This sudden change in Jagger's career aspirations was actively opposed by her parents. Fortunately, she had a school music teacher who provided the support and encouragement needed to make up for lost time.

Jagger's interest in music came at a very late stage compared with most other musicians. She admits:

> As a child I felt confident with academic work and words, but totally unconfident musically.[79]

Jagger was working for her A-levels when she realized that she wanted to study music at university. Yet her school strongly discouraged her from trying to pursue music study. In the end a compromise was reached, in that she attended New Hall Cambridge, to study Moral Science and Music.

Jagger married Richard Phillips in 1971. Although she had planned to continue her studies, the responsibilities of marriage intervened:

> I was accepted to do an M.Mus at Cardiff after I left Cambridge, but I then got married and my husband had a scholarship to Harvard, so I had to ditch my career and go to the USA with him. I wasn't too happy about this [. . .][80]

The couple returned from the USA in 1972 so that Phillips could embark on a Ph.D., again at Cambridge. Jagger used the opportunity to enrol on the BMus course but she became pregnant before she could complete it. Jagger now has two daughters, the first born in 1973 and the second in 1986. She has found domestic responsibilities intensely demanding on her energy. Unlike some female artists who play down this demand on their time and resources, Jagger is adamant about its effect on her work:

> Domestic responsibilities and a husband unkeen to do his share of babysitting shut me up in the home and stopped my performing, which was probably to the detriment of my composing [. . .] I find child care demanding, and it tends to dampen creativity.[81]

In 1975 Phillips was offered a job at the University of Auckland, New Zealand and so the whole family moved there with him. The couple were divorced in 1990, and this has affected Jagger's creative work completely:

> [. . .] the departure of my husband [. . .] for whom I had sacrificed various career opportunities [. . .] has thrown me into a near-breakdown and virtually stopped my composition [. . .][82]

The burden of coping alone has also reduced her creative drive:

> Undoubtedly the reality of being a solo mother [. . .] without a decent night's sleep for four years did not help my ability to compose music in recent years.[83]

For those who ponder the lack of female composers or their comparatively small outputs, the above statements provide clear evidence that certain aspects of the feminine social and familial function continue to create many injustices. Far too often, arguments 'explaining' why women are less prolific than men as composers (or why they tend to compose smaller-scale works) assume an innate lack of ability, instead of scrutinizing the sociological reality of female existence, which to a large degree accounts for these differences.

This brief examination of the influence of domestic responsibilities reveals that even today a married woman's freedom to focus on her chosen career can still be severely limited.

Bryony Jagger echoes many of the sentiments expressed not only by other women composers born in the first part of the twentieth century but also by women composers of 100 or 200 years ago:

> I think being female is a disadvantage until male attitudes change considerably. A man with a family expects his wife to run the house so he can compose in peace; a woman is expected to run the house and keep the children quiet while the man does his work – she has to fit her work in as she can amidst the family noise.[84]

Compare this statement, written in 1993, with the following, written in 1841 by Clara Schumann (1819–1896), the renowned pianist and composer who was married to the composer Robert Schumann:

> My piano playing is falling behind. This always happens when Robert is composing. There is not even one little hour in the whole day for myself. If only I don't fall too far behind [. . .] I cannot do anything with my composing.[85]

The pressures on female composers and artists seem to have remained. The attitudes of those closest to the composer can have a huge bearing on how a creative woman can develop. The social system which assigns men and women such rigid roles is surely damaging to both sexes. When couples find individual solutions to the problem of mixing home life and professional work, conflict for the female can be alleviated.

In conclusion, I would like to identify some common themes that can be seen in the lives of the study group of composers. All the women come from upper and lower middle-class families. Although family incomes varied within this class, all had enough income to provide musical instruments and music lessons. Table 3.1 summarizes the parental occupations and musical training of the study group.

Many of the most successful female composers from previous centuries were born into families of professional musicians and composers, since this was the only type of environment in which women could gain the necessary instruction and opportunities:

Table 3.1 Parental occupations of the study group

	Occupation of the composers' mothers
Coleridge-Taylor	Housewife (trained as a musician)
Williams	Schoolteacher (housewife after children)
Maconchy	Housewife
Keal	Book publisher/housewife
Gipps	Music teacher
Kirkwood	Housewife/singer (untrained)
Luff	Housewife/teacher
Bailey	Housewife
Jagger	Housewife
	Occupation of the composers' fathers
Coleridge-Taylor	Composer
Williams	Schoolteacher
Maconchy	Unknown (but not a musician)
Keal	Book publisher
Gipps	Various (trained as a musician)
Kirkwood	Army officer
Luff	Church minister
Bailey	Baker
Jagger	Schoolteacher

> Women musicians typically came from a limited number of backgrounds: the convent, the aristocracy, in which case women could command education although in many instances only with men's consent; and finally those families of musicians who nurtured their daughters' talents as well as their sons'.[86]

These were the only circumstances in which a woman would have had access to the sort of training needed to develop into a practising musician. As my selection of twentieth-century-born composers reveals, the wider opportunities afforded to women through greater access to education outside that of the family environment can be decisive. Only one of the composer's fathers was a professional musician, whereas three of the mothers studied music to varying degrees, two gaining employment as professionals.

A common feature, not at first apparent in this selection of paternal occupations, is that all these families provided musical stimulation and access to musical instruments and education. The value placed on music in the family environment is an important factor relating to the development of musicians, regardless of their sex. It is interesting to see that out of the three who had no active musical role model, either in the family or extended family, two started serious music study later in life (Jagger aged 18 and Luff aged 34). The exception to this pattern is Elizabeth Maconchy, for neither of her parents nor her close family were trained or active in music. However, they did own a piano and as Maconchy herself admits, her father was musical.[87] The key point here is that music was valued by her parents. The unsurprising conclusion is that most composers and musicians are more likely to develop their full potential and embark on a career in music when brought up in an environment where music is offered as a serious learning option.

Early family attitudes are of great importance in terms of access to, and interest in, music, and also for the patterns of behaviour they instil in children. Many of the women composers in the present study came from families in which the mother did not have employment outside the home, even if she worked before marriage. Two of the composers (Coleridge-Taylor and Luff) were impeded by repression of their creativity by their mothers, who had themselves been similarly repressed. Five of the composers (Coleridge-Taylor, Keal, Jagger, Luff, Kirkwood) were discouraged from, or denied, a thorough musical education – not particularly because they were female, but because a career in musical composition was viewed as an impractical aspiration. This is a problem faced by many male composers, but the lack of female role models no doubt compounds the situation for women.

Seven out of the nine composers are, or have been, married. Two of these women have been married twice. Of the two single women, Grace Williams had a serious commitment to a partner for a number of years. All but one of the eight other composers' husbands/partners were non-musicians. However, two of these were keen amateurs, and each composer (Luff and Jagger) has written works for these partners. Antoinette Kirkwood's husband was a writer, with whom she collaborated on a number of works. Examination of the study group reveals that marriage can often introduce a conflict of interest resulting in partial or total cessation of composition, usually for a number of years. Perhaps this problem is aggravated by the fact that many of the husband/partners were non-musicians. As noted earlier, composers seem more likely to succeed when their talent and work is understood by the people closest to them.

Society continues to reinforce the ideal of the wife as support to her husband and his career. The wife bears the brunt of necessary domestic chores, leaving the husband free to pursue his career without distraction. One might presume that the gradual introduction of legal enforceable equal rights throughout this century would leave women better placed to pursue their careers. However, the reality is that new opportunities for women have come without the necessary change in the division of domestic responsibilities. In most cases the woman is left to juggle her domestic and career responsibilities. This is a daunting challenge for many women. For the creative artist who needs time and space to submerge herself in her work, these distractions can be psychologically devastating.

From the experiences cited above it is clear that domestic and child-care responsibilities, which still inevitably fall to women, can affect profoundly their creative development, education and output. Indisputably, there are factors lying outside the domestic area which can also affect creative output. Different composers do indeed have varying levels of aptitude and creative drive and talent. Further potentially relevant factors include the time and energy taken up by employment outside composition. For example, although Judith Bailey has never married, she has found the constraints of teaching (undertaken chiefly to earn a living) difficult to combine with composition. This is a pressure well known also to male composers: there are very few composers of either sex who actually make a living from composition only.

On the whole, however, domestic responsibilities do not affect male composers to anything like the same extent. On the contrary, the married male composer can very often benefit from the experience of having a wife in the customary supporting role. Indeed, in the past a great deal has been said about the wives of composers and the 'special' part they play in facilitating their partner's creativity. The importance of wives and mistresses to male composers is vast in terms of both emotional and practical support:

> Among the women who have influenced music without actually creating it [. . . are] the wives of the famous composers. Often they have been endowed with no inconsiderable musical genius themselves, but have sacrificed their claim to renown upon the altar of domestic duty. Sometimes, in rare instances, they have had the ability to perform the double task of caring for the household and continuing their own musical labours [. . .] to the present day, they have played a large part in shaping the musical destinies of the world.[88]

Talented women often have had to be satisfied with helping in someone else's work, putting the needs of others before their own. Indeed, in the wider historical context women have often been involved in music by supporting and encouraging other (male) musicians' work. If the definition of musical patronage were expanded to cover the kinds of encouragement and environment women have always provided for their children and husbands, an invisible but vital female contribution is revealed. For hundreds of years the role of helper was largely imposed on women by their debarment from public and professional life.[89] In the twentieth century social trends still make such a supporting role very difficult for a male; domesticated men are still portrayed among their peers and in the media as demasculinized and weak.

When the wives of a number of contemporary British male composers were interviewed about their husbands, some fascinating views were expressed.[90] Jane Ayres, wife of Richard Ayres, spoke of the difficulties partners often encountered in understanding how a composer works:

> It is easy for the partner [. . .] to think that writing music is like extended play, turned on and off at leisure, and particularly when work takes place 'at home'.[91]

If female partners find difficulty in leaving male composers free to work because their work schedule appears to be flexible, a woman composer's problems are sure to be compounded further by the distractions present in her domestic function. The enormous amount of domestic, unpaid work shouldered by women is often 'invisible' work fitted in around paid employment. It has been observed that the less paid employment a woman has, the more 'invisible' domestic work she undertakes.[92] As most composition is also carried out as unpaid work, women composers are possibly in a worse position domestically than, for example, female performers, who at least receive conventional remuneration.

Jane Ayres sees her role as helping her partner to achieve recognition for his work:

> When one has a deep conviction about the importance of one's partner's music one is keen for it to be performed [. . .] I take on the role of Secretary and Publicity Person for my husband's music; and I notice that a recent spate of letters to composers had been answered by their wives (Indeed, one commented that female composers were at a disadvantage, since she thought men less likely to take on their wives' correspondence).[93]

The traditional role of a wife as the supporter and champion of her husband's work, without doubt allows male composers a much greater freedom to concentrate on their composition. The wives of composers continue to relieve their partners of the mundane but time-consuming tasks and burdens, in addition to providing intellectual support. For example, Jonathan Harvey's wife:

> Rosalind Harvey [. . .] will not ask Jonathan to do housework, feeling his composition is more important.[94]

Obviously, in any successful partnership there has to be compromise and cooperation, but sadly many men find great difficulty in fitting into the corresponding role of supporters of their wives' work. For example, Minna and Bill Keal developed problems when Minna was composing, since this disturbed Bill:

> Minna was banished to the garage by Bill ten years ago 'because he didn't like the strange noises I was making on the piano when composing. He said he could hear me in the next village, though you have to remember he doesn't like contemporary music much'.[95]

A similar problem was felt by Linda Hammond, the wife of Julian Hammond, but her concerns were rather different:

> I wish that we had a room which Julian could use solely as a music room; having the piano in our sitting room is not ideal since I feel at times that it prevents him from working as much as he wants to.[96]

When Minna Keal returned to composition after her 46-year silence, her husband Bill unselfishly took on most of the domestic chores. Since the couple were retired, this was a practical strategy, yet the press played up this role-reversal for its oddity:

> She appears on BBC news with her house cleaning husband who believes that his wife, who neglected her musical talents for 50 years, should now concentrate on her composing talent.[97]

In a *Radio Times* article (21–27 October 1989) Bill is portrayed as a 'handbag-carrying' assistant to his wife, he is demasculinized, demoted to the 'feminine' supporting role of a woman. He is 'Mr' Minna Keal. This illustrates the problems faced by men who do try to assist their wives: society, as reflected in press commentary, views the consequences of gender-role-reversal as degrading to men and subtly discourages against any deviation from the conventional gender roles.

Another example of the imposition of gendered social roles on women composers by the media is an article about Ruth Gipps. The report was belligerently headlined: 'She composes in the Kitchen':

> To the milkman, the grocer, and the baker [. . .] Mrs Ruth Baker is just another customer. In the world of music she is Ruth Gipps, housewife composer [. . .] Her next big work is now being completed in the intervals between making the beds, cooking the breakfast and preparing lunch.[98]

Ruth Gipps is described in rather mocking terms: the implication is that this woman, whose prime function is that of a housewife, is merely a part-time composer. Ruth Gipps was then aged 25; she had already completed about 50 works including two symphonies; she had had her first composition published at the age of eight. At the Royal College of Music she had collected all the composition prizes, becoming one of Vaughan Williams' most promising students. This disturbingly flippant account allows the reader to suppose that Gipps is a rank amateur, and that her attempts at composition may well be less than competent. The article endorses the traditional priorities of women: professional work has to be done in the intervals between domestic tasks. The message to other women seems to be: regardless of your talent and career, your most valued role is as a wife and mother. It also conjures up long-established notions of the amateur 'lady' composer, who writes and plays to entertain others as part of her wifely duties.

Attitudes of this kind have continued to underlie many of the debates about female composers throughout the twentieth century. In the light of such assumptions it is hardly surprising that the two composers in the study who remained unmarried (Williams and Bailey) based their decisions to a large extent on their perceived need to concentrate on their musical careers. How far a woman's creativity is affected by marriage is often connected to the attitude of the husband towards the woman's work and his level of participation in child-care. Women themselves frequently give domestic life priority over their 'work' life, but obviously, how far others encourage and value the woman's work by giving practical assistance (which can in turn release the woman to concentrate on composition) is of immense importance.

The first section of this book concluded that there was little or no evidence of any biologically dictated reason why women should take sole responsibility for their children. Every child has two parents, and men are not genetically programmed against housework! There are some who continue to dispense pseudo-scientific theories to provide infallible biological (and therefore 'natural') underpinning for women's domestic role:

> Biology *exonerates* men (and 'society') by explaining male [. . .] success in terms of innate, uncoerced differences in ability and desire. It provides a better theory of the behaviour of the sexes than does the oppression theory [. . .] Given innateness, women's assumption of domestic tasks and men's dominance in the work place are the aggregate effect of the sexes' different choices.[99]

But in reality, the overwhelming effect of the socializing process, which advocates domestic responsibility in women whilst scorning it in men, can be clearly identified as a massive underlying obstacle to female composers (whilst, conversely, being of some benefit to male composers). As we saw in Chapter 2, this socialization has to be regarded as something more 'cultural' than 'natural', since it shows great variation between societies.

As the accounts of the nine women composers demonstrate, the division of domestic labour within families has continued to be segregated in the twentieth century in the same way as it was previously. This trend has continued up to the present day despite the popular myth that a woman's domestic experience has changed:

> In our society, a woman's identity is still organized around the home, domestic work and child-rearing. These features of her life provide her identity whereas a man's identity is given at least partly by his work [. . .] the majority of women are engaged at least for part of their lives in *full-time* domestic work, especially while their children are young. Such a position is very unusual for men.[100]

In many marriages a woman is still found to be dependent on her husband's attitude to her work and this can be the case, no matter how well educated and informed the wife or husband may be.[101] Often, the emotional burdens which are a major part of much married life are borne by women and have a draining effect on creativity. As many of the composers have stated, the interruptions and distractions of child care are particularly difficult for a composer.

The accepted division of labour within marriage is gender-based, the wife at home rearing the children and economically dependent on her husband, who works outside the home to provide for the family. This type of marriage has benefited two of the composers (Maconchy and Luff), who have been spared the necessity of taking employment outside the home to finance their composition work. Yet even in these cases domestic responsibilities have had to take priority. Elizabeth Maconchy, who has a very supportive husband, only managed to complete her compositions in between all her domestic duties, as her daughter Nicola LeFanu recalls:

> When my mother put me to bed at night, she'd walk away down the passage singing a lullaby [. . .] And then I'd hear her playing the piano [. . .] Now I know that was the only time she had to herself.[102]

Enid Luff stated that her work became far easier in her middle years, when her child-care responsibilities were reduced after the children left home. Other marriage patterns have involved the woman's taking work outside the home (Keal, Gipps, Jagger). Sadly, as the youngest example in the study (Jagger) reveals when both partners have careers, the husband's is still usually given priority. It is often assumed that when a woman has a career, her input into the family is increased and that she will also take a greater part in making important family decisions, but even in the present day this is not the case:

> There is some evidence from studies of families in which both wife and husband have careers that even in these situations the husband dominates decision-making, partly because his job is granted more importance.[103]

Obviously, there are many factors which affect a composer's opportunity to compose. Many would argue that men, too, face domestic problems such as balancing family needs against their own and caring for partners and children. But in reality, motherhood and fatherhood are still found to be two very different roles:

> [. . .] mothers are on the front line in looking after children, having much greater involvement [. . .] the main characteristics of motherhood were responsibility and constant availability. Fathers were, in practice, regarded merely as helpers.[104]

This also applies to other caring responsibilities:

> A government survey found that, of those elderly people who were having some difficulty in coping with tasks of everyday life about half were helped by a member of their family [. . .] In practice, family care of this kind is usually provided by women.[105]

Ruth Gipps and Elizabeth Maconchy seem to have been the least affected by personal domestic responsibilities. Both have continued to compose consistently and continuously throughout their careers. It is perhaps not coincidental that both were imbued with great self-confidence in their talent as children, receiving unusual amounts of encouragement and support. In the case of both women their musical education was considered of the highest priority by their respective families. The concept of having enough confidence in one's own abilities is very important in overcoming the many obstacles faced. This was the case for Minna Keal. Initially she did not have enough belief in her own talent to think it worthwhile to try to continue to compose against the wishes of her family. This may also be said of Luff and Jagger, who were pushed to study subjects other than music as children and only in later life gained the confidence to assert their own desires.

The social status of women and the 'feminine' personality, both in the main culturally imposed, makes competing in a society structured to the advantage of men very difficult. In addition, the feminist gains which have allowed more women to choose to go out to work are constantly under threat. Throughout the 1980s there has been a growing backlash; the hard-won ground of the previous hundred years seems constantly threatened in many areas by traditionalist right-wing politicians, the Christian evangelical movement and the Press.[106] Against this background, women who wish to free themselves of domestic labour and full-time care of children face two options: they can either reduce their own career expectations or employ other women to take on their domestic work and child care – a displacement rather than a removal of the problem. The idea of renegotiating home life with a male partner is very rarely considered. The inequalities which can be so evident within family life are also the most difficult to eradicate, as they require people to change the way their personal relationships function, when this obviously involves criticism of family members. The observation that:

> For many people their family life is positively harmful and, probably for the majority of people, their experiences with families bring a good deal of pain as well as pleasure.[107]

seems, sadly, to hold true.

The issues surrounding the social inequalities of marriage and child care reveal that many women are expected by those around them to sacrifice their own needs for the sake of others. It is only in recent times that some women have even become consciously aware of this aspect of their lives – a sentiment summarized by Enid Luff:

> I was brought up to believe that I belong to anyone but myself, that I had no right to myself and this is very, very serious and damaging [. . .] I came to understand that I was responsible for myself [. . .] if you sacrifice yourself you give away something that you have no right to give away. You know this in theory, but there comes a point in your life when you have to realise that you are responsible for what you do, what you give away and what you keep of your own personality [. . .][108]

'Feminine' values, which make women feel guilty for satisfying their intellectual and emotional needs, are passed on from generation to generation, by both women and men. It is impossible to deny that the responsibilities related to marriage and child care hinder many creative women both practically and psychologically and that, generally, women are only just beginning to feel that it is to no one's benefit if they sacrifice their talents or personal fulfilment.

Notes

1 Bel Mooney, 'Between the Pit and the Pendulum', *Sunday Times*, 5 November 1989.
2 Marcia J. Citron, *Gender and the Musical Canon* (Cambridge, 1993), 208.
3 The composers were chosen as a cross-section of British female composers born within the first 50 years of the twentieth century. They have written widely varying amounts of music with varying degrees of success, the connecting factor being that they have all written at least one symphony.
4 Bonnie S. Anderson and Judith P. Zinsser, *A History of Their Own: Women in Europe from Prehistory to the Present* (London, 1988), 2, 366–367.
5 For example, in 1931 the annual rate of divorce was under 0.5 per 1000 marriages, whereas by 1981 it had risen to 12 per 1000 marriages. See Nicholas Abercrombie and Alan Warde, *Contemporary British Society* (Cambridge, 1994), 294.
6 Abercrombie and Warde, *Contemporary British Society*, 295.
7 *Ibid.*, 135.
8 Jane Lewis, *Women in England 1870–1950: Sexual Divisions and Social Change* (London, 1984), 7.
9 *Ibid.*, 149.
10 More recent statistics show the maternal mortality rate now to be at around fewer than 25 deaths per 100,000 live births. Joni Seager and Ann Olson, *Women in the World: An International Atlas* (London, 1986), Section 10.
11 Pat Jalland, *Women, Marriage and Politics 1860–1914* (Oxford, 1986), 159–160.
12 Jane Lewis, *Women in Britain since 1945* (Oxford, 1992), 109.
13 *Ibid.*, 102.
14 Michael Levin, 'Women, Work, Biology and Justice', in Caroline Quest (ed.), *Equal Opportunities: A Feminist Fallacy* (London, 1992), 15–16.
15 Abercrombie and Warde, *Contemporary British Society*, 210.
16 Evidence of Avril Coleridge-Taylor's family background and adult life are taken primarily from her book *The Heritage of Samuel Coleridge-Taylor* (London, 1979) and it is acknowledged that this may lead to a singularly subjective view of events.
17 Avril Coleridge-Taylor, *The Heritage of Samuel Coleridge-Taylor*, 103.
18 *Ibid.*, 101.
19 *Ibid.*, 96.
20 *Ibid.*, 103.
21 Coleridge-Taylor, *loc. cit.*
22 *Ibid.*, 113.
23 *Ibid.*, 106.
24 *Ibid.*, 107.
25 *Ibid.*, 108.
26 *Ibid.*, 109.
27 *Ibid.*, 117.
28 *Ibid.*, 116.
29 *Ibid.*, 117.
30 *Ibid.*, 118.
31 Coleridge-Taylor, *loc. cit.*
32 *Ibid.*, 119.
33 Malcolm Boyd, *Grace Williams* (University of Wales, 1980), 10.
34 Malcolm Boyd, *loc. cit.*

35 Letter from Grace Williams to Gerald Cockshott (April 1950) quoted in Boyd, *Grace Williams*, 74.
36 Boyd, *Grace Williams*, 74.
37 Letter from Grace Williams to Gerald Cockshott (postmarked 10 August 1945) quoted *ibid.*, 28.
38 Letter from Grace Williams to Vivien Cutting (17 August 1970) quoted *ibid.*, 75.
39 Lewis, *Women in England 1870–1950*, 3.
40 Lisa Tuttle, *Heroines: Women inspired by Women* (London, 1988), 97.
41 William LeFanu, interviewed on 'Elizabeth Maconchy: A Video Portrait' (directed and produced by Margaret Williams, sponsored by the Arts Council, 1987), author's own transcript, 9.
42 Hugo Cole, *The 80th Birthday of Elizabeth Maconchy* (London, 1987), 3.
43 Abercrombie and Warde, *Contemporary British Society*, 282.
44 'Elizabeth Maconchy: A Video Portrait', author's own transcript, 8.
45 Fiona Maddocks, 'The Composer Breaks Her Silence: An Interview with Elizabeth Maconchy', *The Guardian*, 26 July 1983.
46 Minna Keal, 'Memories of the Royal Academy' (unpublished typescript), 17.
47 *Ibid.*, 4.
48 Minna Keal, interviewed by the author on 22 June 1993 . Author's own transcript, 3.
49 *Ibid.*, 3–4.
50 *Ibid.*, 21.
51 *Ibid.*, 2.
52 *Ibid.*, 12.
53 *Ibid.*, 14.
54 *Ibid.*, 18.
55 *Ibid.*, 14.
56 Jill Halstead, 'A Study of Dr Ruth Gipps illustrating her Musical Development through Detailed Reference to Symphonies Two to Five' (M.Phil. thesis, University of Sheffield, 1991), 4.
57 *Ibid.*, 18 and 19.
58 *Ibid.*, 28.
59 *Ibid.*, 29.
60 Antoinette Kirkwood, taped oral response to a questionnaire dated 5 November 1993. Author's own transcript, 1.
61 *Ibid.*, 4.
62 Antoinette Kirkwood's written response to a questionnaire sent by the author, dated 10 March 1994, 2.
63 Enid Luff, interviewed by the author on 21 June 1993. Author's own transcript, 23.
64 *Ibid.*, 10.
65 *Ibid.*, 12.
66 *Ibid.*, 11.
67 *Ibid.*, 11.
68 *Ibid.*, 2.
69 *Ibid.*, 3.
70 *Ibid.*, 24.
71 *Ibid.*, 18.
72 Judith Bailey, interviewed by the author on 15 June 1993. Author's own transcript, 30.
73 *Ibid.*, 29.
74 *Ibid.*, 30.
75 *Ibid.*, 26–27.

76 *Ibid.*, 28.
77 Bryony Jagger, written reply to a questionnaire, dated 16 July 1994, 1.
78 *Ibid.*, 3.
79 *Ibid.*, 2.
80 *Ibid.*, 4.
81 *Ibid.*, 5.
82 *Ibid.*, 9.
83 *Ibid.*, 5.
84 *Ibid.*, 9.
85 An extract from the Schumanns' marriage diary cited in Nancy B. Reich, *Clara Schumann: The Artist and the Woman* (London, 1985), 110.
86 Neuls-Bates (ed.), *Women in Music; An Anthology of Source Readings from the Middle Ages to the Present*, xi–xii.
87 Tuttle, *Heroines*, 97.
88 Arthur Elson, *Women's Work in Music* (Maine, 1976: original 1904), 61.
89 For more extensive discussion of this subject see Linda Whitesitt, 'Women's Support and Encouragement of Music and Musicians' in Karin Pendle (ed.), *Women in Music: A History* (Indiana, 1991), 301–302.
90 I would like to express gratitude to Dr Rhian Samuel for bringing the article cited here to my attention.
91 Jane Ayres, 'The Other Half', *Composer*, 92 (1987), 22.
92 Abercrombie and Warde, *Contemporary British Society*, 288–292.
93 Ayres, 'The Other Half', *Composer*, 92 (1987), 22.
94 Ayres, *loc. cit.*
95 Arthur Pearce, 'The Music Maker: An Interview with Minna Keal', 1991. Place of publication unknown (source: British Music Information Centre).
96 Ayres, 'The Other Half', 22.
97 Alan Blyth, 'Late Developer', *Daily Telegraph*, 6 September 1989.
98 'She Composes in the Kitchen', *Daily Mail*, 24 October 1946.
99 Michael Levin, 'Women, Work, Biology and Justice', 14.
100 Abercrombie and Warde, *Contemporary British Society*, 291.
101 Discussing the domestic and personal lives of any person is an extremely delicate procedure. In some cases events and attitudes which have affected some of the composers, although vastly important to the argument of women's disadvantage in this area, have been omitted in accordance with the wishes of the composer. Obviously, if a much-loved family member has hampered a person's progress, to reveal such intimate and disturbing information is often felt to be a betrayal of family confidence.
102 Nicola LeFanu, interviewed by Alix Coleman in 'A Talent to Compose', place of publication unknown (source B.M.I.C), 1987.
103 Abercrombie and Warde, *Contemporary British Society*, 293.
104 *Ibid.*, 284.
105 *Ibid.*, 286.
106 For a full discussion of these issues see Susan Faludi, *Backlash: The Undeclared War Against Women* (London, 1991).
107 Abercrombie and Warde, *Contemporary British Society*, 270.
108 Enid Luff interview transcript, 21.

4 Education, Opportunities and Professions

> No, women have not produced great music, not even remarkably good music. What is the reason? [. . .] the question is promptly answered by saying that they have not been given the opportunity, or that opportunity has not as yet been theirs long enough to show their full capabilities. But this reply will not serve the present case. If there is one thing outside of household affairs, the pursuit of which has been permitted to woman in all ages, that thing is music. Whatever else was denied her, this was granted.[1]

> Social learning theory does not adequately explain why a proportion of women do occasionally achieve [. . .] in certain areas (e.g. literature and politics) but not in others [. . .] Music composition is an interesting case in point, since it is a male-dominated profession despite the fact that girls are given more than equal encouragement to learn music at school [. . .] British composer Peter Maxwell Davies recalls asking to study music at high school in Manchester and was told very firmly [. . .] 'This is not a girls' school!' For hundreds of years European ladies have been expected to sing and play [. . .] yet the great composers have without exception been men.[2]

These statements were written nearly one hundred years apart, but they resonate with the same basic assertion: it is not social or educational disadvantage which has led to a lack of women composers but rather a lack of natural aptitude to create music. Women's unequal participation and success in many disciplines and professions can be traced directly to their exclusion from education, knowledge and opportunities, yet on the surface this would seem not to be the case with music. There is an undeniable historical link between women and music tuition, yet the music profession in virtually all areas remains male-dominated. For many women who lived before the twentieth century, music tuition was one of the few accessible areas of education. It has been established that in Britain, music has long been viewed as a 'feminine' subject, and there is a tradition of music study, along with other artistic and aesthetic subjects, amongst middle-class girls. Many have seized on this apparent contradiction as proof of women's inherent lack of ability in music. In this chapter I intend to examine women's traditional involvement in music education and the effect of this on their subsequent careers. As in the previous chapter, I have illustrated the discussion by drawing on the experiences of the study group of nine composers. From their specific experiences I will illustrate clearly the often hidden difficulties and discriminatory attitudes which affect the training of female musicians.

In any discussion of the education of women as a group it is vital to understand the historical perspective. It must be remembered that for much of history, in many different cultures, women have been denied *any* kind of education. Moreover, in more recent times, when access to education was granted, the education received by most women was very different from that received by men. The roots of sex-differentiated education lie in beliefs and attitudes about women's intellectual and physical inferiority (discussed in Chapter 1) and the socially constructed 'feminine' personality (discussed in Chapter 2). From these discriminatory and restrictive ideas a distinctively oriented education for women was fashioned. The belief that the two sexes were very different in temperament and needed education which would equip them for two completely different social roles has always threatened the quality and status of female education.

For centuries, the idea of educating women on an equal footing with men has provoked fierce debate. The foundations of modern sex-differentiated education can be traced back at least as far as the eighteenth century. One of the most influential (and supposedly progressive) educational philosophers of his time, Jean-Jacques Rousseau (1712–1778), felt that the function of women's education was mainly to benefit men and children:

> A woman's education must [. . .] be planned in relation to man. To be pleasing in his sight, to win his respect and love, to train him in childhood, to tend him in manhood, to counsel and console, to make his life pleasant and happy, these are the duties of woman for all time [. . .][3]

His general educational philosophy enjoyed wide influence in Britain and throughout Europe.

In Britain elementary education became compulsory for all children, regardless of sex, in 1870.[4] The advent of compulsory education did not, in the short run, change attitudes to women's position in society. In reality, the education received by girls at school was quite restrictive and took account of the prevailing beliefs about the female personality and function:

> Formal education did not and could not free women from the constraints of socially-defined concepts of 'femininity' and feminine behaviour. The new schools and colleges in some ways even reinforced these concepts and helped to reproduce the very same ideas and forms of behaviour which girls had learned from childhood onwards in the family.[5]

In the state-run schools attended by working-class and lower-middle-class children, attendance by girls was often very poor. Most parents thought that their daughters were better occupied in domestic and child-care duties, practising the skills they would later need to run their own homes:

> Although the Acts of Parliament gave girls an equal right to education by law, in practice they did not get it. Attendance by girls was lower than that by boys [. . .] Fewer efforts were made to ensure that girls attended school regularly.[6]

Many girls from upper-middle-class families, up till the 1920s, were also kept away from communal schools and were instead tutored at home in the traditional way by governesses. Thus the early gains made in the education of females proved more limited than might at first appear.

The biggest question raised by the compulsory education of girls was, however, what was suitable for them to learn. Many of the female reformers were divided over whether girls should receive the same education as boys:

> Generally, European women pushed first for a differential education which stressed special training for 'womanhood' primarily in the form of less science and mathematics and more religion and needlework. But by the third quarter of the [nineteenth] century it was apparent that with a differentiated education, a young woman would never be admitted to university [. . .][7]

With the securement of elementary and secondary education for women, educational pioneers such as Frances Buss (1827–1894) and Dorothea Beale (1831–1906) began to campaign for women's entry to higher education, where similar arguments about the appropriateness of sex-differentiated education continued. The concept of educating females to the same level, and in the same subjects, as males went against the whole philosophy of 'feminine' education, which for centuries had centred on enhancing 'femininity' through a concentration on domestic and artistic subjects considered intrinsically 'feminine' in nature, as opposed to mathematics and science, which were viewed as 'masculine'. The fear that a curriculum copied from the male educational model would, when taught to girls, destroy their 'femininity' was very real; consequently, by the beginning of the twentieth century a sex-differentiated curriculum had become common educational policy:

> By the time of the 1914–18 war the new emphasis which had emerged suggested that practical training in domesticity should [. . .] take priority over a more general approach. It was a principle which assumed the necessity for a gender-differentiated curriculum.[8]

Correspondingly, many schools taught girls only basic literacy and numeracy, the main emphasis being placed on domestic subjects such as needlework, 'mothercraft' and home economics. These subjects were thought essential to prepare girls for marriage (or, in the case of working-class girls, the declining tradition of employment in domestic service).

Well into the twentieth century, beliefs about women's physical and intellectual inferiority were used to justify this sex-differentiated curriculum. In 1923 a report to the Board of Education on the differentiation of the curriculum for boys and girls stressed:

> [. . .] the danger of 'over pressure' in the education of girls. It recommended that the pace of girls' education be slowed [. . .] and that allowance be made for the effects of menstruation which condemned many girls 'to a recurring and temporary diminution of general mental efficiency'.[9]

The argument that women were, by virtue of their physique, unsuited to a full education recalls the popular doctrine of the seventeenth century and earlier:

> [. . .] a woman's intellect is normally more feeble [. . .] Their bodies as well as their minds are less strong and robust than those of men.[10]

The biological justification of women's educational unsuitability was extended to bar women from attempting to study high-status 'intellectual' subjects. For example, in 1908, Janet Campbell, the chief woman medical adviser to the Board of Education, opined that for females:

> Lessons requiring much concentration and therefore using up a great deal of brain energy, Mathematics, for instance, should not be pushed [. . .] Such subjects as cookery, embroidery or the handicrafts may well be introduced into the curriculum as they cause comparatively little mental strain.[11]

A small amount of mentally undemanding education was thought a refining influence for middle-class girls, but well into the twentieth century it was suggested that women who undertook study to the same extent as men risked putting too much strain on their physiques. An Educational Consultative Committee report in 1923 held that shorter school hours for girls were necessary to stop them overstraining themselves physically, and even suggested that academic competitiveness should be avoided, along with too much homework.[12]

Such discriminatory attitudes lay at the heart of female education: it is clear that against prejudices of these kinds women could not enjoy equality in education. In addition, since education and training were also bound up closely with aspirations for employment, women's education became doubly restricted. The formal employment of middle-class and upper-class women was both socially unacceptable and sometimes legally impossible, so in reality they were rarely trained seriously for any occupation or profession. The typical middle-class female's education centred instead around the learning of 'feminine' refinement. This gave them superficially the cultural gentility thought essential to attract a well-placed, middle-class husband; it was not intended to be thorough training which would enable a woman to establish a career. The once flourishing institution of the 'finishing school' catering only for senior girls and located for preference on the Continent (to equip them with a practical knowledge of foreign languages and customs), conforms to this specifically 'feminine' mode of education. There was a long tradition of educating women in basically superficial artistic skills which could be carried on as hobbies and used as a way of passing their spare time. The middle-class lady's abundance of free time marked her off from the working classes, who had to work both domestically and in paid employment. These artistic, 'unpractical' accomplishments acted as a status symbol – the wife could concentrate on social refinements since she did not have to take paid employment if her husband was able to provide all her financial support.

When boarding schools for girls became fashionable with well-off middle-class families in the late eighteenth century, their sole purpose was to provide tuition in 'ladylike' behaviour (how to walk, make conversation, dress and so on), supplemented with a diet of 'accomplishments' which included French conversation, dancing, drawing, needlework and music (and, later in the century, domestic science). Music (that is, instrumental or vocal tuition) was central to these accomplishments.[13] The Roussellian ideal of the woman 'educated' to entertain, care for, and generally be a pleasing ornament to, those around her condemned millions of women to a degrading, unfulfilled and unproductive lifestyle. Their education served only to reinforce this position as it was 'anti-intellectual' and so of little value in building any sense of independence or competence.

Historically, the position and importance of music in a 'lady's' education is clear, yet it is also apparent that this type of musical education would in no way enable a woman to compete as a professional musician. For hundreds of years the term 'music education' could be more accurately termed 'instrumental tuition'. Female music tuition up until the later decades of this century consisted primarily of learning to sing or play a keyboard instrument, lute, violin or guitar. Any instrument that demanded an unusual posture, energetic movement or distortion of the face was discouraged as 'unladylike'. Before the present century we scarcely ever encounter female players of the oboe, the French horn or the trombone. The study of musical instruments was thought to suit women both intellectually and socially. To play a musical instrument was considered an employment of the hands rather than of the intellect. Today this may seem an amazingly simplistic view, but it was precisely music's practical element that made it an acceptable pastime for the supposedly less intellectual female. The mechanical, repetitive aspects of playing seemingly suited the placid and malleable female temperament, as did the long hours of repetitive practice required for proficiency. Patience had long been understood to be a quintessentially 'feminine' virtue. Learning to play an instrument had the added advantage of being home based; lessons and practice rarely required the woman to leave her home. Performances on her instrument were mainly for domestic enjoyment, access being controlled by her husband. This perpetuated the view of women as amateur (private or domestic) rather than professional (public) musicians.

The disproportionate emphasis on practical instrumental or vocal proficiency (as opposed to theoretical or compositional studies) in women's musical education is a tradition observable over many centuries. For example, Katherine Basset, daughter of the Governor of the garrison in Calais, had a typical female education in the 1500s:

> [. . .] Katherine learned to play the lute, the virginals and the spinet [. . .] They did not teach her to write her name.[14]

That women received only cursory music tuition was later noted by the influential reformer Mary Wollstonecraft (1759–1797):

> Girls learn something of music, drawing and geography; but they do not know enough to engage their attention, and render it an employment of the mind. If they can play over a few tunes to their acquaintance [. . .] they imagine themselves artists for the rest of their lives [. . .] Exterior accomplishments are not to be despised, if the

> acquiring of them does not satisfy the possessors and prevent their cultivating the more important ones.[15]

Proficiency on musical instruments enabled women to enhance their 'femininity' by using their skill to entertain and charm suitors, husbands and family. As Wollstonecraft observes, the study of music was not a liberating or life-enhancing part of education; it served, rather, as a hobby to amuse – in fact diverting women from any 'serious' study which would put them in direct competition with men. With only rare exceptions, women received no serious or rigorously theoretical training in music until the first part of the twentieth century.

In general, musical education had developed a reputation for 'frivolity' and for this reason was scorned by the early reformers of women's education. Two very influential campaigners, Hannah More (1745–1833) and later Frances Power Cobb (1822–1904), both criticized the excessive emphasis placed on music, which left girls with little time to study 'academic' and 'serious' subjects.[16] With such eminent reformers regarding music as intrinsically of little value to women, the inferior standard of women's music education (in relation to men's) was largely ignored. At the turn of the century, it became clear that if women were to prove their intellectual ability and gain access to higher education, it was essential that they be successful in subjects revered and valued by male academics: for example, mathematics, classics, science, law and medicine. It seemed inevitable that music, given its reputation as a 'ladylike' amusement, would be avoided by the serious female student who wished to prove her intellectual worth vis-à-vis males. In this sense, music's reputation as a 'feminine' pursuit was damaging for women.

Into this long-established female tradition of practical musical study and amateur music-making the first four composers in the study group were inducted. Avril Coleridge-Taylor (b. 1903) attended school irregularly. Her elementary school attendance was very poor, since she was required to do domestic work at home. She recalls:

> [. . .] I continued with the routine of the house, as I had grown used to it. Even as a little child, I was made responsible for a large share of the cleaning – even cooking. I was also expected to run errands throughout the day. All these chores had to be fitted in between the hours of a little private school I attended – albeit with considerable irregularity.[17]

This illustrates the point made earlier which stated that even in lower-middle-class families a female child's domestic work was often given priority over her education.

Shortly after the death of her father in 1912, both Avril and her older brother were sent briefly to the Guildhall School of Music, primarily because her brother had shown talent as a violinist.[18] The Guildhall School of Music had, like the other London music colleges, been established in the nineteenth century; at this time, it was primarily an institution which trained amateurs (above all young girls) in piano playing and singing.[19] The Coleridge-Taylor children's attendance at such an obviously amateur-orientated music college is surprising, considering the professional standing of their father.

In 1915 Avril received a scholarship to Trinity College of Music. Her attendance at a music college was in no way unique or unusual for a middle-class girl. Trinity College of Music was not then considered a prestigious institution at which to study in comparison with, say, the Royal Academy of Music or the Royal College of Music. The tuition it offered varied widely: from the elementary training of young children to the training of adults for entrance for a university degree. Both amateur and professional students could select their own teachers, and there often seemed to be a lack of distinction between the two groups. Trinity was famous for having set up a system of testing musical proficiency by examination, and many of its examinations and diplomas were sat without formal attendance at the college. For example, in 1913 28,000 examinations were taken, with approximately 400 pupils attending classes in London.[20] These diplomas were not highly regarded. Avril's tuition at Trinity consisted of piano lessons with Agnes Winter and singing lessons with Norman Notley. Winter encouraged her to compose piano pieces, but there seems to have been no special instruction in composition at this time. Her education was essentially limited to practical studies.[21] In keeping with the educational fashion of the time, Coleridge-Taylor took up dancing in addition to her music study.

Although at Trinity Avril was one of a number of female students, the college's policy was to segregate the sexes. Indeed when Trinity was founded in 1872, it at first barred women from entering the college, but by 1877 women were accepted:

> Like the local examinations, the public ones at the College were now open to all, 'without restriction of sex or creed'. Special Higher Musical Examinations of Women were also instituted at the College, 'in response to an increasing demand for a system of Certificates guaranteeing the musical proficiency of Governesses and other Female Teachers and practitioners'.[22]

The sex-differentiated curriculum for women students was given practical effect via separate classes, as evidenced by an advertisement for the College published in 1881:

> Each student receives individual instruction and separate classes are formed for Ladies in all subjects.[23]

The attitudes of the previous 30 years continued well into the twentieth century, as recalled by Avril Coleridge-Taylor. She remembers how her time at the college was marred by 'excessive' restrictions placed on the students. A female student had only to speak to a male to set off ugly rumours:

> I remember how when I was seen talking to a young Australian [. . .] I was reported as being seen to 'flirt'. That word, of course, has a period ring, and has been replaced by something stronger.[24]

For female students, social interaction with males was difficult, almost daring; contemporary moral codes were zealously adhered to. It is often overlooked that although women were now experiencing a greater freedom than had been known to their Victorian predecessors, 'normal' social contact between the sexes was greatly restricted in many settings, and these included music colleges. Indeed, the restrictions were regarded as the necessary precondition for women's attendence in the first place. A high degree of sex-segregation marked music college life and the tuition provided there between 1900 and 1920.

This outlook was reflected across a wide range of education institutions. From the beginning of the century, and indeed up to the 1960s, females and males were educated separately. Usually, only state-run schools were mixed – but this happened only for reasons of economy. These schools used the same buildings for both sexes but were often not in the full sense co-educational; outside the classroom, boys and girls were kept away from each other as much as possible and even had separate playgrounds and entrances to the schools.[25] All nine composers in the study were educated at all-girls' schools; this segregation continued in varying degrees during their later experience of music colleges and universities.

Avril Coleridge-Taylor's music education was also restricted in terms of access to knowledge. She appears to have been excluded from formal tuition in harmony, counterpoint and theory, which doubtless limited her development as a musician and hindered her participation in professional life. Her early career seems to have been limited to local performances, mainly of her father's vocal music. Only through her work as a composer did she eventually gain the opportunity to expand her musical experience. When her work *To April* was accepted for performance by the Municipal Orchestra at Eastbourne in 1929, the orchestra's regular conductor insisted at the rehearsal that the composer would be the most suitable person to conduct the music. Avril had never conducted before, but she managed to get through the rehearsal and subsequent performance with no actual technical knowledge of conducting, explaining modestly: 'After all I did know the music [. . .]'[26]

This, her first experience of conducting, inspired her to learn more:

> [. . .] I went to see Sir Henry Wood. I explained what had happened and that I wanted his advice, for I was anxious to learn a proper technique so that I could become a real conductor with full knowledge of all that was required.[27]

Consequently, she went to study privately with Ernest Read. Following this, she gained numerous offers of conducting work, which gave her employment for a number of seasons. Significantly, she became the first woman to conduct the Royal Marines Band. In 1936 she came to know the conductor Albert Coates, with whom she later studied privately. During the Second World War Coleridge-Taylor worked with the RAF, for whom she conducted music in Scotland. After the war, along with her second husband, she founded the Coleridge-Taylor Musical Society and the Coleridge-Taylor Symphony Orchestra. It seems certain that she embarked on these ventures to give herself opportunities as a conductor and musical director.

Following the dissolution of the Coleridge-Taylor Musical Society and the breakdown of her marriage, Avril was offered conducting work in South

Africa. She was accepted to conduct two concerts with the South African Broadcasting Corporation Orchestra in Johannesburg in May 1952 and received further engagements with the Cape Town Symphony Orchestra. At first, opportunities abounded in South Africa as they had never done in England, and Avril gained invaluable experience, including that of conducting live and studio concerts. Since then Avril Coleridge-Taylor's career has moved freely between spells as a performer, composer and conductor. Making assumptions about her career and education is rather difficult, since her autobiography often lacks precise factual recollections, but, on the whole, it seems clear that her genuine talent for composing and conducting were badly served by her limited instruction at music college and the lack of family support for her education generally.

Ironically, although Grace Williams (b.1906) came from an altogether less musical family, she benefited from a more serious and thorough education. After junior school she gained a scholarship to Barry County School for Girls in 1917:

> She did well there, excelling in English, French, mathematics and of course music.[28]

Grace Williams was tutored in music at secondary level by the school's geography teacher. However, for her advanced level studies a full-time music specialist was employed. Her teacher, Miss Rhyda Jones, was one of the first wave of university-educated women teachers. She successfully tutored Williams through her Higher School Certificate (equivalent to A level), which enabled her to gain a scholarship to attend University College, Cardiff. Grace certainly profited from the model of a well-educated female teacher. This encouragement was vital, especially when one considers the value placed on music generally in the school education system at this time. Music was regarded as a very low-status subject for girls, this status being reinforced by educational legislation.

In 1917 the School Certificate examination replaced the university Local Examinations system, as the qualification gained by school leavers. The Certificate was divided into four subject groups:

1 English, Scripture, Geography and History.
2 Latin, Greek and Modern Languages.
3 Mathematics and Science.
4 Music, Art, Crafts and Practical Subjects (such as Domestic Science).

Students had to pass five subjects from groups 1–3; however, Group 4 subjects did not count towards the Certificate.[29] It is no coincidence that all the subjects in Group 4 were high priorities in female education. Their non-academic status was indicative of the general lack of regard for, or prestige accorded to, such 'feminine' subjects. The lowly-status of Group 4 subjects was damaging in terms of female success in the School Certificate precisely because of the great emphasis placed on these subjects in the curricula of girls' schools. Consequently there would have been little opposition to girls, like Grace Williams, who wished to study and achieve success in music as a school subject. Only in

1929 were Group 4 subjects actually included in the School Certificate – but only on the condition that two Group 4 subjects be the equivalent of one of the Group 1–3 subjects.[30] Even in 1938, when the 'groups' system was revised, music did not win equal status with the other subjects. Up to the present day, after the introduction of the GCSE examination system, music still does not enjoy parity with all other subjects. Along with art, music is not tested as part of the assessment requirements for the National Curriculum, and in 1991 it was announced that music could be dropped from the age of fourteen.[31]

Grace Williams went on to study music at University College, Cardiff, in 1923. Music at Cardiff University had a somewhat chequered history, having been 'axed' by the university around 1880 on the grounds that:

> The popular music classes not only attracted men who could show very little evidence of any general education, but also introduced a fresh complication by bringing women students into the college for the first time.[32]

The standard of male music students was believed to be below par, again reinforcing notions that music was not a subject which attracted suitably academic students. The additional drawback of its preferential attraction of women students further confirmed music's suspect credentials as an academic subject, and led to its discontinuation for a number of years. It is understandable that women first entered this university as music students, for artistic subjects with a 'feminine' reputation would obviously be the easiest starting points for women's participation in higher education.

It is reasonable to assume that Williams's attendance at university was undertaken to prepare for her for a career as a schoolteacher, not as a professional composer. Both of Williams's parents were trained schoolteachers, who would have had no objection to her training for a career as a respectable music schoolmistress. Unlike some of the other provincial universities, the Welsh colleges made specific provision for the admission of women in their Royal Charters.[33] However, the number of female students who actually attended was tiny for a number of reasons – not least, the fact that most women did not have access to the sort of 16-plus education which qualified them for university study. As noted earlier, when Grace Williams desired to study music at school to an advanced level, a teacher had to be employed specially for the purpose.

The music curriculum Grace Williams studied at Cardiff University was quite typical of the time, with strong emphasis placed on the study of harmony and counterpoint. In this way Williams' music education was quite different from that of most of her female contemporaries at music college. She had many opportunities to compose; indeed, the final 'exercise' she completed for the B.Mus. degree was a composition for soloists, chorus and string orchestra entitled *To Night*.

After graduating from university Grace was encouraged to go to the Royal College of Music in London. Between 1926 and 1930 she began studies with Vaughan Williams. At the Royal College, Williams found many like-minded female contemporaries:

> [. . .] the time spent in the company of fellow students at the Royal College of Music was at least as important to Grace Williams' development as the formal teaching she received. It happened that her contemporaries included several of the same age and sex as herself, and together they made a formidable circle of young women composers [. . .] Dorothy Gow, Imogen Holst, Elizabeth Maconchy, and Elisabeth Lutyens[. . .][34]

Perhaps, by 'banding together', these female composition students found much-needed support and encouragement which they did not receive from any other quarter. Indeed, this was the start of a long friendship between Grace Williams and Elizabeth Maconchy. They corresponded regularly for 50 years, supporting each other by commenting on each other's work and discussing other topical musical issues.

Despite gaining an Octavia Travelling Scholarship in 1930 (which enabled her to study with Egon Wellesz in Vienna for a year), on her return to London in 1931 Williams' only employment opportunities were as a part-time visiting tutor at Southlands Training College in Wimbledon and as a music teacher at Camden School for Girls. Despite the fact that Williams's musical education was extensive for a woman of this time (she had specialized in music study between the ages of 16 and 25), her only option for employment was as a schoolteacher. Throughout the 1930s the vast majority of professional women were teachers or nurses; these two careers above all others were accepted as respectable for women, emphasizing a woman's 'natural' ability to care for others and teach children. This is a characteristic of Grace's personality which is often emphasized:

> Grace Williams's interest in children and young people was instinctive and genuine, and she made an unusually good teacher.[35]

Nevertheless, the investment of so much time in work at such an elementary level must have been a frustrating experience for a highly skilled, highly trained musician. Her composition work had to be fitted around teaching – mainly in the evenings, at weekends and in the school holidays. Williams spent the next 15 years working in this way. Unsurprisingly her health began to suffer, and in 1944 she was admitted to hospital for a short time. The illness made her decide to stop teaching. Grace applied unsuccessfully for a number of higher-status jobs, including a lectureship at University College Cardiff and an Assistant Inspectorship with the London County Council. However, in May 1946 she was offered a post with the BBC Schools Broadcasting department. Sadly, her health continued to deteriorate. Only four months after starting this job, she was advised to move back to her home in Wales, where she could be cared for by her parents.

From this time onwards, Williams survived by writing and composing for the BBC. She produced scripts for schools' broadcasts and incidental music for the BBC and numerous film companies. She also arranged many folk songs and carols for the BBC schools' programme 'Rhythm and Melody' between 1946 and 1954. In 1949 she considered moving back to London to find full-time employment but was unsuccessful in her attempt to find work. In January

1950, to supplement the small income she received from this work, she took a part-time teaching job at the Welsh College of Music and Drama. In 1954 she was forced, for financial reasons, to take work as a copyist. This kind of tedious and time-consuming work had a dampening effect on her own creativity. The last 20 years of Grace Williams's life saw her reach maturity as a composer; it is in this time that she is considered to have completed many of her best works.[36] After she had dispensed with much of her part-time employment, she had much more time to spend on original composition and produced a succession of larger-scale works.[37]

For any composer to continue to develop and produce works regularly, he or she must have some degree of financial security, either via composition or via some other area of the profession. For many years Williams had to struggle with employment outside 'autonomous' composition which hampered and distracted from her work. Despite Williams's impressive qualifications and training, she found great difficulty in gaining the kind of high-status employment which might have assisted her work. Williams's career mirrors exactly the type of employment opportunity available to women from the 1930s to the 1950s. Working with children as a teacher or in some other capacity was widely regarded as the only desirable employment for a woman outside nursing. For a male of similar qualifications and experience, the career opportunities would certainly have been much greater.

The early education of Elizabeth Maconchy (b.1907) was of the very traditional upper-middle-class variety in that she was taught entirely at home:

> I had a very good piano teacher [. . .] And I studied musical theory in Dublin. Other than that, my teachers had been governesses, and governesses who didn't know very much.[38]

The music tuition Maconchy received would have been very much a normal part of this type of upper-middle-class female education. The role of the female governess was usually to teach general knowledge and 'ladylike behaviour'. In addition to taking piano lessons, Maconchy studied harmony and counterpoint with a teacher in Dublin. This kind of specific theoretical study of music was extremely unusual amongst girls at this time. But, ironically, Maconchy's wider experience of music was very poor. She grew up without having access to the gramophone or the radio and at the age of 16 had only once heard a symphony orchestra (but never a string orchestra or a late Beethoven quartet).[39] Nevertheless, Maconchy gained a place at the Royal College of Music, where all classes were open to her. But the narrowness of her musical experience meant that she was at first ill-equipped for a more sophisticated level of study.

Elizabeth Maconchy studied at the Royal College of Music between 1923 and 1929. Like Grace Williams, she studied with Vaughan Williams and Charles Wood. As at the other national music colleges, women were allowed access to the Royal College of Music, but they were generally segregated from their male peers. Female students were considered different in their motivations and aspirations to study music, which further intensified their segregation, even though women made up a large proportion of the students right from the college's inception (for example, the pupils' concert programme of 2 July 1884 lists seven performances, four of which were by female students). Noteworthy and outstanding women students, however, are non-existent (or possibly merely invisible) in the Jubilee record of 1933.[40]

The physical segregation of female students had been evident at the Royal College from its foundation in 1894; women had to enter the College through a separate entrance and use separate staircases.[41] An indication of the intellectual segregation imposed on female students was the nature of the Royal College of Music Debating Society founded in 1896. It was described as 'entirely an affair of the male pupils'. Many distinguished members, such as Gustav Holst, Vaughan Williams, John Ireland and Herbert Fryer, attended its debates. The society provided a much-needed forum for students to get together, discuss academic issues and debate theoretical questions.[42] The total exclusion of women conveys the magnitude of the perceived differences in the interests and abilities of the male and female students. Such attitudes, resting on long-established traditions, affected many generations of female students.

A short time after Elizabeth Maconchy had attended the Royal College, sex segregation was documented as being more relaxed:

> [. . .] the present Lady Superintendent does not, like her predecessor, spend time in sitting through lessons or peering in at the glass doors, and makes no attempt to break up little groups of boys and girls who chat in the corridors [. . .][43]

The glass doors mentioned above reveals another problem faced by women students at this time. The 'see-through' doors were introduced when the principal violin teacher was 'found demonstrating his affection for a student', which caused his prompt sacking. This scandal was actually cited as a reason why some of the more competent teachers avoided teaching positions in institutions with many female students.[44]

While at the Royal College, Elizabeth Maconchy sensed no prejudice against women students, primarily because these totalled nearly half the number. However, her recollections reveal that there was a general feeling that female students were not of the highest standard:

> [. . .] there were plenty of women students, but not very many outstanding ones. And they were almost all instrumentalists or singers, not composers.[45]

Obviously, Maconchy to some extent went along with the prevalent view that female students were not outstanding, and that the women's main preoccupation was still the study of instruments. Ironically, she did not see this as a result of discrimination against female students. Maconchy perceived discrimination only at the point when she tried to establish herself as a professional composer:

> At the College [. . .] there was no prejudice against girls or women, one was completely equal. Then when one left, one found that there was a great prejudice against girls.[46]

While at music college, most of the female music students were obviously not considered in any way as direct competitors of their male contemporaries. The question of the seriousness of female aspirations to a full-time career in music was an important factor in how women students were treated. For example, while at college Maconchy applied unsuccessfully for the Mendelssohn scholarship. Sir Hugh Allen, the then Head of the College, consoled her by saying that the scholarship was of little consequence, since she would only get married and never write another note. Although some years previously the award had been given to a female student (Maude Valerie White, in 1879), the attitudes of many remained that the study of music was a thing for a woman to undertake only before marriage; music should continue after marriage as a hobby, not a professional career.

As mentioned in the previous chapter, Elizabeth Maconchy has never taken any form of professional employment apart from her work as a composer. With the financial support of her husband, she has been able to concentrate solely on composition. But to be considered a professional composer requires more than full-time commitment to composition. Success, public acclaim and professional authority are acquired only when works are performed regularly, published, and given critical and public attention. It is the mixture of these functions which goes a long way to provide the degree of esteem with which a composer is viewed. In the time after leaving the Royal College, when she won numerous prizes and scholarships, Maconchy recalls:

> But what did one do next, particularly if one were a girl? [. . .] Publishers would not consider seriously publishing anything by a young woman – except possibly some little songs. In the London of the 1920s no-one had given a thought to helping a composer to establish himself – still less herself [. . .][47]

Sir Henry Wood, a great promoter of new composing talent, picked Maconchy's suite *The Land* for a Proms performance in 1930. It was greeted with great acclaim by the critics – but no more:

> It received, though I say it, staggeringly good press notices – but that was all. No-one gave me a commission, or a grant, or a chatty interview, or another performance.[48]

But Maconchy was fortunate to have her works performed with some regularity in the Macnaghten-Lemare concerts. These concerts were established in 1931 by three women – Anne Macnaghten, Iris Lemare and Elisabeth Lutyens – to promote works by young British composers. It has been noted that these concerts contained a fairly large proportion of music by women, and Maconchy's involvement in these concerts did much to expose her work to the artistic establishment and thereby improve her status as a professional 'serious' composer. Becoming established as a composer was more difficult for women, who tended to be overlooked or ignored even when they obtained exposure. Only through a 'joining forces' of like-minded women could female musicians at that time gain much-needed professional experience. Since her student days Maconchy has worked alone, keeping in contact with current musical developments often through her daughter Nicola LeFanu, who is also a composer.

Maconchy's most extensive work outside composition has been with the Composers' Guild (of which she became the first woman president in 1959) and the Society for the Promotion of New Music.

Minna Keal's (b.1909) education had the potential to make her the most advanced of all the composers in the study group born before 1910. Yet, although her very liberal education was encouraged by her parents, family demands and domestic work, as we saw, eventually took priority. After attending an ordinary, elementary school, Keal won a scholarship in 1919 to Clapton County School in Hackney, run by Dr O'Brien-Harris, a Fabian socialist. Correspondingly, it was an extremely progressive school, both in its attitudes to girls' education and its informal regime. Fabians believed strongly in women's equality and right to independence. They spoke against the prejudiced definition of femininity as physical frailty; they also campaigned against the inequalities of a sexually based division of labour.[49] For the time, these were extremely progressive ideas and illustrate the almost revolutionary atmosphere at this school. Consequently, many aspects of this political radicalism had a lasting effect on Keal's beliefs.

Minna studied Music alongside a full range of subjects at school (she took ten subjects at matriculation); again, this was exceptional in the educational context of the time. There was a strong emphasis on academic achievement for girls, with earlier students even gaining scholarships to Oxford and Cambridge universities. This, too, was highly exceptional for the time.

The acceptance of women into British universities had begun in 1875, when legislation which allowed universities to award degrees to women was passed. The first university to do so was London University in 1878. However, the most prestigious universities, Oxford and Cambridge, did not award degrees to women until 1920 and 1921 respectively. (Cambridge University did not allow women the full voting rights which usually accompanied graduation until 1948.)[50] More specifically, Elsie Baron Briggs, who in 1915 became one of the first women to fulfil the requirements for the Cambridge B.Mus., was not actually awarded the degree until 1927.[51] Restrictions on the number of female students allowed to enter Oxford and Cambridge were not lifted until 1956.[52] Even for middle-class girls, the continuation to higher education was extremely rare. Throughout the 1920s, it is estimated that only 0.5 per cent of girls reaching the age of 18 years went into higher education.[53] Keal seemed unaware that, at the time, women attending university were pioneers, who had only just been granted degrees on a par with men.

After being forced to abandon university because of family pressures, Keal began in 1927 to attend the Royal Academy of Music instead. Like the previous composers, she found herself one of a number of female students at the Academy. Keal states that one of the main reasons why she decided to study at the Royal Academy of Music was its close proximity. Studying full-time at the Royal Academy fitted easily with her work at home, since it entailed attendance only twice a week.[54] She studied two subjects: piano with Thomas Knott and composition with William Alwyn. Keal had initially wanted to study only piano, but the rule was that students had to study at least two subjects, so she added composition. She did not enrol on any validated course, and her attendance was really that of an interested amateur:

> I wasn't vocationally-minded at the time – all I wanted to do was to study the piano and study composition. I didn't follow a course. Nobody suggested anything to me [. . .] you see, I wasn't moving in musical circles at home – I wasn't moving in musical circles anywhere: I just had a love of music.[55]

Once she started the lessons in composition, this immediately became her overriding passion.[56]

Keal benefited from having many of her student works performed at college concerts. She confirms that the music college experience of the time was in no way stacked against women and that in reality men were in the minority. Keal recalls, looking back at the student concert programmes of 1929:

> [. . .] if anything there was a very, very strong case for discrimination against men: in these three [student concert] programmes, more than half of the performers and *all* the composers are women. There are no men students at all.[57]

Yet even though females were well established in the college system, Keal acknowledges the lack of ambitious or extensive work attempted by them:

> When I analysed these programmes, nearly all the composers were girls, but they were writing songs. But of course I couldn't write a song: I started off by writing a violin and piano piece![58]

This seems to indicate that, at the time, Keal sensed that to prove herself a 'serious' composer, she should not conform to the expected 'feminine' pattern of small-scale composition, as most of her female contemporaries did. Like Elizabeth Maconchy, she viewed other females' work as having low status.

When Keal left the Academy to help with the family business, she always continued to play the piano, although she cut herself off from composition altogether:

> My sister used to say, 'Why don't you compose in your spare time?', but it's not the sort of thing you could do [. . .] I either do it or I don't, so I had to cut if off completely.[59]

After the war Keal attended piano lessons with Norman Anderson at the Guildhall School of Music, where she obtained an LRAM (teachers) diploma. This low-key and commonplace involvement in music (playing and teaching the piano privately) was Keal's main experience of music for most of her working life, and it conforms exactly to the most widespread social stereotypes of women's involvement in music.

Keal's employment record consisted of full-time clerical jobs. Although her secondary education was exceptional, the curtailment of her studies left her with an education of only 'O' level standard. The jobs that she found most rewarding were as a Progress Chaser in an aircraft factory during the Second World War and as the Examinations Secretary for the Institute of Management Association in London. When she reached the age of 60, in 1969, Keal retired from full-time work but continued to give a small number of piano lessons at home. Her chance meeting with the composer Justin Connolly in 1973 marked the start of her return to composition.

Minna Keal has, in recent years, had a great deal of success in terms of being perceived as a professional composer. For example, she has managed to have all her works performed, and because of her remarkable story has received a relatively large amount of exposure in the media. There was intense press interest when her Symphony Op.3 was performed by the BBC Symphony Orchestra under Oliver Knussen in 1989:

> I immediately became a sort of celebrity; the press descended on me [. . .] it was like a thunder cloud bursting. It was the human element; it was the fact that this old lady who had given up for 46 years starts composing again and gets things performed.[60]

Keal has had the time and energy to follow up opportunities afforded by the performance of her works. Since her rededication to composition she has completed six works. Her only commissioned work has been a Cello Concerto completed for the 1994 Aldeburgh Festival.

When we turn to the three composers in the study group born between 1920 and 1940, we see that many of the old educational patterns and attitudes in relation to female music students remained. It must be stressed that the composers born between 1900 and 1940 had exceptional educational experiences in terms of the female population generally. For example, during the 1930s only about 15 per cent of girls aged 11 to 17 went to secondary school.[61] Most girls stayed in the elementary education system only until they were 14 (minimum school leaving age). The numbers going on into higher education were proportionally minute.

After attending kindergarten Ruth Gipps (b.1921) became, in 1927, a weekly boarder at Brickwall school in Northiam. She then changed from this boarding school to one she could attend from home each day, The Gables in Bexhill. This school had originally been exclusively for boys, only admitting a very select group of girl students (usually the sisters of boys who attended the school). This type of co-education was very rare, even in junior schools. Gipps, who was very much a 'tomboy', immediately felt at home in the male-dominated environment, where the usual standards imposed on girls were for once largely ignored. It is quite clear that Gipps even then disliked being classed as a 'female', a conviction that she has kept all her life:

> [. . .] I felt the same pleasure at being called a 'Gable-Boy' that, in years later when I became an orchestra player, I felt on being included in a conductor's 'Now, Gentlemen [. . .]'[62]

In 1932 Gipps moved to the County School. This school was geared solely to academic achievement. In this school music, along with other artistic study, was frowned on. The school's attitude was that academic achievement could be sought only through a curriculum which excluded the arts. This can be seen as a direct reaction against 'feminine' subjects, which throughout this time were considered a wasted opportunity for the brighter female student. Understandably, Gipps hated this environment and at the age of 12 was removed from school on medical grounds, continuing her education at home with a female tutor.

The greatest single influencing factor in Gipps' musical education was, of course, her mother. Having a mother who was a music teacher was both a tremendous benefit and an enormous influence. Mrs Gipps seems to have been confident from the start that Ruth should be trained to be a musician. From the time when she began studying at home, Ruth's general education seems to have been very much fitted around music. She continued to study music at home with her mother and by 1934 was spending at least three hours daily on piano practice in addition to intensive tuition in music history, harmony and aural perception. This full and thorough formative training was paramount in instilling Ruth with confidence in her own abilities. It also placed her ahead of many of her peers when she entered the Royal College of Music at the age of 15.

She studied at the College between 1937–1942, taking piano lessons with Arthur Alexander and Kendal Taylor, oboe lessons with Leon Goossens and composition with R.O. Morris, Gordon Jacob and Ralph Vaughan Williams. In addition to studying for the standard college diploma, Gipps worked for an external B.Mus. degree from Durham University. The degree consisted of two sections. The first was a written examination; the second a compositional 'exercise'. To fulfil the second requirement, Gipps completed her Quintet for oboe, clarinet and strings, Op. 16, in 1941.

On leaving the Royal College, Gipps had her orchestral work, *Knight in Armour*, Op. 8, performed at the last night of the Proms in 1942. In a repetition of Elizabeth Maconchy's experience, despite the good reviews including one in *The Times*, no further opportunities came her way as a result.[63] Determined to make her mark in the profession, Gipps used her versatility as a musician to full advantage. Throughout her long career she has worked as an orchestral player (oboe and cor anglais), a solo pianist, a lecturer and a conductor in addition to her work as a composer.

Of all the composers in this study, Ruth Gipps has had the most varied and extensive professional career. Significantly, she has also had the most thorough and wide-ranging education. Without doubt, those women who received only instrumental tuition would have had neither the training nor the confidence to compete successfully in the musical profession. Gipps gained a position as an orchestral oboe player in the City of Birmingham Orchestra between 1944 and 1948. There has been a long tradition of prejudice against women who play in orchestras. Some of the extreme prejudices vented earlier in the century lingered into the 1950s and 1960s. It was suggested even then that there was 'medical evidence' that women were poorer quality players because females had one muscle missing from the arm and therefore 'lacked power of tone and firmness of attack'.[64] In 1916:

> Women were accused of lowering wages [. . .] and standards [. . .] A typical editorial attack in the [musicians'] union journal deplored their lack of 'vim [. . .] particularly in the climaxes and anti-climaxes necessary to a proper performance'.[65]

After the Second World War more women joined orchestras, but resentment of their presence was still harboured by many male players.[66]

Gipps spent these unhappy years in Birmingham alone, since her husband was away fighting in the war. While she was alone and vulnerable, it was easy for damaging rumours to spread. George Weldon, the conductor of the then City of Birmingham Orchestra, was a kind and supportive friend, but their relationship was misinterpreted by some. The situation came to a head in 1945, when Weldon planned a performance of Gipps' First Symphony. Weldon was accused of programming the work because Gipps was his mistress. This led Weldon to vow never again to program a full concent of Gipps' works in case any similar rumours started. Gipps' unpopularity with the orchestra eventually led to her being asked to leave.

In 1946 Gipps decided to further her training and career by taking the D.Mus. degree at Durham University. She failed the first part of the examination but, undaunted, resat it successfully in 1947, two months before her son was born. The second part of the doctoral examination required the composition of a large-scale work. Gipps produced a cantata, *The Cat*, which was accepted in 1948. Very few women scaled these academic heights in the 1940s – it was simply Gipps' outstanding determination to succeed at the highest level of the music profession which drove her to accomplish so much.

The doctorate led to her being offered a minor conducting post. In the summer of 1948 she became the 'Chorus Master' of the City of Birmingham Choir. Two men had previously turned down the position since they were unwilling to do all the hard rehearsal work, only to let someone else conduct the actual performance. It was suggested to Gipps that, as a woman, she would be satisfied with this arrangement since she would be less ambitious to conduct concerts! However, Gipps was very ambitious, and the experience she gained from conducting this choir encouraged her to take on other work, including the conductorship of the Birmingham Co-Operative Amateur Orchestra and the CBO Listeners' Club Ladies Choir. Naturally, some colleagues encouraged her to consider expanding into work with professional orchestras:

> [. . .] in spite of encouragement from professional orchestral players I didn't think of turning into a professional conductor; for a woman conducting was unthinkable, almost indecent.[67]

When she eventually applied for a job as assistant conductor and accompanist at BBC Midland, she passed the accompanying part of the audition but was informed by the panel that she would never be able to command, from the male-dominated orchestra, the respect required to do the job and was not even allowed to take the conducting audition![68] In addition, Gipps' conducting career was hampered in other ways. Although George Weldon gave her a crash course in conducting before she took the amateur choir jobs, he completely disagreed with the idea of professional women conductors. Undeterred, Gipps sought lessons instead with Stanford Robinson in 1953:

> To a chorus of disapproval and hatred, I became a woman conductor.[69]

In 1954 she made her professional début with the Boyd Neel Orchestra. There followed in 1957 her London conducting début with the Pro Arte Orchestra and Goldsmiths' Choral Union in a programme which consisted of her own cantata *The Cat* and Beethoven's *Choral Symphony*. Sadly, there was little press interest in the concert, and her professional conducting career was halted for want of opportunity. In the 34 years that followed, Gipps applied for every kind of conducting job across the country, but it was not until she was 68 years old that she secured a position as Conductor of the Heathfield Choral Society.

Resilient as ever, Gipps decided to form her own orchestra as a vehicle for her talents. When she returned to London from Birmingham, she realized that there was a gap in the education of young players in terms of sight-reading and repertoire study. Consequently, she formed the One Rehearsal Orchestra, later known as the London Repertoire Orchestra. The idea was to perform works with only one or two rehearsals, as is in any case often the situation in professional orchestras. Gipps remained their conductor for 31 years. In addition, she formed the professional Chanticleer Orchestra in 1961 (this meets only sporadically due to financial constraints).

In her later years (1960–1980) Gipps started a full-time career as a music lecturer in higher education. She was employed as a tutor on the B.Mus. course at Trinity College of Music (1959–1966). In 1966 she became the second women to chair the Composers' Guild. Between 1967 and 1977 she was a tutor at the Royal College of Music, where she occasionally conducted the first and second orchestras. Between 1977 and 1979 she was a principal music lecturer at Kingston Polytechnic. The added burden of this teaching work led to a fall in the number of compositions completed during this period.

On reflection, Gipps herself feels that she has never really succeeded in her professional career, particularly as a conductor:

> I thought when I was young I would never marry or have children. I imagined that I would have to give up all the things I wanted for music [. . .] Life is funny: I have got everything apart from the music. I have never had the job I wanted, not any job I wanted.[70]

Gipps' varied and full professional life pursued in addition to composition has without doubt exposed her to a whole variety of prejudices visited on women right across the musical profession.

There can be no greater contrast to the career of Ruth Gipps than that of Antoinette Kirkwood (b.1930). Her education and experience reflect some of the limitations of female music education previously discussed. Kirkwood attended only one school, the Merrion House School, in Finchley, London (which was primarily a ballet school), for a period of about six months. Kirkwood recalls her mother's rather unconventional reason for removing her from institutional education:

> She was appalled at my obedience and rigorous adherence to the school rules and decided that school must be a grave mistake for me.[71]

After this time, all Kirkwood's education was undertaken at home. Until she was 12 years old, her tutor was a Mr David Thomson, and thereafter a Mr Thomas Crowe. She studied a reasonable range of subjects, including mathematics, natural science, bible study and music. Kirkwood received much encouragement from her parents to practise music at home:

> I was encouraged to play for my mother and also to play my own compositions.[72]

This type of encouragement was not remarkable. For a girl to gain a basic education plus a few 'accomplishments' (rather than a rigorous academic education fitting her for higher education) was still a normal perspective in the 1950s.

At the age of 12, in 1942, Kirkwood entered the Royal Irish Academy of Music to study piano, harmony and cello with Clyde Twelvetrees and Claud Biggs. Kirkwood continued to take lessons from Twelvetrees when she left the Academy. At the age of 15 years she went to London where she played for Irene Scharrer, who advised her to enter the Royal Academy of Music to study piano. On hearing the string playing of Arthur Grumiaux and Maurice Raskin, Kirkwood was inspired to audition at the Brussels Conservatoire, where Grumiaux taught:

> I would have been accepted for cello and composition but I did not feel happy in the place.[73]

Kirkwood returned to Ireland, uncertain of her next step, but she seems to have attempted to further her musical education in the same way as her early education: that is, mostly by studying privately with no overt vocational aim. She recalls that before her family moved from Ireland to London in 1947:

> I wanted to extend my studies and had no idea how to go about it so I wrote to Casals – not expecting to get an answer [. . .] I received a card saying 'I would recommend Monsieur Paul Tortelier as a teacher to you'.[74]

Quite by chance, the new conductor of the Radio Eireann Symphony Orchestra, Jean Martinon, invited Kirkwood to a rehearsal to hear an up-and-coming cellist play. This was Kirkwood's first meeting with Paul Tortelier. She asked if he would be willing to teach her, and he agreed:

> I studied with Tortelier in my own house where he stayed with us whenever he came to London, which was quite a lot.[75]

To avoid conscription into the Land Army, Kirkwood supplemented her sporadic study with Tortelier by enrolling at the private London Violoncello School. The school had close ties with the Royal Academy of Music, and students were sent for private lessons with RAM professors. In this way, Kirkwood had composition lessons with Dorothy Howell, who was a great inspiration to her.

Ironically, despite all her private study with well-known musicians, Kirkwood never took any formal music examinations – mainly on the advice and insistence of her parents:

> [. . .] having been very successful in examinations herself she [her mother] had made up her mind they were a useless waste of time and I was not going to take *any*. My

father [. . .] had a very low opinion of them. He used to say: 'Anyone can pass exams. It doesn't mean you are any *good* at anything'.[76]

This seems a rather odd attitude, bearing in mind that qualifications, and, more importantly, validated full-time study, were the keys to success in any non-manual career. Strangely, however, Kirkwood did actually take two examinations:

The only exams I ever took were in Poetry and Elocution. For some reason Mother didn't feel they represented any threat to me as I wasn't likely to benefit from them![77]

This statement perhaps sheds a little more light on the situation. The idea that formal examinations represented a 'threat' to Kirkwood was not an untypical attitude, although, admittedly one more prevalent earlier in the century. It is clear that too much education was still viewed by some as damaging to a woman's 'femininity' or of no real value to a middle-class 'lady'. (A similarly cavalier attitude to examinations has never characterized the world of non-aristocratic men.) The middle-class status of a family demanded implicitly that the wife did not take paid employment and remained dependent on her husband. All the better, therefore, if she was formally unqualified, so exempt from temptation.

Kirkwood has never taken any employment, musical or otherwise, to supplement her work as a composer. She has never received any awards or scholarships for her work. Despite the unquestionable calibre of some of her teachers, the periods of private, unvalidated study have never really provided career opportunities, a situation doubtless compounded by her lack of formal qualifications and domestic responsibilities. Kirkwood's work has, no doubt, suffered to some degree from this isolation.

Enid Luff (b.1935) was strongly encouraged to gain a full academic education. Since her mother had benefited from a university education, it was a natural progression that Enid should follow the same path. Luff started piano lessons when she was five. As a teenager she gained a three-year music scholarship for piano lessons with Douglas Miller from the Birkenhead Education Authority. Her ability for music was obvious. However, at her secondary school, Birkenhead Girls' Grammar School, her teachers saw her passion and talent for music as a threat to her academic potential. Luff was pushed to take languages instead of Music at A level:

I think the music teacher didn't have much say. Also, they gave my parents funny advice like, 'Music is not a very good career' and 'She can do her music afterwards' [. . .] I was brought up to be too obedient. Lots of women are – not so much nowadays, but in those days you were brought up to be a doormat and just do what people told you.[78]

Indeed, Luff had to stop the lessons with Miller after six months as:

[. . .] the pressure to take up languages resulted in my being sent to France to au pair. The whole thing was disastrous really, if I'd been older and just understood what was going on I wouldn't have done it.[79]

Although the idea of music as a 'feminine' subject encouraged many women to learn the basics, there seems to have been a kind of backlash against the idea of very bright girls taking music in higher education. This was probably aggravated by music's continued low status as a school subject. Consequently, Luff entered Newnham College, Cambridge, to study modern languages in 1953.

Throughout the first fifty years of this century there was a gradual increase in the total number of school leavers who went on to study at university. In 1952–1953 there were around 81,000 students in higher education. In the academic year 1957-1958 females accounted for 25 per cent of students enrolled on full-time first degree and diploma courses.[80] Throughout the 1960s higher education expanded substantially, but this did not diminish the relative scarcity of women students, especially at the more prestigious universities. For example, in 1964 only 10 per cent of Cambridge University undergraduates and 14 per cent of Oxford University undergraduates were female, whereas female students made up 25 per cent of the enrolment at large civic universities and 35 per cent of that at smaller civic universities.[81]

Women who, like Luff, attended Cambridge University in those years were very much an elite group. It must be stressed that although female students were allowed to study at the University, there were no mixed colleges at this time. Luff found the all-female environment of Newnham College dull and much preferred to socialize at one of the 'male' colleges, where her future husband was a student. Luff was very unhappy in her work at the University, having been forced to drop music; her language studies seemed to offer little compensatory fulfilment. She recalls that at university:

> I was abnormally withdrawn and the reason was because anything I really deeply wanted to say was completely impossible [. . .] psychologically it had got to the point where I stopped writing [. . .][82]

Luff finally found the confidence to return to music in the late 1960s. In 1965 she started to take piano lessons with George Hadjinikos in order to gain an LRAM teachers' diploma. Hadjinikos proved pivotal in the rediscovery by Luff of her real calling:

> [. . .] he was an extremely good teacher [. . .] He helped me to develop my musicality and I began to realise that really I was a composer, that I had to do something about it.[83]

In 1968 Luff extended her musical studies by enrolling on a B.Mus. course at University College of North Wales at Bangor, which she completed in 1971, aged 34. Following this, she took an M.Mus. at Bangor, for which she completed her Symphony (1974). The successful outcome of these two courses was a real achievement, bearing in mind her domestic situation. Academically, Luff was given wonderful support and encouragement from the younger members of staff, especially Sebastian Forbes and John Hywel. However, there was a feeling that some of the other members of staff took her aspirations less than seriously, disadvantaging her doubly, as a mature, female student.[84]

During 1973 Luff had four piano pieces broadcast on BBC Radio 3. Fellow Welsh composer Grace Williams heard them and was so impressed by the works that she encouraged Luff to continue her composition studies. Williams wrote to the Welsh Arts Council; at her suggestion it provided Luff with a grant. Between 1975 and 1977 Luff used the money to study with an established female composer, Elizabeth Lutyens. Although in her later years Lutyens was recalled by many as a very difficult and bitter person, Luff has different memories:

> I think now we are more in a position to sympathise with her because she was a pioneer woman, having to fight against a social background and a set up which did not include women. She had been very badly hurt and [. . .] it is a fact she was bitter [. . .] But I have to say, to me personally she was very kind and supportive.[85]

As a teacher, Lutyens emphasized precision of musical thought and clarity of line – virtues which are evident in most of Luff's works after this time. Unfortunately, Lutyens became ill, and Luff had to continue her studies with Anthony Payne. In 1977 she obtained another bursary from the Welsh Arts Council, which she used to spend a number of weeks studying with Franco Donatoni in Milan.

In 1979 Luff's husband was offered the position of Precentor of Westminster Abbey. Having to re-establish herself as a composer in London proved a great strain. Self-promotion, which is so often the key to successful performances of a composer's music, was extremely difficult for Luff, mainly because of her lack of confidence. In 1980, to aid the production and distribution of her works, she founded the Primavera publishing company with another composer, Julia Usher:

> I felt that I really had to establish myself and it was a real battle [. . .] it is just a fight from beginning to end. You write to people and you phone [. . .] you have to push and push. I had to learn how to do this but it took it out of me because I am not a pushy person and I developed high blood pressure.[86]

The promotional side of a composer's activity, which for the most part has to be undertaken by the individual artist, is vital work which is often overlooked. The battle to publish works and gain performances and commissions can be very demanding and demoralizing. Knowing people within the musical 'establishment' is a great asset. Here, women are often disadvantaged by being isolated and lacking the relevant connections. To overcome this, some women composers have 'banded together' and set up their own networks to perform and promote their work: for example, the Women in Music organization. Luff, like many others, feels that this kind of promotion is of great benefit:

> I have been given openings that I wouldn't have got otherwise, but I am not ashamed of that because it is a hard enough road anyway.[87]

Like Kirkwood, Enid Luff has never held any full-time paid employment.[88]

Even in the case of the composers born after 1940, the educational system continued to soft-pedal the claim for equality in female education. Many authorities continued to believe in education for women almost on the Roussellian model:

> Even if a woman has no economic need or any wish to earn her own living after marriage, a sound education must be regarded as a necessity. Over and over again,

> throughout the centuries, people have urged that properly educated women make not only better and more understanding wives, but mothers infinitely better able to fulfil the most important function of their existence – the proper training of their children.[89]

Throughout the 1960s and 1970s the study of music at secondary level continued to suffer from the stigma of being an unacademic subject most suited for girls. Then, as now, music's grouping among the 'practical' subjects reflected – and perpetuated – its lack of academic status. The result was that the more able (that is, academically oriented) students, both male and female, tended to be channelled into subjects with greater intellectual prestige.

It is clear that a gender-divided curriculum which views subjects as 'masculine' or 'feminine' in bias automatically provides them with an intrinsic value and prestige. The traditional perception of males as more academically able is neatly parallelled by the fact of the brightest boys having the least access to music education. It is therefore unsurprising that during the sixties and seventies, many more females than males studied Music at O and A level. For example, some 70 per cent of the students who took music at O level in the summer examination of 1961 were female. In the same examination session 64 per cent of students who sat A level music were likewise female.

Judith Bailey (b. 1941) attended Truro High School. Music formed, in the main, part of the external school activities and the school had established links with the Royal Academy of Music in London. Bailey received much encouragement and had the opportunity to be involved in external music activities, participating in choirs and orchestras. Although the school gave music space within the curriculum, its place on the overall curriculum of an individual student was not assured, since it could only be studied in place of another subject:

> [. . .] they didn't mind you missing needlework for music so I would have clarinet lessons instead of needlework, which was fabulous [. . .] you could also have music lessons instead of art lessons [. . .][90]

The quoted subject choices reflect their place and perceived educational value in the curriculum. In the 1950s the feminine 'accomplishments' of needlework, art and music were still seen as interchangeable and equally valued skills.

Interestingly, some education reports at this time renewed the emphasis that women should be educated in the areas that 'interested' them and also happened to be of 'practical' use to them. For example, the Crowther Report on the education of 15 to 18-year-olds, published in 1959, reiterated some traditional notions of the type of education that girls and boys should each receive:

> [. . .][it] recommended courses for less able girls in personal appearance, fashion and human relationships [. . .] stating baldly that 'the incentive for girls to equip themselves for marriage and home-making is genetic'. As for boys, 'at this stage their thoughts turn more often to a career [. . .]'[91]

Implicit in most of the ideas put forward at this time was that female interests and aspirations were defined by biology and were therefore immutable. Many experts still seemed to endorse the well-worn belief that education should fit women for their 'natural' aptitudes and social role rather than offering new opportunities and training which would expand a young woman's horizons.

Bailey attended the Royal Academy of Music between 1959 and 1963. In order to receive a grant from her county council, she had to enrol for the Graduate Diploma Course (GRSM). Bailey found this course less than challenging, and as a supplement she started to work for a B.Mus. (validated externally by London University), which she completed successfully in 1964. Obviously, many able students like Judith Bailey craved greater intellectual study as part of their music course. This is evidenced by a study of music education provision carried out in 1959, which showed courses in music colleges (the so-called *conservatoires*) to be varied in character and often inadequate compared with university music degrees. The conservatoires offered diplomas on the basis of an examination, but often students would study at the college without sitting any examinations. Standards varied according to the vocational bias of the subject. High standards were found in classes which had a direct bearing on professional careers (orchestra and opera), whereas non-vocational classes in subjects such as harmony and music history were of a lower standard.[92] University degree courses in music offered quite different instruction. The emphasis was on techniques of composition, general history and analytical skills, some universities also offering a considerable performance element.[93]

Bailey felt that it was essential to gain teaching qualifications in addition to the B.Mus. degree; she accordingly worked for, and gained, both the LRAM and ARCM diplomas. She was committed from her student days to a professional career in music, and she was well aware that to gain academic qualifications and high standards would provide much greater opportunities in this direction. Like some of the composers discussed previously, Bailey experienced no discrimination against women during her time at the Royal Academy. She states:

> I did not expect (or notice) any particular discrimination against me as a woman, but perhaps it was harder to prove oneself than it might have been for the male students.[94]

This seems to be a recurrent theme. Although, in general, female music students were not in any sense 'unusual' at the national music colleges, they were perceived collectively as being of a lower standard than their male contemporaries – hence the feeling that a woman had to work harder to rise above the level of the 'average' student.

On leaving the Royal Academy, Bailey found, as did Grace Williams some years before, that the only practical career option was to teach. Her first job was as a peripatetic woodwind teacher with Hampshire County Council (1962–1971). In addition to this, Bailey continued to play professionally as a clarinettist within a county ensemble. In 1969 she was appointed the conductor of the Southampton Concert Orchestra. Entering this most male bastion, she encountered some very blatant sexual discrimination:

> After I had conducted them for about six months there was a lot of unrest and things became unpleasant in (perhaps) the hope that I would resign [. . .] Apparently the reason for this was abundantly clear: it was in this case discrimination against a woman.[95]

Women conductors have had a consistently difficult time; in this role their obvious status and position of power (usually over a male-dominated orchestra) frequently stir up uncomfortable feelings about the accepted power relationships. Confronted by this kind of working environment, it is perhaps unsurprising that Bailey does not push too far the issue of being a woman:

> I have just concentrated on the job in hand and tried to let other things fall into place. I think too many women perhaps bother too much with male attitudes instead of getting on with the job and showing by what they produce that they can be just as good.[96]

In 1971 she was appointed conductor of the Petersfield Orchestra. Her work with this organization was less fraught, since the orchestra's founder had also been a woman, Kathleen Merit. Other appointments followed, with the conductorship of the Haslemere Musical Society (1977–1980) and of the Petersfield Choral Society (1981–present).

Bailey's conducting career has definitely been of benefit to her composing work. Her orchestras have, on a number of occasions, performed both small-scale and large-scale works of hers; this has acted both as an encouragement to the composer and as a vehicle for her musical development. But working in the area of amateur orchestras obviously lacks the prestige of professional conducting. The whole philosophy of amateur music-making is a world away from the market-led outlook of professional orchestras. Bailey feels that her temperament inclines her to be more interested in getting the most out of the players rather than being involved in the high pressure, competitive professional world:

> I think the 'womanly' qualities which were a disadvantage to start with have turned out to be the right things for this sort of orchestra [. . .] I don't need qualities of competition, its musical expression, I just want to conduct [. . .][97]

It is clear that she has been discouraged from seeking professional conducting work because of her perception that success in this area calls for an aggressive, competitive and sometimes ruthless personality.

The youngest composer in the group, Bryony Jagger (b. 1948), attended Mary Datchelor Girls' school in London. Unsurprisingly, music was a valued part of the curriculum of this long-established girls' school:

> [. . .] the policy was to try and ensure that all girls were musically literate and able to sing a musical part in a choral situation.[98]

Jagger was a very bright child who was picked out as university material from an early age. Her initial lack of interest in music is very unusual, as most budding musicians show ability within the first five years of life. In her final A level year Jagger suddenly decided that she wanted to abandon her initial intention to apply to Cambridge University to study classics in favour of studying music. However, she was strongly discouraged:

> [. . .] my father and I had big rows in my teenage years about my wish to compose music [. . .] My headmistress wanted me to apply for Oxbridge [. . .] I was not prepared to abandon the music.[99]

Jagger's school music teacher, Mary Rose Seldon, was an Oxford University graduate herself and encouraged Jagger to pursue her music along academic lines:

> I probably would not have had the strength or determination to go against parents' and school's wishes to pursue my composing career if she had not been so supportive. I consider that she has been the most important teacher in my life.[100]

For a woman to continue into higher education was no longer unusual in the late 1960s. Jagger attended New Hall, Cambridge, between 1967 and 1971 to read for a joint Music and Moral Science degree. In Britain the academic year 1967–1968 saw some 250 students graduate with degrees in Music, 36 per cent of whom were women.

At Cambridge women were in a much smaller minority than the national average. Jagger recalls:

> New Hall was an all-female college. I liked the atmosphere. I spent most of my time playing music in the male colleges or attending lectures with a ratio of ten or more men to one woman, so it was good to get away from men occasionally.[101]

Jagger was offered a place on the M.Mus. degree course at Cardiff University, but marital commitments made this impossible. In 1972, finding herself back in Cambridge, she enrolled on the B.Mus. course but, disillusioned, left within one term.

Jagger has continued to study privately but on the whole is very wary of music tuition:

> Most of what I know has not been taught to me and most of the teaching I have had, and seen in action, has been destructive of creativity.

In addition to her work as a composer and writer, Jagger has taken a number of part-time jobs, ranging from tutor in General Studies and Chinese History at the University of Auckland to proof-reader on a suburban newspaper. She has never taught music or obtained paid music-related employment. When trying to obtain commissions or paid composing work, Jagger has often found difficulty:

> The attitude in the 70s was that I didn't need to be paid, because I had a well-paid husband . . .] the paid commissions tended to go to men because they had families to support [. . .] Even now I have a family to support the attitude lingers on and people are surprised when I point out that I can't *afford* to compose.[102]

This echoes the experience of Elisabeth Lutyens some years earlier:

> [Elisabeth Lutyens was] trying to earn a living by writing for radio and composing film scores (at a time when there were virtually no female music directors, or producers). Lutyens was informed by a producer that he had turned her down for four films as she had 'solved her economic problems by marriage'.[103]

Bryony Jagger is currently trying to secure a composer-in-residence job so as to be able to fund her work further.

When one considers the education and employment experiences of the nine women composers, certain central issues become apparent. Primarily, there seem to be many obstacles which hinder their transition from talented music students to full-time, high-profile music professionals. There continues to be an enormous gulf between women's involvement in music education and their subsequent employment in, and contribution to, professional music. This is corroborated by the wider statistics of the numbers of professional female musicians. For example, in 1992 the Musician's Union membership was only 19 per cent female.[104] This represents a mere 9 per cent increase over the 1926 figure.[105] Accurate statistics are often difficult to uncover. For example, in 1951 there were some 26,000 musicians in England and Wales, of whom 12,000 (46 per cent) were female. Yet these figures are misleading, since 70 per cent of these women were music teachers (many part-time or private), whereas only 20 per cent of the men were teachers.[106]

It is clear that women have made their greatest impact on the world of professional orchestral players. For example, in the 1994–1995 season female personnel accounted for between 17 per cent and 35 per cent of the total number.[107] Although this is not anything like equality, it is certainly an improvement. However, on closer inspection of these figures, the familiar pattern of women occupying the lowest, least prestigious positions is apparent, with female principals accounting for between only 6 per cent and 13 per cent.

On the wider scale, there is a hierarchy imposed on all individuals involved in the creation, recreation and consumption of music. This system of value and prestige is applied to the musicians themselves, greatest importance being given to the creator (composer) or 'conceptual' interpreter (conductor); next comes the physical recreator (instrumental performer and singer), and at the lowest level we encounter those who demonstrate only the passive ability to enjoy music (listeners).

Traditionally, men have always dominated the apex of this hierarchy. Leading composers and conductors, in particular, have been branded with the mark of 'genius', a status almost unattainable by women. The possessor of musical genius is commonly presented as genetically gifted, temperamental, emotionally turbulent and capable of unbelievable feats of intellect, memory, virtuosity and musical proficiency. This grand status is far removed indeed from the historical female musical role of instrumental recreator and amateur entertainer. Since musical genius is perceived to be born, not taught, the value of music education in creating such exceptional individuals can but be viewed as limited. Just as music has suffered from low status and academic under-valuation in the general education of males, so, as we have seen, it has remained uncontested as a 'feminine' educational pursuit. Accordingly, the (at first sight) contradictory low status of music as an educational subject has not really affected its high standing in the professional and cultural arenas, since the two levels are seen to have little in common. Culturally, the traditional gendered music stereotypes are enormously powerful. For women to cross these established boundaries would seem to require a change in society's fundamental beliefs about the value of male and female products, functions and cultural contributions.

The nine composers in the study illustrate the point that few composers are employed exclusively, or even mainly, in composition. Yet, ironically, the status and success of any composer relies heavily on his or her reputation as an apparently full-time professional. Professionalism implies not only competence, respect, status and prestige: it also implies commitment to, and focus on, the work of being a composer to the near-exclusion of everything else. Where other work is undertaken, this is directly supportive of the main effort:

> [. . .] the Western composer has usually been involved in other musical activities as well, be they teaching, conducting, performing, or writing. One could argue that these often constitute the principal professional pursuit [. . .][108]

Indeed, it is often with the help of these other types of work that composers gain opportunities, reputation and fame. It is interesting to note that only three women in the study (Gipps, Williams, Bailey) have, or have had, what can be described as full-time professional music careers on the 'male' pattern. A large proportion of the work of the others involved teaching in various capacities; even then, conducting work was virtually confined to amateur music-making. Coleridge-Taylor took sporadic part-time music employment; three composers (Kirkwood, Maconchy, Luff) took no form of paid employment; and two (Keal, Jagger) have taken non-musical employment.

Full-time commitment to one occupation, let alone two or more, is often difficult enough for most women, considering their domestic and child-rearing responsibilities. All the issues outlined in Chapter 3 have a negative effect on women's ability to take on full-time professional employment. The traditional career pattern set up by males is particularly difficult for females to follow; at the very time when it is vital to become firmly established in the profession (early twenties to early thirties) most women have their children. Moreover, in addition to the distinct social inequalities in the domestic division of labour, other factors emerge to work against women musicians.

For most of the century, there seems to have been an obvious difference in both the type of music education given to females and the social value placed on it. Well into this century, it is clear that although many women studied music, their training was not on a par with that of men. But the large numbers of females in music education created the illusion of equality. Their limited tuition in the intellectual aspects of music was founded on the premise that women could not benefit from such training because they lacked originality and were not fully capable of comprehending complex ideas. A vicious circle was thus set up in which the results of women's inferior training served as a theoretical justification for its perpetuation. In continental Europe, too, these attitudes were reflected in educational practice. The famous music conservatoires in Paris and Munich allowed women some access, but many women students encountered a great deal of prejudice if they attended anything other than instrumental lessons. The American composer Mabel

Daniels (1878–1971) attended the Munich Conservatory in 1902. Her letters home reveal many of the discriminatory attitudes of the time:

> You know that five years ago women were not allowed to study counterpoint at the conservatory. In fact, anything more advanced than elementary harmony was debarred. The ability of the feminine intellect to comprehend the intricacies of a stretto, or cope with double counterpoint in the tenth, if not openly denied, was severely questioned. The counterpoint class is now open to women, although, as yet comparatively few avail themselves of the opportunity.[109]

Indeed, Mabel Daniels was the first woman to attend a counterpoint class at the conservatory.

In Britain similar attitudes were apparent. Many commentators lamented a fall in music education standards in the early part of this century, as more and more women flocked to the national music colleges. For example, the Royal College of Music offered numerous instrumental scholarships – which were won mainly by women. The success of women in winning scholarships over the heads of men was put down to lack of male availability to compete:

> An 'epidemic' of scholarships had resulted in the profession's overcrowding, and increasing domination by women, because men are 'obliged to take to professions which pay or promise a career, and to shun those which do not'. English musical institutions were becoming ladies' schools, the men 'confined to departments for which there is a market and a demand, the orchestra and the organ loft'.[110]

The perverse implication here is that women were 'freer' to pursue music study since they had no real need to earn a living from it and thereby prove the seriousness of their commitment, whereas the poor male students were obliged to find professional employment in music and therefore had to limit themselves to education which would be of practical advantage in career terms.

Others lamented the huge number of female music students who seemingly had no prospects:

> The *Gazzetta Musicale di Milano* had referred to 2,000 female students at the Guildhall School of Music [. . .] as 'poor young girls' without prospects. Only a small proportion of them, retaliated *Musical News*, expected to become professionals, as was the case for most English Colleges, except for the 'two great schools' [. . .] Many of the women would marry and give up work, their culture, 'if not carried beyond prudential bounds', benefiting future generations.[111]

Again, the overriding attitude is that professional prospects were of little significance to women. Blatantly, the vast majority of female music students were not taken to be serious contenders in the professional world, an assumption confirmed by many composers in the study group. Despite the group's general belief that there was no *direct* discrimination against women at the music colleges, more than one qualified this, stating that women were assumed to be less able. Significantly, the composers in the study group did not regard themselves as fundamentally similar to the general mass of female students: instead, they either identified with the male students or eschewed any group identification. On leaving music education, most of the composers soon became aware of the underlying prejudice towards their work and career aspirations.

Since females are regarded in many ways as inferior to males, they are less valued socially. The practical consequence of women's position is that anything in which they dominate is automatically devalued in the eyes of society. This has occurred in a number of occupations, as women have increasingly become part of the workforce.[112] The social devaluation of music education could be seen as in part due to female domination at the lower levels. Music has always been an essential part of female socialization and training; accordingly, it has held little value in male academic circles. The depreciation of music's relevance to education because of women's traditional involvement in it stands in contrast to the wide social appreciation of the male 'intellectuals' who dominate the music profession (composers, conductors, critics and professors). The fact that women have been given music education has acted as a foundation of proof that, even with assistance and opportunities, women simply do not became 'great' composers and musicians.

Against a tradition which portrays women as amateur musicians of average ability, it is unsurprising to find a general lack of self-confidence in female music students. In a recent survey on the attitudes and expectations of A level music students the traditional areas thought unsuited to female students are highly visible as the ones in which girls feel least confident:

> Girls are [. . .] less confident than boys about the harmony part of the course, as well as aural training, and, perhaps as a result not so sure that other people perceive them as musicians.[113]

It seems that the traditional notion that girls have less ability for the intellectual and theoretical elements of music leads them to underestimate themselves and thereby undermines the development of their potential and self-perception as professional musicians. A further repercussion of this lack of confidence can be observed in terms of generally lower examination results, despite female domination in student numbers. That female students in the past did less well than male students is clear, but this is far from proving any lack of ability. The changing face of music examination results over the past 30 years reveals a gradual fulfilling of female potential, which was obviously suppressed in earlier times.

For example, in 1968 females made up 36 per cent of university music students. Yet females predominated in the school examinations which led to university entrance. Females made up 65 per cent of music O level candidates and 63 per cent of music A level candidates. But closer analysis of the examination results shows a clear difference in grades awarded to the two sexes in these examinations. For example, at A level 8 per cent of females gained an A grade, compared with 16 per cent of males.[114] Eleven years later, in 1979, females still made up 64 per cent of students taking the O level music examination. At A level females made up 61 per cent of music examinees; yet the results again reveal that male students were still obtaining generally better grades, with 7 per cent of females and 12 per cent of males receiving A grades. For the S level music examination of the same year, the results show an even greater disparity, only 25 per cent of candidates being female. While 49 per cent of male examinees received distinctions at S level, only 23 per cent of females entrants did so.

When one compares these figures with the most recent ones (1993) for GCSE and A level music examinations, one notes that some interesting changes have occurred. In 1993 the number of females sitting GCSE music had fallen slightly to 58 per cent. At A level it has remained at 64 per cent. Yet the proportion of female students receiving the top grades at both levels has increased substantially. In the O level Music examination of 1979, 10 per cent of females and 11 per cent of males gained an A grade but by 1993 21 per cent of females and 16 per cent of males gained A grades. At A level the number of males gaining an A grade has remained steady at 11 per cent in 1993 compared to 12 per cent in 1979, yet females have improved from 7 per cent A grades in 1979 to 12 per cent in 1993.

Undergraduate music degree results for 1979 reflect the same trend. Even though female music undergraduates accounted for 48 per cent of music undergraduates, only 3 per cent of women compared with 6 per cent of men gained First Class degrees. In 1979, at postgraduate level, the trend is even more marked, with women accounting for only 16 per cent of postgraduates (significantly, no females received a Ph.D. that year).[115] In the latest available figures (1992–1993) females make up 58 per cent of the undergraduate music students, a figure which has remained unchanged since 1984, while women make up 47 per cent of the total number of undergraduate students in all subjects.[116] The number of female postgraduate music students has been increasing steadily since the 1960s. For example, in 1967–1968, females made up 11 per cent of postgraduate music students, this figure rising to 20 per cent in 1977, with a significant 8 per cent increase in female postgraduate students between 1989 and 1990. Yet as recently as 1992–1993 only 37 per cent of postgraduate music students are female – a figure which has remained static since 1990.

The analysis of the range of music examination results shows that while women have long predominated numerically in the secondary-level music examinations, they began to dominate music higher education only in the early 1980s. This is not, however, the case at the two leading higher-education music colleges. Traditionally, females have dominated at the Royal Academy of Music and the Royal College of Music. For example, at the Royal Academy of Music in 1945 females made up 73 per cent of the total number of students – a figure which has been falling steadily, with the most recent figure, that for 1994, standing at around 50 per cent.[117] In comparison, the Royal College of Music figures from 1990 to 1995 reveal that females make up around 58–60 per cent of the total number of students.[118] This consistent majority of promising female musicians is overturned completely in subsequent professional life.

Females are now excelling in secondary-level examinations and have drawn level in university examinations, in terms of receiving an equal percentage of the top grades. This improvement suggests in itself that women were being disadvantaged in a number of ways in the past. These inequalities appear to have been rectified as awareness of the discrimination against women in education has become more widespread. The gains in music education for females have taken many years to achieve, and it remains the case that women are a minority at research degree level.

To suggest that simply because females are now obtaining better results in music examinations, the male domination of the profession will wither away is rather optimistic. This academic success has not substantially altered the numbers of women who attain the middle or top ranks of the music profession. Moreover, the underlying attitudes to female musical ability remain unchanged:

> [. . .] *despite appearances* and indeed despite public examination results, which suggest that girls have a high level of musical autonomy and success in schools, girls in fact fulfil musical roles which are ultimately circumscribed by deeper historical definitions of femininity as musically inferior.[119]

That both teachers and students perceive male and female music students differently is clear. The stereotyped gendered personality traits are superimposed on many aspects of the education process, including styles of and approaches to work, willingness to learn, general interests and classroom behaviour. It is clear from the most recent research that male and female school students are perceived and treated as quite different by music teachers. Primarily, they view girls as more passive and recreative, amenable to hard work, displaying high levels of concentration and producing neat and well-presented work, whereas boys are viewed as more active and creative in their approach to work and more affected by negative peer pressure, more interested in technology and popular music:

> [. . .] given that they [the boys] are seen to be more imaginative, creative, and active, many teachers perceive boys, not the more hard-working and persevering girls whose success and enthusiasm are everywhere so evident, but boys to be ultimately or naturally more musically successful, or at least equal.[120]

Obviously, in the crucial formative years of schooling children develop strong ideas about the gender appropriateness of certain work styles and activities, no doubt internalizing the subconscious message about perceived gender differences in musical ability and success. These differences are then reinforced by a society and culture which are still in many ways the product of the male imagination.

It is clear that the massive gains made in women's education by their mass entry into higher education during the 1980s and 1990s have enabled a whole generation of women to be educated to a much higher standard and correspondingly to have a much better chance of fulfilling their potential. But on the whole, women's increased achievements in education have not been matched by increased numbers of women in high-paid, high-status employment in many areas:

> Gender inequalities in educational achievement had been almost entirely eliminated by 1990, with females performing as well as or better than males until aged 18 + . Inequality becomes very apparent, however, on entry into the labour market.[121]

This is also the case in musical professions. Obviously, the reasons why so few female music students progress into professional life are numerous and complex, but the traditional stereotyped ideas of women's musical aptitude and customary participation have left an enormous legacy. Lucy Green sums up the problem as follows:

> [. . .] although on the face of it girls do better than boys at music in schools, there is a hidden agenda existing at the interstices of pupils' behaviour and teachers' perceptions, which partly explains and partly perpetuates the exclusion of women as a large group from the highest ranks of the musical world.[122]

That girls are now consistently achieving better results than boys across a wide range of examinations is clear from the recent results.[123] There seems to be hard evidence that the gains made by females across all areas of education are branding scholarly success as 'feminine', with the result that boys have become disillusioned and uncooperative, undermining the education system generally because of society's consistent undervaluation of women's ability, intellect and potential. Recent media speculation that boys are now suffering from the 'excessive' concentration on improving female education could give rise to a backlash against women, which might halt the long-delayed gains made in their education. Moreover, although many people felt that women's equal education would naturally ensure their fulfilment and place in professional and cultural life, there seems little evidence that women are making the transition to the highest levels. Even though women have now proved their equality in the education system, the professional and social system remains stacked against them beyond a certain level because of its patriarchal structures and traditions. While women remain devalued and discounted by society at large, they will never achieve their potential as equal contributors to the cultural world.

Notes

1 Edith Brower, 'Is the Musical Idea Masculine?', *Atlantic Monthly*, (March 1894), 333.
2 Wilson, *The Great Sex Divide*, 99.
3 Jean-Jacques Rousseau, *Emile*, translated by Barbara Foxley (London, 1984), 328.
4 It must be stressed that in Britain a child's social class has always to a large extent dictated the quality of education, regardless of gender. As with many of the contemporary social reforms, many of the early educational reforms benefited mainly the middle and upper classes.
5 Carol Dyhouse, *Girls growing up in Late Victorian and Edwardian England* (London, 1981), 175.
6 Ann Mountfield, *Women and Education* (Hove, 1990), 34.

7 Anderson and Zinsser, *A History of Their Own*, 2, 185–186.
8 Felicity Hunt, 'Divided Aims: The Education Implication of Opposing Ideologies in Girls' Secondary Schooling 1850–1940', in Felicity Hunt (ed.), *Lessons For Life: The Schooling of Girls and Women 1850–1950* (Oxford, 1987), 16.
9 Board of Education, *Report of the Consultative Committee on the Differentiation of Curriculum for Boys and Girls Respectively in Secondary Schools* (HMSO, 1923), cited in Lewis, *Women in England 1870–1950*, 101.
10 François Fénelon, *Fénelon on Education*, translated by H.C. Barnard (Cambridge, 1966), 6, cited in Anderson and Zinsser, *A History of Their Own*, 2, 337.
11 J.M. Campbell, 'The Effect of Adolescence on the Brain of the Girl', a paper presented to the AUWT meeting in London, 23 May 1908, 5–6, cited in Dyhouse, *Girls Growing Up in Late Victorian and Edwardian England*, 134.
12 Dyhouse, *Girls Growing Up in Late Victorian and Edwardian England*, 134 and 135.
13 A good example of the type of education offered is shown in a typical school advertisement in a 1711 issue of the *Spectator*, cited in Mary Cathcart Borer, *Willingly to School: A History of Women's Education* (Guildford, 1976), 184.
14 Flora Fraser, *The English Gentlewoman* (London, 1987), 35.
15 Mary Wollstonecraft, *Thoughts on the Education of Daughters* (originally published London, 1787), cited in Janet Todd and Marilyn Butler (eds), *The Works of Mary Wollstonecraft*, 4 (London, 1989), 12–13.
16 Cathcart Borer, *Willingly to School: A History of Women's Education*, 163.
17 Coleridge-Taylor, *The Heritage of Samuel Coleridge-Taylor*, 104.
18 *Ibid.*, 106.
19 Cyril Ehrlich, *The Music Profession in Britain Since the Eighteenth Century* (Oxford, 1985), 114–115.
20 *Ibid.*, 118.
21 In the Coleridge-Taylor book the sleeve notes suggest that the scholarship she received from Trinity College of Music was for the study of piano and composition, yet there is no mention of any composition lessons nor of a composition tutor, so it seems more likely that she took only practical lessons.
22 Harold Rutland, *Trinity College of Music: The First Hundred Years* (London: 1972), 14–15.
23 *Musical Times* (1 January 1881), 8.
24 Coleridge-Taylor, *The Heritage of Samuel Coleridge-Taylor*, 111.
25 Mountfield, *Women and Education*, 34.
26 Coleridge-Taylor, *The Heritage of Samuel Coleridge-Taylor*, 119.
27 *Ibid.*, 119.
28 Boyd, *Grace Williams*, 11.
29 Hunt, 'Divided Aims: the Education Implication of Opposing Ideologies in Girls Schools 1850–1940', 19.
30 *Board of Education Annual Report 1929*, 13 (1929), 37.
31 Gordon Cox, *The History of Music Education* (Aldershot, 1993), 172.
32 D. Emrys Evans, *The University of Wales: A Historical Sketch* (Cardiff, 1953), 22.
33 *Ibid.*, 52.
34 Boyd, *Grace Williams*, 12–13.
35 *Ibid.*, 18.
36 *Ibid.*, 36.
37 *Ibid.*, 36–37.
38 Tuttle, *Heroines*, 97.
39 Cole, *The 80th Birthday of Elizabeth Maconchy*, 3.
40 H.C. Colles, *The Royal College of Music 1883–1933* (London, 1933).

41 *Ibid.*, 26.
42 *Ibid.*, 34.
43 *Ibid.*, 51.
44 Ehrlich, *The Music Profession in Britain Since the Eighteenth Century*, 112.
45 Tuttle, *Heroines*, 98.
46 Elizabeth Maconchy, quoted by Robert Maycock, 'Inheriting the Land', *The Listener*, 12 March, 1987, 30.
47 Elizabeth Maconchy, 'A Composer Speaks', *Composer*, 42 (1971–1972), 24.
48 Elizabeth Maconchy, *loc. cit.*
49 Dyhouse, *Girls growing up in Late Victorian and Early Edwardian England*, 146.
50 Anderson and Zinsser, *A History of their Own*, 2, 497.
51 Eugene Murray Gates, 'The Woman Composer Question: Four Case Studies From the Romantic Era' (D.Ed. thesis, University of Toronto), 34–35.
52 Josephine Kamm, *Hope Deferred: Girls' Education in English History* (London, 1965) , 265.
53 Gail Braybon and Penny Summerfield, *Out of the Cage* (London, 1987), 138.
54 Keal, 'Memories of the Royal Academy', 2.
55 Keal, *loc. cit.*
56 Keal interview transcript, 3.
57 Keal, 'Memories of the Royal Academy', 8.
58 Keal, interview transcript, 4.
59 *Ibid.*, 5.
60 *Ibid.*, 8.
61 Braybon and Summerfield, *Out of the Cage*, 138.
62 Ruth Gipps, 'Autobiography: Before Conducting' (unpublished typescript), 23–25.
63 *The Times*, 24 August 1942.
64 Ehrlich, *The Music Profession in Britain Since the Eighteenth Century*, 158.
65 *Ibid.*, 188.
66 Gipps, 'Autobiography: Before Conducting', 213.
67 Gipps, 'Memoirs 1942–1989', 3.
68 Halstead, 'A Study of Dr Ruth Gipps', 33.
69 Gipps, 'Memoirs 1942–1989', 3.
70 Ruth Gipps, interviewed by the author on 30 August 1990. (Taped conversation.)
71 Antoinette Kirkwood, written response to a questionnaire, dated 10 March 1994, 1–2.
72 Kirkwood, transcript of taped oral questionnaire response, 5 November 1993, 2.
73 Kirkwood, written response to questionnaire of 10 March 1994, 3.
74 Kirkwood, transcript of taped oral questionnaire response, 5 November 1993, 3.
75 Kirkwood, written response to questionnaire of 10 March 1994, 3.
76 *Ibid.*, 2.
77 Kirkwood, written response to questionnaire of 10 March 1994. *loc. cit.*
78 Luff interview transcript, 1.
79 Enid Luff, interviewed by Toni Calam, *Contemporary Music Review*, 11 (1994), 194.
80 *Education Statistics 1968* (HMSO, 1968), 8.
81 Roy Lowe, *Education in the Post-War Years: A Social History* (London, 1988), 93–94.
82 Luff interview transcript, 17.
83 Luff, *Contemporary Music Review*, 195.

84 *Ibid.*, 21.
85 *Ibid.*, 4.
86 *Ibid.*, 7.
87 *Ibid.*, 16.
88 Apart from occasional piano teaching and work as an accompanist for dance classes.
89 Cathcart Borer, *Willingly to School*, 305.
90 Bailey interview transcript, 10–11.
91 Mountfield, *Women in Education*, 40–41.
92 Long, *Music in English Education*, 150.
93 *Ibid.*, 118–120.
94 Correspondence between Judith Bailey and the author. Letter dated 16 November 1992.
95 Bailey, *loc. cit.*
96 Bailey, *loc. cit.*
97 Bailey interview transcript, 35.
98 Bryony Jagger, written response to a questionnaire dated 16 July 1994, 1.
99 *Ibid.*, 1 and 3.
100 *Ibid.*, 1.
101 *Ibid.*, 3.
102 Correspondence between Bryony Jagger and the author. Letter received 8 August 1994.
103 Mooney, 'Between the Pit and the Pendulum', *Sunday Times*, 5 November 1989.
104 *Trade Union Congress Annual Report*, (London, 1992).
105 *Trade Union Congress Annual Report*, (London, 1926).
106 Ehrlich, *The Music Profession in Britain Since the Eighteenth Century*, 235.
107 The orchestras involved in this survey were the London Symphony Orchestra (17% female) , the London Philharmonic Orchestra (25% female), the City of Birmingham Symphony Orchestra (35% female) and the BBC Philharmonic Orchestra (29% female).
108 Citron, *Gender and the Musical Canon*, 82.
109 A letter from Mabel Daniels to a friend, dated 4 October 1902. Cited in Neuls-Bates (ed.), *Women in Music*, 220–221.
110 Ehrlich, *The Music Profession In Britain Since the Eighteenth Century*, 112.
111 *Ibid.*, 125.
112 For example, in the 1920s and 1930s the occupation of bank teller was a reasonably high paid employment; however, as it has become increasing female-dominated, it has become relatively less well paid and respected. Another striking example of this phenomenon is that of doctors in the former Soviet Union. Unlike in the West, the medical profession in the Soviet Union was staffed mainly by women, who were accordingly renumerated on the same level as schoolteachers. For full discussion see Dorothy McBride Kipnis, 'Intelligence, Occupation Status, and Achievement Orientation', in Archer and Lloyd (ed.), *Exploring Sex Differences*, 95–122.
113 Sarah Maidlow, 'Attitudes and Expectations of A Level Musicians', *British Journal of Music Education*, 10 (1993), 209.
114 *Education Statistics 1968*.
115 *Education Statistics 1979*.
116 University Statistics 1992–1993 (HMSO, 1993), 7.
117 Students numbers supplied to the author by the Royal Academy of Music. Letter dated 13 March 1995.
118 Student numbers supplied to the author by the Royal College of Music. Letter dated 18 November 1994.

119 Lucy Green, 'Music, Gender and Education', *British Journal of Music Education*, 10 (1993), 250.
120 *Ibid.*, 249.
121 Abercrombie and Warde, *Contemporary British Society*, 374.
122 Green, 'Music, Gender and Education', 222.
123 Linda Grant, 'First Among Equals', *The Guardian*, 22 October 1994, 37–46.

Part Three:

The Gendered Politics of Music

5 Establishment and Anti-establishment Attitudes

The three chapters which form the final part of this book concentrate on the range of issues which surround music written by women and its place in the musical tradition. The influence of political stances or discriminatory motivations on the judgement and evaluation of musical composition is a new and controversial area of music research. The very idea is strongly disputed by many, since it has long been believed that music is an abstract medium which transcends cultural or social issues. Many commentators are adamant that no factors other than qualitative or directly musical ones can affect the standing or success of a piece of music, or of a composer. However, the creation and dissemination of music cannot be undertaken by an individual in isolation: they are brought about only by the cooperation and contribution of a wide variety of individuals and institutions which operate within accepted social parameters. For example, music is heard through the efforts not merely of the composer but also of performers, teachers, publishers, critics, academics, concert managers, government bodies, music festivals, radio producers, the general public, symphony orchestras and administrators. By moving beyond the myth of the great artist working alone and by acknowledging the role of socially constructed systems both in present-day musical life and throughout musical history, we come to appreciate the importance and influence of our social system. Since our artistic and cultural set-up is patriarchal, its relationship and attitude to women must be acknowledged and any bias or hidden political agenda revealed.

In this chapter I intend to discuss the attitudes towards, and beliefs about, women composers and their work, as evidenced in the writings of musicologists, music critics and the media. Examination of the canon of music literature quickly confirms the subjective attitude of the male-dominated musical establishment. Their patronizing and discriminatory beliefs have played a major part in reinforcing women's inferior and peripheral position in music and in the wider culture. In the second part of the chapter I will examine what effect these traditional views have had on the study group of women composers, their work, their sense of identity and their self-esteem.

As in most areas of musical life, the business of writing about and analysing music has been controlled by men. Yet the idea that this may affect the evaluation of women's work has always been masked by the emphasis placed by musicologists on the abstract nature of music. Musicologists have set themselves above (or apart from) debates about cultural context and meaning. They have claimed the same immunity that has often been granted to music itself: musicologists, as it were, are pure, untainted by human vices and prejudices. However, one traditional function of the musical establishment, with its ecclesiastical and aristocratic connections, has been to uphold and shape cultural elitism

> Musicology has the reputation of being an extremely conservative discipline [. . .] There are obvious connections between its patriarchal structure and the politically stabilising function that 'high' music had for centuries. Music, more than other arts, has formed an alliance with the interests of the state and has been a disciplinary force.[1]

In the secular world of the twentieth century the 'classical' music tradition has served to reinforce the cultural hegemony of the white, middle-class male.

It is unsurprising that this culturally dominant group did not (and in some cases still does not) view the absence of contributions from individuals different from themselves by gender as problematic or unjust. Women's absence from musicological discussion has been justified by the argument and assumption either that their numbers are too insignificant for registration or that their music simply does not merit analysis or commentary. Women composers are viewed as isolated individuals who have contributed little to the overall evolution of music, making their music a 'minority' interest outside the mainstream. But in the light of our patriarchal culture and the value placed on art music as the ever-present proof of male superiority, the exclusion of women could be seen as part of a larger political gesture.

As the discipline of musicology has developed over the twentieth century, its general stance has adapted to the increasing awareness of female liberation. Consequently, three different approaches have been taken to women composers and their work. First, they have been completely ignored by some writers, thus rendering them 'invisible'. Second, many writers who do cite women composers then define them only in terms of how much they reveal or camouflage their 'femininity', this quality itself being a sign of inferiority. In such instances, women composers are usually measured on a scale using sex, temperament and nature as the essential reference points to 'understanding' their work. Third, women composers have most recently been marginalized as a minority 'interest group' producing generally inferior works. In the following discussion the persistence with which these criteria are used reveals a pattern of consistent opposition to women composers' inclusion in the mainstream.

The most obvious way of suppressing awareness and encouragement of female creativity is by denying its existence. Although it is now clear that women have participated in music as composers throughout history and across cultures, the term 'composer' has usually been understood to denote a male creator. Only with the gradual recognition of women's rights in the twentieth century has the buried history of their participation in and contribution to musical composition gradually begun to be acknowledged. Since music literature acts as a window on past musical tastes, trends and valuation, women's invisibility becomes all the more significant. At the turn of the century very little had been written about women composers or their work; their contribution to music on a number of levels had been ignored by virtually all the major musicological texts. This reinforced the belief in women's inability to compose music, thereby discouraging many potential women musicians.

In music literature, the attitudes and opinions expressed play a huge role in the recognition and acceptance of a composer. Women composers' continued low standing in the minds of many people stems, in part, from the fact that most standard music histories make little or no reference to women composers. Their absence leaves an impression that the entire evolution of Western music has been undertaken without women's involvement and could no doubt continue that way. Since musicology is influential on a number of levels, not only helping to preserve a musical work or composer for posterity but also generating interest, criticism, analysis and discussion, inclusion in the discourse of musicology is in itself a mark of recognition and participation. Women's inclusion in music literature is vital for their validation and acceptance into musical life.

Many of the most widely available and widely read music history texts written in English over the last 30 years make absolutely no reference to women composers. Some examples: Alec Harman and Wilfred Mellers, *Man and His Music* (1962); Donald J. Grout, *The History of Western Music* (fourth edition, 1988); John Russell, *A Short History of Music* (tenth edition, 1981); David D. Boyden, *Introduction to Music* (second edition, 1971); William Lovelock, *A Concise History of Music* (1981 edition). It has been asserted that women's absence from this type of music history book is simply an accurate reflection of the rarity of female composers before the twentieth century: yet they do not mention women composers in their analysis of recent music either.

Indeed, it is disturbing that little of the most recently published material reflects the increased numbers of women composers working in this century. In mainstream musicology it is still difficult to see discussion of any of the work being done by women, so perpetuating the invisibility of women's contribution. For example, Paul Griffiths' *Modern Music: the Avant-Garde since 1945* (1981), cites no women composers. In the same author's *Concise History of Modern Music: Debussy to Boulez* (1978, reprinted 1992) there is merely a very brief reference to Ruth Crawford-Seeger. The 1991 edition of the *Kobbé Complete Opera Book* even omits a previous reference to Dame Ethel Smyth. Arnold Whittall's *Music Since the First World War* (1977) mentions no women composers; neither does Michael Nyman's *Experimental Music* (1977). A recent survey of music appreciation textbooks shows a similar pattern.[2]

As the end of the present century draws near, there have been a number of publications charting the major musical contributions and developments during this most turbulent century. In this selection of material women composers are slightly more visible. *A Twentieth Century Composer Speaks: An Index of Interviews*, edited by Mari Nismura (1993), contains references to 34 women composers out of a total of 1000 (4 per cent). *Twentieth Century Music*, by Elliott Antokoletz (1992), mentions more than 300 male composers and only five female composers – approximately 1.6 per cent of the total number of composers.

Twentieth Century Music: A History of Musical Styles in Modern Europe and America, by Robert P. Morgan (1991), cites eight female composers. This may seem very encouraging; however, only three of these composers are dealt with within the main text, the rest being summarized in the following way:

> An important development, closely tied to the pluralistic character of recent music, is the growing number of composers from more diverse backgrounds [. . .] the enfranchisement of various ethnic and other minority [*sic*] groups forms a major issue of our day [. . .] Many gifted women are [. . .] contributing significantly to the contemporary musical scene. Along with the others already named [Anderson, Oliveros, Monk], the Americans Ellen Taaffe Zwilich (b. 1939) and Joan Tower (b. 1938), the Scot Thea Musgrave (b. 1928), the Frenchwoman Betsy Jolas (b. 1926) and the Russian Sofia Gubaidulina (b. 1931) might be mentioned as representative of a group that, at least in the younger generation, approaches parity in size and importance with its male counterpart.[3]

The language used is most encouraging as it suggests that women composers are finally receiving equality: for example, 'an important development' and 'a major issue of our day'. Yet if Morgan really believes that the talented group of female composers 'approaches parity in size and importance with its male counterpart', why does he accord them so small a place in his discussion? Since the discussion of male composers otherwise takes up the entire book, this single paragraph covering women composers certainly does not approach parity with the male group. Despite its ostensibly good intentions, this book is in danger of assigning women composers' contribution in the twentieth century to a mere footnote. After all, actions speak louder than words. To devote not much less than 50 per cent of the discussion of the younger generation to female composers would be a more eloquent and sincere statement than such a throwaway paragraph!

Sadly, all these books make exceedingly scant reference to the work of women composers who have emerged this century. As more women composers have been working in the twentieth century than at any previous time (in both absolute and relative terms), the small regard for their contribution, or even for their appearance in larger numbers, would not seem to bode well for the future. When subsequent generations turn to musicology to learn what was contributed, developed and valued in twentieth-century musical life, women composers will be seen almost as insignificant as they were in the seventeenth and eighteenth centuries.

Often where musicologists *do* include female composers and their music a common language of descriptions and criticisms can be identified. Sexual aesthetics were (and still are) commonly used to judge the work of women, most critics obviously feeling that music composed by women can only confirm or *try* to deny 'femininity'. If a woman composer writes delicate, refined, melodic music in a small form, this immediately 'confirms' beliefs about her feminine temperament of which such musical expression and content is an extension. However, if a woman composes music that is dramatic, large-scale and intellectual in character, this only 'proves' that she was adopting a masculine style in order to step beyond the limitations of her sex. Either way, the composer reinforces her 'natural' position as inferior. Moreover, the music could be judged and discussed in terms different from male composers' work, so denying it entry into the normal discourse of musicological debate. The socially-imposed 'masculine' and 'feminine' personality characteristics (discussed at length in Chapter 2) are utilized as a method of controlling behaviour often exhibited in reality by both sexes. So-called feminine characteristics are largely negative, passive and inferior, and so, by extension, is the product of the woman composer. The product of female creativity is safely restricted to symbolization of black and white sex-determined temperaments. This idea, in its most overt form, was widespread amongst critics and composers, as this statement by the French composer Camille Saint-Saëns (1835–1921) illustrates:

> Women are curious when they dabble seriously with art. They seem preoccupied above all else with making you forget that they are women and displaying an excessive virility, without realizing that it is precisely that preoccupation which betrays the female.[4]

The musical establishment simply reflected society's wider attitudes when it incorporated this destructive dichotomy and presented women composers with a scale of reference within which they could not win – that is, by being successful or mainstream. This situation has been termed the double bind of sexual aesthetics, through which women cannot be judged fairly.[5]

Encouragingly, Peter J. Pirie's *The English Musical Renaissance* (1979) names Ethel Smyth, Elizabeth Lutyens, Thea Musgrave, Elizabeth Maconchy and Priaulx Rainier (1903–1986). Yet Pirie muses:

> Why women should not be great composers is one of the mysteries, but, although in the latter half of the twentieth century there are many women composers none of them is in the front rank.[6]

So the inclusion of the women composers is qualified by a statement proclaiming the inferior status (in practice and, by implication, also in theory) of women's music. This is an important aspect of musicology's confirmation of beliefs: women may be composers, but they are not 'great' composers, and therefore pose no threat to the established order, Pirie goes on to state:

> Elizabeth Maconchy had won a prize for a string quartet in the 1930s [. . .] Her style is somewhat crabbed; like many women composers she seems to be trying to outdo the men in stern and dry music.[7]

It is not coincidental that the criticism of Maconchy's style is that it is 'crabbed' (meaning difficult to understand, complicated). Maconchy ventured into genres considered 'serious' and 'masculine' by writing a number of string quartets, concertos and symphonies. Pirie views Maconchy's reason for attempting such large-scale, intellectual compositional expression as inspired by hostility: she is a woman composer who writes complex music only in an attempt to 'outdo' men! Pirie reflects the threat to established thinking which women composers pose.

Women composers who stick to what is accepted as feminine music – uncomplicated, lyrical, melodic, undemanding and written on a small scale - are disparaged for being able to portray only their essential nature, whereas women who venture to write in masculine genres risk being condemned as unnatural, since they attempt to express emotions which are unfitting or unladylike: they attempt to compete with men. The underlying sentiment is that women composers cannot simply 'join' the musical tradition which was created by men. In every way women are castigated: they are outsiders in relation to the musical tradition, which they cannot significantly contribute to or develop in their own right, at best only copying music already created by males. Time after time, this criticism is levelled against women composers. Often, it takes the ostensible form not of criticism but of a compliment. For example, in his book *Grace Williams* (1980) Malcolm Boyd states:

> The fact that no-one surveying the whole range and character of her music would be able to tell, without prior knowledge, that it was the work of a woman rather than a man is in part a measure of her success [. . .][8]

Once again, a woman composer is judged effective only when she writes music which sounds ordinarily male. Grace Williams would have failed had she betrayed her identity as a female. It also betrays the contempt with which the female musical contribution of the past is regarded.

In Michael Trend's *The Music Makers: Heirs and Rebels of the English Musical Renaissance* (1985), the only woman composer mentioned is Ethel Smyth. Her contribution to British music is summarized:

> She is now best remembered for her autobiographical writings and for her association with the Bloomsbury group [. . .] It is as a character and a celebrated sapphist that she is likely to continue to be best known [. . .] for her music – the chief interest of her life – has gone into almost total eclipse, and there are no grounds for believing that this position will or should be reversed.[9]

The notion that women composers are unusual and eccentric 'characters' is another way of belittling their contribution. Ethel Smyth and Elisabeth Lutyens seem to suffer most from this charge. Ethel Smyth was outspoken in her views on sexual discrimination. Her homosexuality and 'masculine' style of dress were the main focus for comments on her outrageous personality. Elisabeth Lutyens could also be completely outspoken, sometimes being aggressive and very fond of using bad language, all of which habits were (and are) totally unacceptable in a woman. Lutyens had a very difficult domestic life, and in later years her attitude was coloured by bitterness over her lack of recognition as a composer. These two tremendously talented women had to fight hard against prejudice and discrimination: they were pioneers. It seems unsurprising that they succeeded in withstanding the tremendous difficulties which faced them only because they both had determined personalities: they were unwilling to let other people's views of what they should or should not be affect them. But some writers observe:

> The general picture of the woman composer that emerges from these two lives, [Smyth and Lutyens], probably the most well-known women composers of their day, is not encouraging [. . .] Elizabeth Maconchy [. . .] would seem a more positive source of inspiration than most, because she has successfully combined composition with more ordinary living.[10]

This statement could be construed as reactionary. It is unclear what is implied by 'ordinary living', although it is clear that neither Smyth nor Lutyens conformed to traditional stereotypes – Smyth was a lesbian and Lutyens was divorced and often abrasive about her children. The fact that they both refused to conform to a traditional mother/wife role is, however, far from 'not encouraging' and was probably part of the reason they were able to succeed as much as they did. Surely these women can act as a great inspiration to many, and their 'unconventional' lives should in no way limit the respect and admiration due to them. Would we penalize Wagner or Satie similarly?

The notion that previous women composers have been odd or figures of fun, serves only to demean their work and damage their potential as role models for other women. This portrayal of them as eccentrics has been absorbed by some younger composers. For example, Rhian Samuel (b. 1944) states:

> I have always been aware of women composers [. . .] Not that they were considered normal; they were considered absolute freaks, but they did exist.[11]

It is quite obvious that often women composers were devalued and humiliated for not being 'normal' women in that they pushed against accepted norms and refused to become submerged in domesticity.

Another destructive way of writing about women is, ironically, to make an obvious overestimation of their work. In the introduction to the 1991 edition of David Ewen's *The World of Twentieth Century Music*, written by Stephen Pettitt, it was stated that:

> Two women composers have been pre-eminent in the British scene.[12]

The two composers in question, Elizabeth Maconchy and Thea Musgrave, then received only a six-line description of their styles, compared with the half- to full-page discussion of male British composers. Pettitt's estimation of these women composers as 'pre-eminent' is not corroborated by any suitable analysis or discussion in the text. Why do they receive so little attention in this volume, if indeed they are so important? Once again, actions speak louder than words. This merely rhetorical praise of the two composers is not an isolated occurrence. Germaine Greer was the first to note this type of commentary in relation to women artists:

> When men begin to persecute and exclude women, they acknowledge their own insecurity. When they patronise and flatter them they assert the unshakeability of their own superiority.[13]

Greer noted that male critics would often flatter and 'talk-up' the work of a woman artist. Gallantry and chivalry seem, in some cases, to have clouded their judgement of a woman's work. This is only an extension of the accepted social positions of men and women where 'compliment is the recognized commerce of the sexes'.[14] Although I have found little evidence of this occurring on a widespread basis in twentieth-century music literature (there is a hint of it in Boyd's remark about Grace Williams), it is clear that when men discuss the work of women, their attitude to it is different from that shown towards a male composer. Social codes and behaviour no doubt influence how some men feel they should address women. There is a reluctance to refer to women composers, even of the past, by surname alone. As with most modern composers, male or female, the insistence on retaining the given name is a coded way of implying that their position in the 'canon' is only probationary. In the case of women, this usage coincides with the traditional code of social politeness, which disguises its other function.

In *The English Musical Renaissance* (1966) Frank Howes states:

> A point of some social significance was the emergence [in post-war Britain] of women composers who had no need of Ethel Smyth's militant feminism to win them recognition [. . .][15]

The message here is that making a political statement about being a woman composer was no longer necessary. Howes implies that women in the period after the 1940s could now be judged on equal terms and that the battle for the recognition of female composers was over. The insinuation that there was no longer a need to make gender an issue in music seeks to silence any further accusations of injustice. Predictably, Howes goes on to cite Elisabeth Lutyens, Elizabeth Maconchy and Phyllis Tate, using sexual stereotypes to describe their personalities and music:

> Maconchy made her mark with string quartets and shows a disposition towards an intellectual source of inspiration rather than sensibility or emotion. If this is regarded as a masculine trait it corresponds to a robust trait in her personality which enabled her, for instance, to represent English composers in Moscow as president of the Composer's Guild.[16]

Maconchy is described as a 'quasi-masculine' composer who uses her intellect to compose rather than being guided by her 'feminine' emotions (as, by implication, most other women composers were). The supposedly masculine aspects of Maconchy's personality are corroborated by the fact that she travelled to a foreign country in a professional capacity; apparently this is the ultimate proof of 'masculinity'!

As in other discussions of women composers, a contrast to Maconchy's pseudo-masculinity is found in Phyllis Tate:

> Tate's [music] on the other hand is a more feminine talent. She began with light-fingered and light-hearted music [. . .] But she developed and went on to more deeply felt works [. . .] of which *Nocturne* [. . .] enshrines disturbing emotions of war, all the deeper because so quietly and quiveringly imagined [. . .][17]

Phyllis Tate's description as feminine is deduced from her 'light-hearted' keyboard works. The reference to Tate's music depicting war paints a rather pathetic figure of the woman at home with only her imagination for company. She is passive, inactive, 'quivering' in comparison with the male, who can experience war at first hand. The idea that women's only experience of the tragedy or horror of war was imagined is simply untrue. The author seems at pains to point out that this was war only from a woman's perspective.

Many generations of music students have never entertained the possibility that women might have been significant composers, because of their lack of recognition and validation in musicology. Although the absence of women composers from many musicological texts condemns them to a history without contribution, their rare inclusion often serves only to reinforce beliefs about the irrepressible 'feminine' personality, the discriminatory views about women's nature being once again sustained. To presume that musicologists and musicians are somehow immune to society's biased opinions about women is unrealistic. This is surely demonstrated by the comments and attitudes exposed in the above citations. On the whole, musicology has managed only to reflect the commonly held views about women's accepted behaviour and social role. Texts which attempt to discuss women's work objectively or fairly are very hard to find within the mainstream of music literature. For most of this century, discussions of women composers and their work have become bogged down in reflections about gender. Since being a serious composer is viewed as a masculine occupation, any woman attempting such a career is bound to be considered in terms of her motivations for wanting to stray from the 'natural feminine' path. The constant reference to the implicitly unchangeable role played by women's temperament and nature underlines the perceived threat the female composer presents to traditional notions of femininity. This stands in complete contrast to the idea of women as musical performers or entertainers, which confirms femininity. (This apparent contradiction will be discussed in Chapter 6.)

Modern attitudes towards women composers are often encapsulated in newspaper articles and reviews of their work. Critical reviews of works by the study group of composers are rather thin on the ground, since many of them have had only a few works performed. However, a common thread of attitudes can be observed in articles written about Grace Williams, Elizabeth Maconchy, Minna Keal and Ruth Gipps.

When Elizabeth Maconchy's *The Land* was performed in 1930, one review proclaimed it as 'A Masterly Work':

> The suite [. . .] is declared by Our Music Critic to be 'one of the best pieces of orchestral music written by any woman in recent years' [. . .][18]

But this is surely damning with faint praise! Note that Maconchy's work is kept safely defined as 'good for a woman', with all the connotations that implies in music criticism. More encouragingly, Herbert Hughes, in the *Daily Telegraph*, wrote on the same occasion:

> Not only is this one of the best pieces of orchestral music written by any woman in recent years, but by far the most important [. . .] so far at the Promenade Concerts during the present season.[19]

Hughes then goes on to define the work more closely within the usual frame of sexual aesthetics:

> Modern it is [. . .] the method direct, terse economical; the harmony at times acid and biting – never luxurious or sentimental or (in the pre-war sense) feminine.

Again, a demonstrably successful work, when written by a woman, has to be described as 'never feminine'.

In a 1947 review of a concert featuring works by Ruth Gipps it was stated:

> Miss Gipps does not make the mistake of trying to beat male composers at their own game, but instead makes the most of the virtues of her own sex. There is a distinctly feminine grace and delicacy about all her work [. . .][20]

In direct contrast to Maconchy, Gipps' work can express only her 'feminine grace and delicacy'. If she deviated from her femininity, she would obviously be 'trying to beat male composers'.

The same concert provoked reflection in the *Birmingham Post*:

> The concert of chamber music by Ruth Gipps [. . .] raises once more the curious question of the comparative rarity of the creative faculty in members of what it used to infuriate Dame Ethel Smyth to hear described as the fair sex [. . .] Can we account for it by the fact that it is women's special mission and privilege in life to be even more nobly creative than it is possible to be in the arts? [. . .] very few [women composers] appear who have been mothers [. . .][21]

The argument that a female's true creative role is biologically dictated once again reduces a woman to being bound by her 'nature'. Women who create are seen to do so only as a surrogate for pregnancy.

An article which featured the work of Grace Williams appeared in *The Musical Times* in May 1956. Even here, the composer's gender is hinted at shyly when her First Symphony is discussed:

> The score contains plenty of full-blooded themes and effective climaxes, but there remains the impression that such things do not come easily to the composer and that other modes of expression would be more congenial to her.[22]

Immediately after this passage the author describes Williams' 'more successful' works as the 'evocative' *Sea Sketches*, the 'romantic' Violin Concerto and the 'delicately beautiful' *The Song of Mary*. Once again, sexual stereotypes are being applied to an aesthetic judgment.

The treatment of Minna Keal, some 40 years later, shows that the musical establishment has changed little in how it treats women composers. Keal made headlines in 1989, when her First Symphony was performed at the Proms. Her previously discussed life story made good copy: a promising music student forced to stop her career as a composer because of family pressure and finally able to continue her compositional studies only when she retired. Aged 80, she completed her First Symphony, which was subsequently given a high-level professional performance.

The most striking thing about the numerous magazine and newspaper articles which were written at the time is that only one or two make any reference to the real tragedy of Keal's situation: the talent left dormant for 46 years; the missed opportunities; the sheer waste of musical ability dissipated instead into clerical and domestic work. This was not only a tragedy for Keal personally but also a loss to the musical world, if only in Britain.

Stephen Pettitt, writing in *The Times* on 5 September 1989, however, saw the whole situation as rather tiresome:

> Minna Keal is 80. After a promising start to a career as a composer, she wrote nothing for nearly 50 years. Then, suddenly, a chance meeting with Justin Connolly, the composer, lessons with him, a few pieces circulating among those in the know, and the first complete performance of her symphony at the Proms. Marvellous story. The question, however, is whether the music is good.

Pettitt curtly dismisses Keal's circumstances and promptly concludes that the symphony did 'not quite add up'. Yet if one is to dwell on some of the attitudes he revealed in this short paragraph, many of the really important issues raised by Keal's experience are either trivialized or omitted. He writes, 'She wrote nothing for nearly 50 years', yet gives no explanation of why this might have been. The implication is that she had nothing of interest to say during this half-century. Obviously, there was no burning creative urge to satisfy; this in turn proved that she was no tortured artistic genius. The impression is that she was satisfied and content with not composing.

He continues: 'A few pieces circulating among those in the know'. Is he implying that Keal had some sort of preferential treatment? That she knew (or by implication, Connolly knew) how to pull strings to get her work performed? The trivialization of this woman's life and experience is expertly encapsulated in two damning words: 'Marvellous Story'. But this is not a 'marvellous story': it is real; it is 46 years of composing lost forever; it is 46 years of silence!

Stephen Johnson, in *The Listener*, was quick to state that Keal's life made an 'inspiring tale'. But:

> Nevertheless, if you enter the arena with the top players, you must expect to be judged by the highest standards. Keal's symphony is plainly an accomplished piece of scoring, which didn't seem to tax the BBC Symphony Orchestra unduly.[23]

Johnson's odd remark, which implies that Keal's symphony was not complex enough for the players to find it difficult to play, carries a further hint that the music was 'uncomplicated' and therefore perhaps technically deficient or shallow. That complexity should be an index of quality is, for a start, highly controversial outside certain modernist circles; that the orchestra found it not too demanding may in reality show only how accomplished the players were (or how practically minded the composer was).

The overriding attitude to Minna Keal could be paraphrased as: 'Your nice story does not make any difference to how we will judge the music.' The fact that some critics felt a need to stress this point is patronizing in itself. It suggests – unfairly – that Keal had pleaded for some sort of special treatment because of her circumstances, when this was never the case. Minna Keal has a remarkable talent and spirit. She sacrificed nearly a lifetime's work in music for the sake of others: her mother, the family business and her own family. Yet most of the music media miss the true point of Keal's story. They see it as a plea for her music to receive special consideration. Her story should question only the society which tolerates, or expects, this sort of sacrifice. Yet the critics do not wonder how many other potential Minna Keals there may be – those who never had a second chance. At best there is a gloomy acceptance and, at worst, an underlying sentiment of: 'So what?'

In other reviews of Keal's Symphony, a common slant was to superimpose images of the woman composer's physique into the discussion, these serving to reinforce the perceived 'otherness' of the female. There is incredulous wonder that someone of Keal's sex, slight physical stature and age is actually able to write a large-scale 'serious' work for many instruments. The physicality of the female remains for some the mark of their inferiority:

> This birdlike lady – 4ft 11in in her size three shoes and weighing just seven stone – is now 80 [. . .] She is now at the Albert Hall, her face aglow, a tiny figure in a blue trouser suit.[24]

Can you really imagine this being said of a male composer? Such a patronizing attitude reveals that there is a continued belief in correlation between physical size and mental capability. Also, there is some disbelief that this 'dear little old lady' did not produce pretty, tuneful, tonal music but instead dissonant, angular music, full of explosive anger. That many male composers have continued to work well into old age and in a similar style does not draw forth the same kind of incredulity. Take, for example, the articles written recently in celebration of Sir Michael Tippett's continued work in his 90th year.[25]

I have chosen these examples of how music critics and other members of the press react to women composers to make a point about attitudes. These are not just the attitudes and beliefs of a minority of, perhaps, ill-informed or uneducated people, but those of an establishment reflecting Society's worst fears about female liberation. Reviews and articles that take women composers seriously simply as composers are hard to find. This simply confirms that attitudes towards women – among them, women composers – have not really changed that much in modern times. There is strong discrimination at work here; it is not the outright misogyny of 100 years ago, but it is just as dangerous, just as limiting.

The opposition to these outmoded attitudes, spearheaded by the movement now known as 'feminist musicology', has gradually emerged. In the course of the century, the growing awareness of the inequalities and discrimination faced by women has developed into a thorough re-examination of women's musical history. The emerging ranks of female musicologists in the 1970s began to reassess the accepted reasons for the invisibility of women's contribution to music. Writers began to research and uncover a number of women composers, both past and present. This work, which has become known as 'compensatory history', has provided basic biographical and instructive information about women creators and musicians and has provided evidence to counter the claim that women composers did not exist before this century. This type of pioneering documentation forms the bulk of the research on women in music undertaken so far.

Fair reassessment of women's historical and contemporary contribution to music has become a growing field within musicology in recent years. Discussions about 'women in music' can be viewed as falling into three basic categories: first, historical surveys, which cover brief biographical details of a number of composers in various countries throughout history; second, studies of the life and works of individual female composers; third (the most recent type), studies which relate issues of social history, politics and feminist aesthetics to musicology. The latter have focused on women as a group, highlighting the specific problems and obstacles they face working within a male-dominated profession and tradition.

The reconstruction of music history to include women is vital, not only for our understanding of women from the past but also for future women composers. The convenient absence of women as a force to be reckoned with is fundamental to the continuation of the present male-dominated musical canon. When women become visible, when the validity of their experience is asserted, patriarchal values in society are threatened. It is vital to the fragile self-esteem of womankind that they should feel the sense of confidence, the sense of liberation, which men totally take for granted when they encounter their own past and find themselves central.

In the English language two of the earliest musicological texts about women were George Upton's *Women in Music* (1886) and Otto Ebel's *Women Composers: A Bibliographical Handbook of Woman's Work in Music* (1902). These texts give brief biographical details about a number of composers but often manage only to trivialize and patronize the subject. Arthur Elson's *Women's Work in Music* (1904) includes chapters on 'The Wives of the Composers' and 'Musical Romances', acknowledging, albeit in an entirely patronizing tone, women's role as supporter and assistant to male composers. These early books are marked by an implicit acceptance of women's subordinate, inferior role in music.

It was not until after the Second World War that another text about women's work as musicians was published. Sophie Drinker's *Music and Women: The Story of Women in Their Relation to Music* (1948) was an innovative study looking at women's contributions from ancient times. More importantly, it began to acknowledge and question the particular prejudices faced by women. Sadly, it had little impact on the attitudes of the musical establishment at the time, and after its publication there was a long pause in the discussions about women composers.[26]

Indeed, it was only as a result of the new wave of feminist awareness, which took hold at the end of the 1960s, that women were encouraged to research the contribution of women composers and musicians once again. American musicologists took the lead in this endeavour, a pattern which has continued up to the present day. The cultural climate in America seems currently to be far ahead of Britain with regard to attitudes towards sexual and racial discrimination. Americans' greater awareness of social problems has been reflected in extensive debate and discussion among academics in a variety of fields. The late 1970s and early 1980s were marked by many substantial texts on women composers and musicians in American music. Good examples are: Adrienne Fried Block and Carol Neuls-Bates' *Women in American Music: A Bibliography of Music and Literature* (1979), Christine Ammer's *Unsung: A History of Women in American Music* (1980) and Mildred Denby Green's *Black Women Composers: A Genesis* (1983).

In the 1980s a number of valuable source and reference materials were published. Aaron Cohen's *Encyclopaedia of Women Composers* (1981) makes reference to around 6000 women composers from around the world from 30 BC to the present. *Women in Music: An Anthology of Source Readings from the Middle Ages to the Present* (1982), edited by Carol Neuls-Bates, takes a different approach, in that it allows the composers to speak for themselves by quoting from letters, published material and interviews. This text has continued to be a highly valuable contribution to feminist research. It highlights women's involvement in a wide range of musical capacities and brings out the social underpinning, which has always affected women in a different way from men. *The Anthology of Music by Women* (1987), edited by James Briscoe, contains music by 37 women composers from Hildegard von Bingen (1098–1179) to Ellen Taaffe Zwilich (b. 1939) and provides 'a single accessible source of compositions by women suitable for mainstream music history teaching'.[27] This has proved to be a valuable contribution, since the scores concerned are very often difficult to obtain, most remaining unpublished. Jane Weiner LePage's *Women Composers, Conductors and Musicians of the Twentieth Century: Selected Biographies* (published in three volumes: 1980, 1983, 1988) again includes composers of all nationalities. But its style is often popular rather than academic. Continuing the line of 'compensatory' history texts offering material for inclusion in secondary and undergraduate music studies is Diane Peacock Jezic's *Women Composers: A Lost Tradition Found* (1988). Although this book has been criticized for conforming a little too much to the periodization of traditional music histories, its accompanying cassette of recordings of women's music is a very useful addition.

The 1980s also saw the publication of a number of biographies of individual women composers, of which Nancy B. Reich's *Clara Schumann: The Artist and the Woman* (1985) provided an excellent example of full and thorough research into all important aspects of a woman composer's life. Also noteworthy were Leonie Rosenstiel's *The Life and works of Lili Boulanger* (1978) and Judith Rosen's *Grazyna Bacewicz: Her Life and Works* (1984). However, some biographies of women composers (and indeed some of the historical overviews) often merely imitate the traditional methodology applied to male composers and therefore avoid discussion of any of the more controversial issues of discrimination. Texts on other women composers include the Greenwood Press Bio-Bibliographies series, which includes Donald L. Hixon's *Thea Musgrave: A Bio-Bibliography* (1984); more recent texts include work on Cécile Chaminade (1988), Radie Britain (1990) and Peggy Glanville-Hicks (1990).

The Musical Woman (1984, 1987, 1991), edited by Judith Lang Zaimont, Catherine Overhauser and Jane Gottlieb, currently stands at three volumes and is an ongoing publication covering every aspect of women's work as musicians in a wide range of music (classical, ethnic, popular). The contributed material ranges from the life and works of individuals to surveys of women composers from various countries and a more specific examination of women's role in music and society.

Contributions by British authors in the 1980s were, in contrast, often rather low-key. Derek Hyde's *New Found Voices: Women and Music in the Nineteenth Century English Music* (1984) was published by the author himself and has received little attention. The book contains information about women as performers, composers (one chapter is devoted to Ethel Smyth), educationalists and writers. Nicola LeFanu's and Sophie Fuller's *Reclaiming the Muse: A Select Bibliography of English Language Writing on Women in Music* (1991) was produced by the Music Department of King's College London. Aelwyn Pugh's *Women in Music* (1991) is a more glossy publication aimed at informing students at GCSE level of women's work across a range of popular and classical music.

In Britain most other research has taken a more traditional approach by examining the life and work of a single woman composer. Worthy of note are Christopher St John's *Ethel Smyth: A Biography* (1959), Malcolm Boyd's *Grace Williams* (1980), a short but vital account of this composer's life and music, and Meirion and Susie Harries' *A Pilgrim Soul: The Life and Works of Elizabeth Lutyens* (1989), a full and uncensored examination of Lutyens' troubled life and career. In addition, a small number of British composers have published autobiographies, notably Liza Lehmann's *The Life of Liza Lehmann* (1919), Ethel Smyth's account of her life (which runs to seven volumes published between 1919 and 1940), Elisabeth Lutyens' *The Goldfish Bowl* (1972) and Avril Coleridge-Taylor's *The Heritage of Samuel Coleridge-Taylor* (1979).

In the 1990s a number of ground-breaking works focusing on women in music and on what has been termed 'feminist musicology' have appeared. It is encouraging to observe that feminist ideas and discussion seem to have gained a foothold in musicological discourse. *Women and Music in Cross-Cultural Perspective* (1987), edited by Ellen Koskoff, provides enlightening cross-cultural analysis of power structures, genre and women's roles in traditional music-making. Examination of women's social and cultural position and its relationship to their work in music is gradually becoming established practice. Moreover, writers have begun to venture into analysing music, particularly music with a literary context, in terms of how it may represent and symbolize sex and gender. Two convincing examples are Catherine Clément's *Opera or the Undoing of Women* (1989) and Charles Ford's *Cosi? Sexual Politics in Mozart's Operas* (1991).

Women in Music: A History (1991), edited by Karin Pendle, is a collection of essays covering a time span from ancient and medieval music to the twentieth century. In the main, these essays 'rediscover' women's involvement in traditional Western art music and are placed alongside discussion of other genres of music such as non-Western, jazz and popular. Some other interesting issues are raised, including women's position as patrons of music and the possibility of a feminist aesthetic. This book moves away from using certain categorizations found in traditional musicology, since it is claimed that these often have little connection with critical periods in women's music history.[28] For example, the categorization of periods such as the Renaissance and Romantic, both understood to be 'great periods' for male artistic development, were actually very restricting and containing times for women:

> Traditional periodization reflects the history of men, as constructed by men [. . .] traditional historical periods not only make women invisible but frequently distort what was really happening to them [. . .] women actually fared worse in so-called progressive eras, especially the Renaissance [. . . and] the beginning of the nineteenth century, a time of expanding opportunity for men, was 'the nadir' for European women.[29]

This example suggests that simply to apply accepted methodology to the study of women can be problematic and entirely inappropriate. Reassessing history in the quest for women composers and their contribution often requires a different approach and points to the extensive rethinking which has to accompany the evaluation of women's work in music.

Susan McClary's *Feminine Endings: Music, Gender and Sexuality* (1991) is perhaps the most controversial addition to the gender and music debate. The book is made up of a collection of essays covering a diverse range of topics from Monteverdi to Madonna. Significantly, McClary begins to formulate a number of theories about the possible gendered nature of music. She argues that for women to be 'added' to musical history there must be a restructuring of musicology and its methods. Moreover, she asserts that music written by women will be truly successful only when women stop trying to create like men. Because of the all-embracing male culture, many women composers find it extremely difficult, even distasteful, to try to express images of their sex in music:

> [. . .] not only do women not have a musical language of their own upon which to rely, but they often have internalized a strong distaste for the idea of permitting their identities as women to be apparent in their music. The category 'woman' in music is already colonized and is overcrowded with caricatures concocted by male artists.[30]

McClary believes the abstract and formalistic analysis of music, which to a large extent does not cover what the music is actually expressing, must be replaced by a different reading:

> The intellectual obstacles that have impeded the development of feminist music criticism are rooted in the assumptions that have long informed and sustained

academic musicology in general. It is important to remember that there really is very little resembling criticism *of any sort* in musicology.[31]

McClary's assertions were viewed by many as extremely contentious, and the book provoked a number of responses. For example, in *The Journal of Musicology* (Summer 1991) an article titled 'Politics, Feminism and Contemporary Music Theory', by Pieter C. van den Toorn appeared. In this, van den Toorn is scathing of suggestions that music may be gendered and is sceptical of feminist ideology generally:

> Arguments about sex and music are largely a form of propaganda, an attempt to advertise blanket claims of special disadvantage and oppression which, in contemporary life in the West generally, are dubious and farfetched.[32]

Van den Toorn believes that the most disturbing aspects of McClary's feminist critique are its feminist propaganda and detestation of male sexuality:

> Fanned by an aversion for male sexuality, which is depicted as something brutal and contemptible, irrelevancies are being read into the music. In due course, these feelings of distaste are allied to a larger critique, to a more comprehensive feminist argument. They become symbolic of women in general, of the victimization of all women, their plight in a world conditioned by the sexual inclinations of the male. And tonal music becomes an instrument of oppression, a part of the dark conspiracy of men and their relations with women.[33]

A measure of the depth of feeling provoked by this article came in the form of a reply published in the Fall issue of the same journal, entitled 'What Do Feminists Want? A Reply to Pieter van den Toorn', by Ruth Solie. In this article Solie rejects van den Toorn's reading of music as only an 'individual and immediate response':

> He wants [. . .] to inhabit the secure, transcendent space of art. He doesn't want to be implicated in sexism, colonialism and racism – and who can blame him? He's given us a passionate, even poetic, defense of musical formalism – a description of an autonomous and non-referential music whose 'meanings [are] beyond the reach of metaphors, analogies and symbols' [. . .][34]

Van den Toorn also implied quite wrongly that all feminists hold the same opinion.[35] Rightly, Solie points out that he has obviously read very little feminist literature, since it is a discipline alive with vigorous debate on a wide range of topics; in no way do all feminists agree with McClary's thesis.

A fine example of this pluralism is Rhian Samuel's response to feminist musicology and feminist music criticism as exemplified by Susan McClary's book. Samuel, a composer and co-editor of the *Grove Dictionary of Women Composers* (1994), herself worries that feminist musicology could become alienated on account of its 'political stance'. A straightforward biography of a composer who happens to be female fits into the standard pattern of biographical texts, yet when such a piece of writing occurs within a text about other women composers, although more of the problems faced by women as a group can become clear, the framework becomes more controversial:

> [. . .] whether a piece of musicology is feminist or not depends not only on the perceived political aim of the author but on the context in which it appears. Should

> this matter? Yes, if such a categorisation results in segregation from the mainstream [. . .] For any group, a perception [. . .] that its members are victims or outsiders, that their interests do not extend beyond the group, results in ghetto-isation.[36]

Samuel voices a concern felt by many women composers. On the whole, they do not want to break with traditional musicological styles and methodology, even if this step would result in readings of their lives and works in a more sympathetic and comprehensive manner. Most women composers do not want their music to be branded as carrying a 'political' message: they simply want their music to be judged as music, to be accepted as part of the established musical tradition. Samuel regards the most disturbing aspect of McClary's work as its dictatorial line of 'how' women composers should think and, more importantly, compose and structure their music:

> [. . .] beyond its negative tone, there is something in McClary's thesis which rings a sinister note for women composers. At the end of her appreciation of an avowedly-feminist, contemporary piece of music, McClary wonders why other women composers have been reluctant or unable to pursue parallel explorations (that is, to create works that insist upon the fact that they were created by women and by implication break with the classical male-dominated tradition) [. . .] The implication is that women composers would compose in her way if only they knew better.[37]

Like van den Toorn, Samuel views McClary's work as exerting direct pressure on women composers to take up a particular feminist stance and express it in their music. Both view this new type of feminist reading as a call to make a conscious break with male traditions and styles. This fear of a 'political line' which commands women composers to reject and scorn all things male is certainly a misinterpretation. Surely, McClary's work offers merely an alternative way of looking at composition and the musical traditions which inform us. There are still many musicologists who are unconvinced that music is representational or expresses human emotions, while others disagree. I believe that the writing of McClary and others open up a huge new area for debate, which is a good thing in itself. Naturally, their views are uncomfortable, for (feminist issues apart) an attack on the premises of musical expression and the foundation of the whole Western art tradition utterly undermines conventional beliefs.

That our musical heritage has principally been created by men and passed on by men is indisputable. Historical re-examination of this heritage in the light of feminist theory provides a new set of questions about our culture: who produces it; why they produce it; what they are expressing; whom they are expressing it to; why certain works and forms have become valued and mainstream; why others have remained outside it; what the function of music in past and present societies is. I do not feel that society can continue to accept unquestioningly and monolithically the dominant traditional culture, be it in history, art, literature, drama or music. A more liberated appraisal of our musical tradition may eventually create a musical culture which has a place for individuals from many backgrounds, groups and ideologies, all of whom can be represented and appreciated alongside the inherited mainstream canon. This should not be seen as an 'either/or' situation: there is no suggestion that if women are included, men will automatically be excluded. In other words, there is room for a composite tradition.

Marcia J. Citron's *Gender and the Musical Canon* (1993), is another recent ground-breaking text. Citron focuses on how certain composers and 'masterpieces' become valued and are passed on as culturally important. To understand how musical works become part of the musical canon (that is, respected, regularly performed and analysed), she takes an interdisciplinary approach. Citron feels that the belief that music, and composers, become part of the musical canon only through purely qualitative and value judgements, is incorrect

> Music [. . .] appears to be removed from debates about social relations and cultural identity; it deals with abstract sound, not concrete issues. But music is indeed socially contingent and participates in the dynamics of culture. Which music is deemed canonic says a great deal about the image a society has of itself.[38]

The music (and composers) deemed to reflect our culture are white, male, middle-class and European. So the reflection is partial. Citron argues that the adoption of musical 'masterpieces' is not an objective choice and can be determined by a number of groups, including performing organizations, the academy, the musicological community, the public, art foundations and government agencies.[39] The main issues raised in Citron's work provide the starting point for other research into music as a gendered discourse, the methodology of musicology and approaches to women's incorporation in the mainstream or the creation of alternative, female-centred canons and traditions.

Other important texts published in the early 1990s include *Rediscovering the Muses* (1993), edited by Kimberly Marshall. This is an important contribution to our knowledge of women's participation in ancient civilizations, ethnic music and early European music. *Musicology and Difference* (1994), edited by Ruth Solie, contains a range of articles which examine issues of power, difference and meaning in music. The *Grove Dictionary of Women Composers* (1994), edited by Julie Anne Sadie and Rhian Samuel, contains listings for around 800 women composers and can be seen as a valuable successor to the Cohen *Encyclopaedia*. Sophie Fuller's *The Pandora Guide to Women Composers: Britain and the United States* (1994) continues the tradition of short summarizations of the 'life and works' of a range of British and American composers.

Cecilia Reclaimed (1994), edited by Susan Cook and Judy Tsou, is a collection of essays covering a number of gender-related topics. It is marked, like other recent texts, by an interdisciplinary and multi-genre approach. Topics include chapters on individual composers, female images in Rap music, power and gender in the American ballad song, women in the English musical Renaissance and feminist approaches to musicology. This unconventional approach in terms of musicology, which freely crosses boundaries, disciplines, musical eras and musical genres, has become a vital component in the creation of a feminist reading of musicology. In previous decades the kind of information disclosed by this approach had often been impossible to uncover because of the retention of traditional patterns of anthologizing, periodization and methodology.[40]

It is perhaps stating the obvious to observe that the majority of books written on the subject of women in music and feminist musicology are by women. This fact has enabled some in the musical establishment to dismiss the writers as a 'minority' or self-interested group, yet this assertion could just as easily be made about male musicologists. There is a blanket assumption that although most music commentators, critics and academics are male, this fact cannot in any way influence their judgement over 'objective' and 'abstract' musical matters. Many feminists disagree:

> The critical establishment has been overwhelmingly male. The absence of women has meant the absence of a female voice and a female point of view [. . .] It is also important to remember that male critics internalized musical values from male predecessors and contemporaries, and that conditions of response formed a pre-evaluative context for the structuring of their discourse.[41]

It is evident that women themselves are subjected to this same acculturation, but their relationship to it will always be different. It is very difficult to deny that individuals are not influenced in their outlook by their education, background and experience, be they male or female.

On the whole, the musicological establishment is, and has always been, dominated by men. It has tended to ignore women composers and musicians, together with the issues surrounding their absence. The roles of academic commentator and music critic have been notoriously difficult ones for women to penetrate. Obviously, in the past there were practical obstacles, such as the lack of an appropriate education, but in addition there have also been:

> [. . .] ideological reasons why women have not functioned in that role. The role of critic implies authority. It connotes mind, wisdom, and judgement: an epistemological foundation for dispensing knowledge to others.[42]

It is true, however, that in Britain throughout the nineteenth century some women did publish books on music. But it has also to be stressed that these writers were a very tiny minority. Derek Hyde, in his review of writings by women in nineteenth-century Britain, mentions a few, including Mrs Bray, Mary Wakefield (1853–1910), Florence May (1844–1923), Fanny Raymond-Ritter and Georgina Weldon (1837–1914).

Arthur Elson's *Women's Work in Music* (1904) concludes with a brief discussion of women musicologists working in Germany, France and England. He observes:

> Many of the women fall into the bad habit of imbuing all their work with a romantic tinge of exaggerated sentiment. One example of this fault is Elise Polko, some of whose sketches are very pretty reading, but almost wholly misleading to the new student.[43]

The work of female musicologists is analysed and criticized for its 'bad habits', which reveal the true female nature, flawed by illogical 'romanticism' and 'sentimentality'. The cultural stereotype of the female personality as irrational, subjective and emotional (yet 'very pretty') appears to be read into everything touched by the female hand. Interestingly, the small number of women who did manage to publish musical literature in the nineteenth century avoided women composers and their music. Elise Polko, Lina Ramann and Marie Lipsius (who at her father's insistence published under the pseudonym La Mara) stuck with mainstream ideas and avoided any of the crucial questions about discrimination against women and their relatively small role as creative musicians.[44] Finally, the very respected French music historian Marie Bobillier (1858–1918) wrote under the pen-name of Michel Brenet, no doubt with the intention (shared by the writers George Eliot and Georges Sand) of passing permanently for male and so avoiding this kind of criticism.

The contemporary debates about how women composers should be represented, portrayed and judged are reflected in the actual views, ideas and work of female composers. The opinions voiced by female composers are diverse, ranging from those of avowed feminists to those of avowed anti-feminists. In my study group of composers there seems to be a strong vein of more traditional ideas about women and a reticence, by some, to take any stance over sex discrimination. Many express contradictory ideas about women composers, often exposing a split by virtue of which they view themselves as quite different from 'other' women.

It has been asserted that to overcome the cultural discrimination against female creativity:

> A sense of relating or belonging to a palpable tradition is crucial [. . .] a tradition of the present, especially support groups promoting women composers and their music; a sense of a future tradition for which one can function as a precursor to subsequent women composers [. . .][45]

Nevertheless, none of the composers in my study group felt any sense of female tradition or thought that such a thing was possible or desirable. On the whole, they knew very little work by other female composers, either past or present, and with this lack of knowledge (or, indeed, interest) they often failed to recognize a thread of problems common to women composers' experience. The invisibility and lack of understanding of women's work, in part inculcated by the musical establishment, have left each generation of women to believe that they are indeed the 'first' women composers.

A number of women composers (outside the study group) do have, however, a much stronger sense of the benefits that arise from recognizing the difficulties women composers face as a group. Indeed, women composers have, throughout this century banded together to promote themselves in a number of organizations. In 1911 the Society of Women Musicians was founded by musicologist and critic Marion M. Scott. Its function was to 'represent the interests of works by women'.[46] The Presidents of the society included a number of composers, such as Liza Lehmann and Cécile Chaminade (Ethel Smyth was an honorary vice-president from 1925 until her death in 1944). However, the society disbanded in 1972, feeling that its aims had been fulfilled.

It was succeeded by the Women in Music organization set up in 1987 by Nicola LeFanu. LeFanu (the daughter of Elizabeth Maconchy) has been outspoken in her defence of active promotion of the work of women composers:

> [. . .] I want to try and get across what I feel to be positive about the act of singling out women composers [. . .] I believe [. . .] that any art is much richer, much stronger if it is practised by both sexes. If music has anything to offer this destructive, divided society of ours, won't it need to spring from both men and women [. . .]?[47]

In America, the International League of Women Composers was formed in 1975. In much the same way as the British organization, it received a mixed reaction from composers:

> The League has elicited two types of response from the women themselves. Many welcome establishment of the organization. Others feared that being associated with it will tend to minimize their past accomplishments. They argue that recognition should come to them solely as composers, not as *women* composers.[48]

Different groups of male composers work together, influence and help each other; in this way music evolves and schools of thought develop. Yet many women have difficulty in working with each other in the same way. Perhaps this is made harder by their relatively small numbers and the internalized lack of respect for women's work generally. Basically, many do not want to see themselves as part of a culturally inferior sex. Since women have great difficulty in being directly included in the 'male' schools of thought and influence, this often leaves them altogether isolated.

The lack of a widespread communal female sense of identity is typified by what is perhaps the most controversial question affecting female composers: Should they be classified at all as 'women composers'? Many believe passionately that the whole issue of a gendered qualification to the term 'composer' acts only to confirm women's marginalization and perpetuates their place outside the mainstream. For example, Elizabeth Maconchy has stated:

> I have always said 'I am a composer' – one does not say a 'man-composer' so why say 'a woman composer'?[49]

The fear of being categorized outside the mainstream, or of being part of a special interest group, makes many composers very wary of attempts to class them by gender. On the other hand, Antoinette Kirkwood takes quite a different view:

> I don't think I have ever been referred to as a woman composer, it would not worry me if I were [. . .] When I was young nobody ever resented being called an actress, although I believe some do now.[50]

Kirkwood sees the description of women composers as part of the movement for political correctness. She sees objections to being termed a 'woman composer' as rather ridiculous, since for her this is simply a matter of fact, akin to being termed 'Mrs or Miss' instead of the maritally unexplicit 'Ms'.[51]

In an ideal world there would be no strong need for gender categorization, but most of our language and culture has an inbuilt assumption of women's invisibility. This fact cannot be avoided, and in some way the issue needs to be confronted. Blatantly, the unqualified term 'composer' is so saturated with the notion of the male that it does not need a gender qualification; rather, it carries within itself an intrinsic gendered notion. This is also true of many other areas of our language:

> Masculinity is the unmarked form: the assumption is that the world is male unless proven otherwise. Femininity is the marked form: it is the proof of otherwise.[52]

Once again, analysis of women's position becomes subject to a double bind. Our language is constructed in such a way that:

> [. . . women] must signify that the norm, the positive, does not apply and so she becomes a *lady* doctor, a *female* surgeon, a *woman* lawyer [. . .] There is no space for a woman to be positive.[53]

This also applies to *woman* composer. The expression creates a dilemma, since not identifying a composer as female merely continues to imply the male, yet to qualify a composer specifically as female serves, in some people's minds, as a pointer to, and validation of, 'otherness' and inferiority. Even the construction of our language makes it difficult for women composers to take an equal place in musical life. But despite these and other difficulties, the fact that gender is an issue in music remains. The reality that women have been largely invisible from traditional musical life makes it an unavoidable issue.

Many women composers feel that because men do not make an issue of their gender, if women are to be accepted into the musical establishment, neither should they. The British composer Diana Burrell (b. 1948), in response to the formation of the Women in Music organization in 1987, wrote:

> We should not be seen as a group; probably the only thing we have in common with each other is our gender [. . .] I do want my music chosen to be played in concerts; I do *not* want it chosen because it was written by a woman.[54]

Burrell stressed her understanding that women composers need to take their place in the concert repertoire. However, she fears the alienation which may occur if women composers are automatically classified as 'different' from their male contemporaries. She therefore views gender classification as potentially divisive and self-defeating.

In reality, we live in a society which is informed by, and constructed on the basis of, a long history of male domination; thus only part of the real social make-up is reflected. It is crucial first to observe that women have been absent from cultural life and then examine the reason for this. Women are truly a 'class' separate from men in society, no matter how much we might wish it otherwise. If the problems of sexism, or indeed racism or class bias, are to be tackled, such classifications need, as a first step, to be exposed as real and valid. The musical establishment in Britain, which is largely white, male and middle class, has created a norm which is so all-embracing that those who conform to it do not need to be defined further: they have already defined themselves as the central, dominant group. Those who find themselves outside this 'standard' consider it important to bring to notice the fact that their qualification by sex or race has *already* been performed. They argue that an issue should be made of such distinctions so that fair, non-discriminatory representation of people of every sort can be accepted into the mainstream, allowing widespread validation of their expression and experience. Although many, both men and women, continue to feel that prefixing composers as 'women' automatically sets them apart from the music tradition and norm, a failure to recognize the fact that society has *already* placed women in this position serves only to perpetuate their past invisibility and inequality. Not recognizing women composers as a group actually denies their present existence, their exclusion and their potential future inclusion.

Grace Williams clearly absorbed many of the prejudiced attitudes towards woman composers. She wrote in 1949, at the age of 43:

> Ten years ago I thought that no one could ever possibly want to hear music written by a woman in her forties. Well, the two Elizabeths [Elizabeth Maconchy and Elisabeth Lutyens] have proved me wrong. But I still feel the same way about women of 50 + . There does seem something revolting – and perhaps a bit pathetic – in the thought of a symphony by a woman of 50.[55]

This statement is not only puzzling but also entirely contradictory, since Williams completed her Second Symphony in 1956, the year of her fiftieth birthday. She implies that people would, in contradistinction, want to hear large-scale works composed by a male composer of 50-plus. It is unclear whether she feels that it would not be so 'revolting' for a younger female composer to write such works. What is clear, however, is the entirely negative view of women's creativity she has internalized. The statement becomes more significant when one considers Society's general belief that older women lose much of their purpose and attractiveness when they reach an age when they can no longer bear children. This view becomes even more significant when one takes into account the previously quoted arguments that women cannot compose 'great music' because their ultimate creative purpose is to 'create life'. Williams had no children, which possibly made her more receptive to the opinion that a woman who can no longer create children and who creates instead a musical product is pitiful and 'pathetic'.

Some of the most prominent female composers, among them Elisabeth Lutyens, have notoriously opposed being labelled as a woman composer:

> Feminists who come to her [Lutyens'] North London house with tracts get as short shrift as those who label her a woman composer. 'Instead of writing useless information about women being abused why not build a nursery school so women could have two hours a day without Mum, Mum, Mum [. . .]?'[56]

Lutyens, like other women, acknowledged the difficulties she suffered as a woman composer but seems to resent the debate and categorization that accompanied it. This despite the fact that, time and again, Lutyens makes clear her first-hand knowledge of the prejudices faced by female composers:

> I am 15 years behind any man. If Britten wrote a bad score they'd say, 'He's had a bad day'. If I'd written one it was because I was a woman.[57]

She then seems to sense that this statement requires an immediate disclaimer that she is in no way 'anti-men'. Her situation seems to expose a predicament that most women find difficult to resolve satisfactorily. Men have indeed been instrumental in creating a culture in which women are oppressed, but openly to criticize those who are in power – and by implication those men they are close to – leaves many women in a precarious and contradictory position.

Ascribing blame is the most arduous part of the process by which discriminatory attitudes are exposed and reformed. The reason for women's near-absence in music (other than as performers) has traditionally been laid at the door of women themselves. They have been accused of deficiency in a variety of abilities including intellect, creativity, motivation and the inspiration to compose music. Women's deficiency, in comparison with men's proficiency, has consistently been held up as their main obstacle to cultural 'greatness'. But when it is asserted that the reason for women's absence is not women, but men – that it is not that women cannot, and have not, contributed anything, but rather that men have both barred the way and doctored the records – reality undergoes a remarkable change, as does the argument. Defending womankind against allegations of deficiency and inferiority is one thing, but to go on the offensive and attack mankind for its part in this behaviour is altogether more problematic for many women. Feminist writer Andrea Dworkin summarizes:

> The nature of women's oppression is unique: women are oppressed as women, regardless of class or race [. . .] women live with those who oppress them, sleep with them, have their children [. . .][58]

Clearly, women's intimate involvement with men in a variety of personal relationships unsurprisingly leaves many unwilling or unable to level criticism at men, even as a broad group.

Music is not detached from cultural and social reality. A point of some interest is to understand how women composers regard the feminist movement or its concepts of discrimination against women. This would seem to be of direct relevance to how they see themselves in musical life. Those who are more aware of, and sympathetic to, broadly feminist beliefs usually carry this consciousness into their work as composers. How the study group of composers view the feminist movement reveals some interesting and surprising attitudes. Enid Luff has always been aware of discrimination against women composers:

> I received the overwhelming impression that women didn't do it [compose], that they couldn't ever do it properly and that I was a (regrettable) square peg.[59]

Her subsequent discouragement from studying music and her perception of the bias against female creativity has instilled in her a sense that the musical world is not immune to wider social inequalities. She is therefore a close follower, although not an active member, of the women's movement.

In contrast, Antoinette Kirkwood has had little time or sympathy for the women's movement:

> I think it has been quite counterproductive in many ways.[60]

Indeed, her views on appropriate male and female behaviour may be considered by some as reactionary:

> It is known that men are stronger and more aggressive than women, why try and pretend otherwise? If women persist in making out that they can be treated on equal terms physically they will only find themselves further victims of rape and violence as men insist on proving them wrong.[61]

Minna Keal's opinions about feminism were directly informed by her early involvement in the Communist Party, but in a broader context she states:

> I have just been a personal feminist. I fought my own battles. I don't like some things about the feminist movement, as they have become almost anti-men, and I don't like that.[62]

Similarly, Bryony Jagger in the past described herself as a feminist, although she now feels that the aims of the women's movement are suspect. Jagger perhaps sums up the general feelings of the other composers in the group when she states that the contemporary feminist movement has become a 'bigoted chauvinist anti-men movement'.[63] This popular perception has done much to harm the cause of women's liberation, to the extent that many women composers feel that by making an issue of sexism or the lack of women composers, they are in fact subscribing to the 'anti-men' groups.

> It is only in the last couple of years that women composers have segregated themselves off into private women ritual festivals – I'm afraid I've avoided such scenes as I don't like the segregation idea, which will, in the end, drive us from the ordinary concerts [. . .][64]

In many statements Jagger acknowledges the discrimination and difficulties she has faced as a woman who composes music:

> I think of myself as a person and I dislike the idea of segregating things by sex [. . .] It would annoy me to be referred to as a woman composer. I think sex is irrelevant in occupations of the mind [. . .][65]

This seems somewhat contradictory, since to highlight the difficulties faced by women, sex/gender has to become a category of distinction in order to make a comparison with men possible. Certainly, many female composers certainly feel that segregation (even in a merely analytical rather than practical sense) is self-defeating; but to make no issue at all of the simple fact that a composer is a woman merely evades some of the major problems women face.

Judith Bailey is extremely wary of what she sees as the political aspects of the 'Women in Music' movement:

> I was slightly put off the 'Women in Music' movement when it first came out, because it seemed so militant. I thought it could put people's backs up.[66]

Bailey often quotes Elizabeth Maconchy's attitude that it is more productive just to get on with composing instead of making a stand on women's issues:

> It's like Elizabeth Maconchy said: 'You must get on with the job and not be feminist about it'. I think there is such sound sense in that.[67]

Ironically, Bailey has expressed opinions which appear to accept that women's position and comparative lack of success are due to 'nature':

> Possibly women, overall, don't have the drive to say, 'I must be successful' and 'I must get to the top' [. . .] Because, I think, no matter what anybody says, these are more male qualities [. . .] I still think they [women] have the ability to do these things, and that is what they should be concentrating on [. . .] more so than just telling everybody: 'I am a woman, why don't you give me a chance?'.[68]

Bailey's attitude is accommodating towards traditional attitudes. She believes that women composers should just compose and accept the fact that men are better equipped temperamentally to succeed. She sees making a fuss about being a woman as self-defeating and in some way proving inferiority. Possibly, this view somewhat oversimplifies the matter. On the whole, feminism focuses attention on the position of women in society and the extent to which this disadvantage affects equal opportunities and participation. When discussing her work as a lecturer in further education, Bailey clearly embraces a belief that in her experience the best students are usually male:

> I don't know how much of this is actually because of the system, or men's fault or whatever [. . .] if I had any class where the students had to extemporise or improvise, the boys were always better on the whole. Now some might say that the girls [. . .] couldn't do it because they felt silly, but that still doesn't alter the fact, really.[69]

Bailey believes the girl students to be less good in certain areas. However, while she evidently concedes that the reason could be social or discriminatory, she nevertheless feels in the final analysis that males are 'better on the whole' than females. Without wishing to question the genuineness of Bailey's perception, I would argue that this attitude invites a number of challenging questions about how she, also a woman, views herself in relation to her female music students.

Most of the women composers in my study group therefore wish, or seem to wish, to dissociate themselves from feminism. Obviously, many feel that the feminist movement, whatever its usefulness elsewhere, has no relevance to their work in music. This generates a particularly strange contradiction when many of the women composers are nevertheless willing to state that women are at a disadvantage because of their social position. The denial that society still needs to alter the way in which it treats women is unfortunate, in that it undermines a process of change that is in fact going on, however fitfully. It is clear that many women composers are still coming to terms with their own position within musical life:

> [. . .] women, like men, have been socialized to think of music as an art-form beyond gender, and that includes its composers and its history. Until recently music history was conceived as a history of composers, not a history of *male* composers. So a woman might not recognize that there is a problem.[70]

It is clear that the huge obstacles which can be placed in the way of women who wish to compose can result in a general lack of confidence by them in their own abilities. The diffidence exhibited by a number of women composers is commented on by Rhian Samuel:

> One very real barrier to the success of women composers is female prejudice itself. Women commonly feel inadequate to assume dominant roles over their peers; it is but a small step to project such feelings onto other women.[71]

This lack of confidence and tension about their role as creator or authority figure leads to what some have termed the 'anxiety of authorship':

> The anxiety often translates into ambivalence: contradictory statements or actions about one's relationship to the creative process.[72]

Marcia Citron cites many well-known female composers of the nineteenth century who struggled with a lack of confidence in their creativity. These include Clara Schumann and Fanny Mendelssohn. Perhaps it is this lack of confidence coupled with lack of recognition that leads some women to dissociate themselves from women composers as a group.

It is clear that many women composers feel more comfortable if they can view themselves as token men. This is no surprise, since women are acculturated in patriarchy, just as men are. Moreover, their views are often coloured by the same unthinking prejudices. Hence, many find it easier to view themselves as unique; different from most other members of the weaker, less creative, less successful sex. Placing themselves in this position makes some guard their place as individuals fiercely. If other women achieve similar success or status, this becomes a threat to their position. It can result in their dissociation from the general problems faced by other women composers and even make them consistently unhelpful to other women. A similar phenomenon can be observed among members of ethnic and religious minorities who find themselves the only representatives of their 'kind' in the workplace. Having achieved a satisfactory personal position (in their own perception), they may be reluctant to jeopardize it by identifying themselves with others of the same minority, in case dominant prejudices are stirred up or they are accused of partisanship. Isolated members of minorities often state forcefully, and with apparent sincerity, that they have not, personally, suffered prejudice or discrimination. In such cases, one always needs to consider whether the denial of discrimination is not, perversely enough, being used as a mechanism of ingratiation for the purpose of fending off latent (or mitigating actual) prejudice.

An extreme form of this type of attitude is found in a composer who has achieved a considerable amount of exposure and acclaim from the mainstream musical establishment. The Scottish composer Thea Musgrave (b. 1928) stated in a BBC Radio Three interview broadcast on 8 December 1988:

> I don't think any more we [women composers] have a raw deal. Perhaps if you lived 100 years ago, it would have been a different story, but in this country from Dame Ethel Smyth onwards [women] have fought the battle, so one's more of a rarity – so you have much more of an advantage [. . .]

This seems a highly significant statement in the light of the many facts and statistics I have quoted previously about the treatment of women composers and the continued minority status of their music. By stating that she feels it is advantageous to be a woman composer, I presume Musgrave is implying that she can gain some sort of 'novelty' value from her minority position. She has a higher profile because she is one of the very few women working in a male-dominated field. However, this comment raises a number of more disturbing issues. Can being treated as a novelty be seen as anything other than patronizing? And indeed, if composers of Ethel Smyth's generation won the battle to gain a place for women composers, why are women composers, such as Musgrave, still such a rarity? Surely, the continued 'rarity' of female composers cannot be glibly dismissed in the light of the tradition of attitudes against their creativity and involvement.

Musgrave's views are often quoted by those who want to 'prove' that there is no such thing as sexual discrimination in music. Possibly, the most damaging thing is the message it sends to those other women who stand up and speak of discrimination and claim that being a woman composer is a decided disadvantage. It trivializes their experience because it implies that if one is not successful and accepted, one has only a lack of talent to blame – all the more so if, as Musgrave would have it, it is much 'easier' to be noticed if one is a woman composer. The position of Musgrave, as one of the few women who have attained a measure of recognition within the musical establishment, makes her message all the more potent. Her case shows that submitting to the novelty stereotype is easier than trying to change things, although basking in this novelty value serves only to perpetuate tokenism and keep most women safely in their place. It is clear that many women composers do not want to make an issue of their gender, feeling that this category leads only to accusations of special pleading, when they know that they have the ability to be compared and judged by purely musical criteria. Statements which assert that being a woman composer is actually advantageous can only discourage women from airing the discrimination they have faced.

It seems that the cornerstone of contemporary women's distrust of, and objection to, being labelled 'woman' is simply that they consciously or unconsciously do not wish to be burdened with its negative implications and double binds. This is true also of objections to the concept of a female-centred, as opposed to a male-centred, musical aesthetic. There is, without doubt, a fine line between reinforcing cultural and social stereotypes of masculine and feminine temperament, which can be damaging, and searching for a genuine meaning and expression of sexual identity held in music. Clearly, the musical establishment has often used the categorization of 'women' against women composers. The gendered term, when used by male musicologists and critics, has automatically imposed on the composer all the traditionally bigoted arguments and beliefs about female creativity and its supposed inferiority. The prefix of 'woman', often weighted and poisonous, has attempted to keep 'women composers' in their place – in a subsidiary tradition outside the mainstream. Obviously, the relatively new feminist arguments which make a point of accepting, but reinterpreting, the concept of 'women composers' are intended to undermine the original purpose of the old categorization, but at the same time they run the risk of provoking a reconfirmation of the traditional ideas, making it more, instead of less, difficult for female composers to be accepted universally. The dilemma parallels that of ethnic minorities (blacks, Jews and so on) choosing between 'separatist' and 'assimilationist' programmes. One thing is certain: each approach works against (and is seen as an embarrassment to) the other. In the statements made by many women composers there emerges a distinct need to feel part of the tradition by which they are surrounded, a system in which, despite its bias, they have learned all their musical and cultural values. Most of all, they do not wish to alienate men and have a strong need to be accepted and valued by traditional methods and criteria. Feminist writers and commentators should be aware that their work is often viewed by composers of their own sex as a marginalizing influence which complicates still further the debates which surround their experience.

Notes

1 Eva Rieger, 'Dolce Semplice? On the Changing Role of Women in Music' in Gisela Ecker (ed.), *Feminist Aesthetics* (London, 1985), 137.
2 Diane Peacock Jezic, *Women Composers: The Lost Tradition Found* (New York, 1988), 224–227.
3 Robert P. Morgan, *Twentieth Century Music*, (New York and London, 1991), 286.
4 Camille Saint-Saëns, *Harmonie et mélodie*, third edition (Paris, 1885), cited in Eugene Gates, 'The Woman Composer Question' (Doctor of Education thesis, University of Toronto 1992), 44.
5 Jezic, *Women Composers*, 4–5. A fuller discussion of sexual aesthetics as applied to music is deferred to Chapter 7.
6 Peter J. Pirie, *The English Musical Renaissance* (London, 1979), 177.
7 *Ibid.*, 185.
8 Boyd, *Grace Williams*, 10.
9 Michael Trend, *The Music Makers: Heirs and Rebels of the English Musical Renaissance: Edward Elgar to Benjamin Britten* (London, 1985), 93.
10 Marie J. Counter, 'The role of stereotypes in the relationship between composers and society: an enquiry into the extent to which the composers output is affected by environmental pressures, with particular emphasis on the perspective of women composers' (Dissertation, London University, 1990), 7.
11 Rhian Samuel, interviewed by the author on 29 June 1993. Author's own transcript, 18.
12 David Ewen, *The World of Twentieth Century Music* (first edition: London, 1968; second edition, 1991), xxxi.
13 Germaine Greer, *The Obstacle Race* (London and New York, 1979), 68.
14 *Ibid.*, 68.
15 Frank Howes, *The English Musical Renaissance* (London, 1966), 293.
16 *Ibid.*, 293.
17 Howes, *loc. cit.*
18 'Girl Composer's Triumph', place of publication and author unknown, included in the British Music Information Centre's collection of reviews of Elizabeth Maconchy's work.
19 Herbert Hughes, 'The Land', *Daily Telegraph*, 1 August 1930.
20 Editorial, *The Strad*, January 1947.
21 'Women Composers', *Birmingham Post*, 2 December 1946.
22 A.F. Leighton Thomas, 'Grace Williams', *Musical Times*, May 1956, 241.
23 Stephen Johnson, 'Review', *The Listener*, 14 September 1989.
24 Eithne Power, 'Life Begins at 80!', *Radio and TV Times*, 21–27 October 1989, 10.
25 Andrew Clements, 'A Child of Our Time', *The Guardian*, 2 January 1995, 4–5.

26 Susan Cook and Judy Tsou, *Cecilia Reclaimed* (Urbana, 1994), 3.
27 James Briscoe (ed.), *Historical Anthology of Music by Women* (Indiana, 1987), xi.
28 For a more extensive analysis of this aspect of feminist musicology see Citron, *Gender and the Musical Canon*, 213–214.
29 Citron, *Gender and the Musical Canon*, 212.
30 Susan McClary, *Feminine Endings: Music, Gender and Sexuality* (Minnesota, 1991), 115.
31 *Ibid.*, 19–20.
32 Pieter C. van den Toorn, 'Politics, Feminism, and Contemporary Music Theory', *The Journal of Musicology*, 9 (1991), 297.
33 *Ibid.*, 293.
34 Ruth Solie, 'What Do Feminists Want: A Reply to Pieter van den Toorn', *The Journal of Musicology*, 9 (1991), 401.
35 Van den Toorn, 'Politics, Feminism, and Contemporary Music Theory', 293.
36 Rhian Samuel, 'Feminist Musicology: Endings or Beginnings?', *Women: A Cultural Review*, 3 (1993), 66.
37 *Ibid.*, 68.
38 Citron, *Gender and the Musical Canon*, 3.
39 *Ibid.*, 192.
40 Worthy of mention is the forthcoming publication by Margaret Ericson: *Women in Music: A Selective Bibliography on the Collective Subject of Women in Music* (Boston: G.K. Hall).
41 Citron, *Gender and the Musical Canon*, 181.
42 *Ibid.*, 182.
43 Elson, *Women's Work in Music*, 241.
44 Rieger, ''Dolce semplice'? On the Changing Role of Women in Music', 148–149.
45 Citron, *Gender and the Musical Canon*, 78.
46 Stanley Sadie (ed.), *The New Grove Dictionary of Music and Musicians*, xvii, 432.
47 Nicola LeFanu, 'Master Musician: An Impregnable Taboo?' Paper read to the Women in Music Conference, London, 6 February 1987, 2.
48 Nancy Van De Vate, 'The American Woman Composer: Some Sour Notes', *High Fidelity/Musical America*, 25/6 (1975), 19.
49 Correspondence between Elizabeth Maconchy and the author. Letter dated 14 November 1992.
50 Kirkwood, transcript of taped response to questionnaire, 5 November 1993, 8.
51 Correspondence between Antoinette Kirkwood to the author. Letter dated 1 March 1993.
52 Dale Spender, *Man Made Language* (London, 1980), 20.
53 *Ibid.*, 20–21.
54 Diana Burrell, 'Accepting Androgyny', *Contact*, 32 (1988), 52.
55 Letter from Grace Williams to Gerald Cockshott dated 22 January 1949, quoted in Boyd, *Grace Williams*, 42.
56 Mary Blume, 'Elisabeth Lutyens', *International Herald Tribune*, 9–10 January 1982.
57 Blume, *loc. cit.*
58 Andrea Dworkin, *Woman Hating* (New York, 1974), 23.
59 Correspondence between Enid Luff and the author. Letter dated February 1993.
60 Kirkwood, transcript of response to a questionnaire dated 5 November 1993, 8.
61 Kirkwood, *loc. cit.*
62 Keal interview transcript, 20.
63 Bryony Jagger, written response to a questionnaire dated 16 July 1993, 8.
64 Jagger, *loc. cit.*

65 Jagger, *loc. cit.*
66 Bailey interview transcript, 1.
67 *Ibid.*, 38.
68 *Ibid.*, 53.
69 Bailey, *loc. cit.*
70 Citron, *Gender and the Musical Canon*, 178.
71 Rhian Samuel, 'Women Composers Today: A Personal View', *Contact*, 23 (1988), 53.
72 Citron, *Gender and the Musical Canon*, 54.

6 Tradition and Genre

> From conception to completion, Wagner's Ring Cycle took thirty-four years to compose, a remarkable example of persistence and determination. Many women have written successful songs [. . .] but they have seldom put together musical works on a grander scale such as operas, symphonies or even musical comedies. It is difficult to escape the conclusion that some factor such as intrinsic motivation or 'scale of thinking' is another contributor to artistic genius.[1]

> An awareness of the gendered 'difference' of music requires a dismantling of the discursive authority that maintains such difference. Only through such dismantling will those situated 'differently' – including women – be able to recuperate music as a cultural practice of power and consequence. What is required is not the politics of opposition, resistance and negation [. . .] What is required, rather, is a politics of articulation, a politics based on understandings of those fused and confused, messy, paradoxical, and contradictory cultural practices that have come to be discursively constituted as different genres of music.[2]

In this chapter I intend to examine how a male-dominated musical tradition built on a discriminatory social system has both affected and restricted the work of female composers. The legacies of women's traditional roles in music-making, which have been largely dictated by their social status, form an important link in the chain of understanding that illuminates contemporary attitudes towards music written by women. At the heart of the discussion of women's musical traditions lies the concept that the compositional genre used by a composer can be affected by non-musical as well as musical considerations. Furthermore, compositional genre can be seen as a powerful indicator of composers' place in musical life and their access (or relation) to institutions which can bring their music to public attention.

To understand women's position in musical culture in the twentieth century, many aspects traditionally considered purely musical, and therefore natural or unchangeable, need to be analysed and understood in the context of the patriarchal society which produced them. This poses many problems, since musical creation is habitually presented as an entirely autonomous process untouched by the effects of culture or society, when this is surely not the case:

> Musical production, that system by which we collectively produce divided musical products, is regarded, not as an expression of our social history, but as the fulfilment of pre-extant, autonomous requirements laid down by the nature of music. The ideology of autonomy denies the fact that it is necessary for us to have socially-derived, learnt familiarity with inherent meanings, in order to recognise music at all: this denial makes the materials of music and their organisation appear to be

> understandable by virtue, not of social knowledge and historical being, but by nature.[3]

It is frequently asserted that a piece of music is judged only on its 'natural' merits – its quality, construction and content dictating its musical worth. However, musical valuation is far from a purely musical consideration and should be understood as a much more complex matter, very much connected with who is creating and consuming the musical product. Consequently, throughout the twentieth century music has continued to be defined along lines of social status and authority:

> Within the contemporary industrialized world, music is conceptualized and managed either as cultural capital, the property of those with power and influence, or as leisure and entertainment, a diversion and distraction for those without power.[4]

The concept that music, of whatever style or genre, has no 'inherent' qualities which 'naturally' dictate musical worth shifts the burden of valuation and categorization from the neutral 'musical' to the social and often political: it falls to those who are in social authority to dictate what is, and what is not, of musical value.

The construction of the value system which categorizes musical styles and genres can be seen as reinforcing social and political constructions rather than purely musical elements:

> It is questionable [. . .] whether there *are* 'classical', 'popular', 'folk', and 'traditional' musics. It seems more likely that there are *discourses* constructed around concrete musical practices, and that those discourses group such practices into categories that render the music amenable to various forms of social, political and economic control.[5]

Music, when it lies in the hands of those who hold power and authority, reinforces their cultural superiority; yet when it comes into the hands of those without power, it is rendered of little worth. This is the first and most basic categorization of musical value. Clearly, artistic contribution to art, be it in words, visual images or aural statements, is categorized as either high or low culture. High cultural art is usually produced by the ruling group and generally embodies those concepts which are valued by society at large. Low cultural art, on the other hand, can be produced by anyone and is usually not widely valued by society. Within the Western European tradition high culture music is defined by the 'classical' music tradition. Low culture music has been defined as everything from 'popular' songs to rock and roll, music hall and folk idioms. Since women have been without significant power or status for centuries, their access to, and position within, high culture has been limited. Consequently, the high culture/low culture divide is in some measure a gendered divide (although it is also structured along race and class lines) and is of significance to the current discussion.

Within every art form a high-low cultural divide can be observed. Correspondingly, within these wider artistic genres a myriad of compositional genres exist; these, too, often have a corresponding gendered appropriateness and value:

> Certain areas of cultural territory have been marked out as the province of women, while others have been colonized by men. Professional male artists were expected to paint female nudes, while amateur women produced delicate watercolours of landscapes or flowers; men composed symphonies, women songs; men wrote epics, women novels.[6]

These divisions form potent indicators of the relative social role the creator of art holds across culture. In music there is a clear segregation of compositional genres into those which are formal and informal, elite and popular, complex and simple, valued and not valued, public and private, large-scale and small-scale: in each case the former is rated above the latter. The dimensions of a musical composition; its complexity and form; the forces needed to reproduce it; its performance sphere and level of dissemination are all important factors in the potential 'value' which can be ascribed to the work, regardless of its actual content.

To gain a general overview of the traditions and genres evident in the work of women composers I have used *The Encyclopedia of Women Composers* (1987) compiled by Aaron Cohen. This, as we saw, contains a comprehensive list of some 6000 women composers from across the world dating back to 30 BC. Appendix 8 of Volume II contains listings of composers according to the instruments for which they have written and the musical genres to which they have contributed. Although this appendix does not in any way provide a complete listing of *all* compositions ever written by women (or, indeed, by the women listed) it nevertheless provides a very interesting approximate guide to the musical genres cultivated by women, primarily within the Western art music tradition, in different centuries. Of significance is the clear profusion of female work in smaller forms and for a limited range of instruments, even when male composers were gradually developing larger and more complex musical systems. If a general comparison is made with the corresponding male compositional patterns and traditions, it becomes evident that, whether by circumstance or choice, women have not often written in musical genres, such as the symphony, which were considered important in the period of musical history in question (Table 6.1).

The differences between male and female musical contributions are important, since they have often been used as 'proof' of women's intellectual, artistic and spiritual inferiority, many believing that these differences could not have a social cause.

Table 6.1 Women's work in music by genre

Century	18th	19th	20th	Total
Songs	87	665	1969	2721
Keyboard	49	344	2013	2406
Symphonies	3	95	247	355

Source: Cohen, A. (ed.), *The Encyclopaedia of Women Composers*, Second Edition (New York, Books and Music, 1987)

The idea of a distinct female music tradition is an uncomfortable and often unimaginable concept for many, both male and female. However, when the work of past European women composers is surveyed, certain important themes are apparent and these are distinct from the traditional patterns of work produced by male composers. The areas of art inhabited by the female composer, artist and writer have many common characteristics, most noticeably their lack of artistic 'value'. They are stereotypically small scale, simple, modest, undemanding, amusing, charming, less serious and 'pretty'. Such genres usually require less formal training and can often be cultivated with little financial expenditure or contact with public institutions. From this state of affairs two points arise. First, why have women chosen to create music in these genres and, second, why have these genres been considered less important than those which seem to be primarily male dominated?

Before one examines either of these points, it is important to understand women's traditional relationship to compositional genre and how they have customarily functioned in music practices around the world.

Women's contribution to music, when examined across a number of cultures, reveals certain typical patterns. Primarily, this is because globally the pattern of social contribution and experience generally dictates the respective musical spheres of the sexes.[7] Cross-cultural research has shown that women, in virtually all cultures around the world, have tended to be restricted to the private, domestic, usually functional sphere, whereas men tend to occupy and dominate the public sphere. Vocal music has always been an accessible and important part of female music-making. Women tend to sing while they work, to themselves or their children, at weddings, funerals and other family-based events. For women of many cultures, music is undertaken as an accompaniment to other essential, usually domestic, activities. Correspondingly, music has never been marked out as an individual event for women, as it has been for men. This has been suggested as the reason for women's limited participation in instrumental music across a number of cultures. Women, typically, do not have their hands free to play instruments as they create music while they work.[8]

Jennifer Post's research into women's performance spheres provides a vital insight into women's traditional access to musical life in a range of cultures. Table 6.2 devised by Post in relation to female performers, provides a useful model for analysis of women composers' work sphere. From this table a relationship between the composer's social situation and the level of access to music, including the genre of music in which he or she chooses to create, can be traced.

In this light, social restrictions and roles, compositional genre and musical opportunities all have obvious links with gender divisions in society and social relationships.[9] Women's restricted access to certain genres seems to be the musical reflection of the confined social and musical spheres within which they have traditionally operated. The male composer has been universally characterized by his position in the wider 'public' culture, his work dictating and

Table 6.2 Access to musical life

Men's sphere	Women's sphere
Work outside home Limited family contact Group orientation	Work in the home Strong family contact Solitary or limited Small-group limitation
Resulting in Freedom Social Repertoire Musical medium	*Resulting in Restriction* Social Repertoire Musical medium
Domination In an ensemble Decisions about music Integration	*Subordination* In an ensemble Decisions about music Segregation

Source: Post, J., 'Erasing the Boundaries between Public and Private in Women's Performance Traditions', in S. Cook and J. Tsou (eds), *Cecilia Reclaimed: Feminist Perspectives on Gender and Music* (Urbana: University of Illinois Press, 1994)

creating the course and content of high culture music in most societies. Obviously, men will compose music which functions, and is valued, in this public sphere and usually will have access to the establishments which possess the resources to realize music on a larger, public scale. In our Western culture the public domain has traditionally been male dominated. Therefore it is unsurprising not only that more men than women compose in high culture musical genres, but also that these genres have acquired greater musical value.

On the other hand, the private, low-culture traditions of music-making (and other arts) within families and local communities, are an area with which women have been traditionally involved. This type of low culture music has been available to everyone regardless of class, race or sex, but its genres (for example, peasant dance music, celebratory and work songs, lullabies and folk songs) are not considered representative of the real or 'pure' aesthetic value of music. Music created for private, domestic consumption has occupied a very different place from the public music created by, and for, socially powerful individuals and institutions. The choice of compositional genre, in this context, becomes a choice influenced not only by educational and ability orientation, but also by social and political factors.

High culture, public music plays a complex role in contemporary society, but its status and authority remain largely unquestioned. The categorization of high and low culture music, along with the scale of valuation of the many musical genres which make up these areas, plays an important role in women's marginalized access to musical composition as a means of intellectual authority. That women have had access to create music which reflects more functional creative motivations has always been indicative of their social sphere rather than their mental capabilities. For example, there have been women composers whose work has achieved remarkable levels of dissemination and popularity without their music ever receiving 'official' recognition on account of being perceived as low culture, simple or commonplace. A pertinent example of this is provided by two of the most widely known (and performed) songs of the twentieth century: 'Happy Birthday to You', written by Mildred and Patty Smith Hill, and 'Rock-a-bye Baby', written by Effie Canning. These songs show that there are female composers who have written music which has gained immense 'success' – yet their work has not attracted the respect and admiration of musicians and scholars (the musical establishment). The immense success of these songs, in terms of dissemination amongst the population and number of performances in everyday life, has not been judged as any measure of the quality of the compositions. The reasons why these songs have been dismissed as cultural capital reveals much about our system of musical value. So often, these values are accepted as natural, but they can in fact be seen as largely socially constructed and, moreover, working to the disadvantage of women and other groups who hold little power or authority within society.

'Happy Birthday to You' is not widely recognized as a 'great' piece of music for a number of reasons. The genre essentially illustrates all the elements we least value in music: it can be realized by one untrained individual; it is socially related in its lyrical content; it is specifically functional, being a 'celebration song'; it is melodious and simple, and can be passed on aurally rather than by means of notation. All these elements determine the music's frame of reference: low culture music.

Along these lines there has evolved a definite hierarchy of compositional genres: at the top, the world of large-scale (in terms of length of musical duration and instrumental forces), abstract instrumental music, and at the bottom folk or popular songs. This categorization can be observed within both high and low cultures. For example, 'popular music' is usually considered part of low culture music but within popular music instrumental jazz music is seen to hold greater 'musical value' than a commercial pop song or a traditional lullaby. Indeed, in both high and low culture the same system of values can be seen to work; that is, the further from the solo vocal, small-scale, simple, functional and domestic plane a piece of music moves, the greater its perceived musical worth. Of particular importance is the idea that 'great' or 'good' music should be free of social signs and references:

> [. . .] it has been taken as a mark of value in the assessment of much 'serious' ['classical'] music that it can be seen to be asocial, unmarred and untainted by the forces of mass social existence. 'Popular' music, on the other hand, has traditionally been seen as less valuable by aestheticians and musicologists precisely because it is not possible to easily deny the social meaning implicit in many of its genres.[10]

However, 'serious' or high culture music is far from asocial in either its function or its conception. Creating the idea that serious art music transcends social or political content or context is one way in which those who form the musical establishment acquire an unchallengeable authority. Denying music's social roots and political functions gives it an almost God-given autonomy. Hence, relating women's invisibility within high culture music to their socially disadvantaged position has been very difficult, leaving women open to the charge of 'natural' musical inferiority. It is clear that in a musical system where functionality and social relatedness are seen as inferior traits, women's immersion in the domestic and home-based spheres has traditionally kept them functioning within this 'lower' frame of reference.

The compositional genres permitted to, and inhabited by, women have formed an important foundation for the damaging stereotype of the artistically limited and non-prolific female composer. The opportunities, capital and education needed to create high culture music have traditionally been monopolized by the ruling group (white, male, upper and middle-class) in order to reinforce perceptions of their position as the social elite, so strengthening their power base and system of values.

The social and political authority of those who produce and consume high culture music is most strongly signified by its close early association with the church and the aristocracy, both patriarchal power bases. Correspondingly, the role of music in both the sacred and the secular traditions has played a part in creating and reinforcing the views and values of those in power:

> [. . .] music was viewed as a powerful enterprise as well as a source of entertainment and pleasure. The spiritual power and moral suasion ascribed to music gave it special significance and encouraged its regulation.[11]

It also implied women's exclusion from its creation. Music composed to glorify God or uplift the intellectual sensibilities of the rich and powerful was quite distinct from music produced in the home and local community to accompany ritual and work or for simple entertainment.

Music and the status of the composer have always been shaped along social as well as musical lines. The changing social fabric of Europe, including Britain, through the seventeenth, eighteenth and nineteenth centuries saw a corresponding change in the position and valuation of music. Throughout the seventeenth and eighteenth centuries the category of public, high culture music was destined for three main areas: religious, theatrical (operatic) and chamber. At this time the role of the composer was often little more than that of a servant/employee of the church or of a wealthy aristocrat. Music was usually written for a specific event or purpose (sacred, ceremonial or aristocratic), its value and message becoming symbols of the institution for which it was written and its message becoming relatively widespread and public. Women's position outside these institutions of authority, whether political, intellectual or religious, presupposed their exclusion from the artistic realization of music which represented such powerful institutions. Hence women composers' contribution to high culture musical genres up to the end of the nineteenth century was heavily circumscribed on account of their exclusion from positions of authority and power.

The social status of women and the restrictions imposed on them as individuals can also be linked to their early exclusion from many domains of music. For example, debarring women from public music and high culture genres was often directly connected to the suppression and control of female sexuality. Music was, and still is, an essentially social practice which places its creators and performers in a position of physical and mental exhibition, where they become the centre of attention, often 'exposed' to a number of strangers. Consequently, for women of many eras musical participation has been viewed as brazen and immodest behaviour. Through music women could gain contact with and be on 'display' to any number of individuals, often men. This was clearly linked with sexual promiscuity; indeed, safeguards 'protecting' women against such dangers have been imposed on them in a number of ways.

From around the fourth century the injunction *Mulier in ecclesia taceat* (Let women keep silence in church) was enforced, excluding most women from the creation of sacred music, at that time the music of greatest power and influence. Denied this artistic outlet, many potential early women composers were silenced.[12] However, women were sometimes allowed to make music inside the confines of their nunneries. Indeed, this formed an important outlet for female creativity, and over half the sacred and secular music published by women before 1700 was written by nuns.[13] Some of the earliest known composers in the Western art tradition were such nuns as Hildegard of Bingen (1098–1179) and Isabella Leonarda (1620–1704). Even so, convents could in no way compete with the facilities available for music-making in male monasteries.[14]

Moreover, music-making by nuns was constantly under threat by the church authorities and was never fully accepted. For example, in 1563 convents were banned from cultivating polyphonic music and the playing of instruments. In 1686 Pope Innocent XI issued a sterner decree:

> [. . .] forbidding all women – single, married, or widowed as well as nuns – to learn music for any reason from any man, including their fathers or husbands, or to play any musical instrument, 'because music is completely injurious to the modesty that is proper for the [female] sex'.[15]

This decree was even renewed in 1703 and gives an indication of the extent to which music-making was considered a dangerous and damaging practice for women to engage in. It also explains how for many women a limited amount of 'simple' vocal music and singing was the only accepted musical outlet.

In direct contrast to the prevailing attitudes of the church, it is a fact that between 1450 and 1600 most wealthy or aristocratic women were expected to be able to read music, play an instrument and sing. The fact that this was undertaken primarily within the confines of the home obviously lessened the dangers believed inherent when a woman created or performed music for a wider audience.[16] Indeed, domestic music-making was a very important part of life for many wealthy and educated families across Western Europe. This domestic music-making functioned generally on two levels, both of which are connected with the female role. First, music acted as simple entertainment: it charmed and distracted from the drudgery of everyday life. Second, it acted as an accompaniment to courtship and sexual attraction. Music allowed a female to 'display' herself for suitors to admire. Directly linked to this courtship and marriage ritual, musical attainment in women was also considered a demonstration of a family's wealth and position. If a family had sufficient wealth to train a daughter in a fundamentally inessential pastime, it sent out positive signals about its financial situation and social position.

Unsurprisingly, the first women composers of the seventeenth and eighteenth centuries came from privileged aristocratic backgrounds; most were from families of musicians. Obviously, the women who were able to embark on any sort of musical career needed to be born into a family which not only had the necessary resources but also encouraged and developed their musical and artistic abilities beyond the accepted levels of female attainment. Such were the backgrounds of the early female composers Raffaella (*ca* 1570–*ca* 1646) and Vittoria Aleotti (*ca* 1573–*ca* 1620), Francesca Caccini (1587–1640), Barbara Strozzi (1619–1664) and Elisabeth-Claude Jacquet de la Guerre (1666–1729).

Similarly, it was usually as performers, primarily singers, that the earliest British female composers were able to emerge. Mary Dering (1629–1704), admittedly, was not a performer, but she did have direct access to the artistic circles of the day. Three of her songs published in a volume of works by her teacher, the composer Henry Lawes, are probably the oldest surviving published compositions by a British woman.[17] For a woman to seek the publication of her compositions was viewed as fundamentally immodest; indeed, it was only at the insistence of Lawes that these songs were published at all.[18] Examples of early British female composers who made their names initially as singers are Harriet Abrams (1760–1822) and Maria Barthelemon (1749–1799), to whom we may add Jane Guest (1765–1824?), who was a keyboard-player.

At this time most women developed their creativity via their performance skills. Playing an instrument or singing (performance skills) were, and still are, the first point of contact most individuals have with music, and from this platform the creative (compositional) skills evolve in either an improvisatory or a notated shape. But this simple progression was often the last as well as the first contact women had with musical creativity. Their musical development was often confined to their experience as musical performers, since for the vast majority, instrumental (or vocal) tuition was their only route to musical training in the wider sense, as was discussed in Chapter 4. Consequently, women's compositions tended to be limited to these instruments.[19]

> Women's work in composition in the past was directly related to the restrictions placed on them as singers and instrumentalists [. . .] Typically these women wrote the kinds of music that fit into their situations, which were more limited than men's.[20]

This put early women composers at a severe disadvantage. The major 'serious' genres of the sixteenth and seventeenth centuries lay within sacred and secular vocal polyphony (Mass, motet and so on), later joined by opera.[21] If composers did not write in the fashionable and valued genres of the day, they could not be considered serious or worthy. In this connection, it is not coincidental that Maddalena Casulana (*ca* 1540–*ca* 1590) managed to gain attention as a composer precisely because she worked in a genre which was engaging many of the leading composers of the time: the madrigal. Casulana was, indeed, the first woman ever to have her music published.[22]

Many other women composers were, however, much more restricted in their scope. For example, although Barbara Strozzi was a singer of some renown, she never sang in, or wrote, opera:

> While her male contemporaries functioned in the public sphere, Strozzi never left her enclosed domestic one. Perhaps this accounts for the limited genres in which she composed.[23]

Generally, restrictions in the social sphere translated directly into restrictions in the musical sphere of performance, repertoire and compositional genre. During the seventeenth century, particularly in Italy, it gradually became more acceptable for women to perform in a greater number of public spheres.[24] The fashion of the day was for performers to create, through improvisation or embellishment, large sections of the music they performed and women's wider role allowed them greater scope to become more skilled creators. It is recorded that some female performers had the knowledge and ability to improvise an entire piece, although this evidence of early female participation in musical creativity has not been left for posterity to regard and value.[25]

During the sixteenth and seventeenth centuries music was an accepted part of court life for some women:

> The famous courtesans of this era counted music making an indispensable skill. Courtesans were not simply prostitutes, but women who also wined, dined and entertained their male guests with music and witty conservation.[26]

Again, a historical link between the control and availability of female sexuality and music is observed. The vision of the sexually available female employing music as part of the seductive process became, in inverted form, the vision that the female musical performer was sexually available and of low morals. The association between music and female sexuality is both powerful and long-held. Indeed, the widespread cultural vision which identifies women as either virgins or whores can be applied also to the broad stereotypes of women musicians current until the twentieth century. On one hand, women composers emerged from the convent, just as later (especially in Britain and America) women were allowed access to music because it was considered a force which could create and preserve moral and religious purity. Directly opposing this concept is the role music has played as a signal of female availability (as a skill which enhanced the position of prostitutes who were sexually available or in young single women who were maritally available). On a professional level we encounter the female musician (usually a performer), who was considered brazen and sexually promiscuous by the mere fact that she 'exhibited' herself to the public.

Leading *prima donnas* of the last 200 years have often lived up to the image of the sexually promiscuous performer, some being renowned for their sexual freedom and multiple affairs in an era when these would have meant social suicide for most women.[27] Yet taking on such a 'visible' profession sometimes left women extremely vulnerable to sexual exploitation, regardless of their inclinations:

> In general [. . .] actresses, opera singers and ballerinas were not regarded as honourable women, and many were able to support themselves only by also being the mistress of an artistically inclined male patron.[28]

The idea of the 'brazen' woman can also be applied to women composers. To present one's work to be displayed and performed to the public was seen as immodest in a epoch when women were valued for their timidity, naïveté and lack of assertiveness.[29] The cultural belief that a woman should be modest at all times remains even today, but during the last three centuries it has been a powerful restraining influence on women's participation in music and other areas. These contradictory images of women can also be seen to have a direct musical translation, giving rise to musical models which have served only to reinforce further the potent stereotype of the female character:

> [. . .] in European classical music – a code developed and transmitted by men [. . .] women are either docile and passive (Monteverdi's Euridice, Bizet's Micaëla, Mozart's Pamina) or else man-devouring harpies (Monteverdi's Poppea, Mozart's Queen of the Night, Bizet's Carmen, Strauss' Salome). Because these pernicious musical images of women – the Madonna or the whore – have been the only ones available, generations of women training to be performers or composers have learned not to let themselves 'sound like women' in their playing, conducting or composing.[30]

Similar images surrounded female involvement in the rise of the salon in the seventeenth century. The salon was a setting, outside court, where men and women could meet and socialize, discussing a range of subjects from the mundane to the highly intellectual. By the early 1800s salons were established across Europe, and as well being important as social gathering places, they had become important forums for the work and ideas of their era's best-known composers, poets, writers and philosophers. Although women were very much involved in the creation and organization of salons in their homes, their perceived role in salon culture was often far from that of artist or intellectual:

> A woman could reap greater rewards by forming a sexual liaison with a talented or titled man than she could by refusing one [. . .] Social pressures and traditional attitudes about the impossibility of women and men relating other than sexually contributed to many salonières' use of sexual liaisons. Even if a salonière remained chaste, she would be gossiped about unmercifully: it was assumed that relations between men and women, however intellectual or artistic they might appear, could not remain platonic.[31]

So although part of the artistic circles of the time, women in salon life often held a precarious position. It seems that, for some men, women were accommodated within salon culture for their sexual rather than artistic or intellectual contributions. Clearly, this is not true of all salon women, but the bad reputation was influential – the accusation of sexual promiscuity was the risk many regarded as part and parcel of salon culture.

In Britain, specifically during the seventeenth and eighteenth centuries, musical participation for women was defined by similar gendered associations. The discussion in Chapter 4 highlighted that music (as a profession in Britain), although always male-dominated, has not always been highly regarded:

> Activities viewed as non-developmental and expressive of stationary time, such as music, were peripheral to men's lives [. . .] But for females such activities were considered *by men* appropriate and important, as delineators both of gender difference and of gender hierarchy. Music helped produce an ideologically correct species of woman: in the eyes of men music accordingly contributed to social stability by keeping women in the place that men had assigned them.[32]

Far from being a liberating experience, music was initially part of the restrictive socializing process which shaped most middle-class and upper-class women and actually acted as a further controlling element in their lives.

For British women, too, the demonstration of musical skills was considered an integral part of family entertainment or the courtship ritual but of little further value. Women were expected to play, sing, and compose small pieces to entertain and charm men:

> Not surprisingly, many women gave up their music when they married, though music was often used as a symbol of marital bliss, its harmony a parallel to marital harmony. We have few comments on the reasons for this from women [. . .] so cannot judge whether they lost interest in an 'accomplishment' that was specifically promoted as a way to win a husband, or simply had no time because of domestic responsibilities.[33]

The role music has traditionally taken in the lives of many women has been as an accompaniment to the various stages of their development. These undercurrents are important in their influence on women's participation in music leading into the twentieth century.

The essence of the music education received by most females in Britain up to the end of the nineteenth century reiterated their position at the centre of home and family. The musical education received by women was usually channelled into domestic music-making, whereas the musical education received by men was channelled for preference into intellectualism and public display. These socially dictated attitudes to musical education and training were then translated, both directly and indirectly, into the different compositional genres in which men and women felt they could, and should, compose.

The musical genres which accompanied the idealized notions of the feminine character consisted primarily of simple, short songs and keyboard pieces. In the domestic, home-based performance spheres, the function of the female performer and composer (often one and the same person) was that of ornament, decoration, entertainment and pleasant distraction. Their music served to reinforce women's position as subservient to the needs and pleasures of men. It maintained them in the position of amateurs rather than professionals and ensured that the creative work of women was never seen to encroach on the established male territory.

In nineteenth-century Britain the compositional genres practised by women were predominately solo songs, part-songs and piano pieces.[34] Indeed, the one area of composition where women were fully accepted was in song-writing of the parlour ballad variety. Significantly, this type of song was easily distinguishable from the high culture 'art song' type and was considered the vocal equivalent of the character piano piece:

> The drawing room ballad was composed for both public and private consumption and here was a form of music-making that women could experience at first hand in their homes, unlike the performance of most other forms of music which was largely male-dominated and not of easy access to women.[35]

This type of ballad was extremely popular with middle-class English society, but this very popularity marked it as low culture, high culture music being seen as reinforcing musical and social elitism. Since ballads and songs revealed their domestic and social origins, they were consigned to the bottom of the musical establishment's value system.

Yet despite the lack of musical value placed on the popular ballad song by the musical establishment, its importance in shaping and encouraging the acceptability of women's making music should not be undervalued:

> For the first time ever, a large number of English women were involved in the performance of music without social restriction [. . .] using their detailed observations of the domestic scene as a basis for music of their writings, so the drawing room ballad allowed women full participation in their own homes both as performers and as creators.[36]

Some drawing room ballads written by British (or American and European) women sold vast amounts of sheet music and became widely known. For example, Lady Arthur Hill's 'In the Gloaming' (1877) sold 140,000 copies; songs by such composers as Claribel (1830–1869), Amy Woodforde-Finden (1860–1919) and Alicia Ann Spottiswoode (1810–1900) were also extremely popular. Often, the lyrical content of the ballads reflected women's experiences and was based on socially or domestically relevant themes, so providing a much-needed outlet for the female perspective. The ballad's humble musical status also ensured that female composers could produce vast quantities of music in this genre without their creative work ever having to be recognized by the musical establishment – so the wide dissemination of women's songs and ballads in the nineteenth and early twentieth centuries did not after all result in an increase in women's wider musical influence or acceptance.

Vocal music had always been an easily accessible area for female musical participation, but with the introduction of the piano into many middle-class homes from about 1830 onwards, many women gained access to an instrument. The piano was suitable for women, because it was based in the home environment and afforded an excellent vehicle for family entertainment.

Significantly, although women composers wrote a substantial amount of works for piano throughout the nineteenth century, most avoided the formal 'high culture' structure of the piano sonata:

> Middle-period Beethoven and Schubert are the models for several [piano] sonatas written by women composers and most do not achieve any degree of personal conviction: the rather ernest, self-consciously academic first movements tend to discourage [the listener . . .] It is however, when we turn to the smaller piano piece that [. . .] some attractive and worthwhile piano pieces by women [are found].[37]

This type of criticism of women's work is particularly significant when viewed in terms of the historical arguments against women composers' capabilities. Even when looking back from the vantage point of the late twentieth century, the brand of musical intellectualism demanded by sonata form is considered 'forced' and 'unnatural'.

Women composers tended instead to keep to less rigid (some would say less serious) forms, with pieces being of the 'character, lyrical' type exemplified by Mendelssohn's 'Songs without Words'. An influential factor was doubtless the point that many women lacked the formal knowledge and confidence to attempt serious piano genres. Generally speaking, to create a musical form which reflects the subject matter of a programme requires more inspiration and creativity but perhaps less formal training and knowledge of other works.

Another strong factor in the choice of musical outlet was the sexual stereotype which dictated what was suitable for the feminine temperament to produce. Undemanding, entertaining and charming: women's music, it seemed, should simply match their 'personalities'. In small-scale piano works women could create music which was virtually guaranteed a performance and an audience. Piano pieces had the added advantage of being self-contained, because they could be produced and consumed in the home without reference to the male-dominated music profession or institutions.

In the late nineteenth and early twentieth centuries differing patterns of female and male musical contribution could be distinguished. During the nineteenth century the high culture musical genres used by men covered a wide range from symphonies to solo sonatas, from operas to string quartets and from small-scale piano works to song-cycles. All these genres provided music of artistic insight and aesthetic value, rather than pleasant distraction. Although they varied in their demands, they had in common a 'respected' and established place in high culture music. For example, they were often vehicles for originality, developments at the cutting edge of music; they were extended in time span and extension of musical ideas; they were complex and less easily digested by the public: in cultural terms, again, aspects which emphasized their place as valued and elite.

Female composition, on the other hand, was commonly viewed as low culture 'popular' composition, defined by its social relatedness, small scale and simplicity of form. The few compositional genres to which this description applied gradually began to represent the natural modes of composition for women, reflecting both the female physique and the 'feminine' personality.

However, it must be acknowledged that in all genres male composers have outnumbered female composers:

> It would be futile to argue that the choice of a small format and a minor medium is quintessentially feminine. Men have outnumbered women in all the minor modes too [. . .] The tendency of women to work in the minor modes [. . .] is not simply a matter of their inferiority as artists [. . .] Such modes are presented to them both as eminently suitable for women and as impeccable sources of artistic satisfaction.[38]

Male composers have covered the whole range of genres from the largest symphonic works to small lyrical pieces. For men, the creation of music was not just an extension of their personalties: it was, rather, an intellectual display or an expression of the spirit and emotions.

Despite many difficulties, some women did, however, manage to work in large-scale genres at the end of the nineteenth century, but even then their choice of appropriate musical genres could be influenced by the 'feminine' social status of such works. For example, in nineteenth-century Britain music was viewed by many social reformers as a vehicle for religious teaching and moral influence. Involvement in music as a religious experience or to pass on a religious message made this type of recreational activity a more socially acceptable outlet for female emotion and energy:

> The moral goodness of music, particularly as expressed in the oratorio and the 'serious' ballads may account for the very large number of women who took to music in the nineteenth century.[39]

Although religious choral music was very much in vogue among male composers in Britain throughout this time, it provided a particularly significant outlet for women in that through choral and religious genres those who had managed to gain the requisite education could express themselves on a larger canvas via a socially accepted medium. British women composers who gained some recognition through having their religious works published include Ethel Smyth, Elizabeth Nunn (1861–1894) and Mary Grant Carmichael (1851–1935).[40]

It seems that the compositional genre adopted by a composer can be viewed as a very important, even political, decision, influenced by many social factors. Musical genre dictates the place and purpose of performance, the audience and the scale of value by which the work will be judged. There was strong social disapproval of women who attempted to step outside the circumscribed position of an entertainer of family and friends.[41] Since the genres which functioned as part of private and 'low key' entertainment were, on the whole, the main genres available to women, their work was – and is – judged and categorized correspondingly as insignificant and localized.

Indeed, the time-honoured question 'Why are there no great women composers?' concedes that women have been composers while assuming that their contribution has been inferior. This was the base from which women's involvement in the Western art music tradition developed into the twentieth century. The restricted and subservient position of women often denied them real opportunity to create and use music as a powerful medium. The social restrictions of the past and women's subsequent involvement with low-prestige genres has had an immense impact on the perceived value of 'women's work' up to the present day. Women composers throughout the twentieth century have been continually marginalized and criticized by the stereotype of their work as being simple and small, typified by songs and piano pieces, music considered of relatively little cultural worth. Although this stereotype has been exaggerated, it is clear that only a small minority of women composers throughout the nineteenth and early twentieth centuries wrote either large-scale or small-scale instrumental or solo works in high-prestige 'academic forms'.[42]

The result of women composers' concentration on smaller, less academic genres has served in the minds of some as proof that women are inherently incapable of producing large-scale serious music – in particular, abstract instrumental music as typified by the symphony. At the end of the nineteenth century many articles were published in an attempt to explain this supposed lack of success and greatness in women composers. Some asserted that it was women's natural lack of mathematical ability which hindered them in the creation of great music:

> Music may be defined as an imaginative and emotional structure, built on a mathematical foundation. Now we all know that woman, as a rule, is not a mathematical animal [. . .] Far the greater number of lady-composers, however, have devoted themselves to song-writing and in this department they have done good work.[43]

The composition of large-scale genres was considered a process governed by the 'masculine' mental traits of intellect and logic, whereas the composition of songs was thought to require far less mental ability and stamina. When an overtly anti-women statement such as this is delivered, it is often all the more potent when the sentiments are uttered by a woman. Although this article is anonymous, its wording shows that it was written by a woman. The note of resigned inferiority rings clear in the closing paragraph:

> One word of consolation [. . .] If we may never hope to rank high as creators, we may do almost what we like as interpreters. Still more, we may love the art passionately, if not to us shall be accorded her highest favours.[44]

The spectacle of a woman 'admitting' inferiority leaves no doubt that the opinion should be taken as a fact. The impact of such a demoralizing article should not be underestimated, not least because it was published in one of the most important and respected music journals, the *Musical Times*. It is perhaps coincidental that this article was published at a time when women composers were working in greater numbers than ever before. Its message served to reinforce the idea that the creation of great music was impossible for women.

A similar article, again written by a woman, summarized many of the opinions of the era:

> Why, among the thousands of unmarried girls of leisure and education, has no musical genius even approaching the first rank arisen? I answer, that because woman

> as the lesser man, is comparatively deficient in active emotional force, she cannot for this reason produce that which, at its best, is the highest and strongest of all modes of emotional expression [. . .][45]

Despite the many stereotypes which exist of the female as the more emotional, irrational being, in this context female emotionalism was viewed as but shallow and superficial compared to men's (which can ultimately be controlled by logic). Only men can harness their 'true' spiritual, intangible emotionalism and channel it into music. As far as these Victorian commentators were concerned, at the dawn of the twentieth century women still had no soul, intellect or spiritual depth.

Well into the twentieth century such philosophies have continued to be restated. It seems that the growing numbers of active women composers has ensured that from some quarters reminders to women of their proper musical place have periodically been issued. In an article written in 1958 a conciliatory note was sounded. It was now asserted that women were not able to be 'great' composers because:

> [. . .] women are themselves music, earthly harmonic systems that make the music of the world, whose greatest compositions lie in the creation of harmonic human beings attuned to the unuttered music that is in the soul of everyone. The most beautiful music in the world is made by the loving mother to her child.[46]

Women cannot create music because they create children – the oldest and most persistent charge against female creativity! Moreover, it reinforces the idealized image of the domesticated mother and child: in this world, singing to a child is a woman's true and *valued* creative outlet. Exhibited, once again, is the ever-present requirement that women be essentially defined and restricted by their biology. This type of physical objectification confirms woman's role as muse to the male creator, who is conveniently left free to inhabit the superior spiritual and mental space which transcends nature.

Clearly, in the twentieth century these idealized Romantic concepts have continued to exist. Society seems to need to maintain the distinct gender-differentiated roles in the artistic sphere just as it needs to preserve them in the domestic sphere. Some, however, perceived the Romantic era as blurring these strongly gendered roles. Romantic visions of the composer/artist, which have formed the basis of twentieth-century ideas, contain many stereotyped 'feminine' aspects in terms of both musical content and the personality of the composer/artist (a point made in Chapter 2). This, coupled with the fact that by far the largest number of female composers entered the musical scene at this time, reinforced the perception that even under these promising conditions women composers still did not become pre-eminent. Yet although attitudes towards certain 'feminine' characteristics may have changed over time by their increasing acceptance by some men, this bore little relation to the wider position of the female:

> What gives the Romantic contribution to the anti-female traditions a distinctively new feel is that women continued to be represented as artistic inferiors [. . .] even through qualities previously downgraded as 'feminine' had become valuable as

> consequence of radical changes in aesthetic taste and aesthetic theory [. . .] cultural misogyny remained (and even intensified) despite a reversal in attitudes towards emotionality, sensitivity and imaginative self-expression.[47]

The birth of the Romantic movement in the early 1800s contained a number of aesthetic contradictions which became reflected in the type and scale of the genres cultivated by many male composers:

> A number of characteristic themes of the Romantic movement, such as those of love or longing for nature, found their appropriate expression in an intense lyricism embodied in short pieces [. . .] The song and the one-movement piano piece were excellent vehicles for Romantic lyricism [. . .][48]

Some commentators have seized upon the fact that many of the leading male composers were respected for their small-scale songs and solo instrumental works, which appears to imply that women had the same opportunities in this area. But it must be acknowledged that although the work of some male composers concentrated on smaller forms, their output was usually supplemented by a quantity of larger-scale works. For example, composers renowned for their work in small forms such as Schubert, Schumann, Brahms and Liszt were all at the same time revered for their symphonies, concertos and use or development of complex formal structures such as sonata form. Indeed, they liked to group works that in themselves were small-scale into over-arching 'higher' entities. For example, some Schubert songs were organized in much longer song-cycles. Schumann then transferred this concept to such piano cycles as *Papillons* and *Carnaval*.

On the whole, the later Romantic period was a time of musical excess rather than of restraint and contraction. Genres which had evolved in the Classical period underwent tremendous development during this time. The symphony, in particular, often took on gigantic proportions as either an absolute or a programmatic work, and through it many of the core musical values of the era were reflected. Everything about the symphonic genre was made larger and more complex. Examples of this can be seen in the symphonies of Bruckner, Mahler, Mendelssohn, Schubert, Brahms, Tchaikovsky, Berlioz and Liszt. The tonal and harmonic structure became more complex and challenging; the melodic lines became more extended, as did the overall length of movements, the size of the orchestra and the duration of the whole work: a massive musical entity came into being.

The size, scope and pretensions of a work of this order of magnitude were then reflected back on to the individual composer, making the expressions 'great composer', 'genius' and 'masterpiece' essential terms of valuation and reference for entry into our musical canon. The composer who was defined by the formidable status of the 'great' composer was almost synonymous with the creator of music for vast instrumental forces, along extended compositional lines: music which challenged the listener in many ways, not least by its originality. Indeed, the greatness of a composer is a concept today (and even more in the recent past) bound up primarily with the cultivation of large-scale, large-dimension musical genres:

> The very word *greatness* contains a strong element of pure bigness. Usually, the simple preference for size is expressed in other terms, such as scope, profundity, scale, importance and the like. The artist who undertakes projects of due scope, significance and grandeur or size must have a masterful attitude not only to his subject, but also to the beholder whose attention he claims; insofar, such a concept of art may be called masculine.[49]

These 'masculine' dimensions of art mean that the composer must hold some kind of artistic authority to challenge the listener. Not only must the composer perceive and create his (or her) music on a vast scale: he or she must be capable of bearing the vast implications that such high-prestige art demands. This creates a doubly difficult position for women composers, since they have had neither the opportunity, the resources nor the cultural authority to attempt such works. This relationship between 'great' composers and 'great' music is typified by a number of musical genres, yet none more so than the symphony.

The symphony has been one of the most influential and prestigious genres, at the top of the high culture musical value system, for over two centuries. In the light of the previous discussion women's lack of contribution in this 'valued', large-scale, musical genre has been perceived as indicative of their secondary cultural significance. Obviously, the genres favoured by composers have changed greatly over time, but the domination of Western music by the symphony in the late eighteenth, nineteenth and twentieth centuries has left a huge legacy in terms of how music is valued and judged both by the public and by academic commentators. The symphonic tradition stands at the centre of the European musical canon of male composers and can be seen as having a powerful influence on the determination of the parameters of what is, and what is not, specially valued in music.

However, many of the issues which will be raised in relation to the symphony are by no means confined to it. My intention in highlighting the symphony as a compositional genre is simply to allow for the clear illumination of a number of powerful 'masculine' aesthetic values which are typified by this long-established, large-scale, usually abstract orchestral genre. Valued musical concepts such as complexity, size, duration, developmental scope, profundity and intellectualism can be seen as having been evolved and established in such genres as the symphony. Notably, these vital musical values have long been denied to women in obvious ways, not only through the latters' relative lack of education and opportunity, but also in less obvious ways, such as through their domestic isolation, 'feminine' socialization and lack of social/spiritual authority or power. Moreover, the symphony highlights issues of gender and public/private performance areas, as well as of women's relation to the musical institutions which are so much a part of musical life. My study group of female composers have all written one or more symphonies, in addition to other large-scale works, at some point during the twentieth century. I intend to describe how their works have been received by the establishment, examining how women fit into the generic patterns created by male creativity.

This investigation raises important questions about how the female role still restricts compositional genre, opportunities and ultimately recognition.

It is significant that many of the leading male composers of the twentieth century, from several countries, have written at least one symphony, thus further confirming its place as a 'high culture' genre.[50] However, discussion of the influence of genres and traditions in the context of the twentieth century presents some difficulties. The massive diversification of musical style and traditions in the latter part of the twentieth century is enormous. It is recognized that in the works of some composers concepts of genre, form, harmony, melody, dynamic and instrumentation have been dissolved and reinterpreted. Ironically, however, traditions seem to be more important to modern composers than ever before:

> Long a factor in Western thought, historical awareness has during the twentieth century become increasingly important in shaping musical attitudes. The past is now with us as never before, and the availability of such a breadth of historical repertory has fundamentally affected the way we perceive the past, the way we think about musical tradition, and consequently the way we view the music of our own day.[51]

Concepts and values which have surrounded the symphonic tradition – 'symphonic values' – have exerted an immense influence on a huge number of composers throughout the twentieth century. Even when the symphony as a specific genre has begun to lose its hold on the current generation of composers, its place within musical life and, importantly, its legacies are as important as ever. The continued demand for symphonic music in concert programmes, recordings and radio broadcasts indicates its continued strong and established place in musical life. But perhaps the symphony's real potency lies in the lasting influence on the aesthetic values of contemporary society – musical values long embodied by the genre. It is perhaps these less obvious legacies in terms of concepts of musical development and dimensions, ideas rooted and developed in the symphony, which continue to resound far outside its more traditional bounds.

The evolution of the symphony has played an important part in setting the values and ideals at the heart of high culture music. For example, the concept of music as an independent artistic experience was developed on the back of the symphony. Initially, most music was functional, sacred, ritual, or communicative, but over time it evolved into a more abstract, pleasure/aesthetic-based experience. Indeed, most music written before the eighteenth century was created for a specific purpose: it was functional, practical:

> The idea that music needs only a musical reason to exist and deserves to be heard for its own sake, was utterly foreign to earlier epochs of musical history [. . .] The 'musical work of art' came into being with the symphony, the prototype of autonomous instrumental music.[52]

The abstract music encompassed by the genre of the symphony symbolized for many the apex of male musical achievement throughout the late nineteenth and early twentieth centuries. As stated previously, music which belongs to high culture is generally defined as functionless, not tainted by its social foundations: it is 'pure' music which exists for its own sake. The symphony, with its extended structure and dimensions, proved the ultimate vehicle for this type of aesthetic development.[53] The symphony encompasses all the factors which our society values in music, and so women's limited participation in symphonic composition can be seen as emblematic of their current marginalization in musical life.

In musical terms, an instrumental work of symphonic proportions has been the ultimate test of a composer; the completion of such a work placed him or her in a position to receive the fullest exposure to the musical establishment.

> Like no other genre of composition, the symphony answered the definition of the word 'masterpiece', the foundation stone on which the institution of the 'grand concert' was erected.[54]

The symphony is still, for many, the ultimate demonstration of musical intellect – a symbol of artistic power on account of its size and complexity:

> As a work of exceptional length, technical difficulty and intellectual concentration, as a test both for composers and performers, the symphony was the main attraction and the pivot on which a concert turned [. . .][55]

The value accorded to complexity, and indeed virtuosity, over simplicity lies at the heart of the development process in much Western music. Our musical traditions over the last 250 years have become increasingly complex, up to the point where the inevitable gulf between composer and audience (from which a reaction is currently taking place) has reached unprecedented proportions in recent years. Complexity in composition is a particularly important concept for women composers to confront, since many of the mental skills needed to produce complexity have previously been stereotyped as male psychological preserves. Women's relationship to complexity and, indeed, intellectualism has always been different from men's. There is a long tradition of ideas and beliefs which have asserted female mental and creative inferiority. When any woman attempts any kind of complex composition, in view of these traditions, she puts herself in a position of 'proving' herself. When a male composer attempts such a composition, he is doing so in relation to a tradition of male composers who have 'annexed' the mental capacity of complexity as a 'masculine' trait; so his efforts are more likely to be judged as the fruits of his individual ability and not indicative of men as a group. Women, on the other hand, are viewed as a group who have not 'proved' their ability in complexity and who, as individuals, continue to define and represent notions of the perceived group ability. When a woman attempts a complex musical project such as a symphony, she is 'proving' (consciously or otherwise) not only herself, but also women as a class, because they (through her) are contradicting the feminine musical stereotype. The world listens to music by women with expectations of its inferiority and simplicity. If the symphonic genre is seen as a test, even for male creativity, then surely this test is all the more difficult for a woman to attempt and 'pass'.

Musical complexity requires not only skill, talent, intellect and concentration but also knowledge, education and training if it is to be brought from mere potential to full fruition. Further, women's difficult relationship with complexity has been explained by some in terms of her social position:

> The respect accorded to stylistic complexity after 1800 may result from a socio-political fabric that was itself becoming increasingly complex. In this post-aristocratic era there was greater personal opportunity, but the potential was much more relevant to men than women. This difference could partially explain the interest of nineteenth-century women in musical simplicity and their frequent avoidance of complex music structures like the symphony and opera.[56]

At a more fundamental level symphonic tradition represents, for some commentators, the musical manifestation of 'masculine', even 'macho', ideology. Indeed, it has been proposed that one of the reasons that so few British or European women composed symphonies is the genre's awesome reputation and focus on male preoccupations:

> Nationalism and imperialism served as political pretexts for the development of large musical forces [. . .] Because of the power of the ideological associations, male composers have produced symphonies, opera and other large-scale pieces in proportionally greater numbers.[57]

In Britain imperialist ideology has long been evident; indeed, the British symphonic tradition of the twentieth century was very much tied to the Nationalist revival and the high noon of Empire. Taking up these themes and premises in compositions may in reality be difficult for some women, since they are usually kept outside this sort of patriarchal political ritual. When it is also considered that the prime function of the great majority of musical compositions written by women throughout this time was to act as an enhancer of feminine desirability, their concentration on simplicity and accessibility is even more understandable. However, simplicity is an aspect of musicality which is little valued in the general canon, a fact which kept women safely out of the competitive 'great' artist definition.

The concept of originality as an aspect of musical value has also worked hand in hand with concepts of complexity and of the composer's status as genius:

> The neoclassical view that made human supremacy a matter of mental and physical skill was gradually replaced by various forms of pre-Romanticism in which 'originality' was more important than talent.[58]

The value placed on originality as a measure of compositional success, or 'greatness', has traditionally been a problematic area for women in many fields. Yet the creation of something original or unique is not in itself the really valued concept, since every piece of music which is not a verbatim copy of another piece of music can be defined up to a point as 'original'. Originality is relative and is seen as valuable only when it operates and extends our musical values as hitherto defined by male schools of thought and philosophy. Entry into, and acceptance by, the intellectual and artistic circles that control the definition of 'original' has been notoriously difficult for women; even the most prominent women composers have encounted obstacles to being accepted as equals in such circles.[59] Their marginality in this respect has prevented women from being at the cutting edge of artistic developments.

Another property for which the symphony (and such genres as opera) has been valued is its sheer scope and size:

> This suggests that size in two senses – quantitative and temporal, or vertical and horizontal – has played a decisive role in the determination of value [. . .] As Leonard Meyer has observed, size is 'a sign of power'.[60]

This value based on size, applies not only to the length and fullness of scoring of individual compositions but also to the number of works produced by a composer: the size of the *œuvre*. A 'great' composer has to prove his or her position by producing many large-scale compositions. High productivity is valued in individual composers and increases the esteem in which their work is held. The quantity of compositions completed by composers is often equated with their amount of creative motivation. Indeed, it is, in part, but it may also reflect a number of important facts about an individual's social situation. Musical composition on any kind of large scale has a number of prerequisites. First among these are relatively good health and survival into middle adulthood. In former times women's health and life expectancy were often diminished by the perils of childbirth. Second, the composer must have a full training in compositional techniques and a good knowledge of other music which can act as a model for imitation and development. Here, one may observe that women have (at best) gained full and equal educational opportunities only in the late twentieth century. Third, time, space and minimum distractions are also essential if a composer is to write an extended work (or number of works); everyday diversions from work can be very disruptive for the completion of a large project. That women's domestic position (essential household chores, extended periods of child care and so on) has very often denied them such conditions has been amply illustrated in Chapter 3.

It has also been asserted that women lack the emotional and psychological dedication and sustained concentration needed to compose large-scale works, or a series of large-scale works. As justification of this, it has been claimed that it is this part of the collective female character which limits their work to small-scale compositions and leads to relatively smaller *œuvres*:

> The agony and dedication requisite to serious musical production yields little but the satisfaction of creation [. . .] Women, practical realists, foregoing the solitary intellectual enterprise that is composition, prefer to invest their time and talent in teaching and in performance where social contact is intrinsic, the rewards are tangible, and the exposure ego-satisfying. Of all the women composers who study music, even at length, many will go into other activities and use it little or not at all. Of the more devoted, most will choose marriage and motherhood, including, not stressing teaching or performance.[61]

It seems clear that women have been allowed to use music as part of their traditional work (child-rearing or 'entertaining'), but the musical careers which demand cultural or artistic authority are commonly deemed unsuitable. But can this be ascribed to the feminine personality alone? This kind of description of the female character implies that women never really mature psychologically, since they are always in need of supervision and attention, of immediate gratification, and are unable to work independently. It would be truer to say that the social situation which places women at the heart of family and domestic relations withholds from many of them the luxury of time and space for themselves, even when they might prefer to take the solitary path required of composers.

That the compositional output and success of women composers are affected by domestic relations is reiterated by the British composer Diana Burrell:

> However many opportunities are made for women [composers], however, much positive discrimination is applied, all will be in vain unless we re-assess, with honesty, the way we view our careers [. . .] For most women (though many of them would deny it) their career does take second place to caring for partner and family and organising a household.[62]

The socializing process which imbues women with the sense that home and family are their only real option surely needs to be challenged. As can be seen, to produce large-scale compositions requires concentration and commitment. Yet if women are constantly told that their real commitment lies elsewhere, some female composers will find it impossible to devote themselves to the task single-mindedly.

The composition of large-scale symphonies has thrown up numerous barriers for women composers to surmount. Obviously, levels of creative capacity vary between individuals, but there are clearly few female composers who have produced vast amounts of music in the way male composers have. Closer examination reveals that it is the social position and conditioning of women which have for hundreds of years created this situation. Despite the many problems cited, some women composers have produced large-scale works, including symphonies. But even when this point has been reached there remain further obstacles which make the realization of women's work, on the whole, altogether more problematic than men's. As has already been established, the development of the symphony has played a vital role in the creation of artistic standards in musical life in the twentieth century. In addition to this influence there is the symphony's importance for the creation of concert halls, the development of the orchestra and the standard type of concert programme. Women composers' near-absence from genres like the symphony, which stand at the foundations of musical life, can, again, be seen as integral to women composers' current marginal musical position. Without their contribution to this genre, it has been impossible for women as a group to be serious contenders in the musical arena of high culture. In the establishment view, their non-representation is emblematic of inferiority, no matter what their contribution to other genres.

Finding outlets for performance of any kind of large-scale work requires an immense amount of organization (performers, promoters, conductors, audience) and funding. Without securing an outlet for performance, many composers fail to develop either the musical or the psychological confidence to undertake further large-scale projects. So performance of such works is often vital to the composer's future compositional choices. A fierce competitive element is involved in gaining performances of large-scale orchestral works. This competitive environment in itself works against women, bearing in mind their psychological socialization against competitive, and ultimately aggressive, behaviour. Although it has been stated that many male composers are disadvantaged to an equal extent by this situation, the male composer's relationship to both the behavioural codes and the musical institutions (which have the means to produce such works) is quite distinct.

In producing a work which requires a very large number of people to participate in its realization and performance, the composer becomes a supreme musical authority figure. Large-scale works require large-scale venues, which in turn allow large-scale audience attendance and thus broad dissemination. When a piece of music is produced in such a public arena, the very participation of such forces suggests control, authority and, moreover, the cultural approval earned by the creator. This is a substantial power position traditionally enjoyed by composers active within the symphonic tradition. The privileged power and influence of symphonic music to dictate and shape events and associated musical institutions is apparent. Symphony orchestras in Britain, Europe and America are powerful institutions which lie at the heart of music life. However, the nature of these institutions is frequently far from a purely musical one:

> Symphony orchestras, like other human institutions, require the involvement of many individuals and are therefore in many respects political entities.[63]

The composer, more than any other kind of artist, must rely on many others to interpret, understand, produce, value and distribute his or her work. Any public organization of this kind poses problems for women wishing to join it at any level, but to be the supreme authority figure is a position contrary to women's present and traditional social assignment.

The composer of a symphonic score is the highest point of authority in a long chain linking the conductor, the players and ultimately the audience. All the artistic power and authority held by the composer figure is therefore encapsulated in the notated score:

> Just as the printed word acquires greater importance than the spoken word, so does the printed page of music acquire authority [. . .] The power of the [. . .] printed page of music arises from its seeming permanence – from its potential for outliving the person who created it. It is the power of this permanence which may well lead performing musicians to embrace the authority of the printed page in the realization of a symphonic composition.[64]

The printed score is musical doctrine, musical control. The fact that many works by women composers remain unpublished, even when the works have been performed, is significant in terms of perpetuating the female composer's impermanence and lack of authority. However, taking a broader view, any piece of notated music would seem to define some sort of musical authority. From the musical score all persons in the musical chain of performance take their instruction, including conductors, performers, critics, academics and listeners. Our culture makes it very difficult for women to be at the very top of any authority chain and this is perhaps of vital importance when considering why the positions of conductors and composers are still the two most male-dominated musical professions. William L. Cahn's article about the function of symphony orchestras is revealing for its insight into the political position of the orchestral composer. This author states:

> While the creation of a musical composition is one of the highest forms of personal expression, it is also of necessity a political statement [. . .] in creating a musical score the composer is also asserting authority over the actions of other people [. . .] Does this mean that the composer of music for a symphony orchestra must not only have knowledge of composition and orchestration, but of people as well? Certainly, in today's symphonic musical environment, with literally hundreds of people who may be involved in bringing a new work to performance and with staggering economic considerations in terms of the cost of running an orchestra, the answer is yes.[65]

So another dimension is added to the composition of large-scale works. In addition to all the factors listed previously, knowledge of the organizational structure and individuals who initiate, commission and perform such works is advantageous for the ultimate 'success' of the composer. For women composers, who on the whole have much less contact with powerful musical institutions and hold far fewer residential composition positions, access to such institutions is more limited, which again restricts the chances of their 'success'.

It is acknowledged that getting a large-scale work performed is often a difficult business for any composer, male or female. But the established musical network and connections which make performance possible can place women in a more difficult position entirely because of their gender. Making contacts and pressing for attention can take on a very different aspect for women working within a male-dominated establishment:

> Professional contacts are of the greatest importance to composers. Using contacts to promote new music can be quite respectable, but it can also lapse into simple sycophancy. Women fit awkwardly into the latter social pattern for obvious reasons. A young woman's flattery is subject to unflattering interpretations. A middle-aged woman is too old to join the charmed circle of bright young careerist. Yet many established women composers *are* middle-aged for their entry into the field has been delayed [. . .][66]

The currency of sexual relationships between men and women is often ignored in the discussions of female composers. When operating within a system of male authority, many women have to deal with a very different set of problems which often play on their sexual vulnerability.[67] Women's musical marginalization, stemming from their social and sexual place, hinders in every way their production and performance of large-scale compositional genres. Symphonic music requires the composer to be involved in social structures which involve many people and their prejudices (this kind of prejudice can also work to discriminate along the lines of class and race).

A professional composer who is defined by work in public, large-scale, high culture genres can become as well known for his or her individual personality as for his or her actual music. Any figure, artistic or otherwise, who is authoritative in shaping and sustaining an intellectual or cultural elite may come to be regarded as a genius occupying a God-like position:

> 'I am the author', 'I am male', 'I am God'. Romantic and modernist art binds these three sentences together into a holy trinity. Poststructuralist fashion pretends that a post-modernist artist has no authority, and is far from god-like. But the convention that makes the artist a god was [. . .] 'universally accepted' in the nineteenth century, and as long as we retain Romantic notions of artistic creativity, we retain the author as a pseudo-god.[68]

The position of 'pseudo-god' is, again, one of immense contradiction for women. It stems from patriarchal religious and philosophical traditions which have been further reinforced by the historical 'evidence' of women's lack of (or inferior) cultural contribution. Although the concept of genius has been understood right from prehistoric times,[69] the idea of the modern 'genius' hero composer has been a tradition steadily built up throughout the eighteenth and nineteenth centuries:

> He [the nineteenth century composer] was the new 'ruler' or the middle class [. . .] who was honoured in a way previously reserved for the aristocracy or representative of the church. The artist who [. . .] was the spokesman for a *Weltseele* [universal spirit] became aware of his 'mission', the freedom to practice his art as an end in itself. The commonplace and dull were loathsome to him, so that whenever possible, he withdrew from the demands of society in order to 'live his own life' independently [. . .] or dedicate himself 'to his art' [. . .][70]

The rejection of social codes and standards was permitted to male composers because of their immersion in more spiritual matters, but was, and is, a position virtually impossible for women composers to attain. Women's main role in society has for centuries been to act as the provider of emotional and domestic support. Woman's sphere was delineated by the domestic and 'commonplace'; her mental and physical being was thought entirely dictated to by childbearing and menstruation. In contrast, men's greatest achievements have been seen in their transcendence of the biological and bodily – the ascent into the world of mind and spirit.

Explicitly the Romantic preoccupation with the physical objectification of women acted further as a contrary frame of reference to the concept of male 'genius':

> [. . .] a period that signified the release of the creative genius of the male inaugurated a greater limitation on the energies of the female. The Romantic Era was [a] time of heady, self-conscious freedom for men. They imprisoned women on a pedestal, and they allowed her to perform but not to create.[71]

It also secured two antithetical roles within which the two sexes could exist. For women to come down from the pedestals of sexual objectification, domestic refinement and intellectual restriction (defined musically in their songs and piano pieces) has proved a very difficult process. The tradition of the great composer as a respected and adored musical genius, a role to which musicians should aspire, debarred the creator from being female. Men and women alike frequently find it very difficult to relate to a female authority figure. It is clear that this Romantic notion of artistic genius allowed no female version:

> The element of heroic maleness had always been present in the concept of the artist [. . .] When the inevitable question is asked, 'Why are there no *great* women artists' it is this dimension of art which is implied [. . .][72]

This idea of an autonomous 'hero' artist subservient to no one is one which is very much alive today in the positions of serialist and avant-garde composers, whose music quite clearly does not appeal to the general public but instead satisfies them and the high culture musical elite. This stands in complete contrast to the subservient, sacrificial role stereotyped as feminine. If a woman composer were to withdraw into this 'heroic' mental state, she would be seen as selfish and in contradiction of her most basic function: that of nurturing, giving to and supporting children and men. In theory, there is no reason why women should not inhabit this musical territory, but in reality there is a strong tradition dissuading women from operating in music in this way.

The 'great' male composer, working to satisfy his own spiritual and intellect desires, is a role-model that no composer, regardless of gender, can ignore. The American composer Pauline Oliveros (b. 1932) has throughout her career been very aware of the type of pressure the 'genius' composer concept can exert on many people's creativity:

> [. . .] Oliveros is committed to the belief that everyone is musical. In one of the most animated and vehement statements [. . .] she called the Western concept of talent and genius 'a crock' and said that they have disempowered many people. Empowering people to make music is Oliveros's mission.[73]

Destroying these stereotypes, however, is alien to most composers. All the female composers in my study group have composed symphonies, implying an acceptance and valuation of many past traditions, of which the symphony is perceived the most masculine expression. The compositional genres employed by the study group reveal some interesting points about gender and genre in Britain. Of most importance is the fact that these (and other) women have become active in a number of larger-scale genres, but it seems that women who work consistently in this way are still in a minority. Moreover, their work remains remarkably low-key in our musical life. The performance and broadcasting of women's work remains only a tiny proportion of our musical culture, and it very often consists of small-scale works. For example, BBC Radio Three, over the period of one month, listed 11 women composers in comparison with approximately 840 male composers (in percentage terms, a ratio of approximately 2:98).[74] The Huddersfield Contemporary Music Festival that ran from 16–27 November 1994 scheduled only two women composers (in addition to three others who each composed a one-minute work in honour of Anthony Gilbert's 60th birthday). In reaction to this state of affairs, a number of musical festivals and events specifically focusing on the work of women composers have been arranged by various groups. For example, in 1994 festivals devoted to women composers occurred in Chard, Cardiff, London and Norwich; in addition, a week-long television series about women composers entitled 'Secret Chamber' was broadcast on Channel Four in June 1994. Although these events have provided valuable performance opportunities for women, they validate, by making 'special arrangements', their continued location outside the mainstream.

The compositional output of the oldest composer in the study group, Avril Coleridge-Taylor, can be seen as a reflection of the restricted genres cultivated by women composers in the previous century. Her output is relatively small, totalling fewer than 80 works. Most of her output consists of songs, chamber duos (mainly for piano and violin or flute) and piano pieces. She did, however, complete sixteen orchestral works, mainly suites and descriptive tone poems such as *To April* (date unknown), *To the Hills* (1935), *The Snow Goose Suite* (date unknown) and *Comet Prelude* (1952). Without doubt, her work as a conductor was a vital enabling factor in her use and development of these orchestral genres. Among the most substantial and indeed 'formal' works are the Piano Concerto in F minor (1936) and a *Symphonic Impression Historical Episode* (MacArthur of the Philippines) (1942). The combination of an overall lack of adequate training and lack of performances were perhaps influential in her compositional choices. A selection of Coleridge-Taylor's compositions was written under the male *nom de plume* of Peter Riley, but whether this was to avoid comparison with her father or to avoid sex discrimination is unclear. In her autobiography Coleridge-Taylor discusses in some detail events which affected her personal life; however, direct references to her music are surprisingly scarce. The lack of focused discussion on her compositions generally perhaps indicates some uncertainty about its merits.

From the information available it seems that few of her orchestral works have been performed, although there is a reference to the performance and broadcasting of the *Symphonic Impression* in the United States.[75] Critical commentary on her compositions has also proved very difficult to locate, giving a sense that her compositional work held only low status. For much of her life Coleridge-Taylor seems to have worked to keep her father's music alive. She very much walked in his shadow, and it seems that where possible she promoted his work before her own, especially in her work as a conductor. Her pioneering work as a conductor, working with professional orchestras such as the London Symphony and the BBC Symphony, Theatre and Concert Orchestras, would provide a positive role-model for women of subsequent generations if her work were more widely known.

Grace Williams' compositional output reflects her much fuller education and training. She had the option of working in a number of genres to suit her creativity. Williams wrote 27 large-scale orchestral compositions, including two symphonies. However, the vast majority of her orchestral works are in forms which would be regarded as less 'academic'; they include suites, fantasias and characteristic 'Welsh theme' works, such as *Four Illustrations of the Legend of Rhiannon* (1939), *Penillion* (1955) and *Welsh Dances* (date unknown). Her Symphony No. 1, fully titled *Symphony No. 1 in the form of Symphonic Impressions of the Glendower Scene in 'Henry IV Part 1'*, was completed in 1943. The strong programmatic element distances this work from the more formal symphonic structures sometimes deemed inappropriate for female composers.

The Second Symphony, completed in 1956, is quite different, being a work stemming from Williams' mature period of composition (1955–1961). It appears to have grown out of another orchestral piece, *Penillion*, which was in four movements and had strong symphonic elements, its material clearly developing along evolutionary lines. For many commentators this work occupies an important point in Williams's development as a 'serious' composer:

> As a whole *Penillion* never exactly bursts the more modest bounds of the suite, but it seems natural that Grace Williams should have followed it up with a 'proper' symphony [. . .] The result [. . .] was her most ambitious instrumental work, and the one which most decisively modifies the picture of her as a 'mere' vocal composer.[76]

Obviously, to write even a large-scale orchestral work in the form of a suite did not correspond to the idea of a 'proper' symphonic composition. It is equally evident that a composer who works only in vocal or melodic forms is a poor candidate for greatness. That Williams finally attempted this 'proper' symphonic genre placed her in a different category, almost regardless of whether or not the work was successful. Such a valuation of the perceived hierarchy of orchestral genres acquires greater significance when one considers that women composers have written a great many more orchestral suites and overtures than symphonies. (For example, in the twentieth century women have composed approximately 247 symphonies, yet as many as 720 suites and overtures.)[77] It would seem that a number of women who possessed the innate ability – but were then unable, for various reasons – to compose in 'proper' orchestral genres, have forfeited their chance to join the canon of high culture music.

It is evident that when female composers such as Williams have written in high culture genres, this has often been interpreted as 'unnatural' or 'against their normal artistic personality'. Consider, for example, the following criticism of Symphony No. 2 by Williams:

> [. . .] that the Second Symphony was brought to completion 'against the grain' [is clear . . .] signs of struggle are certainly present in the music, even after its revisions of 1975 [. . .][78]

Others have stated that Symphony No. 2 allowed Williams to express a hitherto unheard side of her musical personality:

> Still more surprising and to many early listeners disconcerting, was the uncompromisingly aggressive tone of much of the music [in Symphony No. 2]. . . But although it is unlikely ever to be numbered among the composer's most popular works, the symphony did reveal hitherto unsuspected dimensions of her artistic personality, and in the context of her music as a whole it can be seen to have played a cathartic role.[79]

Perhaps only in this genre did Williams (perhaps unconsciously) feel able to reveal this more abrasive side of her personality, validating the underlying perception that to work effectively in the symphonic medium a composer needs to demonstrate essentially 'masculine' characteristics. That much of Williams's music is easily accessible, often featuring vivid musical 'storytelling' of legends and narratives, is indeed part of its popular appeal. This popular style is commonly thought to favour the smaller-scale, less demanding genres such as the suite, chamber and vocal music – all traditional genres of acceptably feminine character. We return to the familiar idea that women composers work most naturally in vocal, melodic genres:

> It could be argued that the orchestral music constitutes the most consistently successful part of Grace Williams' output, but it was in the solo song, more than anything else, that her musical personality found natural expression.[80]

Even when a woman composer appears to work 'successfully' in large-scale orchestral genres, it is only small-scale vocal genres which can *reveal* the 'natural' expression of her femininity.

Elizabeth Maconchy's work, like that of Williams, covers a wide range of genres. Her compositional output is marked by its size and embraces mainly high culture 'serious' forms. Again, it must be stressed that Maconchy was able to fulfil this potential to compose only with the benefit of a thorough musical education. Her extensive list of works includes many songs and large-dimension vocal settings such as *Sun, Moon and Stars* (1979) and *My Dark Heart* (1982). Her orchestral works include three symphonies (1948, 1952 and 1980) and a large number of orchestral suites and overtures including *The Land* (1929), Suite for Chamber Orchestra (1930), *Puck Fair* (1940), *Theme and Variations* (1942) and *Proud Thames* (1953). Maconchy has also produced a number of concertos and concertinos: Concertino for Piano and Chamber Orchestra (1928), Concerto for Violin (1937), Double Concerto for Oboe and Bassoon (1957) and *Serenata Concertante* (1962). She has written a number of operas, including *The Sofa* (1956–57), *The Departure* (1960–61), *The Birds* (1967–68), *The Jesse Tree* (1969–70) and *The King of the Golden River* (1974–75); several large-scale choral works including *And Death Shall have no Dominion* (1969) and *Héloïse and Abelard* (1978); a number of sonatas, including two Sonatas for Violin and Piano (1938, 1944) and a Sonata for Cello and Clarinet (1944); and many chamber ensemble works: Oboe Quintet (1932), Quintet for Clarinet and String Quartet (1963) and Oboe Quartet (1972). At the heart of Maconchy's compositional output lies a series of thirteen string quartets (1933–1984).

Although string quartets belong to a chamber genre which inhabits a more 'private' performance sphere, this genre holds far greater significance than any other type of work for small ensembles. Quartets have, through most of their history, been predominantly four-movement structures which employ sonata form and mirror symphonic writing in many ways. The string quartet is considered a 'serious' genre because of this legacy; a work belonging to the genre is expected to be substantial in terms of size, scope and complexity, if not scoring. Maconchy's focus on this respected and valued chamber genre takes her work beyond the usual boundaries imposed by the choice of a chamber medium. 'Genre discrimination' against women composers is something of which Maconchy seems to have been well aware from an early stage in her career:

> The publishers weren't interested [in works by women]. They were all men, of course, and tended to think women composers being capable of only the odd song or two.[81]

With this prejudice in mind, Maconchy evidently chose her compositional genres carefully in order to avoid such comparisons. For example, although a trained pianist, she wrote very little for solo piano. Her decision to avoid traditional 'feminine' patterns was possibly motivated by a knowledge of how stereotypes of female composers' inferiority have become reinforced through their gravitation towards certain musical genres.

Of all the composers in the study group, Maconchy stands as the most prominent and well received by the musical establishment. This is evident from the number of performances of her music, the readiness to publish it and the commissions she received throughout her life. That Maconchy's work was well placed to receive public performance and critical consideration may have been due in part to the fact that the genres to which she contributed were valued musical currency of the time.

Nevertheless, the relatively wide exposure and acceptance of her music has often been undermined by criticism of its lack of originality and thus its lack of a vital element of real 'greatness':

> The [musical] style is as reticent as the woman, and that is surely one reason why it has not received the recognition it deserves. She is indeed a figure who might more easily have made her mark in the eighteenth century, when composers were largely valued for their craftsmanship and romanticism had not yet imposed 'originality' as the supreme value in artistic creation.[82]

Obviously, this is a criticism which has often been applied to male composers – but here, the traditional denial of female originality makes it a more damning perception. Many would understand the comment to 'prove' that a woman's individual lack of musical originality is due to her sex rather than to herself as an individual; clearly, this could never be the implication for a male composer.

Maconchy's development as a composer has been much encouraged by the fact that so many of her works have been performed in public, especially while she was still young. This was partly due to opportunities afforded by the Macnaghten-Lemare concerts, which were organized by women and included a substantial amount of women composers' work. Of course, having the talent and raw ability to compose is in the end decisive, but the impact of hearing her works on a reasonably regular basis at an early stage of her career must have had some impact on the development of Maconchy's artistic confidence later to produce works in large-scale prestigious genres. Most significantly, Maconchy's career stands to dispel the myth that women are able to write only on a small scale, and has secured her work the reward of a degree of recognition by the musical establishment.

Minna Keal has produced only five pieces of music since resuming composition at the age of 60; String Quartet (1978), Wind Quintet (1980), Symphony (1987), *Cantillation for Violin and Orchestra* (1988) and Cello Concerto (1995). This is the smallest *œuvre* of any member of the study group. But it highlights a number of important issues which primarily affect women composers. The fact that Keal started so late draws attention to a problem for many female composers (although in this case in quite extreme form); missed opportunities and compulsory breaks to have and rear children are real and difficult barriers that many women have experienced. It is noteworthy that whereas Keal's student works were small-scale piano/violin and piano works, all her works written since she resumed composition have been on a large scale: it is as if only at this late stage she acquired the confidence and determination to attempt such works. Originally, Keal's first orchestral work (only her third opus) was to be a suite in five movements based on poems written by her husband. But as the work progressed, it became clear that the music was evolving independently of the extra-musical ideas:

> [. . .] it was turning into something different and I came to Justin [Connolly, her teacher] and I said, 'Would it be too presumptive to call this a symphony?'. He said: 'No, a symphony it is'. That's how it became a symphony.[83]

Keal's caution, which made her wary of naming the work a symphony rather than a suite, illustrates the hallowed significance that the genre holds for many composers. In addition to this, Keal's lack of confidence in her ability to write on such a large scale stemmed from her losing touch with contemporary musical developments and her relatively small compositional experience:

> I approached the composition with considerable trepidation and disbelief in my ability to handle such forces.[84]

Keal never thought that she would have the symphony performed, but it was played both at the Proms and as a studio recording for broadcast; this gave her confidence and status an unimaginable boost.

Yet Minna Keal's triumph over the many factors which worked against her completion of such a piece are largely ignored in subsequent reviews of her life and work. What is presented as the remarkable feat is that Keal managed to write a composition which was high inprestige, complex, profound, aggressive, serious and large-scale. Placed in the context of the traditional female compositional genres, the remarks become more powerful:

> [. . .] when her symphony was played, it was of a substance and scale that you might never have guessed from seeing or listening to its author [. . .][85]

> As a slightly dazed-looking photographer put it at the Proms rehearsal of Minna Keal's symphony [. . .] 'I didn't think little old ladies wrote music like that [. . .]'[86]

The fact that Keal composes music is not seen here as the surprising fact; what is, however, is the genre and scale of her composition.

The connected themes of large-scale 'masterpiece' and 'genius' composer traced previously are evident in a number of reviews of the Keal symphony. The symphonic genre brings with it a frame of reference; for the work to be really successful, the composer must produce an 'original masterpiece' and exhibit 'genius'. Alan Blyth of the *Daily Telegraph* summarized the opinions of many:

> I wish I could acclaim [it] a masterpiece. Unfortunately, Keal's 30-minute extravaganza [. . .] sounded like one of those large-scale aggressive symphonies that were written in their dozens a quarter of a century ago [. . .] It needs a genius to say something new on the subject. As it happens, just such a genius [John Tavener . . .] was present in the evening's second half.[87]

In one paragraph most of the implicit discriminatory beliefs about female composers are exposed. The terms 'masterpiece' and 'genius' are traditionally loaded descriptions which have most definitely been categorized as male. Keal is criticized for not being 'original' enough and for being only 'one of many' from a fashion long passed. As in the previous review of Elizabeth Maconchy's work, the critic is at pains to imply that whatever the actual merits of the composition, it is not original and therefore cannot really be 'great' music worthy of serious consideration. The comparison of Keal with John Tavener (b. 1944) is not coincidental; the glaring gendered stereotypes of male genius, female non-genius, are vividly counterposed.

The stand taken by most of the commentators on the actual musical content of the Symphony is informed by incredulity that a woman composer could attempt such a project. Many still believe that the scale and scope of the symphonic genre and aggressive dissonant style used by Keal are not true or credible expressions of a female, whatever her age – a point summarized by a more enlightened review critical of Keal's treatment by the musical establishment:

> [. . .] what she put on paper was not bits and pieces but a masterpiece. For her Symphony *is* a masterpiece. No other word will serve [. . . but] It is not her work we are invited [by the media] to admire, but the amazing spectacle of an aged female person scoring for full orchestra [. . .] It diminishes her. And side-tracks her Symphony as a curiosity.[88]

This kind of blinkered view was lamentable enough in the 1880s, but when, in the 1980s, a symphony written by a woman can still be depicted in this way, it is intolerable.

Ruth Gipps' extensive musical training and uninterrupted career have enabled her to complete a number of both large-scale and small-scale works. She has always tended to work in genres and forms which have been unattainable for many women. Throughout her career Gipps has concentrated much of her compositional energy on large-scale orchestral music, including five symphonies (1942, 1945, 1965, 1972, 1982); a series of concertos: Oboe Concerto (1941), Violin Concerto (1943), Piano Concerto (1948), Horn

Concerto (1968) and Concerto for Violin and Viola (1957). Other orchestral works include a Suite, *The Chinese Cabinet* (1945), and *Sinfonietta for Ten Wind Instruments* (1989). She has also completed a number of substantial choral works, including *The Cat* (1947), *The Prophet* (1950) and *Goblin Market* (1953). Gipps has also written many works for solo instruments and chamber ensembles, including sonatas for clarinet, oboe, cello and violin, a String and Wind Quintet (1941), a String Quartet (1956), and a *Wealden Suite for Four Clarinets* (1991). Gipps, like Maconchy, has tended to avoid the small-scale songs and piano pieces which typified female composers of the past.

At the heart of Gipps' *œuvre* are the five symphonies written between 1942 and 1982. The works are very traditional in style, bearing the strong influence of the prominent British composers with whom Gipps had contact (Vaughan Williams, Arthur Bliss and William Walton). The influence of such leading musicians without doubt encouraged Gipps to write in a number of prestigious genres which would take her music to the widest possible audience. Gipps' domestic circumstances as a child and her adult relationships (she has always kept her marital and domestic responsibilities to an absolute minimum) have been pivotal in her fulfilment of her musical potential and in allowing her to produce the quantity of work that she has.

Also beneficial to Gipps' work in large-scale orchestral genres has been her work as a conductor. This facilitated the performance of some of her works by amateur and professional orchestras. In addition to conducting performances of her Fourth and Fifth Symphonies with her own London Repertoire Orchestra, Gipps became, in 1969, the first woman to conduct her own symphony with the BBC Scottish Symphony Orchestra. Gipps was also seen to 'make history' when she conducted the Pro Arte Orchestra and the Goldsmith's Choral Union at the Royal Festival Hall in a concert programme containing her own cantata *The Cat* and Beethoven's *Choral Symphony.* For a woman to conduct such a programme was hitherto quite unthinkable:

> This work [the Beethoven] is one of the Everests of music. It makes exceptional demands on the conductor's nerve, stamina, intellect, imagination, emotions. A woman is no more expected to conduct it than to build a Great Boulder Dam, pilot a space rocket, buy ten million surplus Army razors, or put up a new deep-sea diving record [. . .][89]

Conducting (or indeed, composing) a large-scale musical work was, in 1956, considered about as feminine as growing a beard! The composing and conducting careers of Ruth Gipps are marvellous examples to other women in many ways, since she consistently refused to be defined and pigeonholed by any 'feminine' stereotypes and has always demanded serious consideration by the musical establishment, although she often did not receive it. Gipps took on the musical establishment on its own terms. For example, when she could not find regular conducting work, she formed her own orchestra. She has obviously faced many of the difficulties posed by being a woman in a male-dominated profession. Ironically, however, Gipps can sometimes alienate women by being unsympathetic to many of the wider problems faced by other women composers. For example, when asked if she found being a musician and a mother difficult, she replied:

> Not a bit of it. The two things go well together in some ways. I got my nursemaids for nothing – girl students who helped me in exchange for unpaid piano lessons.[90]

This seems ironical when domestic responsibilities have been a major restrictive factor hampering many women composers' sustained and concentrated efforts at composition.

Enid Luff's output since her return to composition embraces a range of genres. Thorough training and the opportunity to study with a number of established composers has obviously enhanced her ability to work on a large canvas and in prestigious genres. However, her compositional output is relatively small because of her late start. Significantly, Luff has worked consistently in larger-scale genres even when the instrumental forces are small. Alongside a number of small-scale piano works stand *Sonata: Stormtide for Piano* (1986), chamber works including three string quartets (1970, 1972 and 1976), a wind quintet, *The Coastal Road* (1980), and finally choral and theatre works such as *Rags* (1990) and *Listening for the Roar of the Sun* (1992). Luff has also written a number of vocal works; most of these evolve over extended time-spans: for example, *Lux in Tenebris* (1971), Five Nocturnes (1975) and *Swn Dwr* (1981). Her largest scale instrumental works are her two symphonies, completed in 1974 and 1994 respectively. Luff composed her First Symphony as part of her M.Mus. degree requirements. Her motivation to write for orchestra was very strong, and the initial conception of the symphony was inspired:

> All of a sudden I heard the beginning of my symphony and I thought, 'This is it'. I went to my Professor and said, 'Sorry, I am going to write a symphony' [. . .] He said 'Well, all right, but I hope you know what you are doing'.[91]

Neither of Luff's symphonies has been performed, although she has managed to gain performances (mainly via the SPNM) of her larger-scale ensemble pieces, generally in a chamber setting. Luff's passionate interest in the large-scale orchestral medium has not been stimulated from outside, as evidenced by the lack of performance of these works. Indeed, on the whole, Luff's work has received little exposure.

Antoinette Kirkwood, like Avril Coleridge-Taylor, has tended to write in small-scale genres: songs and piano pieces which typify the stereotype of the female composer. Indeed, her output totals only some 41 works. Works for piano include Sonatina (1946), Suite for Piano (1947) and Six Intermezzos (1951–1956); vocal works have tended to be in the form of individual songs with piano accompaniment such as *The Fly* (1950), *Remorse* (1954) and *The Oyster-Catcher's Song* (1957). However, in addition, Kirkwood has produced a number of substantial vocal works, including *The Akond of Swat* (1986), *The Cummerbund* (1988) and *Snowflake* (1989). In addition to a range of small solo works, Kirkwood completed a Sonata for Cello and Piano (1950).

Her ventures into orchestral music have resulted in three short Fantasias for Orchestra (1958, 1961) and a number of large-scale works: Suite for Strings (1949), Symphony No. 1 (1953), *Musa the Saint* (1958) and a music drama *Alessandro* (1957).

Kirkwood feels that the completion of her symphony and its subsequent performance are her greatest musical achievements.[92] Some have criticized her works as reactionary in the light of modern musical developments. Yet constantly striving for newness and originality are not Kirkwood's main impetuses to compose:

> There is a difference between writing to please the artistic establishment and writing to express yourself and hopefully please other people as well. For me the important thing is to succeed in writing the work as I meant it to be [. . .] I have never had the slightest ambition to be a revolutionary, and I think that used to be a criticism made about me quite often.[93]

For Kirkwood, an important aspect of composition is that the audience understands and enjoys her music. Obviously, the cessation of composition which occurred between 1961–1979 meant that she missed valuable opportunities, not only to increase her list of works and develop her musical style but also to establish herself as a composer, make professional contacts and develop a reputation. Those who dismiss the work of Kirkwood (as of other female composers) because of her relatively small output rarely realize the difficulties that prevent the uninterrupted development of a woman's career.

Judith Bailey's compositional output covers a range of genres but is relatively small, containing fewer than fifty works. There is a rich vein of shorter orchestral pieces, no doubt inspired by her regular contact with orchestras as a conductor. Her orchestral works include two symphonies (1981 and 1983); the overtures *Penmorvah* (1966) and *Penwith* (1987); and what can be termed 'descriptive' works such as *Trencrom* (1978), *Fiesta* (1988), *Havas* (1992) and *Voyage for Orchestra* (1994). Her chamber works include sonatas for clarinet, violin and oboe, two string quartets and a number of wind pieces. The largest scale works are the two symphonies and *Seascape* (1985) for female chorus and orchestra. Small-scale piano and vocal works are scarce in Bailey's output. Her attitude towards both her composing and conducting work seems to be quite different from that of many male musicians:

> I think I am not very ambitious; I was more ambitious when I was young [. . .] but I think of my music as a way of life not as a stepping stone in a career [. . .] I think, if I had looked at it like that I would have entered for many more competitions and tried for prestigious appointments.[94]

Obviously, I am not suggesting that men cannot hold such attitudes – there are no doubt male composers who feel the same way. But in an artistic world which is dominated by men and masculine stereotypes of competition, drive and the ambition to be the greatest, the female relation to such ideas must be different. Our society expects a more circumscribed, less ambitious temperament from women, whilst encouraging such traits in men. Whether one way is better than the other is questionable, but it is clear that culture demands ambition and ego in its artists. In the view of female socialization, this kind of behaviour is less acceptable when displayed by women and makes their climbing the career ladder more arduous.

Bryony Jagger has written a large number of works, many of which are in high prestige genres and are substantial in scope. However, practicalities have limited her options:

> I like writing for large-scale orchestra but I'm unlikely to write for it here [in New Zealand] as we only have small-scale orchestras and large-scale orchestral pieces don't get played [. . .][95]

Jagger has written two symphonies to date. Neither of these has been performed; she feels that her freedom to complete a third is restricted primarily by work opportunities:

> I have had ideas for a Third Symphony but at present it is unlikely to get written unless someone actually wants to perform it. The local orchestra has a composer-in-residence post and I keep applying for it. Should I get it I will undoubtedly write the Third Symphony [. . .] However, the post seems to be reserved for young composers [. . .] so I rate my chances of getting it as low.[96]

Again, opportunities missed whilst concentrating on domestic responsibilities can result in women being somewhat older than men when they reach equivalent stages of their careers. This can create disadvantages in employment which restrict compositional options.

Performances of Jagger's large-scale instrumental works have been few, but performances of her large-scale vocal works have been more frequent; correspondingly, Jagger has written numerous works of this type, including *Birds of Enlightenment* (1978), a theatre cantata for choir, *Chitra* (1980), a lyric opera and *Shosho* (1980), a one act chamber opera. Interestingly, although Jagger has been influenced by many non-Western forms and musical elements, when composing for large-scale orchestra she has continued to employ Western high culture traditional genres:

> I wrote my first symphony because I'd done an oratorio and a big *a cappella* choral piece and wanted to try another big form.[97]

Jagger has often chosen to import topics into her composition which are traditionally perceived as defining the female experience. These issues have rarely been addressed in the musical work of men and mark an important contribution in redressing the balance of cultural recognition of the female experience. Jagger's works such as *Abortion Debate* (1978), *Childbirth* (1979) and *Birthmass* (incomplete) are musical attempts to express the profound experiences which have affected her and other women generally. Jagger is the only composer in the study group to produce work which so overtly deals with issues which reflect the female experience. It is perhaps not coincidental that she is also the youngest of the group; this fact may illustrate to some extent a recent change in the genres and styles into which female composers feel comfortable to channel their musical creativity.

The output of the study group of composers could be considered traditional by contemporary standards, especially in terms of their general use of established genres and musical elements viewed by some as 'blind' to contemporary developments. Whatever the merits of this argument, the important point for women composers in general is that during the twentieth century they have had greater access and opportunity than before to compose in high prestige, large-scale public genres. However, there are still many aspects of the female role and status which inhibit their collective work. Moreover, the quoted selection of comments and views about the work of the study group of composers reveals a continued disbelief that women, as a section of society, can work in such musical genres and a feeling that, even when they do, this is not a true reflection of their temperament and musical personality.

Conspicuously, many of the musical values which excluded full female participation in traditional large-scale genres have continued to be evident in the many avant-garde schools of thought. The avant-garde can be seen still to aspire to many of the previously valued aspects of high culture genres:

> The characteristics of this ideal [avant garde] musical type are formal in the broadest sense, marked by composers' stated and demonstrated concerns for issues of form, particularly complexity, unity and structure.[98]

Our valuation of musical elements is still basically defined by parameters of conventional musical notation. Even contemporary music incorporates ideas which can be considered 'standard' and 'official'. Against this, some composers such as Pauline Oliveros have tried to re-evaluate aspects of composition:

> Oliveros' feeling of being trapped by notation was an important realization, for Western musical notation has served to facilitate the perpetuation of certain musical ideas such as complexity, virtuosity, and large-scale formal structure at the expense of others. In particular, these ideas could tend to be seen as patriarchal, in light of the social and political systems under which they developed.[99]

In rejecting conventional notions of notation, Oliveros is defying the conventions of the authority of the composer and the system of values which has been developed in Western high culture music genres most of which stem from the permanence of the notated score. Within these notated parameters 'masculine' logic, originality, unity and analytical method are still highly prized musical elements. Oliveros' compositions have made a point of emphasizing what she sees as conventional 'feminine' traits such as intuition and emotionalism, so often devalued because of their relation to the female personality.

Outside the study group, some females have worked consciously against the traditional patterns of male composition. For these composers, the dominant 'masculine' ideology of our Western heritage poses very particular problems. They see, instead, much to be gained by upholding the musical values and patterns set by preceding generations of women. Some have decided that the reasons for rejecting women's previous contribution should not be supported. That patriarchal society has created what is valued in our tradition, and has also largely dictated women's contribution is an important matter for subsequent female composers to acknowledge. Some male composers have, for a variety of reasons, also started to reassess musical values, but the feminist perspective on the motivations for certain musical judgements raises distinct and important questions about the authority of our musical traditions.

Music faces a time of rapid development and transformation on many fronts, yet certain aspects have remained consistent with the high culture symphonic values of complexity, size, public performance, authority and elitism.[100] All these aspects still act as excluding factors for women's participation in mainstream musical life. Whatever the stance taken by living female composers, most of them still face a difficult task to be accepted alongside their male colleagues. Their historical positions of invisibility and inferiority have largely denied them the opportunity to contribute in their own right as women to aesthetic developments, and their continued position outside the mainstream can only indicate that this situation persists. The identity and role of the composer as male has constantly been reinforced in the latter part of the twentieth century, primarily via the perspective of the predominance of male composers over the past 400 years. In these terms, the history of women composers is actually quite new, which places them at a disadvantage. In particular, the lack of a substantial female contribution to the realm of the 'masterpiece' and to the ranks of the 'great' composers of genius seems constantly to undermine women's position in twentieth century music.

Many of the restrictions imposed on women, both socially and psychologically, have shaped their artistic contribution to Western art music. It seems important that this is recognized by contemporary women in some way. It is clear that the past invisibility of women's contribution and the downgrading of the genres of music in which they have written has had some effect on the perception of subsequent generations of women composers. In 1973 a Stanford University study concluded that:

> Women appear to be so impressed by the dismal picture history has so far given of their contributions to the arts that they picture creativity as an enduring characteristic of the male role. So long as they retain this picture of themselves, it is likely that relatively few will be willing to put forth the effort essential to sustained creativity.[101]

The historical image of musical works produced by women as inferior, low-level and defined by certain genres and styles worms its way into the morale of women composers and can ultimately undermine their confidence to invest energy and time in the process of composition.

This situation presents problems which many female composers, consciously or unconsciously, would rather not deal with. Some desperately want just to get on with the business of composing music, immersing themselves in purely musical issues and stating that any debate about female traditions and female 'differences' only worsens their position. However, past inequalities affect the present and the future: it is only by coming to terms with the differences which formed the female composer's experience in the past that women composers of the future will eventually take their rightful place at the forefront of public and private musical life.

Notes

1 Wilson, *The Great Sex Divide*, 108–109.
2 John Shepherd, 'Difference and Power in Music', in Ruth Solie (ed.), *Musicology and Difference* (Berkeley, 1993), 65.
3 Lucy Green, *Music on Deaf Ears* (Manchester, 1988), 101.
4 Shepherd, 'Difference and Power in Music', 51.
5 *Ibid.*, 49.
6 Dinah Birch, 'Gender and Genre', in F. Bonner and L. Goodman *et al.* (eds), *Imagining Women: Cultural Representations and Gender* (Cambridge, 1992), 54.
7 Jennifer C. Post, 'Erasing the Boundaries between Public and Private in Women's Performance Traditions', in Cook and Tsou (eds), *Cecilia Reclaimed*, 35–51.
8 *Ibid.*, 40.
9 Janet Wolff, 'The Ideology of Autonomous Art', in Richard Leppert and Susan McClary (eds), *Music and Society* (Cambridge, 1987), 6.
10 John Shepherd, *Music as Social Text* (Cambridge, 1991), 195.
11 J. Michele Edwards, 'Women in Music to ca. 1450', in Pendle (ed.), *Women in Music*, 26.
12 Neuls-Bates, *Women in Music*, xii.
13 Merry E. Wiesner, *Women and Gender in Early Modern Europe* (Cambridge, 1993), 157.
14 Neuls-Bates, *Women in Music*, xii.
15 Wiesner, *Women and Gender in Early Modern Europe*, 158.
16 Pendle, 'Women in Music ca 1450–1600', 35.
17 Sophie Fuller, *The Pandora Guide to Women Composers Britain and the United States 1629 – Present* (London, 1994), 104–105.
18 Fuller, *loc. cit.*
19 Pendle, 'Women in Music ca 1450–1600', 51.
20 Neuls-Bates, *Women in Music*, xiv.
21 This is not to say that the male composers who wrote for solo instruments were unimportant, but works for these instruments usually had more restricted settings and many composers worked in a range of genres to ensure wider recognition and performance of their works.
22 Pendle, 'Women in Music ca 1450–1600', 47–48.
23 Jezic, *Women Composers*, 26.
24 Women were not accepted on stage in Britain until after 1660.
25 Pendle, 'Women in Music ca 1450–1600', 36.
26 *Ibid.*, 37.
27 For example, Elizabeth Billington (1765/68–1818) and Madame Vestris (1797–1856).
28 Wiesner, *Women and Gender in Early Modern Europe*, 158–159.
29 Indeed, male amateur composers, who, like women, lacked a proper professional training, often apologized in the preface of their published works for their audacity in exposing their talents to a wide audience. In this sense, women ranked as 'doubly' amateurs – by profession (or lack of it) and by gender.
30 McClary, *Feminine Endings*, 114–115.
31 Anderson and Zinsser, *A History of their Own: Women in Europe from Prehistory to the Present*, 2, 105.
32 Richard Leppert, *Music and Image* (Cambridge, 1988), 29.
33 Wiesner, *Women and Gender in Early Modern Europe*, 156.
34 Derek Hyde, *New-Found Voices Women in Nineteenth-Century English Music* (Cornwall, 1984), 44.

35 *Ibid.*, 57.
36 *Ibid.*, 57–58.
37 *Ibid.*, 55.
38 Greer, *The Obstacle Race*, 113.
39 Hyde, *Women in Nineteenth Century English Music*, 2.
40 *Ibid.*, 48.
41 Examples of this kind of restriction can be observed in the lives of Ethel Smyth and Fanny Mendelssohn.
42 Obviously, some women did write in these forms, but their numbers are comparatively few.
43 'Women as composers', *Musical Times*, 1 February 1887, 81–82.
44 *Ibid.*, 82.
45 Brower, 'Is the Musical Idea Masculine?', 334.
46 Montagu, 'Why Wagner was no Lady', 137.
47 Battersby, *Gender and Genius*, 23.
48 David D. Boyden, *An Introduction to Music* (London, 1971), 284.
49 Greer, *The Obstacle Race*, 104.
50 These composers include Prokofiev, Tippett, Hindemith, Britten, Lutoslawski, Kodaly, Berio, Scriabin, Stravinsky, Shostakovich and Copland.
51 Morgan, *Twentieth Century Music*, 487.
52 Monika Lichtenfeld, 'The Symphony Concert, Its Origin, Form and Programme', in Ursula von Rauchhaupt (ed.), *Symphony* (London, 1973), 35.
53 The symphony, despite its programmatic dimensions, was less easily attached to social functions than other high-prestige forms such as opera. The presence of words automatically gave music a readily discernible social relatedness.
54 Lichtenfeld, 'The Symphony Concert: Its Origin, Form and Programme', 38.
55 *Ibid.*, 35.
56 Citron, *Gender and the Musical Canon*, 132.
57 *Ibid.*, 130.
58 Battersby, *Gender and Genius*, 71–72.
59 Two examples of this can be seen in the experiences of Clara Schumann and Ruth Crawford (1901–1953). Clara, although accepted as a performer by her eminent colleagues, was often an outsider in compositional terms. For example, Joseph Joachim wrote to her in 1860 of her Trio, 'I recollect a fugato in the last movement and remember that Mendelssohn once had a big laugh because I would not believe that a woman could have composed something so sound and serious' (Nancy B. Reich, *Clara Schumann: The Artist and the Woman*, 228). Ruth Crawford, although a very talented composer in her own right, was not allowed to attend the New York Musicological Society (run by her husband Charles Seeger) for many years.
60 Citron, *Gender and the Musical Canon*, 130.
61 Judith Rosen and Grace Rubin-Rabson, 'Why have there been No Great Women Composers', *International Musician*, 23/2 (1975), 50.
62 Burrell, 'Accepting Androgyny', 52.
63 William L. Cahn, 'Authority and Motivation in the Symphony Orchestra: A Symphony Musician's Point of View', *Contemporary Music Review*, 7 (1992), 27.
64 *Ibid.*, 32.
65 *Ibid.*, 31.
66 Tick and Rubin-Rabson, 'Why have there been No Great Women Composers?', 22.
67 This also seems to apply to female performers. The soprano Jane Manning has stated, 'Unfortunately, the "casting couch" is alive and well in our profession

[. . .] Glaring examples of favouritism based on non-musical factors are all around us'. *Women in Music* (Booklet accompanying the Secret Chamber season on Channel Four 1994), 16.

68 Battersby, *Gender and Genius*, 43.
69 *Ibid.*, 52.
70 Walter Salmen, 'Social Obligations of the Emancipated Musician in the 19th Century', in Walter Salmen (ed.), *The Social Status of the Professional Musician from the Middle Ages to the 19th Century* (New York, 1971), 268.
71 Edith Borroff, 'Women Composers: Reminiscence and History', *College Music Symposium*, 15 (1975), 32.
72 Greer, *The Obstacle Race*, 105.
73 Timothy D. Taylor, 'The Gendered Construction of the Musical Self: The Music of Pauline Oliveros', *The Musical Quarterly*, 77 (1993), 392.
74 Listed in *Radio Times* 29 April to 9 June 1995 (five editions). Male numbers were worked out from the observed fact that on average about 30 male composers are listed each day.
75 Coleridge-Taylor, *The Heritage of Samuel Coleridge-Taylor*, 97.
76 Arnold Whittall, 'Grace Williams 1906–1977', *Soundings*, 7 (1978), 20.
77 Aaron Cohen, *Encyclopedia of Women Composers* (New York, 1987), 2, 903–906.
78 Boyd, *Grace Williams*, 45.
79 *Ibid.*, 44.
80 *Ibid.*, 49.
81 Maconchy interviewed by Fiona Maddocks: 'The Composer breaks her Silence', *The Guardian*, 26 July 1983.
82 Peter Heyworth, 'Climbing the summit of Mount Messiaen', *The Observer*, 22 March 1987, 25.
83 Keal interview transcript, 8.
84 Keal Symphony programme notes from the Proms performance on 4 September 1989.
85 Michael John White, 'Veiled in Innocence', *The Independent*, 6 September 1989.
86 Eithne Power, 'Life Begins at 80!', *TV Times*, 21–27 October 1989, 10.
87 Alan Blyth, 'Late Developer', *Daily Telegraph*, 6 September 1989.
88 Peter Fryer, 'Two who have paid their dues', *Workers' Press*, 16 September 1989.
89 Francis Martin, 'The Night Mrs Baker Made History', *Everybody's Weekly*, 16 March 1957, 10.
90 *Ibid.*, 11.
91 Luff interview transcript, 6.
92 Kirkwood, transcript of response to a questionnaire dated 5 November 1993, 9.
93 Kirkwood, *loc. cit.*
94 Bailey interview transcript, 43.
95 Jagger, written response to questionnaire, 6.
96 *Ibid.*, 6.
97 Jagger, *loc. cit.*
98 Taylor, 'The Gendered Construction of the Musical Self', 394.
99 *Ibid.*, 388.
100 Part of music's rapid change has been brought about by technology. Obviously, there are strong stereotypes of women avoiding technology and science, this stereotype has no doubt affected women composers' relation to this area of

music. However, many women composers have made use of technology. See J. Michele Edwards, 'North America Since 1920', in Pendle (ed.), *Women in Music: A History*, 211–257.

101 Professor Paul Fransworth, cited in Tick and Rubin-Rabson, 'Why Haven't Women Become Great Composers?', 48.

7 Sex, Gender and Music

> Questions of music and gender [. . .] go deeper than the difference in power that women and men typically experience in relation to the world of music. To raise concerns of music and gender is to raise concerns having to do with the socially grounded affect of music.[1]

Throughout this book I have presented some of the issues which have frequently been thought to affect women's creativity and equal participation in music. But what of the music itself? Can musical sounds or the organization of sounds actually express gender or sex differences? If the answer is in the affirmative, it would certainly influence and inform a whole range of musical and non-musical issues which affect male and female composers. How sex and gender might be communicated, symbolized or expressed in music forms part of the latest contribution made by feminist musicologists and others. I intend to review these contributions in illustration of my own ideas. Obviously, the discussion is limited because of considerations of space, but such a concept must surely be examined in relation to the previous discussion of women composers and their participation in mainstream musical life.

It is first important to disentangle the many possible interpretations of the question, 'Can music express gender?' Often, when issues of 'gender and music' are discussed, the term 'gender' is actually used to indicate the unchangeable aspects of biological sex. It is therefore important to make a distinction between the two terms sex and gender. Sex is the biological fact of being either male or female, whilst gender is the range of characteristics, behaviour, roles and values – masculinity and femininity – which are imposed on the sexes through conformity to social norms and through social interaction. Separating sex from gender distinguishes the innate from the imposed, and only through a definite and distinct use of these terms can any clear understanding of the issues be attempted.

The search for possible links between sex, gender and music suggests a range of points for investigation. For the purposes of the current study the issues can be most easily summarized by the following questions:

1 Is the act of musical creation affected by the sex of the creator?
2 Is the act of musical creation affected by the gender of the creator?
3 Does the musical creation reflect in any way the sex of its creator?
4 Does the musical creation reflect in any way the gender of its creator?

5 Can music, through inherent meaning, symbolization, representation or shared understanding, reveal sex (male and female), or gender (masculinity and femininity) *regardless* of the sex or gender of its creator?

These questions focus on two distinct but related areas: the creative act and the musical product. The starting point for any discussion of any sex/gender linked differences in music, the act of creation, must first be understood, since any sex-differentiation of music must surely originate in sex/gender-differentiation of the artist and the creative process.

Why do humans create? What are their psychological motivations? The roots of the human need to produce and consume artistic products (literature, visual arts and music) has been explored through psychoanalytic theories of the development of human behaviour and personality.[2] In Chapter 2 the influence of personality on the fulfilment of musical potential was examined in depth. Although it was concluded that males and females have equal potential for creativity, intelligence and cultural contribution, psychoanalytic theories of the creative act form another significant area of enquiry. These have suggested that there are strong sex-differentiated differences in temperament and personality, which are developed in the unconscious mind. Such developments are proposed as the basis for male, but not female, potential – a factor which would be just as relevant to the realization of musical ability as any other:

> [. . .] discrepancies [between male and female brains] indicate that the correct explanations [of male domination and achievement] are going to lie not in the realms of raw ability, innate or otherwise, but in the interplay between raw ability and motive. At stake are not the various forms of verbal, numerical and spatial intelligence *per se*, but the passionate inclination to use these for particular purposes, and the highly specific powers of intuitive discrimination and judgement that result.[3]

Psychoanalytic theories which have been used to 'explain' proposed difference in male and female motivation or 'inclination' differ from other psychological fields of enquiry (as discussed in Chapter 2) by their focus on the role and influence of the unconscious mind. It is believed that through understanding the mechanisms which develop in the initial perception of babies and children an explanation can be found for most adult behaviour, including creativity. Most of the theories suggest that the normal development of male and female personalities is different and distinct, and that these differences then form the basis for the well documented sex-differentiated behaviour, contributions and roles. Psychoanalysis was initially developed by Sigmund Freud in the late nineteenth century. The basic premise of Freud's theories (and a host of subsequent psychoanalytic theories) is that the development of the male and female personality (and corresponding behaviours and characteristics) stems primarily from sexual (genital) identifications and the comprehension of the difference or similarity with others which then results (social object relationships). In this way, Freud established another sex (anatomical) differentiated approach to the development of human behaviour. Central to Freud's theories was the idea that instincts, primarily sexual instincts, were the key driving force behind human motivations:

> Generally speaking, our civilization is built up on the suppression of instincts [. . .] The sexual instinct[s] [. . . are] probably more strongly developed in man than in most of the higher animals [. . .] It places extraordinarily large amounts of force at the disposal of civilized activity, and it does this in virtue of its especially marked characteristic of being able to displace its aim without materially diminishing in intensity. This capacity to exchange its originally sexual aim for another one, which is no longer sexual but which is psychically related to the first aim, is called the capacity for *sublimation*.[4]

Correspondingly, the complexities of human society and the development of art and culture can be regarded as a result of sublimation of sexual instincts. Through this theory the seemingly unconnected areas of sex and musical creativity become inextricably linked. Through an exploration of psychoanalytic theories an answer to the first question, 'Is the act of musical creation affected by the sex of the creator?', may be found.

Although it has been acknowledged that both sexes have sexual instincts, these were defined differently by Freud (and others). It was suggested that in terms of strength of sexual motivation women have a less strong sex drive, or libido. Freud supported this idea with the observation that:

> [. . .] men are primarily responsible for reproduction, since their aggressive nature enables them to force women to have sexual intercourse whether they want to or not.[5]

Determining levels of sexual drive from this fact would seem flawed, especially when in reality women play such a central role in reproduction. In addition, the proposal that sex drive and desire can only manifest in aggression reflects a misunderstanding of sexuality in its many forms. However, Freud was by no means the first to suggest a link between the sexual drive of males and their supposed creative superiority; it is in fact an age-old belief.[6] Debates about the nature of female sexuality must acknowledge the historical position. Control, denial and repression of female sexuality have been part of patriarchal society's method of oppressing women; similarly, the link between sexuality and the creative process could be seen as a way of denying or controlling female creativity and expression. In addition to their supposed lack of sex drive, Freud suggested that women did not have as strong a need to sublimate any desires which they *did* have:

> We [. . .] regard women as weaker in their social interests and as having less capacity for sublimating their instincts than men.[7]

Women's psychological disposition (based on reproductive sex) here provided less initial drive/motivation in addition to a less strong mechanism to channel effort, energy and concentration into a range of areas.

If the primary motivation to create music (or other art forms) may be derived from, or governed by, sexual (reproductive) drives, and if sexuality and sexual 'drives' are different in men and women, those arguments which state that the relative lack of female contribution to music is a matter only of external discrimination would, once again, be severely damaged. Yet before we accept such an idea, two issues should be considered. First, it is by no means a proven fact that human motivation to invest energy in creative work is purely the sublimation of sexuality or sexual desire. Many feel that the emphasis on sex as the root of human motivations is misplaced and that any differences in sexuality are simply just that. Psychologist Robert Ornstein has stated:

> *Sex differences matter most in matters sexual.* As we consider areas further and further away from sexuality itself, sex differences matter less and less [. . .] In fact if we look to sex as a basis for differences in abilities in mathematics, music, writing, and the like, we are probably looking in the wrong place. The right place is the way in which each of us learns to act in the world.[8]

This suggests that *gender*, the massive and diverse range of socially imposed elements, is much more likely to hold the answers to women's current position. Second, even if it were proved that sex and sexual desires lay behind our motivations to create, this would prove disadvantageous to women only if the psychoanalytic theories which define female sexuality as passive and less pervasive were taken as fact.[9] Sexual intercourse and sexual function are a fundamental part of our human existence and individual being; indeed, these distinctions are the undeniable essence of the differences between the sexes. However, anatomical sex (the fact that women have ova and men have sperm) is not the same thing as sexuality. Before one accepts any of the ideas about the influence sex or sexuality may have on creativity, a more rounded understanding of female sexuality (and, indeed, male sexuality) is necessary. Female sexuality has, throughout history, been repeatedly restricted, feared and denied, and these restrictive beliefs are no less damaging when presented in the guise of 'pseudo-scientific' facts.

Freud's theories have been considered extremely damaging to women in their restrictive and derogatory interpretation of the female; indeed, many female psychologists have sought to reveal the masculine bias of Freud's work.[10] Yet despite this movement, many psychoanalytic theories continue to use Freud's assertions as a foundation for the understanding of male and female psychological development and ultimately, of male and female artistic contributions. A recent example, of particular interest to this study, is *The Way Men Think: Intellect, Intimacy and the Erotic Imagination* (1991) by Liam Hudson and Bernadine Jacot. The theories put forward in this work build on Freudian-based thinking of the last 25 years.[11] Hudson and Jacot believe that male dominance in many fields stems primarily from the distinctive male need to invest people, objects, systems and theories with sexual and erotic significance. Correspondingly, the artistic contribution of males 'may be distinguished [. . .] by their need to produce works which have their point of origin in sexual desire'.[12] This accords with the previously cited Freudian view, which has posited that creativity is the result of sublimation of sexual desires.

Hudson and Jacot suggest that men develop such drives and needs as part of their distinct psychological evolution. Like many other psychologists, they believe that a child's personality develops through the formative understanding of its relationship with the mother (whether biological or not). When a child is born, it is thought to perceive itself as part of the mother. In other words, it has no sense of the boundaries between itself and the outside world (known as ego boundaries). Only as the child develops does it perceive that the mother, to whom it was originally attached, is another entity. Hudson and Jacot state that the male psychological split takes place two to three years after birth, at a time when children of both sexes begin to identify with those around them whilst building perceptions of themselves.[13] Through this process they suggest that gender identity is built on the foundation of similarity and difference of reproductive anatomical sex differences. The male child's development of gender identity is understood to evolve differently because of anatomical dissimilarity between himself and his mother. To develop a male personality, a male child must first dis-identify with the mother, who is different, before con-identification with a male (usually the father) can be completed:

> [Of these two actions] The first establishes the boy's separateness; the second, his maleness. *It is these two developmental processes in combination which we* [Hudson and Jacot] *call the male wound.*[14]

A parallel is drawn between the male foetus's physical divergence from the female foetus (at a specific prenatal point) and a deep psychological divergence until:

> [. . .] early in childhood, the male *separates psychologically.* For the male, this splitting off creates a source of unease we call the *male 'wound'*. The special interest in this wound [. . .] is that it introduces a permanent element of dislocation into the lives of one sex, but not the other. Once experienced, *the wound generates needs and tensions in the male mind for which there is no direct female equivalent.*[15]

This theory seems a reinterpretation of the previously quoted Freudian view that the male is more driven – having certain 'inclinations' or compulsions which the female does not. The 'needs and tensions' for which there is no female equivalent, unsurprisingly perhaps, form the basis for male domination. Primarily, the 'male wound' fosters three important psychological facets which are distinct in men.[16] The first facet brought about in males is a sense of agency and psychological independence. (It should be observed that these stereotypical 'masculine' traits, as discussed in Chapter 2, are here given a new biological justification.) It is the male child's perceived separateness, or difference/distance between himself and his mother, which is thought to be essential for the formation of the ability to treat objects and ideas in an abstract, objective way; indeed, this ability would seem an essential part of the creative act. There are strong parallels here with Freudian theory, which states that anatomical differences are the starting point for psychological differentiation. Basically, Freud suggested that females differ psychologically from males because they perceive that they do not have male genitals and therefore are envious (a phenomenon known as penis envy). Feminists have subsequently pointed out that this concept links a number of psychological assumptions about the female personality:

> [. . .] theories of personality all have something in common: they highlight the sexual bias that determines how psychologists regard the female [. . .] psychoanalytic [. . .] theories treat the male body and personality as the norm. Freud begins with the premise that not having a male genital is a catastrophe almost beyond imagining.[17]

This direct and obvious prejudice lies at the heart of many of the definitions of female. Indeed, Hudson and Jacot elaborate the concept of penis envy thus:

> What women lack [. . .] is not a penis but an in-built sense of agency (of which a penis is sometimes assumed to be symbolic). It is this sense which a woman must subsequently construct, and which, if her own femininity is insecure, she may envy.[18]

Yet this idea presents a theory which, essentially, is built on the same starting point as Freud's penis envy theory. Freud suggested that women do not have an 'in-built' sense of psychological independence because they physically lack male genitals and so are envious of the male who does. Hudson and Jacot suggest that *because of their lack of male genitals* females experience no sense of separation from their mothers, whereas men, *due to their genital difference*, do experience separation from the mother, a process from which they 'benefit' psychologically: a process which women then envy. The Hudson and Jacot theory has, on the surface, moved away from Freud's position, but it still rests on the fact that because males are genitally different from their mothers, they will normally develop a psychological advantage which women cannot but envy.

The second psychological facet which males develop is termed 'abstract passions':

> [This concept . . .] explains [. . . the] ability not merely to think analytically, nor even to think analytically with passionate intensity, but to think analytically and with passionate intensity about topics that have no detectable bearing on our ordinary biological appetites or needs. For the 'male' male [. . .] *such passions will be the more enduringly gratifying the more completely divorced from human relationships they are.*[19]

In this way men have an in-built need to focus on objects and ideas outside social relationships; again, this could be used as an 'explanation' of the predominance of male cultural contribution.

The third consequence of male development cited by Hudson and Jacot is the male's unique source of 'psychic energy'. Freud's theory that human 'drive' or motivation is the sublimation of sexual desires is here reinterpreted as the result of the 'primitive separation' between the mother and the male child.[20] Although this is never stated explicitly, it is implicit that the psychological energy needed to create is entirely male, since it is suggested that females do not experience such a primitive separation. Females are said, instead, to find satisfaction in identification with the mother, who is female – thus confirming a connection which enforces female identity through attachment, without any sense of psychological separation. This is thought to imbue females with a personality which is defined by connectivity, contentment and passivity. Hence the normal female personality is marked by the absence of an active, persistent, driven personality required for full participation in the creation of the arts and science, a point reinforced in a different way by Freud's theories:

> [. . . For] Freud's 'feminine' woman the crisis of puberty that forces her to suppress her curiosity about the nature of her own sexuality also leads to the abandonment of her intellectual precocity. She is envious of the penis, but represses knowledge of this. Without sexual curiosity there is no intellectual or creative curiosity.[21]

This would seem to turn many traditional notions of the 'feminine' male creative personality on its head. It was concluded by Hudson and Jacot that men and women, who embrace a whole range of personality types ('masculine' female, 'feminine' male), have equal amounts of inherent mental ability, but that they are motivated differently in both the expression and fulfilment of intellectual potentials. It is the masculine or 'male' male (the result of 'normal' male psychological development) who has, in his make-up, the motivation to create and achieve:

> [. . .] the male wound and its consequences [. . . are] in no sense reducible to biology [. . .] It does not depend on there being sizeable differences of anatomy or function between male and female brains [. . .] Our claim [. . .] is not that 'male' men are more (or less) gifted than women or androgynous men. Rather, that the 'male' man is impelled towards certain imaginatively charged extremities of thought and action in ways which most women and androgynous men are not. What is at issue is not ability as such, but accomplishment of the kind that only a driven need can bring about.[22]

This implies that women of all personality types (masculine/female, feminine/female and androgynous/female) are denied the 'compulsion' to use their abilities. In this way women are not denied the ability as such, but rather the *ability* to actually develop innate potential, which is just as limiting.

The three psychological consequences of the 'male wound' or male development cited obviously hold significant implications for a range of activities. Much of the evidence considered in this book has suggested that such functions and characteristics are vital to the creation of music. It is clear that composers must have the basic desire to create something – the 'inspiration' or 'psychic energy' which motivates them to expression through the medium of music. To compose music, the creator must have a strong enough sense of self or will to enable the investment of time and energy in creativity: in other words, a sense of agency to satisfy their own internal needs before those of others. Finally, the composer must be able to pursue his creative ideas and products (which are not human or even necessary to human existence) with a passion and energy usually reserved for processes essential to survival. Disturbingly, in Hudson and Jacot's opinion, it is the 'male' male personality that is best placed to contain such psychological traits:

> The more 'male' the male, the greater the imaginative gulf separating him from his sources of primitive comfort [. . .] He is perfectly poised, nevertheless, to heal his wound at one symbolic remove; to use the anxiety his separation provokes in him to create systems of ideas which can stand in the place of lost intimacy and within which he can strive for coherence and harmony.[23]

Clearly, many of the traits which are defined as facets of male psychological development are important to creativity and intellectual development. If all these are consequences of male, but not female, psychological development, this would suggest an innate or 'natural' rationalization of women's relatively limited musical contribution.

The above arguments assert that the creative act is governed by sexual drive and that the channelling of such drive is fulfilled only by aspects of the male personality. These theories exonerate patriarchal society from the accusation of suppression of female creativity, since the male domination of cultural activity becomes a 'natural' phenomenon. However, such ideas cannot be upheld, since they take no account of society's influence on human development and behaviour. Many of the characteristics which are suggested as ultimately sex-related have, throughout history, simply been descriptive of female social oppression. All too often, conclusions are reached which describe women's secondary position as a reflection of women's difference from men, rather than interpreting the effects which women's restricted social role may have had on their collective psychological development.

Psychologist Nancy Chodorow has been instrumental in challenging many Freudian-based accounts of personality, exposing the bias of its viewpoints. In contrast to the psychoanalytic theories cited, Chodorow puts forward a theory of personality which is based on biology but not *determined* by it. Chodorow observes that female development is different from male, but that this is a result of learnt gender characteristics and roles, not an inevitable result of female or male biology or anatomy:

> Ideologies of difference, ideologies that define us as women and as men – and inequality itself – are produced, socially, psychologically, and culturally [. . .] To speak of difference as a final, irreducible concept and to focus on gender differences as central is to reify and deny the *processes* that create the meaning and significance of gender. To see men and women as qualitatively different kinds of people, rather than seeing gender as processual, reflexive, and constructed, is to reify and deny *relations* of gender, to see gender differences as permanent rather than created and situated.[24]

Chodorow's theory of personality development sees the *imposition* of 'feminine' psychology and personality on women as primarily a result of the universal role of female mothering (caring for, rather than actually giving birth), which brings with it a range of imposed social and psychological restrictions. Chodorow concludes that it is woman's position as mother which needs re-examination:

> Women's universal mothering role has effects both on the development of masculine and feminine personality and on the relative status of the sexes [. . .] Social and psychological oppression [. . . are] perpetuated in the structure of the personality.[25]

Female oppression is supported by female psychological development based on an overly strong sense of identification and continuity with the mother, which can lead to a lack of sufficient ego boundaries. However, when a mother has herself developed an adequate sense of ego and self, she will pass this on to her female children. For example, Chodorow observed that in cultures which are matrifocal the female sense of self is more definite:

> The evidence [. . .] suggests that satisfactory mothering, which does not reproduce particular psychological problems in boys and girls, comes from a person with a firm sense of self and of her own value, whose care is a freely chosen activity rather than a reflection of a conscious and unconscious sense of inescapable connection to and responsibility for her children.[26]

However, the continued emphasis placed on women's role as mothers, especially true in middle-class Western society, ensures the perpetuation of psychological dependency in some women:

> The care and socialization of girls by women ensures the production of feminine personalities founded on relation and connection [. . .] Various kinds of evidence suggest that separation from the mother, the breaking of dependence, and the establishment and maintenance of a consistently individuated sense of self remain difficult psychological issues for Western middle-class women [. . .][27]

This results in the fact that women often do not see themselves as distinct from their children and husbands and are content to obtain some sort of satisfaction through the behaviour and lives of others.[28] A woman's lack of self and ego boundaries can result in her assumption of total responsibility for others' happiness. The psychological dependency on others and the lack of self this situation creates would seem to be an extremely inhibiting characteristic, not at all conducive to the fulfilment of artistic potential. However, these characteristics are in no sense an inescapable part of female psychological development but are, more realistically, the result of women's dependent and subordinate social place.

Although females will always be in a position of continual psychological identification with their mothers, the resulting sense of continuity which secures femaleness cannot, in Chodorow's view, be understood automatically to result in a personality defined by lack of ego boundaries, passivity and non-achievement:[29]

> [. . .] these problems are not inevitable products of having a sense of continuity and similarity, since selfhood does not depend only on the strength and impermeability of ego boundaries.[30]

She believes that the development of independence and sense of self does not have to be defined totally in terms of understanding separateness (available only to men, through their difference from their mothers), as was previously suggested:

> The senses of agency, of a true self that does not develop reactively, of a relational self or ego core, and of an internal continuity of being, are fundamental to an unproblematic sense of self, and provide the basis of both autonomy and spontaneity. The strength, or wholeness, of the self, in this view, does not depend only or even centrally on its degree of separateness [. . .] The more secure the central self, or ego core, the less one has to define one's self through separateness from others.[31]

Chodorow suggests that the development of a core gender identity of male and female (the central and unchanging understanding of one's biological sex) is established in the first two years of life and is a process which is different for each sex. She believes that males develop their core gender identity starting from a position of oneness with the mother and that, therefore, their core gender identity and maleness are in a position to be undermined or under threat. Females, on the other hand, have a constant sense of identification with femaleness, so little conflict, frustration or stress arises.[32] The female's core ego seems always to be secure, in that her understanding of her sex is confirmed by her first object relation experience with her same-sex mother. Through continual confirmation of self, a sense of autonomy can securely develop. Chodorow's deconstruction of the traditional psychoanalytic understanding that male psychological separation from the mother gives men a sense of independence and agency which women have difficulty obtaining once again leaves space for female development of creative ability.

Chodorow's theory that the development of ego is gendered (socially imposed through a variety of channels) changes the influences on the act of creation from being ultimately reducible to sex-differences (as was suggested first by Freud and then by Hudson and Jacot) to being, instead, imposed by learnt gendered differences. In this way the wider social and cultural restrictions placed on women become embedded through the process of female psychological development; hence arguments against female creativity become self-fulfilling prophecies. The social oppression of women seems to have consequences which reach to the very heart of female experience and can restrict and confine female energy. More disturbing is Chodorow's finding that women from the middle classes are most vulnerable to loss of sense of self and weaker egos, because of over emphasis on mothering and child care. Since virtually all female composers come from this section of society, it confirms that the challenges faced by female composers operate on a psychological and domestic level. The absorption of creatively restrictive characteristics suggests that it would be more difficult for women to distance themselves from their families and so be free to concentrate on an activity such as musical composition, which in every sense defines the woman as pursuing needs separate from those around her. For a female, the satisfaction of her own instinctual and artistic needs can be psychologically difficult in a culture where mothering is still considered the predominant female role.

Yet despite the difficulties which accompany female psychological development as part of female subordination, some writers view such developments as positive:

> Although there are obvious disadvantageous psychological consequences to being socially subordinated, outside the dominant system, and relatively powerless, there are also some advantages. Outsiders may escape some of the dominant group's weaknesses and may even be able to develop special strengths and insights by virtue of their subordinate position.[33]

In this view, the special facets of female development (empathy, deference, connectivity) are viewed as positive traits which are undervalued. Arguably, no one would deny that this is true but as the previous discussion showed, such traits appear to develop only at the expense of others such as independence, agency and objectivity – all traits which are significant facilitators of the fulfilment of potential. This situation creates a real dilemma. Should the qualities developed in female psychology (whether imposed or innate) be accepted and valued for their true worth, despite their low place in traditional thinking, or should females be made aware that through the development of such traits society denies many women a psychology whereby they will be able to liberate themselves and compete in the current system?

The basis for psychological sex-differentiation in the area of creativity is a far from secure one, since it is often unclear what is real, innate or imposed. While such issues remain unresolved, the assertion of any deep-rooted sex-differences in the creative process will remain without firm foundations. Despite this, debates over how gender and sex are realized in music have been intense. It has long been claimed that the creative product – that is, the musical composition – reveals many sex and gender differences. Suggestions of an audible sex-difference in music must be handled with the utmost care. Any understanding of music which defines women's contribution or expression as distinctive, for reasons of biological or psychological difference, is in danger of reinforcing stereotypes of the female as different and inferior (see Chapters 5 and 6). However, it cannot be ignored that psychoanalytic theory suggests that men and women differ to varying degrees in their psychology and socialization (whether innate or imposed), and that this can have a significant bearing on many areas of experience, expression and motivation.

The differences between male and female development outlined above have been used as the foundation for arguments which insist that there is a female or 'feminine' expression and a male or 'masculine' expression in music:

> The dominance men enjoy in disciplines like mathematics and physics stems from the [male] wound [psychological separation and maleness . . .] in the form of a driven need to create and explore formal structures. Such a need might also account for the superiority men have in the past enjoyed in certain aspects of the arts; musical composition for instance.[34]

The footnote to this statement then elaborates:

> [The . . .] assumption [. . .] is not that men are necessarily better than women at musical composition, but that, in the hands of gifted women, musical composition may take distinctively new forms.[35]

The suggestion here is that musical compositions by women could be generically distinct from those of their male colleagues. The reasoning is that male and female differences are (or, perhaps, ought to be) implanted into male and female musical expression. This is a controversial area, and one traditionally associated with theories which imply female inferiority as an issue of 'difference'. Indeed this is demonstrated in the Hudson and Jacot quotation, since although note 35 states categorically that men are not necessarily better than women at composition, the main text (see note 34) contradicts this with the assertion that male difference 'accounts for the superiority' male musicians have enjoyed in the past. Many femininists have argued strenuously that such 'differences', if they exist at all, are in reality imposed; certainly, this has been the position taken for much of this book. However, other feminists argue in favour of the 'difference' hypothesis. They believe that women *are* different from men and that the plea for 'sameness' serves only to further the politics of patriarchal subjugation. In this view, fighters seeking to gain equality for women should not be tempted to present the sexes as 'the same' just because the 'female' and everything that this category implies have, in the past, been downgraded and derided. (However, this stance, to a certain extent, also implies an acceptance of many patriarchal constructions of the female.)

This leads to the uncomfortable situation where two opposing camps use the same argument for different purposes (that is, those who see women's difference as the basis for their equality oppose those who see women's difference as the reason for their subjection). In relation to music, both camps believe that compositions by men and women will be different by virtue of the sex and gender of the creator, which will unconsciously be transmitted to their work through the psychological sensibilities they have developed as men and women respectively. The crucial point here is that the composer's gender or sex will be stamped on to the musical work in some way and that the composer has *no conscious means* of avoiding or concealing such characteristics. This would seem to reinforce the views according to which female composers' works are infused with their sex and gender (this was brought out in Chapters 5 and 6) – but one femininist camp would suggest that the same is also true of male composers' works.

Identifying exactly what male and female, masculine and feminine, musical expressions may be unsurprisingly finds its starting point in the parallels between musical and sexual experience. Previously quoted theories have suggested that the source of artistic expression may be the sublimation of desires (namely, sexual). In an extension of this concept, it has been observed that the sexual experience has certain parallels with the musical experience. In this way the musical composition is constructed so as to evoke in the listener a sort of pseudo-sexual response:

> [. . .] Freud believed that in adult life a period of tensionless satisfaction followed sexual orgasm. It is obviously possible [. . .] to compare musical experience with sexual experience. Music can cause intense emotional arousal accompanied by a desire for physical movement and [. . . a range of] physiological changes [. . .] When music is over, feelings of peace, tranquillity, and satisfaction may supervene [. . . however] It does not follow that either experience is a substitute for, or even remotely related to, sexuality. The pattern of arousal followed by relaxation is ubiquitous – an inescapable aspect of both human and animal life.[36]

Although the above statement by Anthony Storr rejects the notion that sexuality and music are specifically linked by the emotions and desires they evoke, many feminists have seen the parallel as real and, moreover, part of how sex and gender may be linked to musical expression. Some have identified traditional tonal musical structures as mirroring male sexual experience. The supposition that music can act as an expression of sexuality, and that male and female sexuality differ, is the starting point for Susan McClary's discussion of a composition by Janika Vandervelde entitled *Genesis II*.

The inspiration for the musical premise of *Genesis II* originally came to Vandervelde when she completed a commission for an orchestral work to accompany the children's fairytale of 'Jack and the Beanstalk'. In portraying the story's narrative in the structure of the work Vandervelde became aware of what McClary terms the 'phallic nature' of the music she produced.[37] The features which form this 'phallic' association can be understood primarily as a build-up of musical tension and frustration, which is marked by 'the hero climax of many a tonal composition'.[38] This kind of build-up, marked by striving, climax, release and satisfaction, is found in much traditional post-Renaissance music, yet these features have customarily been perceived as having meaning in terms of purely musical procedures and form:

> In most post-Renaissance Western music and in virtually all of its critical literature, the climax-principal [. . .] has been transcendentalized to the status of a value-free universal of form. Despite the prevalence of this pattern, it is rarely even viewed as sexual (let alone masculine) any longer – it is simply the way music is supposed to be.[39]

McClary asserts that the traditional patterns and constructions of tonal music which structure this musical gesture are reflective of male sexuality. Her understanding relies on explicit reference to the male's physical stages of arousal, penetration and orgasm. If such musical gestures are a manifestation of male sexuality, where does it leave the female composer in relation to creating such musical structures? Or indeed, would it affect a female listener differently from a male? Vandervelde obviously felt strongly enough about her alienation from such structures to construct in her own work a different musical narrative or structure. This would seem to take the presumably unconscious imposition of male sexuality in music and turn it into a conscious exploration of something else. Yet it is stressed that this is not an exploration or position restricted only to female composers, being available to:

> By extension [. . .] any composer – female or male – who has become dissatisfied with the implied contents of received artistic conventions and procedures, especially the standard narrative of tonal striving, climax and closure.[40]

Genesis II is for piano trio (piano, cello and violin). McClary sees the work as providing two kinds of material which are 'rich in metaphysical implication'. First, the piano part, which sets up a cyclic 'clockwork' pattern, changing but basically remaining stable. This pattern is described as making the listener:

> [. . .] continually [. . .] aware of the present moment, as the asymmetries of the pattern attract the ear down into its intricate cross-rhythms; yet the completion of each cycle yields a sense of satisfaction and security and we experience the possibility that the pattern might be replicated indefinitely, infinitely.[41]

This musical structure stresses continuity, change without opposition, evolution from oneness without separation or domination. In the light of the psychological theories discussed above, this is also suggestive of what some would see as the female psychological experience. Against the 'cyclic' pattern, string parts create more traditional musical models which are inherently striving and searching:

> [. . . the string parts] present us with goal-oriented gestures of self-expression and striving that typically characterize Western concert music: gestures that are explicitly *not* content with living in the present moment but that seek to expand horizons and to defy social convention, gestures that trade the very hope of future stability for a never-ending chase after the elusive chimeras of progress, change, and finally the transcendence and obliteration of time.[42]

These gestures are marked by separation, opposition and a driven need. Such descriptions recall certain theories of male psychology and experience. Although McClary does not label either of these musical parts male or female, this implication is more than apparent. McClary does not suggest that the structure or nature of the musical material employed by Vandervelde is unique; rather, it is the organization and 'working out' of the material that suggests a new narrative in musical structure. Vandervelde seems to work against conventional patterns. Instead of the goal-oriented, striving 'aggressive' material being presented first (as it would be in standard tonal or 'sonata' organization) the continuous 'cyclic' material sets up our expectations and is 'intruded' upon by the 'striving' material.[43] The composition culminates in the confrontation of the two types of material, which leads to an 'overwhelming explosion'. But the work does not end on this note of self-destructive climax, as perhaps one would expect from most tonal compositions: instead, we have a 'second prologue characterized by sustained, pulsating energy: the embryonic promise of a new and perhaps different scenario'.[44] McClary sees the importance of *Genesis II* thus:

> [. . .] the significance of Vandervelde's achievement is not *simply* that she has revealed as phallic and sexually violent many of the 'value-free' conventions of classical form (though there is nothing like the appropriation by a woman of [. . . phallic] gestures to make us realize that there are unwritten cultural rules of gender propriety) [. . .] What Vandervelde has accomplished is an approach to composition that permits her – expressly as a woman – to inhabit a traditional discourse, to call into question its gestures and procedures *from the inside*, and to imagine from that vantage point the possibility of other narrative schemata.[45]

Such claims reveal the obvious sense of alienation felt by many female composers, and indeed musicologists, from the traditional musical canon. Without denying the validity of such sentiments, McClary's reading of this work, and by extension her perception of other traditional works, relies on a number of assumptions which need further clarification. The first of McClary's assumptions is that traditional musical structures, patterns and organization are employed as such by men because they parallel the 'effects' felt in sexual arousal (primarily male, since the vast majority of Western music has been created by men). Recalling Storr's citation, tension followed by release can be viewed as ubiquitous to human experience of all kinds. Indeed, slow build up of tension (defined by increased movement or frustration) followed by explosive release (climax, or crisis point), then relaxation could just as well be a physical description of the experience of childbirth. I am not suggesting that music parallels this physical occurrence, but rather that build-up, climax/crisis and release are not only applicable to, or suggestive of, male sexual processes. Moreover, McClary's analysis seems to blur the boundaries of physical sexuality and gendered psychology, along with conscious and unconscious infusions of such concepts in music. A pertinent question not addressed by McClary's research is: 'If musical structures do indeed reflect male sexuality, is this a conscious or an unconscious part of their creative process?' If it is an unconscious manifestation, it could be seen as a brake on their creativity – a reversal of an argument which has long been used against female composers. It has become apparent in the course of the brief discussions in this chapter that such issues must be tackled in a manner that does not reinforce discriminatory ideas about women, most of which are based on similar failures to demarcate what is physically and psychologically inherent or imposed, and what are unconscious or conscious artistic manifestations.

Debates about sexuality, such as those incorporated in McClary's work, must beware of the dangers inherent in generalization. Obviously, there are physical aspects of genitalia and sexual function which are different between the sexes, but this does not necessarily imply that female sexual experience or sexuality have nothing in common with the male. Explorations of male and female sexuality often serve only to polarize further notions of 'normal' sexuality as 'male: active – female: passive'. Considering the centuries of misunderstanding and oppression female sexuality has endured, defining it in any way can be difficult, especially if one rejects the assumption that all women have the same kind of sexual experiences and desires.[46] McClary herself acknowledges that attempts to classify women's sexuality, experience and expression as different from men's imposes enormous problems. The danger is that it can lead to the continued labelling of certain traits and expressions as appropriate for either male or female but not both:

> [. . .] it may encourage essentialist readings: to map femininity onto nature, cycles, and timeless stability and masculinity onto culture, linear time and agency is to risk reinscribing these associations that very much need to be interrogated and resisted.[47]

I would add that, considering the previously quoted psychoanalytic definitions of male and female, these elements and concepts are very much bound up with psychological characterizations which should be closely scrutinized and questioned. Recent reinterpretations of psychoanalytic theories (for example, that of Chodorow) point towards the idea that no psychological characteristics are in principle unavailable to either men or women; but so long as children are raised in a patriarchal culture, males and females alike will tend to live up to the psychological stereotypes imposed on them. (The same would doubtless be true in a one-sidedly matriarchal culture.)

The exploration of perceived differences in narrative agendas in works of literature produced by males and females has attempted to identify the distinctly female and 'feminine' traits in the work of female writers. This in turn has provided a starting point for comparisons with the work of female composers.[48] Renée Cox has imagined a 'translation' of 'feminine' writing modes into musical expression:

> A music modelled on feminine writing would engage the listener in the musical moment rather than in the structure as a whole; would have flexible, cyclical form; and would involve continuous repetition with variation, the cumulative growth of an idea. Such music would serve to de-construct musical hierarchies and the dialectical juxtaposition and resolution of opposites, disrupt linearity, and avoid closures.[49]

Let us first consider why these musical (or literal) traits could be a 'feminine' mode of expression. Immediately, one is struck by the fact that these ideas can be traced directly to the psychoanalytic theories cited above (and indeed in Susan McClary's work). For example, the idea that music based on the 'feminine' would engage the listener with a sense of continual participation, with avoidance of juxtaposition of opposites, using instead continuous repetition with variation, can be traced to the female's supposed psychological connectedness (developed from primary identification with the mother). Through this sense of connectedness with others (mothers and later biological children), women would tend to order their worlds less in terms of opposition but more in those of evolution from oneness – the interest being not in play between two opposites, but rather in the transformation of the one. The description also suggests that the 'feminine' in music might de-construct 'musical hierarchies' – hierarchies that would seem to depend on separation and opposition. The 'flexible cyclical form' advocated by Cox seems to emerge from two areas. First, psychologically, the female's connectedness has been defined as resulting in a flexible sense of self and flexible ego boundaries which make definitions of beginning and end less pressing. Second, the emphasis on 'cyclic forms' recalls the female's bodily experiences of childbirth and menstruation. The 'avoidance of closures' has been linked to female sexuality, in which pleasure and orgasm are viewed by some as 'open ended' or at any rate not geared to 'climax and resolution'.

Many critics (of both sexes) would immediately point out that all of the ideas perceived as reflecting the feminine can be heard in the work of male composers. Accordingly, this type of expression cannot be considered solely an expression of female experience or psychology:

> The predilection for musical organism, for continuous growth and development, can also be found in the music of men, of course, and it is not found in all music by women. But it is especially meaningful in the music of women, for it has been associated with the female or feminine since ancient times.[50]

Underlying Cox's vision is a suggestion that music composed by a female which operates in these ways (reflecting and expressing female psychology and physicality, continuity, connectedness) is, in a real sense, more 'meaningful' than music by a female which does not incorporate such concepts. But to whom is this music more meaningful? I, for one, do not believe that women's music is only meaningful if it reflects their (supposed) psychological developments and experience. But perhaps Cox is suggesting that it would be 'especially meaningful' to the listener – particularly to another woman, who could closely identify with such concepts. The corresponding argument would suggest that manifestations of (supposedly) male psychology and experience in the music of male composers would be 'especially meaningful' as far as other male listeners were concerned. To claim that certain characteristics may be classed as female – especially those reflecting female development and experience under patriarchy – may ultimately be a valid argument, but there is a constant danger of relegating women (and, indeed, men) to a needlessly limited sphere of reference. Since it remains debatable whether these claimed psychological developments and traits describe accurately the unchanging essence of women (or men), extending such ideas into what is, or what is not, meaningful in music is premature, to say the least.

Cox's research also suggests that women, because of their unique physical experiences, are more in touch with their bodies than men. Psychologists have argued that another important factor in female ego development is that, more than the male, the female is, throughout her life, constantly challenged, by bodily experiences, in relation to her physical boundaries:

> Women's biosexual experiences (menstruation, coitus, pregnancy, childbirth and lactation) all involve some challenge of the boundaries of her body ego [. . .] These are important and fundamental human experiences that are probably intrinsically meaningful and at the same time complicated for women [. . .] However, a Western woman's tenuous sense of individuation and of the firmness of her ego boundaries increases the likelihood that experiences challenging these boundaries will be difficult for her and conflictive.[51]

The fact that men do not have these experiences, and that they have traditionally disparaged and feared them, has meant that such bodily experiences can be, for Western women, a source of conflict rather than of strength and self-awareness. Perhaps a factor too often overlooked in this particular debate is that men, too, are affected by their physical realities and experiences. In the context of the mind/male – body/female split, which is traditional in Western thinking, the male mind has been conspicuously placed above such phenomena. In their quest to liberate women from the accusation of limited and confined intellect, some feminists have concentrated on verifying that females are quite capable of reason and intellect in order to counterbalance the emphasis placed on the female's association with her body, emotions and the 'irrational'. However, others have put forward the view that a one-sided emphasis on what are, in effect, imposed 'masculine' values does not deal with the fundamental definitions and understandings of female experiences. A more fruitful analysis would instead break down the patriarchal mind-body split, which, some suggest, is an artificial polarization in the first place:

> Because of the nature of their bodies and their experiences, what women [. . .] may have to offer is the integration of body and psyche, an integration of the mental, emotional, and physical. Such an integration can give rise to authenticity and

> creativity [. . .] because such a creativity would be disruptive to the objectifying and controlling nature of the patriarchal order [. . .] In exploring their bodies, cycles, natural rhythms, sexuality, and emotional life, however, women can examine the impact of these aspects on their reason, the relationships among them, and their thought.[52]

Valuation of fundamental human experiences, be they male or female, might prove a step forward in taking a more balanced view of what are authentic artistic expressions. For a female aesthetic or style to be defined or developed, both men and women need to understand the historical position and cultural legacies of the patriarchal definitions and prescriptions of what is female and male. This is a point reinforced by Cox:

> Perhaps the most difficult problem with the idea of a women's music lies in determining how to distinguish the expression of women's experience from the expression of male constructions of the feminine [. . .] Do women have any authentically female experience unconditioned by patriarchal oppression and constraints? Do the female processes or qualities identified [. . .] arise out of the very social conditions that we are trying to change, such that celebration of these qualities would limit women's progress?[53]

A great deal of care must be exercised when defining a distinctly 'female' or 'male' emotion or sensibility so that neither sex is robbed of its full being. However, when any psychoanalytic theory about the 'nature' of women and men is used to define what is male or female, it must be remembered that such definitions have frequently been formulated from highly biased standpoints which merely reflect patriarchal definitions of, and evolutions from, the present situation. Psychoanalytic theory, it must be remembered, is not a fully scientific discipline that relies, for its statements, on replicable laboratory evidence. It takes results and interprets them neatly, but not necessarily accurately. If females are subject to a common social environment, its psychological effects on them are not easily distinguishable from those of their common biology. In practice, nature and nurture are inseparable as they affect behaviour. Using these understandings of women and men may serve only to reinforce many traditional concepts which, instead, need to be deconstructed. In our attempt to understand how gender identities are formed via identification with those around us, the present discriminatory state of affairs must surely be taken into account. If the female personality and experience have been observed to function along certain lines, this could well be due to the internalization of thousands of years of oppressive conditioning affecting sexuality, intelligence and physicality. We are all products of a system which values the male, both physically and mentally, as the norm, and in this situation there has been no honoured place for the female. If musical creativity is indeed associated with the expression of desires, especially sexual, what effect could being a female living during the past 200 years have had – not only on women's capacity to express themselves but also on the form taken by this expression? The type of psychological maiming which has unquestionably occurred in our society has created an environment which reflects such ideas back through the psychology of individuals or groups. Women's biosexual experiences should not be shunned or repressed, for they are real and important in many women's lives. Yet how far they can be expressed in music remains to be seen.

It seems clear that the case for certain musical elements being true representations of female or male experience, sexuality or behaviour is untenable when such musical elements can be found in the work of both sexes. For example, to state categorically that conflict and striving are 'authentic' male expressions and that continuity and stability are 'authentic' female expressions, serves only to accept and perpetuate restrictive stereotypes. I suggest that, in reality, striving can be 'meaningful' for many women and that continuity can be 'meaningful' for many men, depending on the experience of the individual. If socially imposed constructions of sex-differentiated experience and expression have a potent and wide-ranging influence, I believe that the real issue must be how far such concepts can affect the work of composers. Composers of both sexes employ a variety of musical styles and approaches which have been classed as 'male', 'masculine', 'female' and 'feminine'; the fact that some have made conscious attempts to construct gendered statements in music (as was the case with Janika Vandervelde) reveals only the extent to which they feel estranged from certain traditional musical processes. In this way, music can be 'made' gendered, but only in relation to a theoretical 'ideal' stereotype.

This idea is supported by the observable fact that music has often been understood, and certainly described and written about, by means of sex-specific and gender-specific terms.[54] Sonata form (masculine and feminine themes), cadences (masculine and feminine closures) and qualities of music (for example, soft, lyrical, sensuous sounds, regarded as feminine) are some of the most obvious examples. Although these descriptions are used to refer to different elements of music, they rely on a common understanding of the terms masculine and feminine to underpin their meanings; that is, 'feminine' implies weakness, submissiveness, small-scale, whilst 'masculine' implies strength, dominance and large-scale. It has been argued earlier that such descriptions are invalid, since they are wholly (or in large measure) true of either female or male composers' work. It is altogether clear that, in theory, a whole range of styles and approaches are open to either sex. However, such stereotypes may have some effect, either conscious or unconscious, on what a composer writes. From the information already discussed, it emerges that music is perceived in many ways to reflect gender and sex – but this does not seem in any sense to be as an unconscious manifestation of the composer's personal identity or as part of a universal characteristic which only women or only men are capable of revealing in their music. The more likely explanation is that music can be gendered in the sense that the many elements which constitute music are perceived as part of a wider gender-differentiated or schematized view of the world.

Accordingly, there are examples of discussions about music in sex-specific and gender-specific terms which have been undertaken *completely* in relation to the work of male composers. Although musical practices have changed over time, gendered descriptions of music, and of the responses it evokes, can be traced right back to Antiquity:[55]

> Ruder peoples delight in the harsher modes of the Thracians; civilized peoples, in more restrained modes, though in these days this almost never occurs. Since humanity is now lascivious and effeminate it is wholly captivated by scenic and theatrical modes.[56]

Another example, from the mid-1800s, comes in a statement by Robert Schumann:

> We must speak a word in favour of every one of the more powerful, masculine expressions in music today (which so preponderantly and in its most beloved masters tends to the contrary); as if Beethoven had not lived a short time ago and plainly said ' Music must strike fire from the spirit of a man; emotionalism is only meant for women.' Few remember what he said, the majority aim at emotional effects. They ought to be punished by being dressed in women's clothes.[57]

Unsurprisingly, in the work of male composers anything which is perceived as 'feminine' is viewed as a sign of an inferior musical product. It has been argued in previous chapters that the work of female composers has often been discussed in relation to how far it 'betrays' itself as created by a female, hence suggesting some sort of limit placed on women's musical achievement. Schumann's implication is that some male composers express in their music 'emotionalism', which is seen as a feminine characteristic and therefore unsuitable for a male person. If it were the case that only the male could express what are perceived as masculine traits in music, this statement would clearly not have been necessary. Instead, Schumann provides a *prescription* by which music created by men should contain 'powerful masculine' expressions which evoke a given response in other men. Everything which relates in reality, or by association, to the female becomes monstrous when displayed in the music of a male composer. Schumann's jocular suggestion that male composers who express feminine 'emotionalism' should be punished by being made to wear women's clothes illustrates just how aberrant a male employing 'feminine' musical characteristics was considered. True, composers of either sex can express masculine or feminine traits in their music, but these gendered associations form part of the prescription of what men and women should be, and therefore also of what their expression in music should be. According to Schumann, men should compose 'masculine' music and women presumably 'feminine' music, although it is all too clear that the 'feminine' is inferior, regardless of the sex of the composer. That music can be understood and discussed in gendered terms, even when the sex and gender of the composer is not an issue, reveals the real heart of the debate on sex, gender and music.

It is a fact that only a physical male or a physical female can be unequivocally described as male or female, man or woman: anything else is described as such only by metaphor or analogy. The idea that *only* males can be 'masculine' and that *only* females can be 'feminine', with all that these categories imply, is, in reality, not a fact, no matter how strong the social stereotypes which enforce such ideas may be. Nevertheless, for hundreds of years it has been thought maladaptive for a man to be feminine or for a woman to be masculine. Our world is largely ordered around sex and gender as the fundamental basis for the categorization of a whole range of behaviour and actions. Correspondingly, we are all accustomed to expect such characteristics and behaviour to be displayed by each sex. Such categories become issues in music (and the other arts) because society uses sex and gender not only as categories for the appropriation of human characteristics, skills and behaviours, but also as a tangle of metaphors and analogies which relate to objects, ideas and phenomena far outside the original sex or gender category.

What becomes apparent in many discussions of music is an underlying perception of the whole world in gender-specific terms. Perhaps the essential point in understanding gender's exact relation to music is the proposition that gender associations form a fundamental part of human cognition. Psychologist Sandra Lipsitz Bem has put forward a theory, known as Gender Schema, which seeks to explain this occurrence:

> Gender Schema theory begins with the observation that the developing child invariably learns his or her society's cultural definitions of femaleness and maleness. In most societies, these definitions comprise a diverse and sprawling network of sex-linked associations encompassing not only those features directly related to female and male persons – such as anatomy, reproductive function, division of labour, and personality attributes – but also features more remotely or metaphorically related to sex, such as angularity or roundedness of an abstract shape and the periodicity of the moon. Indeed, no other dichotomy in human experience appears to have as many entities linked to it as does the distinction between male and female.[58]

Through our interaction with a culture which emphasizes gender as a fundamental category (based on the basic reproductive and anatomical sex differences) we develop a gendered cognition of the world: Bem explains:

> [. . .] a category will become a schema if: (1) the social context makes it the nucleus of a large associative network, that is, the ideology and/or practices of the culture construct an association between that category and a wide range of other attributes, behaviours, concepts, and categories; and (2) the social context assigns the category broad functional significance, that is, if a broad array of social institutions, norms and taboos distinguishes between persons, behaviours, and attitudes on the basis of this category.[59]

Gendered organizations and descriptions of the world become part of the way we comprehend reality. Accordingly, our gendered perception of the world is automatically mapped on to music through our network of gendered associations. Every aspect of music – the inherent quality of sounds, the organization of such sounds, their form, our responses to them and, ultimately, their perceived meaning – can be understood as part of this gender schema. In this way, not only human behaviours, emotions and personality are comprehended as masculine and feminine, but also objects, systems and ideas which can be tagged as *descriptive* of either sex, or, perhaps more important, *prescriptive* (more suitable, natural or perfectly evolved) for each sex. It is the way in which all of us see the world as emanating from a sexual or gendered binary division that creates the problems of biased valuations in a musical perception organized around gender. Taking this as a starting point, it can be expected that all our fundamental definitions of masculine and feminine in music will correspond to the array of associative cultural correlates which our awareness of the classes of masculine and feminine conjures up. Yet it must be stressed that when the cultural and social definitions and associations are removed, only reproductive and anatomical differences remain. It is clear that these have no physical reality in musical sounds, thereby leaving all such categories and associations open to reorganization.

This theory suggests an answer to the fifth question posed at the beginning of this chapter: 'Can music, through inherent meaning, symbolization, representation or shared understanding, reveal sex (male and female) or gender (masculinity and femininity) *regardless* of the sex or gender of its creator?' In the light of gender schema theory, the answer would be yes. In terms of a gender-schematic comprehension of the world, musical stimuli are organized in such ways to be understood:

> Gender-schematic processing in particular thus involves spontaneously sorting attributes and behaviours into masculine and feminine categories or 'equivalence classes', regardless of their differences on a variety of dimensions unrelated to gender, for example, spontaneously placing items like 'tenderness' and 'nightingale' into a feminine category and 'assertive' and 'eagle' into a masculine category. Like schema theory generally, gender schema theory thus construes perception as a constructive process in which the interaction between incoming information and an individuals' preexisting schema determines what is perceived.[60]

In a reality where all manner of objects, behaviours, traditions are understood as masculine and feminine equivalence classes, their meaning can ultimately be processed into 'equivalence classes' of gender to be accepted, it would seem, as an inescapable part of our culturally-imposed psychological inheritance. Yet how far any piece of music is perceived and understood as part of a gender schema can depend on the experience of the listener; this would appear true also of the composer's intentions. The process of cognition apparently depends on predetermined factors (background, family, education) interacting with new information. Hence the degree to which music conforms to a gender schema is, in theory, different for each individual, although certain sections of society may be found to process music similarly on account of common factors in their experience – for example, education or social class.

A gender-schema-based perception of music requires the formulation of a set of potential musical equivalence classes of gender. Accordingly, I have postulated a number of possible gender equivalence classes in music (see Table 7.1).

In devising the classes, I have accepted associations which are easily traced to their source in the female and male body, in addition to traditionally 'imposed' components connected with sexuality and psychology. All the terms classified as gendered (male or female) can be understood as actual descriptions of musical sounds: musical forms, musical range (pitch and duration), harmony,

Table 7.1 Gender equivalence classes in music

Source	Male	Female
Body size	Large	Small
Body size	Dominant	Submissive
Body size/voice	Harsh sounds	Mild sounds
Body size/voice	Booming sonority	Soft sonority
Body size	Large gestures	Small gestures
Body size	Slow, sluggish	Quick, agile
Body type	Hard, angular	Soft, rounded
Body type	Strong	Weak
Sexuality	Active	Passive
Sexuality	Striving	Yielding
Sexuality	External	Internal
Psychology	Complex	Simple
Psychology	Transcendent	Bodily
Psychology	Separation	Continuance
Psychology	Abstract	Tangible
Tradition	Norm	Other

melody, the size of a piece of music in terms of instrumentation, duration and so on. Attention should be drawn to the fact that the categories 'male' and 'female' are traditionally exclusive and opposing; accordingly, the same is true of the associations they evoke.

Many of these equivalence classes have obvious musical correlates, low sounds, for example, being associated with the pitch location of the male voice and high sounds with that of the female voice. Others are less readily obvious: for example, male/norm – female/other. This concept can also be seen operating in the organization of musical hierarchies such as tonality or sonata form (thematic organization). Also significant is the fact that, depending on the form of association made, the same concept can be correlated with both sexes. For example, in sexual terms, male is active (moving/quick), female is passive (static/slow); but in terms of body size the male is slow (large), and the female quick/agile (small). To test how far such equivalence classes are part of a shared perception of music, I intend to review a number of recent findings which have explored a range of music and its relation to sex and gender.

The obvious starting point for many of the explorations of how music can express gender has been music with a text or music which accompanies a narrative plot (such as opera, television and film music). Music attached to visual images and language suggests an 'outside' imposition of meaning in the form of a predefined range of characters, emotions, objects and ideas. Music which operates in such a context is employed primarily to elaborate, support and enhance specific meanings.

A gender-schematized perception of music is supported by research carried out by Philip Tagg in relation to television and film music. His article 'An Anthropology of Stereotypes in TV Music?' (1989) reveals how gender-schematized understanding can connect with musical elements which are sometimes far removed from sex or gender. Television music often compacts many commonly understood musical elements which are used to reinforce particular scenarios, characters, emotions and tensions. Understanding the associations people find in particular pieces of music indicates the existence of a widespread and consistent understanding of meanings (or, more probably, associations) in music generally. In Tagg's study a group of students were asked to provide visual verbal associations for ten television and film tunes; no prompts were given, and their choice was completely free. The most striking finding from an analysis of the responses was that the students held very high levels of gender-association with different aspects of music. A summary of the findings is given below:[61]

1 Male music had a faster tempo marking and also uses smaller divisions of the beat, thus giving the impression of much faster movement in the music.
2 Female tunes were *legato e cantabile* melodies using arpeggios or tied-over string chords; male tunes used staccato phrasing and quick repeated notes.
3 Female tunes employed changes in dynamic, whereas male tunes did not.
4 Male tunes contained bass lines which were more rhythmically and intervallically active than female tunes.
5 Male melodic lines featured more rhythmic irregularities.
6 Female melodic material was played on strings, piano or woodwind, whereas male tunes were played by electric guitar and trumpet. Tagg has suggested that this marks the female figures (melodies and characters) as more serious and 'classical', whereas the male ones are more modern. Accompaniments observe similar divisions.
7 Tagg concludes that the tonal language of the female tunes is classical-romantic or classically modal, whereas the male tunes are characterized by popular musics such as rock or fusion. This is paralleled by the use of percussion in male tunes, as opposed to no percussion in female tunes.

Interestingly, in the often stylized medium of television and film music language the 'classical/romantic' tonal styles are interpreted as suggesting the female, with the more rhythmically driving music (in terms of the constant use of percussion) being evocative of the male. This may seem a strange contradiction when both musics are in reality male-dominated in many senses. Yet such associations are reinforced by the more widely perceived cultural status of the respective musical genres. The contemporary reputation of 'classical' music is conformist and somewhat effeminate; consequently, it is linked to the female (the position of 'classical' instrumental tuition as a 'feminine' accomplishment also informs this gender association). On the other hand, the reputation of 'popular' music as rebellious (linked to aggression) and anti-establishment secures its male association.

Table 7.2 Suggested polarities of musical male/female opposition

male	female
fast	slow
sudden	gradual
active	passive
dynamic	static
upwards	downwards
outwards	inwards
hard	soft
jagged	smooth
sharp	rounded
urban	rural
modern	old times
strong	weak

Source: Phillip Tagg, 'An Anthropology of Stereotypes in TY Music?', *Svensk tidskrift för musikforskning*, 71 (1989), 14.

On the basis of the responses generated by the study Tagg compiled a hypothetical listing of the polarities of musical male/female opposition (see Table 7.2).

This characterization of elements reflects back the most conservative and socially restrictive stereotypes of men and women, and yet correlates completely with the gender equivalence classes proposed above. Many of the issues which have been addressed concerning women composers' social and cultural positions are embraced within our perception and associative understanding of music (male/culture – female/nature, male/public – female/private, male/active – female/passive). Some might object that these are simply imposed categories and that they have little connection with what music actually is or means. However, the ways in which music is seen to portray, reflect or symbolize human experience in society, and, in so doing, to reinforce gendered stereotypes so accurately, must be taken as being significant. Tagg concluded:

> If [. . .] the portrayal of 'Woman' in title music is as conservative as our respondents seem to believe musically (less so visually and even less so verbally), then it appears that music in our culture [. . .] can categorise shared subjective experience of and relation to our social and natural environment at deeper, possibly more 'archaic', levels of consciousness than visual and more notably verbal symbols.[62]

Unlike visual or written information, musical associations (often working at a subconscious level) seem able to reinforce many conservative social stereotypes in ways which language and visual images do not.

Susan McClary's research into nineteenth-century opera is completely different from Tagg's study in its methodology and subject, but despite these differences, she has made many similar observations. McClary first points out the misogynous nature of many opera plots, which so often end in the brutal murder of the main female character. These must be regarded as an important issue and reflecting in some way the arts' role in perpetuating restrictive and derogatory images of women. Yet our gendered understanding of opera is not only a question of our understanding of the narratives involved. For any of these operas to work on more than a superficial level, the music itself must in some way be constructed to reflect and reinforce the characters, images and ideas portrayed. Music which accompanies a text (or a visual scenario) usually provides the listener with a set of commonly understood aural references and associations which enhance the range of meanings within the text or scenario.

On the basis of this conjecture McClary used the example of Bizet's opera *Carmen* to demonstrate how the musical construction of the character of Carmen serves to reinforce her position in the narrative:

> The energy of the opera is, of course, located in the musical characterization of Carmen herself: she is the dissonant Other who is necessary for the motivation and sustaining of the plot. Bizet grounds Carmen's music in the physical impulses of exotic, pseudogypsy dance [. . .] Her rhythms suggest she is very aware of her body.[63]

Carmen's musical preoccupation is with dance music – music which features great rhythmic drive, can inspire bodily movement and revels in its blatant connectedness with the body. In addition, this aspect is articulated by Carmen's music in its use of melody, which is marked by extreme (by normal standards, excessive) chromaticism. It often 'teases' the listener by withholding diatonic resolution and satisfaction. Because of these physical 'displays':

> [Carmen . . .] arouses desire; and because she apparently has the power to deliver or withhold gratification of the desires she instills, she is immediately marked as a potential victimizer.[64]

McClary suggests that Carmen's music makes all those around her more aware of her body and their own. Connectedness with the body and an inability to rise into higher, purely mental regions has traditionally defined female intellect. The musical demonstration of this idea can be seen in that:

> [. . .] one of the principal claims to supremacy in European classical music (and other forms of high culture) is that it transcends the body, that it is concerned with the nobler domains of imagination and even metaphysics.[65]

The association of rhythmic movement and the female appears to contradict some of the findings of Tagg's study, which located female associations in slower tempos and less complex rhythmic patterns. However, I would suggest that Carmen's musical depiction relies heavily on her overt sexuality, which is not depicted in the traditional passive 'feminine' sense but is instead suggestive, in the risqué sense, of the stereotype of active 'masculine' sexuality. The musical portrayal of Carmen creates tension by employing musical elements which shift the musical focus to a female body expressing an active sexuality that has needs, can entice, withhold and overpower. This contradicts, certainly, the stereotype of passive female sexuality but has to do so by employing 'masculine' musical associations.

McClary's interpretation of the ending of Carmen is that the dangerous elements of Carmen's music and her physical character have to be destroyed before they contaminate others (characters and listeners). This is achieved through the restoration of firm tonality:

> [. . .] the listener [. . .] longs for this flood of chromaticism to be stopped, for stability to be reestablished – even though we know that the triumph of tonal closure means the violent murder of Carmen. Bizet's musical strategies, in other words, set up almost unbearable tensions that cause the listener not only to accept Carmen's death as 'inevitable' but actually to *desire* it.[66]

The music articulates the power positions and respective characteristics involved in the central relationships between the male and female roles (and, indeed, many other aspects of race and class).[67] The tensions surrounding Carmen are reflected in her active sexuality: specifically, the appropriation by a female of the active 'masculine' sexual prerogative. This factor forms part of the instability which is reinforced by the musical content.

McClary goes on to suggest that many of the musical procedures used to elaborate and enhance meaning in opera (and music with a text) have developed as central to the structure and organization of ostensibly abstract instrumental music:

> [. . .] aspects of *Carmen* [. . .] namely these particular constructions of gender, the ejaculatory quality of many so-called transcendental moments, the titillating yet carefully contained presentation of the feminine 'threat', the apparent necessity of violent closure – are all central to the great tradition of nineteenth century 'Absolute Music'.[68]

McClary's theory is that music has developed its procedures as a way of enhancing tangible meanings (verbal and visual). Therefore, the original meaning of such musical processes can remain even when the imposed meanings are removed:

> The viability of apparently autonomous instrumental music depends on the powerful affective codes that have developed within the referential domains of vocal music. Familiarity with this network of cultural associations permits us to recognize even in textless music traditional signs for grief, joy, or the heroic. But signification extends far beyond the surface in instrumental music: its formal conventions – often held to be neutral with respect to meaning – are likewise socially encoded.[69]

This stance goes against much traditional thought, since music of the Western art tradition has often presented itself as 'above' strict meaning; yet it fits well with the proposition that music is part of a gender schema in which many objects and concepts in reality far removed from male and female can be taken, symbolically, to represent them through gender association.

A good example of this is McClary's idea that the system of tonality has emerged from the inevitable imposition of the order of our patriarchal society. The hierarchal concept of tonality suggests a norm-and-other duality which is an established gender male/norm – female/other association. The vast majority of tonal compositions begin and end in the same key, with the introduction of other keys serving to provide interest, tension and conflict which are later resolved in accordance with the 'natural' hierarchy of tonality; in other words, the home (norm) key will prevail. The 'other' keys and chromatic notes are always extinguished by the final restatement of the original key, so providing the satisfaction which has been anticipated from the beginning of the piece:

> The schema thus outlines a kind of narrative based on identity and certainty on the one hand, and difference and excitement (with at least the illusion of risk) on the other. Each individual piece of tonal music fleshes out the paradigm in its own way [. . .] But all these choices are socially based and socially intelligible insofar as they draw on powerful social conventions of normative tonality [. . .] In other words, Absolute Music enacts a kind of absolutist political narrative merely by virtue of assuming tonality as a natural imperative.[70]

In this way, our perception of tonality can become part of a wider gender-schematized perception. We relate to tonality on the level of self and other, normality and difference. Our social and cultural conventions and traditions ensure that we perceive such ideas in terms of domination and submission, power and subservience, strength and weakness, all of which have become fundamental gender-equivalents of male and female.

Linked to the function of tonality is the role of sonata form, for the sonata concept has been an essential structural tool in music's evolution from vocal to purely instrumental music (that is, the evolution from music which has a predefined set of associations and meanings to music which has no such obvious imposed associations). Sonata form has been adopted in a wide range of music (orchestral, chamber, solo), and its development can be seen as pivotal in enabling instrumental music to be widely understood and appreciated, and therefore accepted. It has now been suggested that sonata form has been a far from value-free concept, although its position in 'liberating' music from the imposed associative meanings of vocal music has traditionally portrayed it as such:

> Having helped displace the supremacy of vocal music, the sonata aesthetic has carried enormous semiotic meaning ever since [. . . however . . .] Without the interference of text and fixed meanings, such music amounted to an embodiment of the absolute [. . .][71]

Basically, sonata form is constructed around the relationship between two opposing themes, of which the principal theme is understood to be 'dominant', and the secondary theme 'weaker' and ultimately subservient to the first. Indeed, the convention of naming the first theme masculine and the second theme feminine was still being used in textbooks of the 1960s.[72] Although some would maintain that such labelling did not amount, at least in intention, to a description of the gendered aspects of sonata form or, indeed of music in general, its wider implications cannot so easily be dismissed:

> [. . .] eliminating this terminology does not erase the issue of gender from the musical structures [. . .] because many of the themes in question draw on the semiotic of 'masculinity' and 'femininity' as they were constructed in opera or tone poems, they are easily recognized in their respective positions within these musical narratives.[73]

In terms of musical equivalence classes, the opposition-associations (self/other, norm/different, dominance/submission) all relate to socially and culturally grounded definitions of male and female:

> Basically the two themes of the exposition are set up as a hierarchy that exhibits stylistic traits considered characteristic of man and woman, respectively. These are constructed in various ways [. . .] but the basic model is one of ideological domination of man over woman. It seems to be an extension of general societal notions of ideal man and ideal woman and their proper relationship.[74]

In this way, through powerful gender-schematized associations, music can, in theory, reinforce essentialist and derogatory ideas about women (and, indeed, men) and also the wider implications of race and class. McClary does not suggest that such musical organizations are available for the use of men only on account of some aspect of their nature; she argues, rather, that these concepts reflect social and emotional constructions. By this means, the use of certain musical structures can be seen as a reaffirmation of the white, European, middle-class, male composer's position in relation to his social, cultural and historical situation. However, McClary asserts that composers who may stand in a different position in relation to the narratives of traditional tonal music can also adapt such systems to express their positions in relation to it; this can apply to men as well as to women.[75] Thinking along similar lines, Marcia Citron has cited the example of Cécile Chaminade's Piano Sonata Op. 21 as revealing a differing construction and placement of musical material that reflect an unconscious rejection of the musical narratives and constructions which have defined Western patriarchal culture.[76]

In the same way, other musical concepts have been suggested as gendered by the nature of their metaphysical associations. Marcia Citron identifies this aspect of absolute music as the 'metaphysical ability to transport one to the infinite beyond all barriers'. Following on from the previously quoted theories, it has been asserted that in order to develop a masculine identity, the male must break free from the environment provided by his mother and, in so doing, strive for that which is 'beyond'. Citron claims that this urge is then strengthened by the social environment, which encourages the male to explore, and be curious about, the public sphere. Thus 'striving' becomes enthroned as part of the male personality. On the other hand, it was suggested that women do not have this need to break away in order to find a female identity, since they find primary identification with the mother; this, coupled with private-sphere social roles, results in a reduced drive to transcend physical and social barriers:

> Meaning and identity [for the female] might be more readily found with the complex of signs associated with mother and other females [. . .] Consequently, the ethos of absolute music might be more unfamiliar and alien, and possibly even repugnant.[77]

Such psychological 'characteristics' can also be seen as linked to the less convoluted concept of active/probing male sexuality and passive/receptive female sexuality. I am not suggesting that such dichotomized concepts are natural, but they are certainly associations long held and ingrained in our collective understanding and which therefore form part of our gender schema and are conceived as such. The research undertaken by McClary and Citron stands at the cutting edge of the theories which explain musical constructions as reflections of social organization and traditions. Although this research is not without its methodological difficulties, it at least provides a starting point for a new insight into our music conventions, how they have developed and why they continue to be presided over, on the whole, by a narrow segment of society.

Many of the initial attempts to understand music as a gendered discourse have concentrated on the organization of the sounds (tonality and rhythm) and the structure and form of compositions as manifesting social and gendered meanings. John Shepherd, on the other hand, has suggested that the way in which we comprehend the actual quality of the sounds (timbre) is gendered, so that there are links between manifestations of musical timbre and constructions of gender. The main thrust of Shepherd's theory is that timbre is the 'nature of sound itself'; through timbre, therefore, the social relatedness of the world is revealed. Timbre, the very heart of musical sound, reminds us, in effect, of our place in the social world:

> [Timbre . . .] can be said to speak to the central nexus of experience that ultimately constitutes us all as individuals [. . .] The existence of music, like the existence of women, is *potentially* threatening to men to the extent that it sonically insists on the social relatedness of human worlds and as a consequence implicitly demands that individuals respond. When this happens music reminds men of the fragile and atrophied nature of their control over the world.[78]

When the connectedness of the world is reaffirmed, it seems threatening to men, who have constructed a culture which is controlled and explained by objectivity and separation.[79] Shepherd sees the emphasis on the visual notation of music as a result of the male's feelings of powerlessness in the process of biological reproduction. The suppression of timbre in musical notation is viewed by him as symbolic of the suppression of the social and human connectedness symbolic in music:

> Control of cultural reproduction compensates for a lack of centrality in biological reproduction, and nowhere is this control more effectively exercised than on the mapping and notational procedures – among which music figures prominently – which both facilitate and constrain processes of cultural reproduction. It is no accident that the vast majority of noetic and scribal elites have been male, for by this means men preserve themselves paradoxically as independent and in control of the very social relations which produce them.[80]

This connects with the previous chapter's discussion of some elements of notated music, which are seen as 'masculine' and have consequently been fostered and valued. In a similar way to McClary, Shepherd feels that the physical phenomenon of sound is a threat to the visual-oriented male scribal elites.[81]

Timbre is an element in Western classical (high culture) music which is most often taken as self-sufficient and natural. The training of any classical performer centres, to a large extent, on the production of a full and pure timbre. Pure timbre is created by employing all the overtones which are accessible on any particular instrument. Popular musics (low culture), on the other hand, make use of 'dirty' or 'impure' timbres; because the timbre produced is often incomplete in its use of overtones, it 'invites completion from the outside'.[82] Classical music's traditional obsession with purity of timbre and sound implies a sense of completeness which allows the listener little sense of 'participation'.

Shepherd takes the vocal timbres employed in popular music as a starting point for examining the role timbre plays in the articulation of gendered identities (not as natural phenomena but as socially constructed realities). He asserts that in forms of popular music which are particularly 'macho' in expression (known as 'cock rock'), the male singer's timbre is distinguished by its hard, rasping quality which is achieved by a harsh use of the vocal chords, the sound being focused in the throat and mouth. In contrast, songs performed by women, which seek to express other experiences, feature warmer, softer, fuller sounds produced by relaxed use of the vocal chords and the focus of sound resonating in the chest.[83] In this way, Shepherd identifies four types of timbre in popular vocal music: the typical male 'macho' sound, which is hard and rasping; the female 'woman-as-nurturer' sound, which is very full and soft; the 'woman-as-sex-object' sound, which employs a more masculinized tone; and the male as vulnerable and innocent, 'the boy next door', which admits more 'feminized' tones. The translation of such relationships into classical music is more difficult, but Shepherd views purity of tone as representative of both male and female.[84] Yet this does not result in the acceptance of the female; instead, it results in a kind of musical androgyny which denies male and female relations:

> Such androgyny, such bourgeois male dominance and recontextualization of gender relations can only occur through a rejection of what the female gender could in actuality offer were this offering not downgraded [. . .] Male culture attempts to be self-sufficient, although the attempt is ultimately doomed to failure because that which is fundamental to human existence can never ultimately be denied.[85]

Shepherd sees the insistence on pure timbre in classical music as reflective of the separateness and unassailability of those with power and influence.

In addition to the range of musical factors, it has been proposed that a view of the roles of composer, conductor and performer also affects how a piece of music is perceived and assessed by an individual. Lucy Green states that once a listener is aware that a piece of music is composed by a woman, that music immediately becomes delineated in terms of femininity.[86] This echoes the discussion in Chapter 5, where it was observed that women's music is very often understood only in terms of how far it adheres to or deviates from, the feminine personality:

> [. . .] part of all musical delineation contains the notion of a male mind. When we discover a woman's mind behind the music, her femininity then enters the delineations, from which position it acts to alter our perceptions, normally unchallenged in

> this regard, of the inherent meanings. The more that femininity is delineated, the less inclined are we to judge the inherent meanings as autonomous essences.[87]

Notions of the sex or gender of the creator or performer serve to strengthen further the gender-schematic perception of music. The sex or gender of the individual involved in the creation or performance of music provides a further basis for gender-equivalences to be mapped on to the music itself. Gendered perceptions of music become, therefore, very powerful, not only in expressing symbolic representations as gendered concepts but also in serving to enforce such concepts:

> Music's incorporation of gender does not reside hermetically in musical meaning, for gendered musical meanings affect our consciousness and experience, not only of music, but through music of ourselves. Gendered musical meanings participate in the construction of our very notions of masculinity and femininity. This means, therefore, that we can use music to confirm and perpetuate our concepts of ourselves as gendered beings.[88]

Again, a gender-schematized view of the world, and hence of ourselves, is confirmed, and reflected back through, media far removed from the basic categories male and female.

To conclude: there seems to be some evidence which suggests that music can be perceived as gendered, albeit not in terms of any mental or creative limitations inherent in the sex of the composer. However, music does indeed seem to be perceived as gendered through the way in which the whole range of elements which together constitute music (intensity, pitch, structure, form, tonality, duration, instrumentation, timbre, style and so on) are processed by the individual into a network of gender-equivalents. In a society where many categories, objects, roles and emotions are commonly classified and understood in terms of gender-equivalences, music is not exempt from the process. The theory that music can, depending on the individual, be perceived and processed according to a system of gendered meaning provides a more tenable position than most for a gendered understanding of music. It will, one hopes, dispel the essentialist view which assumes that any sexual or gendered understanding of music must stem from the encoding of their work, by composers, with some kind of watermark of sex or gender.[89] The main point is that any gendered musical associations are imposed from other, outside influences on composers and listeners alike and are always open to reinterpretation.

I do not wish to intimate that issues of music and meaning are perceived only in relation to gender, sex or sexuality. There are a whole range of variables which can affect the perceived meaning of a piece of music and the response it evokes. Although some researchers have suggested direct links (and many similarities) between music with 'ready-made' meaning (text and images) and music which has no imposed visual or verbal accompaniment, there is clearly a difference in the context in which the listener perceives such music – a context which is highly relevant. Music which allows 'free' association or interpretation, in the light of the above discussion, can be linked in many ways to how we perceive, and relate to, the world around us. The more that this world is structured around the binary division of sex and gender, the more such categories will invade our understanding of music. It has been suggested that only when gender-category associations are reduced (by a narrowing of the parameters which constitute gender), will gender/sex divisions be altered:

> [. . .] the concept of gender-schematic processing directs our attention to the promiscuous availability of the gender schema in contexts where other schemata ought to have priority [. . .] the network of associations constituting the gender schema ought to become more limited in scope and [. . .] society ought to temper its insistence on the ubiquitous functional importance of the gender dichotomy. In short [. . .] society should stop projecting gender into situations irrelevant to genitalia.[90]

The most recent research which insists on gendered interpretations of music tends, perhaps, to reinforce such dubious projections. On the other hand, research into the gendered perception of music has the merit of bringing out into the open concepts which, for the most part, have not yet been openly examined, even though many musical premises unarguably hold strongly gendered associations. Gendered perceptions of (or, more correctly, gendered prescriptions for) the world can exert a deep influence over how we perceive music. Every aspect of music, over and above our knowledge of its composer and performer, plays a part in creating gendered expectations of what the music might mean.

Strong sex-typing of children results in the development of wide-ranging gender-schematized cognition; but such strong sex-typing should not be seen as 'inherent' in either sex:

> [. . .] children would be far less likely to become gender schematic and hence sex typed if the society were to limit the associative network linked to sex and temper its insistence on the functional importance of the gender dichotomy.[91]

Although men and women have for centuries been stereotyped as possessing masculine or feminine characteristics, there is nothing within these categories which is in principle unavailable to either sex. Yet the social forces which deny and discourage male tenderness and female aggression, for example, make male and female relationships to such behaviour very different, a difference which carries over into expressions as they are manifested in music. In this sense, it would seem unproductive constantly to discuss gender as an issue, since this can serve artificially to augment the functional significance of the category. This point introduces a dilemma which faces many feminist researchers. How is it possible to focus on issues of gender, or indeed of sex discrimination, without actually worsening the situation by marginalizing women further through encouraging their segregation and differentiation? The separation of women as a group for special consideration, which has been the basis of this book, often runs into the criticism that it portrays women as 'different' from men, thereby confirming their place outside the mainstream. Certainly, the 'same' versus 'different' debate has been central to many of the issues raised throughout this book. However, neither of these polarized approaches is without its dangers:

> The 'sameness' alternative is insufficiently critical of the status quo. The 'difference' option *is* critical of the status quo, but seems to conjecture that women can exist in some sort of separate world. Seeing women as the 'same' as men prevents us *challenging* the model against which women are being compared; seeing women as 'different' prevents us *changing* it. Talking in terms of 'sameness' or 'difference' skirts the issue, rather than confronting it.[92]

It is clear that the host of complex factors which result in the comparative rarity of female composers can never be reduced to a simple 'same/different' argument, as has so often been proposed. Confronting the issue is to address the reality of women's current and historical position. As the twentieth century draws to a close, Western society, on the whole, holds more opportunities than ever before for women; but the fact remains that a woman's right to equal status and opportunity is far from established or operational, whatever the legal provisions. Women's continued under-representation in musical composition is part of a much wider complex social and cultural phenomenon where many groups, including women, are systematically undervalued socially, economically and intellectually. While this larger problem remains, the major obstacles to female equality in musical composition will prove difficult to surmount.

Notes

1 Shepherd, 'Difference and Power in Music', 65.
2 It is acknowledged that psychoanalysis is a vast and complex area, and I in no way intend to cover the many different theories which have evolved. Rather, I have confined the discussion to ideas and theories which seem most relevant in terms of the understanding and perpetuation of differences between male and female creativity.
3 Liam Hudson and Bernadine Jacot, *The Way Men Think: Intellect, Intimacy and the Erotic Imagination* (Hew Haven and London, 1991), 97.
4 Sigmund Freud, '"Civilized Sexual Morality and Modern Nervous Illness"' (1908), in Elisabeth Young-Bruehl (ed.), *Freud on Women* (London, 1990), 167–168.
5 Joanna Bunker Rohrbaugh, *Women: Psychology's Puzzle* (Sussex, 1980), 92.
6 See Battersby, *Gender and Genius*, 61–70.
7 Freud, 'Femininity', in Young-Bruehl (ed.), *Freud on Women*, 362.
8 Robert Ornstein, *The Roots of the Self* (San Francisco, 1995), 131.
9 For further discussion see Shere Hite, *The Hite Reports: Sexuality, Love and Emotion*.
10 Over the decades since Freud developed his theories a number of feminists have refuted and reinterpreted the psychoanalytic definitions of the female personality. Karen Horney, once a student of Freud, was the first to question his work in the late 1920s, when she reversed some of his main assertions. For example, she believed that, rather than women being envious of male genitals (penis envy), men were in fact envious of female capacity to produce children, a concept she called womb envy. In 1964 Clara Thompson contributed in a similar vein, stating that penis envy was surely only a reflection of women's position in relation to men's power and authority. Women did not envy male genitals but instead envied the male's superior position in society. However, during the 1970s feminists such as

Juliet Mitchell read Freud's theory's not as an 'explanation' of women's position but as a description of how both sexes develop in a patriarchal society. This idea has been furthered throughout the 1980s in the work of Janet Sayers and Helen Block Lewis, who believe that women can use psychoanalytic understanding of the female personality under patriarchy as a foundation in the process of social change.

11 Hudson and Jacot, *The Way Men Think*, viii.
12 *Ibid.*, 139.
13 *Ibid.*, 38.
14 *Ibid.*, 40.
15 *Ibid.*, viii.
16 *Ibid.*, 49.
17 Rohrbaugh, *Women: Psychology's Puzzle*, 80.
18 Hudson and Jacot, *The Way Men Think*, 183.
19 *Ibid.*, 51.
20 *Ibid.*, 49.
21 Battersby, *Gender and Genius*, 134.
22 Hudson and Jacot, *The Way Men Think*, 93–94.
23 Hudson and Jacot, *The Way Men Think*, 49.
24 Nancy Chodorow, 'Feminism and Difference in Psychoanalytic Perspective', in Mary Roth Walsh (ed.), *The Psychology of Women: Ongoing Debates*, 263–264.
25 Nancy Chodorow, 'Family Structure and the Feminine Personality', in Michelle Zimbalist Rosaldo and Louis Lamphere, *Woman, Culture, and Society* (Stanford, 1974), 66.
26 *Ibid.*, 60.
27 *Ibid.*, 58.
28 *Ibid.*, 64.
29 All the previously discussed theories made implicit the idea that the development of strong ego boundaries (that is the understanding of one's own self as distinct and definite from others) is usually considered to be preferable to lack of ego boundaries. Yet, the balance of ego boundaries can be dangerous in both its extremities. Lack of ego boundaries is pathological but too strong a sense of ego (which has been identified particularly in Western men) has been suggested as leading to aggressive masculinity and political system of capitalism based on the Protestant ethic. Overly strong egos and sense of agency can prove damaging to men.
30 Chodorow, 'Feminism and Difference in Psychoanalytic Perspective', 261.
31 *Ibid.*, 257.
32 *Ibid.*, 259.
33 Anne Colby and William Damon, 'Listening to a Different Voice', in Mary Roth Walsh (ed.), *The Psychology of Women: Ongoing Debates*, 328.
34 Hudson and Jacot, *The Way Men Think*, 139.
35 *Ibid.*, 198.
36 Antony Storr, *Music and the Mind* (London, 1992), 94.
37 'Like most beloved fairy tales, 'Jack' [and the Beanstalk] deals with very basic life issues: the beanstalk is accidentally planted when Jack's mother callously rejects his newly acquired magic beans. Overnight the beanstalk becomes erect, grows very big, and penetrates the clouds, permitting Jack to ascend and conquer the Giant/Father. A more obvious oedipal situation is difficult to imagine.' McClary, *Feminine Endings*, 112.
38 McClary, *Feminine Endings*, 112.
39 *Ibid.*, 130.
40 *Ibid.*, 113–114.
41 *Ibid.*, 119.

42 McClary, *loc. cit.*
43 *Ibid.*, 120–121.
44 *Ibid.*, 121.
45 *Ibid.*, 131.
46 For more detailed discussion see Hite, *The Hite Reports: Sexuality, Love and Emotion.*
47 McClary, *Feminine Endings*, 131.
48 For detailed discussion of what has been termed the 'feminine' style in literature see Hélène Cixous and Catherine Clément, *The Newly Born Woman*, translated by Betsy Wing, (Boston, 1985).
49 Renée Cox, 'Recovering *Jouissance*: An Introduction to Feminist Musical Aesthetics, in Pendle (ed.), *Women in Music: A History*, 334.
50 *Ibid.*, 336–337.
51 Chodorow, 'Family Structure and Feminine Personality', 59–60.
52 Cox, 'Recovering *Jouissance*', 337.
53 *Ibid.*, 337–338.
54 See McClary, *Feminine Endings*, 3–34.
55 See Leo Treitler, 'Gender and Other Dualities of Music History', in Solie (ed.), *Musicology and Difference*, 23.
56 Boethius, cited *ibid.*, 23.
57 Robert Schumann, *Gesammelte Schriften über Musik und Musiker*, 2, Fifth Edition (Leipzig: 1914) cited in Konrad Wolff (ed.), *Robert Schumann on Music and Musicians* (London, 1947), 71.
58 Sandra Lipsitz Bem, 'Gender Schema Theory and Its Implications for Child Development: Raising Gender-Aschematic Children in a Gender-Schematic Society', in Walsh (ed.), *The Psychology of Women*, 231–232.
59 *Ibid.*, 237.
60 *Ibid.*, 232.
61 Philip Tagg, 'An Anthropology of Stereotypes in TV Music?', *Svensk tidskrift för musikforskning*, 71 (1989), 13–14.
62 *Ibid.*, 18–19.
63 McClary, *Feminine Endings*, 57.
64 McClary, *loc. cit.*
65 McClary, *loc. cit.*
66 *Ibid.*, 62.
67 McClary (63–66) suggests that the question of race may also be particularly important in readings of *Carmen.*
68 McClary, *Feminine Endings*, 67.
69 Susan McClary, 'Narrative Agendas in "Absolute Music": Identity and Difference in Brahms's Third Symphony', in Solie (ed.), *Musicology and Difference*, 329.
70 *Ibid.*, 331.
71 Citron, *Gender and the Musical Canon*, 142.
72 McClary, 'Narrative Agendas in "Absolute Music" ', 332.
73 McClary, *loc. cit.*
74 Citron, *Gender and the Musical Canon*, 133.
75 For example, see McClary's examination of Tchaikovsky's Fourth Symphony in *Feminine Endings*, 69–79.
76 Citron, *Gender and the Musical Canon*, 145–159.
77 *Ibid.*, 144.
78 Shepherd, *Music as Social Text*, 159.
79 *Ibid.*, 160.
80 *Ibid.*, 156.
81 *Ibid.*, 159.
82 *Ibid.*, 165.

83 *Ibid.*, 166–167.
84 *Ibid.*, 169.
85 Shepherd, *Music as Social Text*, 169.
86 Lucy Green, 'Gender, Musical Meaning, and Education', *Philosophy of Music Education Review*, 2 (1994), 79.
87 *Ibid.*, 79.
88 *Ibid.*, 80.
89 This is not to say that gendered associations in music have no effect (conscious or unconscious) on how composers work; this subject may indeed provide a profitable further avenue of research.
90 S.L. Bem, 'Gender Schema Theory and Its Implications for Child Development', 245.
91 *Ibid.*, 237.
92 Carol Lee Bacchi, *Same Difference: Feminism and Sexual Difference* (London, 1990), 262.

Bibliography

Unpublished Sources

Personal correspondence of Judith Bailey and the author, 1991–1995.
Personal correspondence of Ruth Gipps and the author, 1989–1995.
Personal correspondence of Bryony Jagger and the author, 1991–1995.
Personal correspondence of Minna Keal and the author, 1991–1995.
Personal correspondence of Antoinette Kirkwood and the author, 1991–1995.
Personal correspondence of Enid Luff and the author, 1991–1995.
Personal correspondence of Elizabeth Maconchy and the author, 1991–1994.

Interviews

Judith Bailey, interviewed by the author on 15 June 1993. Interview transcribed by the author.
Ruth Gipps, interviewed by the author on 30 August 1990. Two 90-minute tapes.
Ruth Gipps, interviewed by the author on 9 November 1990. One 50–minute tape.
Bryony Jagger, written response to a questionnaire, dated 16 July 1994.
Minna Keal, interviewed by the author on 22 June 1993. Interview transcribed by the author.
Antoinette Kirkwood, taped oral response to a questionnaire dated 5 November 1993. Interview transcribed by the author.
Antoinette Kirkwood, written response to a questionnaire, dated 10 March 1994.
Enid Luff, interviewed by the author on 21 June 1993. Interview transcribed by the author.

Literature on Members of the Study Group and Individual Composers

Judith Bailey

'Judith Bailey's Second Symphony', *Haslemere Herald*, 3 June 1983.
'New Judith Bailey Work', *Petersfield Herald*, 29 March 1985.

'Petersfield Orchestra Gets its Own Symphony', *East Hampshire Post*, 2 June 1982.

Avril Coleridge-Taylor

Coleridge-Taylor, Avril. *The Heritage of Samuel Coleridge-Taylor* (London: Denis Dobson, 1979).

Ruth Gipps

Gipps, Ruth. 'Autobiography: Before Conducting', unpublished typescript.
Gipps, Ruth. 'Memoirs 1942–1989', unpublished typescript.
Martin, Francis. 'The Night Mrs Baker Made History', *Everybody's Weekly*, 16 March 1957, 10–12.
'Editorial', *The Strad*, 1 January 1947.
'She Composes in the Kitchen', *Daily Mail*, 24 October 1946.
Halstead, Jill. 'A Study of Dr Ruth Gipps illustrating her Musical Development Through Symphonies Two to Five' (M.Phil. thesis, University of Sheffield, 1991).
'Women Composers', *Birmingham Post*, 2 December 1946.

Minna Keal

Blyth, Alan. 'Late Developer', *Daily Telegraph*, 6 September 1989.
Foster, William. 'She Shall have Music', *Saga Magazine*, February 1990, 22–23.
Fryer, Peter. 'Two who have paid their dues', *Workers' Press*, 16 September 1989.
Grier, Christopher. 'Bridging a 50–year Interval', *Evening Standard*, 5 September 1989.
Grove, Valerie. 'In a Hurry at 80 to Catch Life's Lost Chords', *Sunday Times*, 10 September 1989, B5.
Hayes, Malcolm. 'Why they didn't like Minna Keal', *Sunday Telegraph*, 10 September 1989.
Johnson, Stephen. 'Review', *The Listener*, 14 September 1989.
Keal, Minna. 'Memories of the Royal Academy', unpublished typescript.
Maddocks, Fiona. 'Born Again Composer', *The Independent*, 21 March 1988, 13.
Morrison, Richard. 'Heroes, Villains, or Ratings?', *The Times*, 3 September 1994, 5.
Pappenheim, Mark. 'Music and Opera', *The Independent*, 31 August 1989.
Pettitt, Stephen. 'Not Quite on an Even Keal', *The Times*, 5 September 1989, 18.
Pearce, Arthur. 'The Music Maker: An Interview with Minna Keal', 1991. Place of publication unknown (source: British Music Information Centre, Minna Keal File).

Potter, Keith. 'Never too Late to Write', *Classical Music*, 11 February 1984, 19.
Power, Eithne. 'Life Begins at 80!', *Radio and TV Times*, 21–27 October 1989, 10 and 12.
Reynolds, Nigel. 'Chicago Symphony Cancels after South Bank Strike Threat', *The Times*, 4 September 1989.
Sutcliffe, Tom. 'Minna's Music', *The Guardian*, 13 February 1984.
Webster, Valerie. 'See-Sharp Minna', *The Yorkshire Post*, 31 May 1989, 3.
White, Michael John. 'Veiled in Innocence', *The Independent*, 6 September 1989.
'Minna Hits a High Note in the Sunset of Life', *Bucks Free Press*, 22 September 1989.

Enid Luff
Calam, Toni. 'Interview with Enid Luff', *Contemporary Music Review*, **11** (1994), 193–199.
'Huddersfield Contemporary Music Festival', *Music and Musicians*, March 1987, 27.

Elisabeth Lutyens
Blume, Mary. 'Elisabeth Lutyens', *International Herald Tribune*, 9–10 January 1982.
Harries, Meirion and Susie Harries. *A Pilgrim Soul: The Life and Works of Elisabeth Lutyens* (London: Michael Joseph, 1989).
Lutyens, Elisabeth. *The Goldfish Bowl* (London: Cassell and Co.,1972).
Mooney, Bel. 'Between the Pit and the Pendulum', *Sunday Times*, 5 November 1989.

Elizabeth Maconchy
Cole, Hugo. *The 80th Birthday of Elizabeth Maconchy* (London: Chester Music, 1987).
Coleman, Alix. 'An Interview with Nicola LeFanu'. Place of publication unknown (source: British Music Information Centre, Elizabeth Maconchy File).
Dickinson, Peter (ed.). 'Serenata Concertante – An Analytical Note by Elizabeth Maconchy', in *Twenty British Composers* (London: Chester Music, 1975), 50–53.
Heyworth, Peter. 'Climbing the Summit of Mount Messiaen', *The Observer*, 22 March 1987, 25.
Hughes, Herbert. 'The Land', *Daily Telegraph*, 1 October 1930.
Macnaghten, Anne. 'Elizabeth Maconchy', *Musical Times*, June (1955), 298–302.
Maconchy, Elizabeth. 'A Composer Speaks', *Composer*, **42** (1971–1972), 24–28.

Maddocks, Fiona. 'The Composer Breaks Her Silence: An Interview with Elizabeth Maconchy', *The Guardian*, 26 July 1983.
Maycock, Robert. 'Inheriting the Land', *The Listener*, 12 March 1987, 30.
'Dame Elizabeth Maconchy', Obituary, *The Guardian*, 12 November 1994, 19.
'Elizabeth Maconchy: A Video Portrait'(directed and produced by Margaret Williams, sponsored by the Arts Council, 1987). Transcript by the author.

Grace Williams

Boyd, Malcolm. *Grace Williams* (Cardiff: University of Wales Press, 1980).
Leighton Thomas, A.F. 'Grace Williams', *Musical Times*, May 1956, 240–243.
Various. 'Grace Williams: A Symposium', *Welsh Music*, 5, 6 and 7 (1977).
Whittall, Arnold. 'Grace Williams 1906–1977', *Soundings*, 7 (1978), 19–37.

General

Adorno, Theodor W. *Prisms* (Cambridge, Mass.: MIT Press, 1983) [translated by Samuel and Shierry Weber].
Albert, Robert S. (ed.). *Genius and Eminence* (Oxford and New York: Pergamon Press, 1983).
Ammer, Christine. *Unsung: A History of Women in American Music* (Westport, Conn.: Greenwood Press, 1980).
Anastasi, Anne and Charles E. Schaefer. 'Biographical correlates of Artistic and Literary Creativity in Adolescent Girls', *Journal of Applied Psychology,* **53** (1969), 267–273.
Anderson, Bonnie S. and Judith P. Zinsser. *A History of Their Own: Women in Europe from Prehistory to the Present,* **1, 2** (London: Penguin Books, 1988).
Antokoletz, Elliott. *Twentieth Century Music* (New Jersey: Prentice Hall, 1992).
Archer, John. 'Gender Stereotyping of School Subjects', *The Psychologist,* **5** (February 1992), 66–69.
Archer, John and Barbara Lloyd. *Exploring Sex Differences* (London: Academic Press, 1976).
Archer, John and Barbara Lloyd. *Sex and Gender* (Cambridge: Cambridge University Press, 1985).
Askew, Sue and Carol Ross. *Boys Don't Cry: Boys and Sexism in Education* (Milton Keynes, Open University Press, 1988).
Atkinson, Rita L. and Richard C. Atkinson, Edward E. Smith, Daryl J. Bem. *Introduction to Psychology,* Tenth Edition (San Diego: Harcourt Brace Jovanovich, 1990).
Attali, Jacques. *Noise: The Political Economy of Music* (Manchester: Manchester University Press, 1985).

Austern, Linda Phyllis. 'Music and the English Renaissance Controversy over Women', in Susan Cook and Judy S. Tsou (eds), *Cecilia Reclaimed: Feminist Perspectives on Gender and Music* (Urbana and Chicago: University of Illinois Press, 1994), 52–69.

Ayres, Jane. 'The Other Half', *Composer,* **92** (1987), 22–23.

Bacchi, Carol Lee. *Same Difference: Feminism and Sexual Difference* (London: Allen and Unwin, 1990).

Bailey, Walter B. and Nancy Gisbrecht Bailey. *Radie Britain: A Bio-Bibliography* (Westport, Conn.: Greenwood Press, 1990).

Baker Miller, Jean. *Psychoanalysis and Women* (London: Penguin, 1973).

Baker Miller, Jean. *Towards a New Psychology of Women* (London: Penguin, 1986).

Ballantine, Christopher. *Twentieth Century Symphony* (London: Dennis Dobson, 1983).

Barron, Frank. *Creative Person and Creative Process* (New York: Holt, Rinehart and Winston, 1969).

Battersby, Christine. Gender and Genius (London: The Women's Press, 1989).

Beck, Hermann. 'The Symphony: An Historical Survey', in Ursula von Rauchhaupt (ed.), *The Symphony* (London: Thames and Hudson, 1973), 91–94.

Beechey, Veronica and Elizabeth Whitelegg (eds). *Women in Britain Today* (Milton Keynes: OUP, 1986).

Bem, Sandra L. 'The Measurement of Psychological Androgyny', *Journal of Consulting and Clinical Psychology,* **42** (1974), 155–162.

Bem, Sandra L. 'Sex Role Adaptability: One Consequence of Psychological Androgyny', *Journal of Personality and Social Psychology,* **31** (1975), 634–643.

Bem, Sandra L. 'Probing the Promise of Androgyny', in Mary Roth Walsh (ed.), *The Psychology of Women: Ongoing Debates* (New Haven and London: Yale University Press, 1987), 206–225.

Bem, Sandra L. 'Gender Schema Theory and Its Implications for Child Development: Raising Gender-Aschematic Children in a Gender-Schematic Society', in Mary Roth Walsh (ed.), *The Psychology of Women: Ongoing Debates* (New Haven and London: Yale University Press, 1987), 226–245.

Bentley, Arnold. *Music in Education* (Windsor: NFER Publishing Company, 1975).

Benton, R.L. 'The Amusias', in M. Critchley and R. A. Henson (eds), *Music and the Brain: Studies in the Neurology of Music* (London: William Heinemann Medical Books, 1977), 378–397.

Bergeron, Katherine and Philip V. Bohlman. *Disciplining Music: Musicology and Its Canons* (Chicago and London: University of Chicago Press, 1992).

Bernard, Jessie. *Academic Women* (New York: Meridian, 1964).

Bever, T.G. and R.J. Chiarello, 'Cerebral Dominance in Musicians and Non-Musicians', *Science,* **185** (1974), 537–539.

Birch, Dinah. 'Gender and Genre', in F. Bonner and L. Goodman *et al.* (eds.), *Imagining Women: Cultural Representations and Gender* (Cambridge, Polity Press, 1992), 43–55.

Birke, Lynda. *Women, Feminism and Biology* (Great Britain: Harvester Press, 1986).

Blaukopf, Kurt. 'The Symphony, Concerts and the Public', in Ursula von Rauchhaupt (ed.), *The Symphony* (London: Thames and Hudson, 1973), 9–16.

Block, Adrienne Fried and Carol Neuls-Bates. *Women in American Music. A Bibliography of Music and Literature* (Westport, Conn.: Greenwood Press, 1979).

Bonner, Frances and Lizbeth Goodman *et al. Imagining Women: Cultural Representations and Gender* (Cambridge: Polity Press, 1992).

Booth Davies, John. *The Psychology of Music* (London: Hutchinson, 1978).

Borchgrevink, Hans. 'Cerebral Lateralization of Speech and Singing after Intracarotid Amytal Injection', in M. Taylor Sarno and O. Hook (eds), *Aphasia: An Assessment and Treatment* (Stockholm: Almquist Wicksell, 1980) 58–65.

Borchgrevink, Hans. 'Prosody and Music Rhythm are Controlled by the Speech Hemisphere', in Manfred Clynes (ed.), *Music, Mind and Brain: The Neuropsychology of Music* (New York and London: Plenum Press, 1982), 151–157.

Borer, Mary Cathcart. *Willingly to School: A History of Women's Education* (Guildford and London: Lutterworth Press, 1975).

Borroff, Edith. 'Women Composers: Reminiscence and History', *College Music Symposium,* **15** (1975), 26–33.

Bovenschen, Silvia. 'Is there a Feminist Aesthetic?', in Gisela Ecker (ed.), *Feminist Aesthetics* (Boston: Beacon Press, 1985), 23–50.

Bowers, Jane. 'Feminist Scholarship and the Field of Musicology', *College Music Symposium,* **29** (1989), 81–92.

Bowers, Jane and Judith Tick (eds). *Women Making Music: The Western Art Tradition 1150–1950* (Urbana and Chicago: University of Illinois Press, 1986).

Boyden, David D. *Introduction to Music*, Second Edition (London: Faber and Faber, 1971).

Braybon, Gail and Penny Summerfield. *Out of the Cage* (London: Pandora Press, 1987).

Bridenthal, R. and C. Koonz (eds). *Becoming Visible: Women in European History* (USA: Houghton Mifflin, 1977).

Briscoe, James (ed.). *Historical Anthology of Music by Women* (Indiana: Indiana University Press, 1987).

Broverman, I.K., S.R. Vogel *et al.* 'Sex Role Stereotypes: A Current Appraisal', *Journal of Social Issues,* **28** (1972), 59–79.

Brower, Edith. 'Is the Musical Idea Masculine?', *Atlantic Monthly,* March 1894, 332–339.

Budd, Malcolm. *Music and the Emotions: The Philosophical Theories* (London and New York: Routledge, 1985).
Buffery, A.W.H. and J.A. Gray. 'Sex differences in the Development of Spatial and Linguistic Skills', in C. Ounsted and D.C. Taylor (eds), *Gender Differences: Their Ontogeny and Significance* (Edinburgh: Churchill, 1972), 123–158.
Burrell, Diana. 'Accepting Androgyny', *Contact,* **32** (1988), 52–53.
Butcher, H.J. *Human Intelligence: Its Nature and Assessment* (London: Methuen, 1968).
Butler, Marilyn and Janet Todd (eds). *The Works of Mary Wollstonecraft,* **4** (London: Pickering, 1989).
Cahn, William L. 'Authority and Motivation in the Symphony Orchestra: A Symphony Musician's Point of View', *Contemporary Music Review,* 7 (1992), 27–38.
Campbell, Anne (ed.). *The Opposite Sex* (London: Ebury Press, 1989).
Chodorow, Nancy. 'Family Structure and the Feminine Personality', in Michelle Zimbalist Rosaldo and Louise Lamphere (eds), *Women, Culture, and Society* (Stanford, California: Stanford University Press, 1974), 42–66.
Chodorow, Nancy. 'Feminism and Difference: Gender, Relation, and Difference in Psychoanalytic Perspective', in Mary Roth Walsh (ed.), *The Psychology of Women: Ongoing Debates* (New Haven and London: Yale University Press, 1987), 249–264.
Citron, Marcia J. *Cécile Chaminade: A Bio-Bibliography* (Westport, Conn.: Greenwood Press, 1988).
Citron, Marcia J. *Gender and the Musical Canon* (Cambridge: University of Cambridge Press, 1993).
Citron, Marcia J. 'Feminist Approaches to Musicology', in Susan Cook and Judy S. Tsou (eds), *Cecilia Reclaimed: Feminist Perspectives on Gender and Music*, (Urbana and Chicago: University of Illinois Press, 1994), 15–34.
Cixous, Hélène and Catherine Clément. *The Newly Born Woman* (Boston: Beacon Press, 1985) [translated by Betsy Wing].
Clément, Catherine. *Opera or the Undoing of Women* (London: Virago Press, 1989).
Clements, Andrew. 'A Child of Our Time', *The Guardian*, 2 January 1995.
Cohen, Aaron (ed.). *The Encyclopedia of Women Composers*, Second Edition (New York, Books and Music, 1987).
Colby, Anne and William Damon. 'Listening to a Different Voice: A Review of Gilligan's *In a Different Voice*', in Mary Roth Walsh (ed.), *The Psychology of Women: Ongoing Debates* (New Haven and London: Yale University Press, 1987), 321–329.
Colles, H.C. *The Royal College of Music 1883–1933* (London: Royal College of Music, 1933).
Colley, Ann M. and David J. Hargreaves (eds). *The Psychology of Sex Roles* (London: Harper and Row, 1986).
Connell, R.W. *Gender and Power* (Cambridge: Polity Press, 1987).

Cook, Susan C. and Judy S. Tsou. *Cecilia Reclaimed: Feminist Perspectives on Gender and Music* (Urbana and Chicago: University of Illinois Press, 1994).

Cooper, Martin. *Ideas and Music* (London: Barrie and Rockliff, 1965).

Counter, Marie J. 'The Role of Stereotypes in the Relationship between Composers and Society: An Enquiry into the Extent to which Composer's Output is affected by Environmental Pressures, with Particular Emphasis on the Perspective of Women Composers' (Dissertation, London University, 1990).

Coward, Rosalind. *Our Treacherous Hearts: Why Women let Men get their Way* (London: Faber and Faber, 1992).

Cox, David. *The Henry Wood Proms* (London: BBC,1980).

Cox, Gordon. *A History of Music Education in England 1872–1928* (Aldershot: Scolar Press, 1993).

Cox, Renée. 'Recovering *Jouissance*: An Introduction to Feminist Musical Aesthetics', in Karin Pendle (ed.), *Women in Music: A History* (Indiana, University of Indiana Press, 1991), 331–340.

Critchley, Macdonald and R. A. Henson (eds). *Music and the Brain: Studies in the Neurology of Music* (London: William Heinemann Medical Books, 1977).

Curtis, S.J. and M.E.A. Boultwood. *An Introductory History of English Education since 1800* (London: University Tutorial Press, 1960).

Cuyler, Louise. *The Symphony* (New York and Chicago: Harcourt Brace Jovanovich, 1973).

Dahlhaus, Carl. *The Idea of Absolute Music* (Chicago and London: University of Chicago Press, 1978).

Dahlhaus, Carl. *Between Romanticism and Modernism* (Berkeley and London: University of California Press, 1980). Originally published in German in Munich in 1974.

Damàsio, A.R. and Hanna Damàsio. 'Musical Faculty and Cerebral Dominance', in M. Critchley and R.A. Henson (eds), *Music and the Brain. Studies in the Neurology of Music* (London: William Heinemann Medical Books, 1977), 141–155.

Deem, Rosemary. *Women and Schooling* (London: Routledge and Kegan Paul, 1978).

Delamount, Sara. *The Sociology of Women* (London: George Allen and Unwin, 1980).

Department of Education and Science. *Half Our Future: A Report of the Central Advisory Council for Education* (England) (London: HMSO, 1963).

Dervin, Daniel. *Creativity and Culture: A Psychoanalytic Study of the Creative Process in the Arts, Sciences and Culture* (London: Associated University Press, 1990).

Deutsch, Hélène. *The Psychology of Women* (London: Research Books, 1947).

Deutsch, D. (ed.). *The Psychology of Music* (London: Academic Press, 1982).
Diamond, M.C. *et al.* 'Plasticity in the 904 day old Male Rat Cerebral Cortex', *Experimental Neurology,* **87** (1985), 309–317.
Drinker, Sophie. *Music and Women: The Story of Women in Their Relation to Music* (New York: Coward-McCann, 1948).
Durant, Alan. 'Improvisation in the Political Economy of Music', in Christopher Norris (ed.), *Music and the Politics of Culture* (London: Lawrence and Wishart, 1989), 252–282.
Durden-Smith, J. and D. DeSimone. *Sex and the Brain* (New York: Arbor House, 1983).
Dworkin, Andrea. *Our Blood: Prophecies and Discourses on Sexual Politics* (London: The Women's Press, 1982).
Dworkin, Andrea. *Women Hating* (New York: Dutton, 1987).
Dyhouse, Carol. *Girls growing up in Late Victorian and Edwardian England* (London: Routledge and Kegan Paul, 1981).
Ebel, Otto. *Women Composers: A Biographical Handbook of Woman's Work in Music* (Brooklyn, NY: F.H. Chandler, 1902).
Eccles, J.S. and J.E. Jacobs. 'Social Forces Shape Math Attitudes and Performance', *Signs,* **11** (1986), 367–389.
Ecker, Gisela (ed.). *Feminist Aesthetics* (Boston: Beacon Press, 1985).
Edwards, J. Michele. 'Women in Music, ca. 1450–1600', in Karin Pendle (ed.), *Women in Music: A History* (Indiana: Indiana University, 1991), 8–28.
Ehrlich, Cyril. *The Music Profession in Britain Since the Eighteenth Century* (Oxford: Clarendon Press, 1985).
Ellis, Havelock. *Man and Woman: A Study of Human Secondary and Tertiary Sexual Characters* (Boston: Houghton Mifflin, 1929).
Ellis, Havelock. *Psychology of Sex* (London: Heinemann Medical Books, 1947).
Ellis, L. 'Developmental Androgen Fluctuations and the Dimensions of Mammalian Sex', *Ethnology and Sociobiology,* **3** (1982), 171–179.
Elson, Arthur. *Women's Work in Music* (Maine: Longwood Press, 1976). Originally published in 1904.
Emrys Evans, D. *The University of Wales: A Historical Sketch* (Cardiff: University of Wales Press, 1953).
Entwistle, Harold. *Class, Culture and Education* (London: Methuen, 1978).
Ericson, Margaret. *Women in Music 1987–1992: A Selective Bibliography on the Collective Subject of Women, Gender Issues and Music* (Boston: G.K. Hall, forthcoming).
Etzkorn, K. Peter (ed.). *Music and Society: The Later Writings of Paul Honigsheim* (London: Wiley, 1973).
Ewen, David (ed.). *The World of Twentieth Century Music*, Second Edition revised by Stephen Pettitt (London: Robert Hale, 1991).
Faludi, Susan. *Backlash: The Undeclared War Against Women* (London: Chatto and Windus, 1992).

Feather, N.T. 'Positive and Negative Reactions to Male and Female Success and Failure in Relation to the Perceived Status and Sex-Typed Appropriateness of Occupations', *Journal of Personality and Social Psychology,* **31** (1975), 536–548.

Feder, Stuart, Richard Karmel, and George Pollock. *Psychoanalytic Explorations in Music* (Connecticut: International Universities Press, 1990).

Feingold, A. 'Cognitive Gender Differences are Disappearing', *American Psychologist,* **43** (1988), 95–103.

Fénelon, François. *Fénelon on Education* (Cambridge: Cambridge University Press, 1966) [translated by H.C. Barnard].

Fletcher, Peter. *Education and Music* (Oxford: Oxford University Press, 1987).

Ford, Charles. *Cosi? Sexual Politics in Mozart's Operas* (Manchester: Manchester University Press, 1991).

Fraser, Flora. *The English Gentlewoman* (London: Barrie and Jenkins, 1987).

Freeman, J., H.J. Butcher and T. Christie. *Creativity: A Selective Review of Research*, Second Edition (London: Society for Research into Higher Education, 1971).

French, Marilyn. *The War Against Women* (London: Hamish Hamilton, 1992).

Fuller, Sophie. *The Pandora Guide to Women Composers. Britain and the United States 1629–Present* (London: Pandora Press, 1994).

Fuller, Sophie and Nicola LeFanu. *Reclaiming the Muse: A Select Bibliography of English Language Writing on Women in Music* (London: King's College, 1991).

Fuller, Sophie and Nicola LeFanu (eds). 'Reclaiming the Muse', *Contemporary Music Review,* **11** (1994) issue devoted to women composers.

Furneaux, W.D. *The Chosen Few: An Examination of Some Aspects of University Selection in Britain* (London: Oxford University Press, 1961).

Gardiner, H. *Frames of Mind :The Theory of Multiple Intelligence* (New York: Basic Books, 1983).

Gates, Eugene Murray. 'The Woman Composer Question: Four Case Studies from the Romantic Era' (Doctor of Education thesis, University of Toronto, 1992).

Gilbert, G.M. 'Sex Difference in Musical Aptitude and Training', *Journal of General Psychology,* **26** (1942), 19–33.

Gilligan, Carol. 'In a Different Voice: Women's Conceptions of Self and Morality', in Mary Roth Walsh (ed.), *The Psychology of Women: Ongoing Debates* (New Haven and London: Yale University Press, 1987), 278–320.

Goehr, Lydia. *The Imaginary Museum of Musical Works: An Essay in the Philosophy of Music* (Oxford: Oxford University Press, 1992).

Goertzel, Mildred George *et al. 300 Eminent Personalities: A Psycho Analysis of the Famous* (San Francisco: Jossey-Bass, 1978).

Goldberg, S. and M. Lewis. 'Play Behaviour in the Year-Old Infant: Early Sex Differences', *Child Development,* **40** (1969), 21–31.

Gordon, H.W. 'Hemispheric Asymmetry and Musical Performance', *Science,* **189** (1975), 68–69.
Gordon, H.W. 'Degree of Ear Asymmetries for Perception of Dichotic Chords and for Illusory Chord Localization in Musicians of Different Levels of Competence', *Journal of Experimental Psychology: Human Perception and Performance,* **6** (1980), 516–527.
Gould, Stephen J. 'Women's Brains', *New Scientist,* **80** (1978), 364–66.
Grant, Linda. 'First Among Equals', *The Guardian*, 22 October 1994, 37–46.
Green, Lucy. *Music on Deaf Ears: Musical Meaning, Ideology, Education* (Manchester and New York: Manchester University Press, 1988).
Green, Lucy. 'Music, Gender and Education: A Report on some Exploratory Research', *British Journal of Music Education,* **10** (1993), 219–253.
Green, Lucy. 'Gender, Musical Meaning, and Education', *Philosophy of Music Education Review,* **2** (1994), 76–82.
Green, Mildred Denby. *Black Women Composers: A Genesis* (Boston: Twayne,1983).
Greer, Germaine. *The Female Eunuch* (London: Paladin, 1971).
Greer, Germaine. *The Obstacle Race: The Fortunes of Women Painters and their Work* (New York and London: Martin Secker and Warburg, 1979).
Greer, Germaine. *The Madwoman's Underclothes: Essays and Occasional Writings 1968–1985* (London: Picador, 1986).
Griffiths, Paul. *Concise History of Modern Music: Debussy to Boulez* (London: Thames and Hudson, 1978).
Griffiths, Paul. *Modern Music: the Avant-Garde since 1945* (London: Dent, 1981).
Grout, Donald J. *The History of Western Music*, Fourth Edition (London: Dent, 1988).
Hale, Noel V. *Education for Music* (Oxford: Oxford University Press, 1947).
Hall, Calvin S. and Lindzey Gardner. *Theories of Personality* (London: Wiley and Sons, 1970).
Halsey, Albert Henry. *The British Academics* (London: Faber and Faber, 1971).
Hanslick, Eduard. *The Beautiful in Music: A Contribution to the Revisal of Musical Aesthetics* (New York: Da Capo Press, 1974).
Harding, M. Esther. *The Way of All Women: A Psychological Interpretation* (London: Rider and Company, 1971).
Harewood, The Earl of. *Kobbé Complete Opera Book* (London: Bodley Head, 1991).
Hargreaves, David J. 'Sex Roles in Divergent Thinking', *British Journal of Educational Psychology,* **47** (1977), 25–32.
Hargreaves, David J. *A Developmental Psychology of Music* (Cambridge: Cambridge University Press, 1986).
Harman, Alec and Wilfred Mellers. *Man and His Music* (London: Barrie and Rockliff, 1962).

Harris, L.J. 'Sex Difference in the Growth of Language', in E. Donelson and J. Gullahorn (eds), *Women: A Psychological Perspective* (New York: Wiley, 1977).

Hartnett, Oonagh, Gill Boden, and Mary Fuller (eds.). *Sex-Role Stereotyping* (London: Tavistock, 1979).

Hassler, M. 'Creative Musical Talent, Cognitive Functioning and Gender: Psychobiological Aspects', *Music Perception,* 8 (1990), 35–48.

Hassler, Marianne and Eberhard Nieschlag. 'Masculinity, Femininity, and Musical Composition: Psychological and Psychoendocrinological aspects of Musical and Spatial Faculties', *Archives of Psychology,* **141** (1989), 71–84.

Hassler, Marianne, Eberhard Nieschlag and Diether De La Motte. 'Creative Musical Talent, Cognitive Functioning, and Gender: Psychobiological Aspects', *Music Perception,* 8 (1990), 35–48.

Häusler, Josef. 'Between Sonata Form and the Aleatoric Principle', in Ursula von Rauchhaupt (ed.), *The Symphony* (London: Thames and Hudson, 1973), 275–292.

Hayes, Deborah. *Peggy Glanville-Hicks: A Bio-Bibliography* (Westport, Conn.: Greenwood Press, 1990).

Helson, Ravenna. 'Sex Difference in Creative Style', *Journal of Personality,* **35** (1967), 214–233.

Helson, Ravenna. 'Effects of Sibling Characteristics and Parental Values on Creative Interest and Achievement', *Journal of Personality,* **36** (1968), 589–607.

Henschen, S.E. 'On the Function of the Right Hemisphere of the Brain in Relation to the Left in Speech, Music and Calculation', *Brain,* **49** (1926), 110–123.

Henson, R.A. 'Neurological Aspects of Musical Experience', in M. Critchley and R.A. Henson (eds), *Music and the Brain. Studies in the Neurology of Music* (London: William Heinemann Medical Books, 1977), 3–21.

Hirschkop, Ken. 'The Classical and the Popular: Musical Form and Social Context', in Christopher Norris (ed.), *Music and the Politics of Culture* (London: Lawrence and Wishart, 1989), 283–304.

Hite, Shere. *Women as Revolutionary Agents of Change: The Hite Reports on Sexuality, Love and Emotion* (London: Bloomsbury, 1993).

Hixon, Donald L. *Thea Musgrave: A Bio-Bibliography* (Westport, Conn.: Greenwood Press, 1984).

Hood, J.D. 'Psychological and Physiological Aspects of Hearing', in M. Critchley and R.A. Henson (eds), *Music and the Brain. Studies in the Neurology of Music* (London: William Heinemann Medical Books, 1977), 32–47.

Horden, Peregrine (ed.). *Freud and the Humanities* (London: Duckworth, 1985).

Horn, Pamela. *Education in Rural England 1800–1914* (Dublin: Gill and Macmillan, 1978).

Horner, Matina S. 'Toward an Understanding of Achievement-Related Conflicts in Women', in Mary Roth Walsh (ed.), *The Psychology of Women: Ongoing Debates* (New Haven and London: Yale University Press, 1987), 169–184.

Householder van Horn, Susan. *Women, Work and Fertility 1900–1986* (New York and London: New York University Press, 1988).

Howes, Frank. *The English Musical Renaissance* (London: Secker and Warburg, 1966).

Hudson, Liam. *Frames of Mind: Ability, Perception and Self-Perception in the Arts and Sciences* (London: Methuen, 1968).

Hudson, Liam and Bernadine Jacot. *The Way Men Think: Intellect, Intimacy and the Erotic Imagination* (New Haven and London: Yale University Press, 1991).

Hunt, Felicity. 'Divided Aims: The Education Implication of Opposing Ideologies in Girls Secondary Schooling 1850–1940', in Felicity Hunt (ed.), *Lessons For Life: The Schooling of Girls and Women 1850–1950* (Oxford: Basil Blackwell, 1987).

Hunt, Felicity (ed.). *Lessons for Life: The Schooling of Girls and Women 1850–1950* (Oxford: Basil Blackwell, 1987).

Hutt, C. *Males and Females* (Harmondsworth: Penguin, 1972).

Hyde, Derek. *New Found Voices: Women in Nineteenth Century English Music* (Canterbury: Tritone Music, 1984).

Hyde, J.S. and M.C. Linn. 'Gender Differences in Verbal Ability: A Meta-Analysis', *Psychological Bulletin,* **104** (1988), 53–69.

Jalland, Patricia. *Women, Marriage and Politics 1860–1914* (Oxford: Clarendon Press, 1986).

Jezic, Diane Peacock. *Women Composers: The Lost Tradition Found* (New York: The Feminist Press, 1988).

John, Angela, V. (ed.). *Our Mother's Land: Chapters in Welsh Women's History 1830–1939* (Cardiff: University of Wales Press, 1991).

Jones, Derek (ed.). *Women In Music,* booklet published to accompany the 'Secret Chamber' series shown on Channel 4 Television in June 1994.

Kamm, Josephine. *Hope Deferred: Girls' Education in English History* (London: Methuen, 1965).

Kemp, A.E. 'The Personality Structure of Composers and Performing Musicians' (D.Phil. thesis, University of Sussex, 1979).

Kemp, A.E. 'The Personality Structure of the Musician: II. Identifying a Profile of Traits for the Composer', *Psychology of Music,* **9** (1981), 69–75.

Kemp, A.E. 'The Personality Structure of the Musician: III. The Significance of Sex Differences', *Psychology of Music, 10* (1982), 48–58.

Kemp, A.E. and Rosemary Bruce. 'Sex-Stereotyping in Children's Preferences for Musical Instruments', *British Journal of Music Education,* **10** (1993), 213–217.

Kennedy, Michael. *The History of the Royal Manchester College of Music 1893–1972* (Manchester: Manchester University Press, 1971).

Kersey, Shirley Nelson. *Classics in the Education of Girls and Women* (Metuchen, N.J.: Scarecrow, 1981).
Kilmister, Sally. 'Aesthetics and Music: The Appropriation of the Other', *Women: A Cultural Review,* **3** (1993), 30–39.
Kimura, D. 'Left and Right Differences in the Perception of Melodies', *Quarterly Journal of Experimental Psychology,* **16** (1964), 355–358.
Kipnis, Dorothy McBridge. 'Intelligence, Occupation Status, and Achievement Orientation', in John Archer and Barbara Lloyd (eds), *Exploring Sex Differences* (London and New York: Academic Press, 1976), 95–122.
Klausmeier, H.J. and W. Wiersma. 'The Effects of IQ Level and Sex on Divergent Thinking of Seventh Grade Pupils of Low, Average and High IQ', *The Journal of Educational Research,* **58** (1965), 300–302.
Klein, Ethel. *Gender Politics* (Cambridge, Mass.: Harvard University Press, 1984).
Kogan, Nathan. 'Creativity and Sex Differences', *Journal of Creative Behaviour,* **8** (1974), 1–14.
Koskoff, Ellen (ed.). *Women and Music in Cross-Cultural Perspective* (Westport, Conn.: Greenwood Press, 1987).
Kramer, Lawrence. *Music as Cultural Practice 1800–1900* (Berkeley: University of California, 1990).
Krellman, Hanspeter. 'The Symphony, its Listener's and Interpreter's Thoughts on the Institutionalization of a Form and its Performing Apparatus', in Ursula von Rauchhaupt (ed.), *The Symphony* (London: Thames and Hudson, 1973), 293–298.
Kwalwasser, Jacob. *Exploring the Musical Mind* (New York: Coleman-Ross, 1955).
Ladd, G. *Why Women Cannot Compose Music* (New Haven: Yale Publication Association, 1917).
Lamb, Roberta. 'The Possibilities of/for Feminist Music Criticism in Music Education', *British Journal of Music Education,* **10** (1993), 169–180.
Langlois, J.H. and A.D. Downs. 'Mothers, Fathers, and Peers as Socialization Agents of Sex-Typed Play Behaviour in Young Children', *Child Development,* **51** (1980), 1237–1247.
Larue, Jan. 'The Background of the Classical Symphony', in Ursula von Rauchhaupt (ed.), *The Symphony* (London: Thames and Hudson, 1973), 99–110.
Lawrence, Ian. *Composers and the Nature of Music Education* (London: Scolar Press, 1978).
LeFanu, Nicola. 'Master Musician: An Impregnable Taboo', paper read to the Women in Music Conference, London, 6 February 1987.
Lehmann, Liza. *The Life of Liza Lehmann* (London: T. Fisher Unwin, 1919).
LePage, Jane Weiner. *Women Composers, Conductors and Musicians of the Twentieth Century: Selected Biographies*, 3 volumes (Metuchen, N.J.: Scarecrow Press, 1980, 1983, 1988).

Leppert, Richard and Susan McClary (eds). *Music and Society: The Politics of Composition, Performance and Reception* (Cambridge: Cambridge University Press, 1987).

Leppert, Richard. *Music and Image* (Cambridge: Cambridge University Press, 1988).

Levin, Michael. 'Women, Work, Biology and Justice', in Caroline Quest (ed.), *Equal Opportunities: A Feminist Fallacy* (London: IEA Health and Welfare Unit, 1992), 9–26.

Levy, Jerre. 'Lateral Specialization of the Human Brain: Behavioral Manifestations and Possible Evolutionary Basis', in J.A. Kiger (ed.), *The Biology of Behavior* (Oregon: Oregon University Press, 1972).

Levy, Jerre and M. Reid. 'Variations in Cerebral Organization as a Function of Handedness, Hand Posture in Writing, and Sex', *Journal of Experimental Psychology,* **107** (1978), 119–144.

Lewis, Jane. *Women In England 1870–1950: Sexual Divisions and Social Change* (Sussex: Wheatsheaf Books, 1984).

Lewis, Jane. *Women in Britain since 1945* (Oxford: Blackwell, 1992).

Lichtenfeld, Monika. 'The Symphony Concert: Its Origin, Form and Programme', in Ursula von Rauchhaupt (ed.), *The Symphony* (London: Thames and Hudson, 1973), 35–38.

Lindsey, Linda L. *Gender Roles: A Sociological Perspective* (New Jersey: Prentice Hall, 1990).

Long, Noel. *Music in English Education: Grammar School, University and Conservatoire* (London: Faber and Faber, 1959).

Lovelock, William. *A Concise History of Music* (London: Bell & Hyman, 1981).

Lowe, Roy. *Education in the Post-War Years: A Social History* (New York and London: Routledge, 1988).

Lundin, R.W. *An Objective Psychology of Music* (New York: Ronald Press, 1953).

Lyndon, Neil. *No More Sex War: The Failures of Feminism* (London: Sinclair-Stevenson, 1992).

Maccoby, Eleanor E. 'Sex Differences in Intellectual Functioning', in Eleanor Maccoby (ed.), *The Development of Sex Differences* (London: Tavistock, 1967), 25–55.

Maccoby, Eleanor E. and Carol N. Jacklin. *The Psychology of Sex Differences* (London: Oxford University Press, 1975).

Mackinnon, D.W. 'The Nature and Nurture of Creative Talent', *American Psychologist,* **17** (1962), 484–495.

Maidlow, Sarah. 'Attitudes and Expectations of A Level Musicians', *British Journal of Music Education,* **10** (1993), 205–211.

Marshall, Kimberly (ed.). *Rediscovering the Muses: Women's Musical Traditions* (Boston: Northeastern University Press, 1993).

Martin, Christopher. *A Short History of English Schools 1750–1965* (Hove: Wayland, 1979).

Matlin, Margaret W. *The Psychology of Women* (New York: Holt, Rinehart and Winston, 1987).
McClary, Susan. 'The Blasphemy of Talking Politics during Bach Year', in Richard Leppert and Susan McClary (eds), *Music and Society: The Politics of Composition, Performance and Reception* (Cambridge: Cambridge University Press, 1987), 13–62.
McClary, Susan. *Feminine Endings: Music, Gender and Sexuality* (Minnesota and Oxford: University of Minnesota Press, 1991).
McClary, Susan. 'Narrative Agendas in "Absolute" Music: Identity and Difference in Brahms' Third Symphony', in Ruth Solie (ed.), *Musicology and Difference: Gender and Sexuality in Music Scholarship* (Berkeley: University of California Press, 1993), 326–344.
McClary, Susan. 'Reshaping a Discipline: Musicology and Feminism in the 1990s', *Feminist Studies,* **19** (1993), 399–423.
McClary, Susan. 'Of Patriarchs . . . And Matriarchs Too', *Musical Times*, (June 1994), 364–369.
McGlone, J. 'Sex Differences in Human Brain Asymmetry: A Critical Survey', *Behavioural and Brain Sciences,* **3** (1980), 215–227.
McLeish, J. *Musical Cognition* (London: Novello, 1968).
McMillan, Carol. *Women, Reason and Nature* (Oxford: Blackwell, 1982).
Mead, Margaret. *Sex and Temperament in Three Primitive Societies* (New York: Mentor, 1950). Originally published in 1935.
Mead, Margaret. *Male and Female* (Harmondsworth: Penguin, 1950).
Messent, Peter R. 'Female Hormones and Behaviour', in John Archer and Barbara Lloyd (eds), *Exploring Sex Differences* (London: Academic Press, 1976), 185–212.
Metraux, Rhoda (ed.). *Margaret Mead: Some Personal Views* (London: Angus and Robertson, 1979).
Meyer, Alfred. 'The Search for a Morphological Substrate in the Brains of Eminent Persons including Musicians: A Historical Review', in M. Critchley and R.A. Henson (eds), *Music and the Brain: Studies in the Neurology of Music* (London: William Heinemann Medical Books, 1977), 255–281.
Meyer, Leonard B. *Music, the Arts and Ideas: Patterns and Predictions in Twentieth Century Culture* (Chicago and London: University of Chicago Press, 1967).
Millet, Kate. *Sexual Politics* (London: Virago, 1977).
Millet, Kate. *The Loony Bin Trip* (London: Virago, 1991).
Mitchell, Juliet. *Psychoanalysis and Feminism* (London: Allen Lane, 1974).
Montagu, Asley. 'Why Wagner Was No Lady', *High Fidelity Magazine*, March (1958), 34–35 and 137–138.
Morgan, Robert P. *Twentieth Century Music* (New York and London: W.W. Norton, 1991).
Mountfield, Anne. *Women and Education* (Hove: Wayland, 1990).
Mountford, Sir James. *British Universities* (London: Oxford University Press, 1966).

Murray, Penelope. *Genius: The History of an Idea* (Oxford: Blackwell, 1989).
Mursell, J.L. *The Psychology of Music* (New York: Norton, 1937).
Neuls-Bates, Carol (ed.). *Women in Music: An Anthology of Source Readings from the Middle Ages to the Present* (New York and Cambridge: Harper and Row, 1982).
Nicholson, John. *Men and Women: How Different Are They?* (Oxford: Oxford University Press, 1993).
Nismura, Mari (ed.). *A Twentieth Century Composer Speaks: An Index of Interviews* (Berkeley, California: Fallen Leaf Press, 1993).
Nochlin, Linda. *Women, Art, and Power and Other Essays* (London: Thames and Hudson, 1991).
Norris, Christopher (ed.). *Music and the Politics of Culture* (London: Lawrence and Wishart, 1989).
Nyman, Michael. *Experimental Music* (London: Studio Vista, 1977).
Oakley, Ann. *Sex, Gender and Society* (London: Gower/Temple Smith, 1985).
Ornstein, Robert. *The Roots of the Self* (San Francisco: Harper, 1995).
Parker, Rozsika and Griselda Pollock. *Old Mistresses: Women, Art and Ideology* (London: Pandora Press, 1981).
Parsons Smith, Catherine. ' "A Distinguishing Virility": Feminism and Modernism in American Art Music', in Susan Cook and Judy S. Tsou (eds), *Cecilia Reclaimed: Feminist Perspectives on Gender and Music* (Urbana and Chicago: University of Illinois Press, 1994), 90–106.
Peacock, Alan and Ronald Weir. *The Composer in the Market Place* (London: Faber Music, 1975).
Pendle, Karin (ed.). *Women and Music: A History* (Indianapolis: Indiana University Press, 1991).
Pirie, Peter. J. 'The Psychology of Musical Creation', *Music and Musicians,* 20 (March 1972), 36–40.
Pirie, Peter J. *The English Musical Renaissance* (London: Victor Gollancz, 1979).
Pool, Robert. *The New Sexual Revolution* (London and Sydney: Hodder and Stoughton, 1994).
Portnoy, Julius. *Music in the Life of Man* (Westport, Conn.: Greenwood Press, 1963).
Post, Jennifer. 'Erasing the Boundaries between Public and Private in Women's Performance Traditions', in Susan Cook and Judy Tsou (eds), *Cecilia Reclaimed: Feminist Perspectives on Gender and Music* (Urbana: University of Illinois Press, 1994), 35–51.
Pratt, R.T.C. 'The Inheritance of Musicality', in M. Critchley and R.A. Henson (eds), *Music and the Brain. Studies in the Neurology of Music* (London: William Heinemann Medical Books, 1977), 22–31.
Proctor, Charles. *To Be a Professional Musician* (London: Methuen, 1951).

Pugh, Aelwyn. *Women in Music* (Cambridge: Cambridge University Press, 1991).
Pugh, Martin. *Women and the Women's Movement in Britain 1914–1959* (London: Macmillan, 1992).
Quest, Caroline (ed.). *Equal Opportunities: A Feminist Fallacy* (London: IEA Health and Welfare Unit, 1992).
Rainbow, Bernarr. *The Land Without Music: Musical Education in England 1800–1860* (London: Novello, 1967).
Rauchhaupt, Ursula von. *The Symphony* (London: Thames and Hudson, 1973).
Reich, Nancy B. *Clara Schumann: The Artist and the Women* (London: Victor Gollancz, 1985).
Reich, Nancy (ed.). *Women's Studies/Women's Status*, College Music Society Reports No. 5 (Boulder, Colo.: College Music Society, 1988).
Reid, Ivan and Erica Stratta (eds). *Sex Differences in Britain* (Aldershot: Gower, 1989).
Révész, G. *An Introduction to the Psychology of Music* (London: Longmans Green, 1953).
Rieger, Eva. 'Dolce Semplice: On the Changing Role of Women in Music', in Gisela Ecker (ed.), *Feminist Aesthetics* (Boston: Beacon Press, 1985), 135–149.
Robert-Blunn, John. *Northern Accent: The Life Story of the Northern College of Music* (Manchester: Sherratt and Son, 1972).
Roederer, Juan G. 'Physical and Neuropsychological Foundations of Music: The Brain Questions', in Manfred Clynes (ed.), *Music, Mind and Brain: The Neuropsychology of Music* (New York and London: Plenum Press, 1982), 37–46.
Rogers, Lesley. 'Male Hormones and Behaviour', in John Archer and Barbara Lloyd (eds), *Exploring Sex Differences* (London: Academic Press, 1976), 157–184.
Rohrbaugh, Joanna Bunker. *Women: Psychology's Puzzle* (Sussex: Harvester Press, 1980).
Rosaldo, Michelle Zimbalist and Louise Lamphere (eds). *Women, Culture and Society* (California: Standford University Press, 1974).
Rosen, Charles. *Sonata Forms* (London: W.W. Norton, 1980).
Rosen, Judith. *Grazyna Bacewicz: Her Life and Works* (Los Angeles: Friends of Polish Music, 1984).
Rosen, Judith and Grace Rubin-Rabson, 'Why Haven't Women Become Great Composers?', *High Fidelity/Musical America,* **23** (1973), 46–53.
Rosenblatt, P.C. and M.R. Cunningham. 'Sex Differences in Cross-Cultural Perspective', in John Archer and Barbara Lloyd (eds), *Exploring Sex Differences* (New York and London: Academic Press, 1976), 71–94.
Rosenstiel, Leonie. *The Life and Works of Lili Boulanger* (Rutherford, N.J.: Fairleigh Dickinson University Press, 1978).

Ross, W.D. (ed.). *The Works of Aristotle,* **6** (Oxford: Clarendon Press, 1913).

Rothenberg, Albert. *The Emerging Goddess: The Creative Process in Art, Science and Other Fields* (Chicago: University of Chicago Press, 1979).

Royle, Edward. *Modern Britain: A Social History 1750–1985* (London: Edward Arnold, 1989).

Ruppel, Karl H. 'The Extra-Musical in Music', in Ursula von Rauchhaupt (ed.), *The Symphony* (London: Thames and Hudson, 1973), 204–206.

Russell, John. *A Short History of Music*, Tenth Edition (London: Harrap, 1981).

Rutland, Harold. *Trinity College of Music: The First Hundred Years* (London: Trinity College of Music, 1972).

Sadie, Julie Anne and Rhian Samuel (eds). *The Grove Dictionary of Women Composers* (London: Macmillan, 1994).

Saint-Saëns, Camille. *Harmonie et mélodie*, Third Edition (Paris: Calmann Levy, 1885).

Salmen, Walter (ed.). *The Social Status of the Professional Musician from the Middle Ages to the Nineteenth Century* (New York: Pendragon Press, 1983).

Salmen, Walter. 'Social Obligations of the Emancipated Musician in the 19th Century', in Walter Salmen (ed.), *The Social Status of the Professional Musician from the Middle Ages to the Nineteenth Century* (New York: Pendragon Press, 1983), 267–281.

Samuel, Rhian. 'Women Composers Today: A Personal View', *Contact,* **32** (1988), 53–54.

Samuel, Rhian. 'Feminist Musicology: Endings or Beginnings?', *Women: A Cultural Review,* **3** (1993), 65–69.

Samuel, Rhian. 'Women Who Call the Tunes', *The Guardian*, 26 May 1995, 11.

Sayers, Janet. *Biological Politics: Feminist and Anti-Feminist Perspectives* (London: Tavistock, 1982).

Sayers, Janet. *Sexual Contradictions: Psychology, Psychoanalysis and Feminism* (London and New York: Tavistock Publications, 1986).

Scanzoni, Letha Dawson and John Scanzoni. *Men, Women and Change* (New York: McGraw-Hill, 1981).

Scheid, P and J.C. Eccles, 'Music and Speech: Artistic Functions of the Human Brain', *Psychology of Music,* **3** (1975), 21.

Scheinfeld, Amram. *Women and Men* (London: Chatto and Windus, 1947).

Schloss, M.F. 'Out of the Twentieth Century: Three Composers, Three Musics, One Femininity' (Ph.D. thesis, Wesleyan University, 1993).

Schoen, M. *The Psychology of Music* (New York: Roland Press, 1940).

Seager, Joni and Ann Olson. *Women in the World: An International Atlas* (London: Pan Books, 1987).

Seashore, Carl, E. *Psychology of Music* (New York: Dover Publications, 1967).

Seward, John and Georgene Seward. *Sex Differences: Mental and Temperamental* (Toronto: Lexington Books, 1980).
Shaver, Phillip and Clyde Hendrick (eds). *Sex and Gender* (California and London: Sage Publications, 1987).
Shepherd, John. *Music as Social Text* (Cambridge: Polity Press, 1991).
Shepherd, John. 'Difference and Power in Music', in Ruth Solie (ed.), *Musicology and Difference: Gender and Sexuality in Music Scholarship* (Berkeley: University of California Press, 1993), 46–65.
Shepherd, John, Phil Virden, Graham Vulliamy and Trevor Wishart. *Whose Music? A Sociology of Musical Languages* (London: Latimer, 1977).
Sherman, Julia. *Sex-Related Cognitive Differences* (Illinois: Thomas Books, 1978).
Shuter, Rosamund. *The Psychology of Musical Ability* (London: Methuen, 1968).
Simonton, Dean Keith. *Genius, Creativity and Leadership: Historiometric Inquiries* (Cambridge, Mass. and London: Harvard University Press, 1984).
Simpson, Helen. 'Seeking the Female, through the Holistic Study of Music', *British Journal of Music Education, 10* (1993), 163–167.
Simpson, Robert. *The Symphony. Volume One: Haydn to Dvořák* (London: Penguin Books, 1966).
Sloboda, John A. *The Musical Mind: The Cognitive Psychology of Music* (Oxford: Clarendon Press, 1985).
Small, Christopher. *Music, Society and Education* (London: John Calder, 1977).
Smith, Harold L. *British Feminism in the Twentieth Century* (Aldershot: Edward Elgar, 1990).
Smith, J.A. and W.D. Ross (eds). *The Works of Aristotle,* 5 (London: Clarendon Press, 1912).
Solie, Ruth A. 'What Do Feminists Want? A Reply to Peter van den Toorn', *The Journal of Musicology,* 9 (1991), 399–410.
Solie, Ruth A. (ed.). *Musicology and Difference: Gender and Sexuality in Music Scholarship* (Berkeley: University of California Press, 1993).
Spender, Dale. *Man Made Language* (London: Routledge and Kegan Paul, 1980).
Spender, Dale. *Invisible Women: The Schooling Scandal* (London: The Women's Press, 1989).
Spender, Dale and Elizabeth Sarah (eds). *Learning to Lose: Sexism and Education* (London: The Women's Press, 1980).
Squire, Corinne. *Significant Differences: Feminism in Psychology* (London and New York: Routledge, 1989).
St John, Christopher. *Ethel Smyth: A Biography* (London: Longmans, 1959).
Statham, June and Donald Mackinnon. *The Education Factfile* (London: Hodder and Stoughton, 1989).

Steinberg, Michael P. 'Introduction: Music, Language and Culture', *Musical Quarterly,* 77 (1993), 397–400.

Stockard, Jean, and Patricia Schmuck *et al. Sex Equity in Education* (New York and London, Academic Press, 1980).

Storr, Anthony. *The Dynamics of Creation* (London: Secker and Warburg, 1972).

Storr, Anthony. *Music and the Mind* (London: Harper Collins, 1987).

Storr, Anthony. *The School of Genius* (London: André Deutsch Limited, 1988).

Strachey, Ray. *The Cause: A Short History of the Women's Movement in Great Britain* (London: Bell and Son, 1928).

Stradling, Robert and Meirion Hughes. *The English Musical Renaissance 1860–1940: Construction and Deconstruction* (London and New York: Routledge, 1993).

Sutherland, Margaret B. *Sex Bias in Education* (Oxford: Basil Blackwell, 1981).

Swanwick, Keith. *Music, Mind and Education* (London and New York: Routledge, 1988).

Tagg, Philip. 'An Anthropology of Stereotypes in TV Music?', *Svensk tìdskrift för musikforskning,* **71** (1989), 19–42.

Taylor, Clifford. *Musical Idea and the Design Aesthetic in Contemporary Music*, (New York: Edwin Mellen Press, 1990).

Taylor, Timothy D. 'The Gendered Construction of the Musical Self: The Music of Pauline Oliveros', *Musical Quarterly,* 77 (1993), 385–396.

Terman, Lewis and Miles, Catherine Cox. *Sex and Personality: Studies in Masculinity and Femininity* (London and New York: McGraw-Hill, 1936).

Tick, Judith. 'Why have there been No Great Women Composers?', *International Musician,* **79** (1975), 6 and 22.

Toorn, Pieter C. van den. 'Politics, Feminism and Contemporary Music Theory', *The Journal of Musicology,* **9** (1991), 275–299.

Travis, Carol and Carole Offir. *The Longest War: Sex Differences in Perspective* (New York: Harcourt, Brace and Jovanovich, 1977).

Treitler, Leo. 'Gender and Other Dualities of Music History', in Ruth Solie (ed.), *Musicology and Difference: Gender and Sexuality in Music Scholarship* (Berkeley: University of California Press, 1993), 23–45.

Trend, Michael. *The Music Makers: Heirs and Rebels of the English Musical Renaissance* (London: Weidenfeld and Nicolson, 1985).

Trollinger, Laree McNeal. 'A Study of Biographical and Personality Factors of Creative Women in Music' (D.M.A. thesis, Temple University, 1979).

Turner, Barry. *Equality For Some: The Story of Girls' Education* (London: Ward Lock Educational, 1974).

Tuttle, Lisa. *Heroines: Women inspired by Women* (London: Harrap, 1988).

Upton, George. *Women in Music* (Chicago: A.C. McClurg and Company, 1886).

Ussher, Jane M. *The Psychology of the Female Body* (London and New York: Routledge, 1989).

Van de Vate, Nancy. 'The American Women Composer: Some Sour Notes', *High Fidelity/Musical America*, **25** (1975), 18–19.

Walker, Alan. *An Anatomy of Musical Criticism* (London: Barrie and Rockliff, 1966).

Wallach, M.A. and N. Kogan. *Modes of Thinking in Young Children* (New York: Holt, 1965).

Walsh, Mary Roth (ed.). *The Psychology of Women: Ongoing Debates* (New Haven and London: Yale University Press, 1987).

Watson, Sophia. *Winning Women* (London: Weidenfeld and Nicolson, 1989).

Weber, William. *Music and the Middle Class* (London: Croon Helm, 1975).

Weininger, Otto. *Sex and Character* (London, Heinemann, 1906) [translated from the Sixth German Edition].

Wells, Brain W. P. *Body and Personality* (London and New York: Longman, 1983).

Wertheim, N. 'Is there an Anatomical localisation of Musical Faculties?', M. Critchley and R.A. Henson (eds.), *Music and the Brain, Studies in the Neurology of Music* (London: William Heinemann Medical Books, 1977), 282–297.

Whitesitt, Linda. 'Women's Support and Encouragement of Music and Musicians', in Karin Pendle (ed.) *Women in Music: A History* (Indiana: University of Indiana Press, 1991), 301–313.

Whittall, Arnold. *Music Since the First World War* (London: Dent, 1977).

Wiesner, Merry E. *Women and Gender in Early Modern Europe* (Cambridge: Cambridge University Press, 1993).

Williams, Nicolas. 'Behold the Sun: The Politics of Musical Production', in Christopher Norris (ed.), *Music and the Politics of Culture* (London: Lawrence and Wishart, 1989), 150–171.

Wilson, Glenn. *The Psychology of the Performing Arts* (London: Peter Owen, 1985).

Wilson, Glenn. *The Great Sex Divide: A Study of Male-Female Differences* (London: Peter Owen, 1989).

Wing, Herbert D. 'Musical Ability and Appreciation' (Ph.D. thesis, London University, 1941).

Wing, Herbert D. *Tests in Musical Ability and Appreciation* (Cambridge: Cambridge University Press, 1948).

Wolf, Naomi. *The Beauty Myth* (London: Vintage, 1991).

Wolf, Naomi. *Fire with Fire: The New Female Power* (London: Chatto and Windus, 1993).

Wolff, Janet. 'The Ideology of Autonomous Art', in Richard Leppert and Susan McClary (eds), *Music and Society* (Cambridge: Cambridge University Press, 1987), 1–12.

Wolff, Konrad (ed.). *Robert Schumann on Music and Musicians* (London: Dennis Dobson, 1947).

Wyke, Maria. 'Musical Ability: A Neuropsychological Interpretation', in M. Critchley and R.A. Henson (eds), *Music and the Brain. Studies in the Neurology of Music* (London: William Heinemann Medical Books, 1977), 156–173.

Young-Bruehl, Elisabeth. *Freud on Women* (London: Hogarth Press, 1990).

Young, Percy M. *A History of British Music* (London: Ernest Benn, 1967).

'Women as Composers', *Musical Times*, 1 February 1887, 80–82.

'The Wives of Some Great Composers', *Musical Times*, 1 September 1900, 586–589.

'Women Musicians Urge Equal Rights', *New York Times*, 19 May 1938, 24.

Zaimont, Judith Lang, Catherine Overhauser and Jane Gottlieb (eds). *The Musical Woman: An International Perspective*, 3 volumes to date (Westport, Conn.: Greenwood Press, 1984, 1987, 1991).

Index